SALVATION IN THE WORLD

T&T Clark Studies in Edward Schillebeeckx

Series editors

Frederiek Depoortere
Kathleen McManus O.P.
Stephan van Erp

SALVATION IN THE WORLD

The Crossroads of Public Theology

Edited by Stephan van Erp, Christopher Cimorelli
and Christiane Alpers

Bloomsbury T&T Clark
An imprint of Bloomsbury Publishing Plc

B L O O M S B U R Y
LONDON · OXFORD · NEW YORK · NEW DELHI · SYDNEY

Bloomsbury T&T Clark

An imprint of Bloomsbury Publishing Plc

Imprint previously known as T&T Clark

50 Bedford Square	1385 Broadway
London	New York
WC1B 3DP	NY 10018
UK	USA

www.bloomsbury.com

BLOOMSBURY, T&T CLARK and the Diana logo are trademarks of Bloomsbury Publishing Plc

First published 2017

© Stephan van Erp, Christopher Cimorelli and Christiane Alpers 2017

Stephan van Erp, Christopher Cimorelli and Christiane Alpers have asserted their right under the Copyright, Designs and Patents Act, 1988, to be identified as Author of this work.

British Library Cataloguing-in-Publication Data
A catalogue record for this book is available from the British Library.

ISBN: HB: 978-0-5676-7815-7
ePDF: 978-0-5676-7816-4
ePub: 978-0-5676-7817-1

Library of Congress Cataloging-in-Publication Data
LC record available at http://lccn.loc.gov/2015040645

Series: T&T Clark Studies in Edward Schillebeeckx

Typeset by Deanta Global Publishing Services, Chennai, India
Printed and bound in Great Britain

CONTENTS

LIST OF CONTRIBUTORS

Christiane Alpers is a research fellow at the faculty of theology at the Catholic University Eichstätt-Ingolstadt (Germany). She received her PhD from Radboud University Nijmegen (the Netherlands) and KU Leuven (Belgium). Her research focusses on public theology, Radical Orthodoxy, and the Christology of Edward Schillebeeckx.

Thijs Caspers is a researcher at Tilburg University (the Netherlands). Currently, he is participating in the programme 'Catholic Inspiration' led by Prof. Dr Erik Borgman. As a theologian, his main expertise is Catholic social thought. In addition to different articles, he is the author of the book *Proeven van goed samenleven. Inleiding in het katholiek sociaal denken* (2012), a Dutch introduction to Catholic social thought.

Christopher Cimorelli is visiting assistant professor of theology at Caldwell University (New Jersey, USA). He received his doctorate in theology from the Katholieke Universiteit Leuven (Belgium) in the Research Unit of Systematic Theology and the Study of Religions. His research and publications focus on the intersection between theology and history, as well as the life and thought of John Henry Newman. He has a forthcoming book, *John Henry Newman's Theology of History: Historical Consciousness, 'Theological Imaginaries', and the Development of Tradition* (Peeters Publishers, 2017).

Marijn de Jong has a PhD from the Catholic University of Leuven (Belgium). His dissertation focuses on the relation between philosophy and theology, more specifically on the role of metaphysics within theology. Before coming to Leuven he studied law and theology at Tilburg University (the Netherlands), the University of Cambridge (UK), and Boston College (Massachusetts, USA).

Heather M. DuBois is earning a PhD in systematic theology and peace studies at the University of Notre Dame (Indiana, USA). Her research interests include interpretations of the self and their impact on how people experience suffering, violence, and healing. She co-authored 'The Intersection of Christian Theology and Peacebuilding', a chapter in the *Oxford Handbook of Religion, Conflict, and Peacebuilding*. Heather holds an MA in conflict resolution from the University of Bradford (UK) and another in theology from Fordham University (NYC). As a non-profit programme manager, she trained in public health approaches to violence in the United States and co-organized short-term interreligious projects in Sarajevo, Israel/Palestine, and Damascus.

Stephan van Erp is professor of fundamental theology at KU Leuven (Belgium). Among his research interests are philosophical theology, political theology, theology and aesthetics, and the theology of Edward Schillebeeckx and Hans Urs von Balthasar. He is the author of *The Art of Theology* (Peeters Publishers, 2004), and editor of twenty volumes, among which are *Edward Schillebeeckx and Contemporary Theology* (Bloomsbury, 2010) and *Conversion and Church: The Challenge of Ecclesial Renewal* (Brill, 2015). He is the editor-in-chief of Brill Research Perspectives in Theology, managing editor of *Tijdschrift voor Theologie*, and editor of the T&T Clark Studies in Edward Schillebeeckx (Bloomsbury) and of Studies in Philosophical Theology (Peeters Publishers).

Julia A. Feder is an assistant professor of theology at Creighton University (Nebraska, USA). Her book *Trauma and Salvation: A Theology of Healing* (Fortress Press, *forthcoming*) explores healing from sexual trauma as a mystical-political practice. She earned a PhD in systematic theology from the University of Notre Dame (Indiana, USA).

Joshua Furnal is assistant professor of systematic theology in the Faculty of Philosophy, Theology, and Religious Studies at Radboud University Nijmegen (the Netherlands). Previously, he was a visiting research fellow at the Leslie Center for the Humanities and a lecturer in the Department of Religion at Dartmouth College (USA), and a postdoctoral research fellow at Durham University (UK) in the Department of Theology and Religion.

Jan J. Hasselaar is senior lecturer in economics and public theology at the CAH Vilentum University of Applied Sciences Almere (the Netherlands). He is also a researcher on the project 'The Catholic Tradition as a Living Source in the Public Sphere' under the supervision of Erik Borgman (Tilburg University, the Netherlands). Hasselaar was a policy-advisor of the National Federation of Christian Trade Unions in the Netherlands (CNV). He is the co-editor of the book *An Ongoing Conversation: The Green Patriarch in the Netherlands* (Oud-Katholiek Boekhuis, 2015) and chairs the working group 'Ecological Sustainability' of the Dutch Council of Churches.

Eleonora Hof has written her dissertation at the Protestant Theological University in the field of missiology. Her research focuses on a theology of vulnerability in the postcolonial context of World Christianity. Her published articles focus on the definition and implication of World Christianity in a postcolonial context.

Branislav Kuljovsky is a doctoral researcher at the Faculty of Theology and Religious Studies, KU Leuven (Belgium). He is a member of the Research Unit of Systematic Theology and the Study of Religions and the Research Group of Theology in a Postmodern Context. He has previously studied theology at Trnava University in Bratislava (BA, 2010) and KU Leuven (MA, 2011; Advanced MA, 2012), as well as international economic relations at the University of Economics in Bratislava (BA, 2010). He is currently preparing a doctoral dissertation on Joseph Ratzinger's conceptualization of the relationship between faith and culture, under the supervision of Prof. Stephan van Erp and Prof. Lieven Boeve.

Rhona Lewis previously read classics at the University of Bristol (UK) and did a Post Graduate Certificate in Education at the University of Cambridge (UK). Most recently, she taught for the Theology Faculty of the University of Oxford, teaching New Testament Greek and reading biblical texts with undergraduate and postgraduate students. She has done a masters in Christian theology at Heythrop College, University of London, where she is now a PhD student. The focus of her research is the connection between creation and Christology in the writings of Edward Schillebeeckx.

Megan Loumagne is a doctoral student in theology and religion, a Clarendon scholar, and a SCIO (Scholarship and Christianity in Oxford) scholar in science and religion at Christ Church, University of Oxford (UK). Since coming to Oxford to work with Prof. Graham Ward, her doctoral research has been focused on the doctrine of original sin and, in particular, on the challenges and opportunities for the doctrine in a post-Darwinian world. A central task of her research is to construct a doctrine of sin that takes biology and the evolution of sexual difference seriously. Her other theological interests include contemplative spirituality, Teresa of Ávila, and the theology of Edward Schillebeeckx.

Daniel Minch is a postdoctoral research fellow at the Faculty of Theology and Religious Studies, KU Leuven (Belgium). He is the secretary of the Research Group of Fundamental and Political Theology, and his current work focuses on the economic dimension of political theology and theologies of hope. Minch is the co-editor, with Joris Geldhof and Trevor Maine, of *Approaching the Threshold of Mystery: Liturgical Worlds and Theological Spaces* (Regensburg: Friedrich Pustet, 2015). His articles have appeared in *The Heythrop Journal*, *Horizons*, *Louvain Studies*, and *Tijdschrift voor Theologie*.

Kate Mroz is a doctoral student in systematic theology at Boston College (Massachusetts, USA). She holds a master of theological studies from Harvard Divinity School, and a BA in theology and political science from Fordham University. She is currently working on her dissertation, 'No Salvation Apart from Religious Others: Edward Schillebeeckx's Soteriology as a Resource for Understanding Christian Identity and Discipleship in a Religiously Pluralist World'.

Tom Uytterhoeven graduated in 1993 as a teacher in primary education. Since 2003, he has combined a full-time job, first as a teacher and later on as a lecturer in religious education at Thomas More Mechelen University College, with the study of theology at the KU Leuven (Belgium). Since 2012, he is a doctoral researcher preparing a dissertation on evolutionary explanations of religion. He is a member of the Research Unit of Systematic Theology and the Study of Religions at the Faculty of Theology and Religious Studies, KU Leuven.

INTRODUCTION

Stephan van Erp, Christopher Cimorelli, and Christiane Alpers

What happens when Edward Schillebeeckx's theology crosses paths with contemporary public theology? In this book, fifteen emerging scholars from North America and Europe present what they have discovered in traversing these paths. To this end, the contributors to this book delve deeply into the theological heritage which Schillebeeckx has left behind, and critically assess its relevance for the contemporary theological scene. In tracing the way(s) in which Schillebeeckx observed and examined his own context's increasing secularization and concomitant development towards atheism, the authors of this volume indicate the potential directions for a contemporary public theology that pursues the path which Schillebeeckx has trodden. Most contributors agree that today's generation of theologians has much to learn from the direction which Schillebeeckx followed in his times. In traversing and developing the path which he has navigated, they thus respond in their own context to Schillebeeckx's call to theologians, 'to stand at the dangerous crossing of the roads – at the point where faith comes into contact with modern thought and the whole of the new philosophical situation, but where no synthesis has as yet been achieved'.[1]

The nearly unanimous message of this book is that Schillebeeckx's uncompromising attention to the suffering of the world constitutes one of the most striking and inspiring features of his thought. Understanding and proclaiming Jesus Christ as Good News to the poor and marginalized becomes a restless struggle in a world that sadly continues to be broken again and again by meaningless suffering and evil. Maybe the most important lesson to be learned from Schillebeeckx is never to give up challenging Christian theology with these most disconcerting and troublesome realities and, in this way, neither to abandon faith in the Good News nor to become indifferent to the misery that seems to tear the world apart. Given this challenge, many contributors to this book primarily draw upon the way in which Schillebeeckx reflected on finitude, limitations, sin, and evil, as well as how he incorporated the notion of negative contrast experiences into his theology. Many authors argue that, when confronting Christian theology

---

1. E. Schillebeeckx, 'What Is Theology?', in *Revelation and Theology*, trans. N. D. Smith, *CW*, vol. 2 (London: Bloomsbury T&T Clark, 2014), 106 [163].

with the suffering of the world today, this notion continues to be powerful and fruitful. This book moreover helps to clarify how Schillebeeckx's attention to the surrounding public is related particularly to his theology of creation and his soteriology.

In order to understand this book's contribution to public theology, let us very briefly explain what we mean by this term to those who might not be familiar with the discourse. In recent years, the public relevance of Christianity has become a contested issue in many Western societies. Currently, and with the establishment of the *International Journal of Public Theology* in 2007, public theology has been instituted as a Christian theological discourse that is specifically devoted to respond to this new situation.[2] Whereas theology has been relevant for the wider contexts in which it was situated until relatively recently, the specific field of public theology has arisen in reaction to societal pressures that seek to locate faith traditions in a privatized realm.[3] One of the discipline's leading questions therefore concerns how theology, as a particular understanding of God, humanity, and society developed in and for the community of Christian faith, could 'be applicable to the wider, secular and pluralistic society'.[4] Although the nature and tasks of the emergent discipline are still being debated,[5] there is considerable agreement that public theology must be rooted in the Christian tradition, on the one hand, while simultaneously being engaged in secular discourse, on the other.[6]

In this climate of the increasingly questioned status of Christianity in wider public contexts, many contemporary public theologians agree that an adequate

2. W. Storrar, '2007: A Kairos Moment for Public Theology', *International Journal of Public Theology* 1 (2007): 5–25.

3. S. Kim, 'Editorial', *International Journal of Public Theology* 1 (2007): 1.

4. S. Kim, 'Editorial', *International Journal of Public Theology* 3 (2009): 138.

5. For attempts to distinguish public theology from political and liberation theologies, see G. Martinez, *Confronting the Mystery of God: Political, Liberation and Public Theologies* (New York and London: Continuum, 2001) or E. L. Graham, *Between a Rock and a Hard Place: Public Theology in a Post-Secular Age* (London: SCM Press, 2013), 82. For debates about the nature and tasks of public theology, see J. W. De Gruchy, 'Public Theology as Christian Witness: Exploring the Genre', *International Journal of Public Theology* 1 (2007): 26–41; M. Stackhouse, 'Reflections on How and Why We Go Public', *International Journal of Public Theology* 1 (2007): 421–30; D. Smit, 'Notions of the Public and Doing Theology', *International Journal of Public Theology* 1 (2007): 431–54; H. E. Breitenberg Jr, 'What Is Public Theology?', in *Public Theology for a Global Society: Essays in Honor of Max L. Stackhouse*, D. K. Hainsworth and S. R. Paeth (eds) (Grand Rapids, MI and Cambridge: William B. Eerdmans Publishing Company, 2010), 3–20; S. Kim, *Theology in the Public Sphere: Public Theology as a Catalyst for Open Debate* (London: SCM Press, 2011); E. Jacobsen, 'Models of Public Theology', *International Journal of Public Theology* 6 (2012): 7–22.

6. Graham, *Between a Rock and a Hard Place*, xix. For a collection of theological discussions about the (post)secular context, see W. A. Barbieri (ed.), *At the Limits of the Secular: Reflections on Faith and Public Life* (Grand Rapids, MI: Eerdmans, 2014).

reaction would have to be apologetical. They contend that the relevance of the Christian faith must be defended against secularist criticisms. A great deal of contemporary public theological literature thus concerns questions about the translatability of Christian language into publicly intelligible terms or new forms of practical or imaginative apologetics.[7] Building on the theological heritage of Edward Schillebeeckx, the present book opens up a way for a different, non-apologetic public theology. In other words, at the crossing of the roads between Schillebeeckx's thought and the contemporary public theological discourse, the contributors to this book indicate alternative directions for public theology to those already in existence. They unapologetically accept the Christian tradition as a legitimate starting point for thinking about issues of public relevance, and show in this way not only how Christian theology may develop in contemporary contexts, but also how specific public problems may be responded to from a Christian theological perspective.

At the crossing of the roads between Schillebeeckx's theological heritage and contemporary public spheres, the authors of this book demarcate four significant directions for Christian theology to pursue. These directions themselves shed light, more broadly speaking, on the frontiers being engaged by Christian public theology in the contemporary context. The first direction is from the public into Christian theology. Theologians at this crossing are presented with the question of how theology can keep pace with developments in contemporary public realms. The first four chapters in this book analyse what can be learned from Schillebeeckx's devotion to this question and are organized under the heading, 'Theological Renewal in the Public Sphere'. Yet, this impetus for theological renewal immediately raises the question of how to remain faithful to the past and to what has been received. If one is to take the road ahead constructively, as opposed to running around in circles, one must understand whence one has come. Consequently, the five subsequent chapters critically assess the degree to which Schillebeeckx's own efforts at theological renewal have been a successful progress of the Christian tradition. They comprise the second direction – that is, looking backwards in order to move ahead – and appear under the heading 'Faithfulness to the Christian Tradition in the Public Sphere'. A third direction at the crossroads is from Christian theology into the public spheres. Theologians at this crossing are confronted with the question of how developments in the wider public can be criticized from a Christian perspective. Three chapters under the heading 'Theological Critique of the Public Sphere' follow Schillebeeckx in taking on this task, which seeks to contribute critically to public discussions and the promotion of the common good. Finally, the fourth direction features a back-

---

7. Kim, 'Editorial', 3; J. W. De Gruchy, 'Public Theology as Christian Witness', *International Journal of Public Theology* 1 (2007): 26–41; Graham, *Between a Rock and a Hard Place*, 104–14, 177–233; T. Reynolds, 'A Closed Marketplace: Religious Claims in the Public Square', *International Journal of Public Theology* 8 (2014): 201–22; C. Hübenthal, 'Apologetic Communication', *International Journal of Public Theology* 10 (2016): 7–27.

and-forth movement between Christian theology and the public spheres. The frontiers between Christian theology and the wider public can be perceived as more navigable for those attempting to cross from any direction, but especially directions one and three as outlined above. The fourth direction thus conceives of the borders between theology and the public sphere as more porous than one might normally assume. It allows for mutual enrichment, which is fostered – in a manner of speaking – by the reciprocal action of a two-way street. The results of this direction and approach to public theology are presented in the three final chapters, which are summarized under the heading 'Crossings of Theology and the Public Sphere'.

Structure and Content of the Book

Part I: Theological Renewal in the Public Sphere

Public theologians sometimes describe their discipline as being characterized by a particularly dialogical method.[8] If public theology seeks to open up Christian theology self-critically to the surrounding public discourse, the first section of this book might be said to respond broadly to this aspiration. However, while a number of public theologians equate this dialogical openness of Christian theology with the submission to public scrutiny,[9] that is, in the sense of 'procedural norms of public discourse',[10] the chapters of this section indicate a different way of Christian theological self-critique undertaken in response to developments in the public sphere. Instead of displaying a submission to secularist norms, the following four authors engage questions of self-critical renewal *from* a Christian theological perspective.

In setting out on the path of recovering the way in which Schillebeeckx perceived the wider public as directed towards Christian theology, our book begins with Joshua Furnal's chapter, 'Edward Schillebeeckx on Secularization and Public Theology'. In response to the ongoing process of societies becoming less connected with religious matters and institutions, Furnal presents Schillebeeckx's sophisticated ability to handle classical dogmatic positions in debates with the radical theologians of secularization of his day. Schillebeeckx's theology of secularization is explored through a focus on his pastoral and philosophically sensitive engagement with the Anglican bishop J. A. T. Robinson's book, *Honest to God* (1963), and it is recommended as a helpful resource for fostering theological renewal today. Furnal retrieves from this debate Schillebeeckx's wider account of intersubjectivity as an important category for presenting and defending the Christian faith to/in a modern public.

---

8. Graham, *Between a Rock and a Hard Place*, 71; Kim, *Theology in the Public Sphere*, 226.

9. Kim, *Theology in the Public Sphere*, 230.

10. Graham, *Between a Rock and a Hard Place*, 71.

In 'Public Opposition to Ecclesial Involvement in Secular Politics: Schillebeeckx's Grace-Optimism as a Response to Public Theology and Radical Orthodoxy', Christiane Alpers argues that it is Schillebeeckx's understanding of grace which allowed him to comprehend the surrounding public as directed towards Christian theology. This chapter builds further on Schillebeeckx's response to Robinson's *Honest to God* by arguing that this response constitutes a viable alternative to the two prominent and contrasting theological reactions to the contemporary post-Christendom context: namely, public theology, on the one hand, and Radical Orthodoxy, on the other. Through analysis, both are exposed as understanding the crossroad between Christianity and the wider public in too limited a fashion, that is, as a one-way road from Christianity into the public; this trait blinds both reactions from perceiving the path that is led by grace from the public towards Christianity. Edward Schillebeeckx's response to Robinson is then presented as a signpost for a contemporary public theology that both understands the contemporary public as gracefully helping Christian theology on its way into the future and allows Christians to confess publicly the churches' past alliances with evil.

The suggestion of reforming the church through attention to public developments is further refined and concretized in Megan Loumagne's chapter, 'A Theologian Standing with God in the World: Development in Schillebeeckx's Epistemology and Implications for Feminist Theology'. Loumagne revives Schillebeeckx's appeal for theologians to be an 'intense presence in the world', which she regards as being supported in the present by Pope Francis. Schillebeeckx's epistemology is examined regarding how it can navigate impasses related to discussions of gender and the role of women in the church. Loumagne argues that Schillebeeckx provides a theological foundation through which dissenting voices can help to direct the reconsideration and reconstruction of doctrine in the light of changes happening in the public.

In 'Dangerous Theology: Edward Schillebeeckx, Pope Francis, and Hope for Catholic Women', Kate Mroz argues that Christian theology should not shy away from the dangers hidden on its way forward. Mroz emphasizes that both Schillebeeckx and Pope Francis privilege the idea that the church's journey through the world is characterized more properly as risky rather than secure and/or certain, where the church is seen as standing still in order to cling on to some predated security. Pope Francis's papacy is interpreted as a hopeful sign for the future of feminist theology over against the persistence of some exclusionary practices in the Roman Catholic Church. Moreover, Mroz views the papacy of Pope Francis as a welcome reminder that Christian life is praxis-oriented and requires at times endangering one's own life for the sake of the marginalized.

Part II: Faithfulness to the Christian Tradition in the Public Sphere

The subsequent five chapters correspond with the public theological concern not to 'purchase' self-critical openness at the expense of jeopardizing the faithfulness and commitment to the Christian tradition.[11] Nevertheless, there have been legitimate questions as to whether public theologians always succeed in this task, and public theology itself has been called 'self-destructively accommodationist' to the surrounding secular worldview.[12] The five chapters of this section and direction examine more thoroughly the degree to which Edward Schillebeeckx succeeded in leading Christian theology ahead without merely accommodating the Christian tradition to current societal trends.

A counterweight to the enthusiasm for risky theological renewals in pace with developments in the wider public, as it is represented in the opening section to this volume, is offered by Branislav Kuljovsky in his chapter, 'Tradition Hermeneutics: Joseph Ratzinger and Edward Schillebeeckx on the Role of Historical-Cultural Context for the Understanding of Christian Faith'. Kuljovsky critically evaluates Joseph Ratzinger's and Edward Schillebeeckx's respective conceptions of the role of the historical-cultural context in adequately understanding the content of the Christian faith. Schillebeeckx's openness to the surrounding context is problematized in this chapter insofar as Kuljovsky argues that Schillebeeckx thinks about doctrinal continuity in changing cultural contexts from a one-sidedly secular-hermeneutical perspective. By contrast, Ratzinger's 'hermeneutics of reform' is appreciated for its ontological understanding of the continuity of Christian faith. Schillebeeckx's unbalanced embrace of the notion of human historicity, prevalent in his cultural context, is said especially to prevent an adequate understanding of Christian tradition development.

In 'Metaphysical Theology in Hermeneutical Times? Lessons from Edward Schillebeeckx', Marijn de Jong delves deeper into the impact of the post-metaphysical turn on Schillebeeckx's theology; this turn was characteristic of his later philosophical context. De Jong argues that Schillebeeckx's own turn to hermeneutics did not result in a complete abandoning of metaphysics. The centrality of the 'objective dynamism' towards the constitutive ground of reality in Schillebeeckx's earlier work still plays a key role in Schillebeeckx's later, more hermeneutically oriented theology. It provides an 'objective directionality' in interpretations and thereby avoids a reductionist subjective understanding of interpretive experience. As such, de Jong presents Schillebeeckx's transformed metaphysics as indicative of an alternative path to that led by any postmodern wholesale rejection of metaphysics.

In his chapter, 'Re-examining Edward Schillebeeckx's Anthropological Constants: An Ontological Perspective', Daniel Minch examines the implications of Schillebeeckx's hermeneutical ontology for his anthropology. Minch exposes the particular vision of the human being and its ontological structure as it is

---

11. Kim, *Theology in the Public Sphere*, 226; Graham, *Between a Rock and a Hard Place*, 71; R. F. Thiemann, *Constructing a Public Theology: The Church in a Pluralist Culture* (Louisville, KY: John Knox Press, 1991), 19.

12. C. Matthewes, *A Theology of Public Life* (Cambridge: Cambridge University Press, 2007), 1.

suggested by Edward Schillebeeckx's seven 'anthropological constants'. He argues that Schillebeeckx's later focus, on the 'absolute limit' or 'radical finitude' as the single element of human experience that appears to ground all others, is also at the basis of all seven constants. The absolute limit within the framework of Schillebeeckx's hermeneutical ontology is then presented as an essential element of human ontology that should be retrieved for contemporary theological reflection on the (religious) human subject in society.

Rhona Lewis, in her chapter 'Forging a Way through Creation: "God or the World?" or "God and the World?"', argues that Schillebeeckx's anthropology remains, despite its ontological repercussions, fundamentally a Christian theological understanding of humankind. She counters the widespread perception that, in his later theology, Schillebeeckx places undue emphasis on the human at the expense of the divine. Schillebeeckx's focus on anthropology is presented as theologically motivated, posing the question of God's will concerning the human position and responsibility with regard to creation. She argues that the Thomist conception of creation, as a free and continuous divine act, constitutes the basis of not only Schillebeeckx's emphasis on contingency, human finitude, and limitations, but also his conviction that God is absolutely present in the world.

The relation between creation faith and human finitude and sin in Schillebeeckx's theology is further explored in Thijs Caspers's chapter, 'Reflections on the Contrast Experience's Methodological Undercurrent'. Caspers defends Schillebeeckx's notion of the contrast experience against one-sided psychological or anthropological interpretations by highlighting the theological underpinnings of the notion. The continuing relevance of Schillebeeckx's theology of creation and soteriology for his conception of negative contrast experiences allows for a fuller understanding of how human experiences of suffering, pain, and hope are, for him, directly related to God's all-embracing salvation.

Part III: *Theological Critique of the Public Sphere*

Contemporary public theology is particularly concerned with the directionality from Christian theology into the surrounding public spheres, as it seeks to demonstrate the ways in which Christian theology can contribute to the common good of a shared public sphere.[13] The three chapters in this section also look in this direction. Instead of abstractly defending the idea that Christian theology is directed towards the public, however, they critically engage specific developments in the wider public from a distinct Christian theological perspective. If one of public theology's aims is to motivate other disciplines to draw on Christian theology,[14] then this section of the volume indicates how this might occur more concretely. Its chapters take on the issues of climate change, societal conceptions of progress, and evolutionary understandings of the origin and purposes of religions.

---

13. S. Kim, 'Editorial', *International Journal of Public Theology* 6 (2012): 268.
14. Kim, 'Editorial' (2012), 134.

It is fitting that, after Lewis's and Caspers's reflections on the role of creation, finitude, and sin in Schillebeeckx's thought, Jan Jorrit Hasselaar counters both optimistic and pessimistic public reactions to climate change by introducing a theological perspective of hope. In his chapter, 'The Good News about Climate Change', the emphasis on God's presence in and with the world's finitude, which marks Schillebeeckx's theology of creation, is presented as underlying the notion of negative contrast experiences. This reading is possible because the resistance against threats to the *humanum* and nature are understood as supported by an 'open yes'. Hasselaar argues that this open yes underneath human protest allows for a hopeful response to climate change. To bolster this argument, he puts Schillebeeckx's proposed solution of self-restraint and sobriety into conversation with Jonathan Sack's covenantal politics, which is geared towards individual and social transformation. The resultant perspective provides a distinct, critical, and constructive alternative to the binary responses to climate change prevalent in the contemporary public sphere.

This direction is also pursued in Christopher Cimorelli's chapter, 'Development amid Sin: Schillebeeckx and Newman for Today', which introduces John Henry Newman's and Edward Schillebeeckx's respective views of tradition-development as theological considerations that remain critical today, not only within the church's own life and thought, but also in and for the wider contemporary context. Newman's and Schillebeeckx's perspectives on development are able to counterbalance overly progressive and evolutionary outlooks because they hold human finitude and sin clearly in view. By squarely facing the considerations of human finitude and sin – albeit in distinct manners – in the treatment of ecclesial change throughout time, Newman and Schillebeeckx demonstrate their relevance for global humanity today, which faces immense challenges that imperil the very survival of our species. Cimorelli argues that political attempts to confront such challenges can benefit from Christian anthropology, which does not shy away from or ignore the deleterious influence of sin in the world, especially as it may pertain to communal action, development, and notions of 'progress'.

In 'Experience and Critical Reflection in Religion: Schillebeeckx's Theology and Evolutionary Studies of Religion', Tom Uytterhoeven challenges those academic disciplines that talk about religion to take more seriously the questions which theologians could legitimately pose to them in turn. More precisely, Uytterhoeven challenges the retro-reductionist interpretation of religion by evolutionary scientists with Schillebeeckx's theological understanding of the transmission of religious traditions. He then introduces Robert Bellah as a thinker who can bridge the gap between the two conflicting interpretations of religion through his method of situating evolutionary understandings of religion in a larger historical perspective.

Part IV: Crossings of Theology and the Public Sphere

The way has been prepared for the subsequent three chapters that are less interested in a theological corrective of public developments, seeking instead a mutual enrichment between Christian theology and the wider public spheres in which it is set. As such, these chapters accord with the public theological concern to increase the interactions between theology and public issues of contemporary society.[15] They demonstrate how this concern could become manifest in regard to the issues of healing from trauma and racial prejudices in the public sphere. All three chapters relate Schillebeeckx's soteriology to contemporary discussions about wholeness, and, therefore, they respond to the incentive to grant soteriology a central place in contemporary public theological debates.[16] Whereas public theologians tend to connect soteriology primarily to Christian ethics, the chapters in this volume show that Christian soteriology is co-determinative for the way(s) in which Christians interpret the world.

Julia Feder, in her chapter, 'Edward Schillebeeckx and Sexual Trauma: Salvation as Healing', argues that any contemporary articulation of Christian salvation, as the 'total sense' or 'being whole' of human existence, must take into account the reality of widespread, senseless human suffering in our world, including the horrific realities of sexual violence. Feder appeals to Schillebeeckx's notion of negative contrast experiences to show how God is present to the victim of sexual trauma in her suffering, but does not sanctify it. Schillebeeckx's soteriology allows for a comprehensive project of human healing insofar as human beings are commissioned by God to participate in bringing about the realities of human salvation. The view herein developed provides a contemporary framework for articulating the ways in which victims of sexual trauma may work towards their own healing as precisely a salvific task, without eclipsing God's salvific role in the recovery process.

Whereas Feder primarily focuses on the way in which Christian soteriology can help victims of trauma to ameliorate their situation actively, Heather DuBois explores further a complementary aspect vital to trauma therapy: namely, that of enabling victims to experience wholeness before they attain it fully. Her chapter, 'An Ever-Stitched Wholeness: Multidimensional Relationality in Trauma Theory and Schillebeeckx's Theology of Salvation', exhibits the concurrence between Schillebeeckx's anthropological constants and the insights of eminent, contemporary trauma theorists concerning the importance of relationships for any process of healing. On this basis, DuBois then analyses the way in which Schillebeeckx relates critical theory's prioritization of 'the fragment' to a Christian understanding of perceiving the whole. Read in conversation with trauma theory, Schillebeeckx's claim, that humans can and do experience fragments of salvation here and now, even amid ongoing suffering, yields a theology that allows for experiences of psychic health without one's being completely healed.

Finally, Eleonora Hof reacts against a binary understanding of wholeness and vulnerability. In her chapter, 'Towards a Theology of Vulnerability: An Analysis and Critique of White Strategies of Ignorance and Invulnerability', a theology

---

15. Kim, 'Editorial' (2007), 1.
16. Kim, 'Editorial', *International Journal of Public Theology* 2 (2008): 140.

of vulnerability is embraced in order to dismantle white privilege. Whiteness is associated with both strategies of invulnerability and an epistemology of ignorance. With the help of Kristine Culp's work, vulnerability is interpreted as the fundamental openness towards blessing and empowerment by God or, alternatively, distortion and violation. In order to elucidate the former, Hof draws on Sarah Coakley's considerations concerning 'right' forms of vulnerability, or those that allow for empowerment by virtue of the opening up of the self towards the divine. She then argues that this power-in-vulnerability is able to transform the invulnerability produced and maintained by ignorance, thus helping to abolish the mechanisms that ingrain societies with racial injustice.

Part I

THEOLOGICAL RENEWAL IN THE PUBLIC SPHERE

Chapter 1

EDWARD SCHILLEBEECKX ON SECULARIZATION AND PUBLIC THEOLOGY

Joshua Furnal

It is often said that there are many twists and turns in Edward Schillebeeckx's intellectual development, such that no single coherent thread can be traced. This remark can also lead one to expect that it is a difficult task to (re)establish the contemporary relevance of Schillebeeckx's work. But recently there have been some scholars who have embarked upon such a journey, and this chapter is but one attempt to explore *how* Schillebeeckx's theology remains relevant for contemporary debates in public theology.[1] In particular, one of the core debates in public theology is whether theological concepts can be translated without remainder into a secular context. This debate spreads even further into other subfields like political theology, with debates about whether or not it is prudent to *re-theologize* secular political concepts – but this short chapter will not explore this tangential implication of the argument.[2]

Although it might seem anachronistic to read Schillebeeckx in the context of public theology, my claim is that Schillebeeckx anticipates the debates that are going on today, and he makes some important observations that are still worth bearing in mind for pushing debates in public theology forward. To illustrate my point, I will briefly examine Schillebeeckx's early period, in which he began to sketch his theology of secularization in response to what has been called the '*Honest to God*' debate. In the first section of this chapter, after a short introduction to this debate itself, I examine how Schillebeeckx engages with Bishop Robinson

---

1. To date, the most convincing case put forward for Schillebeeckx's enduring relevance for public theology is in S. van Erp, 'The Sacrament of the World: Thinking God's Presence beyond Public Theology,' *ET-Studies* 6, no. 1 (2015): 119–34.

2. For instance, I have in mind current debates surrounding the work of theologians engaging with the following subjects, particularly in regard to the theo-political notion of sovereignty: Radical Orthodoxy, Giorgio Agamben, Gilles Deleuze, Carl Schmitt, and Erik Peterson. For more, see P. Fletcher, *Disciplining the Divine: Toward an (Im)Political Theology* (Farnham: Ashgate, 2009).

on the crucial issue of theological renewal amid secularization, and I observe that Schillebeeckx moves the discussion away from the *reduction* of theology to anthropology, instead pushing it towards the *development* of Christian doctrine. In the second section, I assess how this particular engagement with Bishop Robinson is inflected in Schillebeeckx's early theology of secularization. My overall argument is that what Schillebeeckx does and claims here still lends itself as an important lesson to contemporary debates about public theology.

1. *The* Honest to God *Debate*

In the 1960s, there was a theological fermentation regarding atheism, secularization, and the perceived need for the church to accommodate itself to the demands of modernity. In England, these issues came to the forefront with the publication of the Anglican bishop John Robinson's book *Honest to God*.[3] It is often argued that, although this book is not theologically astute, its appearance is a historical instance where the relevance of theology became a public issue – and this cultural achievement is what many theologians have only dreamed about ever since. This controversial result was certainly a surprise to Bishop Robinson, who had merely raised the question about whether traditional concepts of God, as they are popularly understood, can have any relevance to us today. Bishop Robinson argued that we must dispense with unhelpful and theologically misguided pictures of God, and instead recover more appropriate conceptions that can be understood by the contemporary public. During this same time period in the United States, radical theologians were saying something similar, but were going one step further than Robinson by promoting a Christian form of atheism.[4] It did not help matters that Bishop Robinson often enlisted the aid of these radical theologians in his enthusiastic plea for a new concept of God. From the perspective of public theology, this was a moment in history when secularization, atheism, and the relevance of theology converged in ways that were difficult to untangle and interpret.[5] However, what often goes unrecognized is how the radical theology debate in the United

---

3. J. A. T. Robinson, *Honest to God* (London: SCM Press, 1963).

4. For instance, see T. J. J. Altizer, *The Gospel of Christian Atheism* (New York: Collins, 1967). See also G. Vahanian, *The Death of God: The Culture of Our Post-Christian Era* (New York: George Braziller, 1961). Far from being an outdated theological moment in history, radical theology continues to resurface in contemporary debates, thus showing its ongoing relevance. For more, see K. S. Moody, *Radical Theology and Emerging Christianity: Deconstruction, Materialism and Religious Practices* (Farnham: Ashgate, 2015).

5. The best account of this phenomenon from a sociological perspective is R. Towler, *The Need for Certainty: A Sociological Study of Conventional Religion* (London: Routledge & Kegan Paul, 1984). During the 1960s in Europe, debates about Radical Theology revolved around the resurgence of Ludwig Feuerbach's work and the way secularization featured in the work of Marcel Xhaufflaire.

States and the United Kingdom was engaged by European Catholic theologians like Edward Schillebeeckx.

2. *Schillebeeckx and the* Honest to God *Debate*

Scholars have already mapped the debates going on during this time period regarding atheism, secularization, and the relevance of Schillebeeckx's work for wider post-conciliar changes in the church.[6] Instead of rehearsing these findings, I would like to examine Schillebeeckx's theology of secularization in his two books, *God the Future of Man* and *God and Man*.[7] I assess how Schillebeeckx critiques Bishop Robinson's presentation of theological renewal amid secularization in his book *Honest to God*, in order to show how Schillebeeckx develops his own public theology of secularization in response. Rather than being a mere fragment of vintage theological history, this debate is important for understanding Schillebeeckx's wider account of intersubjectivity as an important category for presenting and defending the Christian faith in modernity. My claim is that, because of Schillebeeckx's sophisticated ability to handle classical dogmatic positions in the debate with the critical questions posed by radical theology, he still offers a helpful approach to fostering theological renewal amid the process of society becoming less connected with religious matters and institutions. For a new generation of Catholic theologians, Schillebeeckx still proves to be a guiding light for engaging critical and contemporary questions regarding Scripture, dogmatics, and philosophical hermeneutics today.

In his preface to *God and Man*, Schillebeeckx reports that there was a growing conviction in his time that 'salvation comes about within [our] daily life, "in this world," in [our] relationship with the strictly "secular"'.[8] By 'secular', Schillebeeckx means 'ordinary everyday life with its joys and sufferings, its fears and its hopes'.[9] Schillebeeckx describes this 'new religious attitude to the world' as 'an objection to the use of any specifically religious language' and a preference to use everyday language to express religious feelings.[10] This new orientation advocates a Christianity without a 'church', but still wants to retain the idea of human solidarity.[11] The stakes were thus high in the *Honest to God* debate that

6. W. T. Cavanaugh, 'Return of the Golden Calf: Economy, Idolatry, and Secularization since *Gaudium Et Spes*', *Theological Studies* 76, no. 4 (2015): 698–717.

7. E. Schillebeeckx, *God the Future of Man* (hereafter *GFM*), trans. N. D. Smith, *CW*, vol. 3 (London: Bloomsbury T&T Clark, 2014); E. Schillebeeckx, *God and Man*, trans. E. Fitzgerald and P. Tomlinson (London: Sheed & Ward, 1969).

8. Schillebeeckx, *God and Man*, v.

9. Ibid.

10. Ibid., vi.

11. Ibid., vii.

raged on during that time period, and it is within this context that Schillebeeckx understands his own authorship (at least at this early stage of his development).

Fifty years on, this 'new' religious sentiment that Schillebeeckx describes does not seem so alien to us. So perhaps it is worth attending to the observations he offers and the fundamental principles he clarifies in order to evaluate whether Schillebeeckx still has something to offer to us today. Schillebeeckx indeed furnishes much for our consideration; but for the sake of time, I will focus on his book-length chapter, 'Life in God and Life in the World', which discusses the debate about Bishop Robinson's book *Honest to God*.[12] Schillebeeckx opens his reflection with two simple questions. First, is 'being a Christian' synonymous with 'being authentically human'? Second, does union with God prevent human solidarity? In doing so, Schillebeeckx highlights the fundamental theological issue of non-competitive divine agency and human flourishing as the fault line of the *Honest to God* debate. Schillebeeckx argues that the tacit assumption is that human flourishing is at odds with divine action, and (as the story goes) we are thus forced to choose between dedicating our lives either to becoming more authentic *or* to God alone. In being forced to make such a choice, the tacit assumption implies that Christianity works against human solidarity and authenticity, rather than promoting it. Judging by the number of empty pews, the *Honest to God* debate suggests that, in practice, ordinary people are choosing the world instead of God. However, for Schillebeeckx, this presentation is too simplistic and requires charitable correction. He says that, for Bishop Robinson,

> theology must therefore be the analysis of the depth of our human inter-subjectivity. A contention is theological not because it purports to tell us something about an individual entity we call God, but because it tells us something about the ultimate sense of our existence. And this deepest ground of our being is love from which no one can separate us. Precisely what is *implicit* in all our historically conditioned human relationships is God.[13]

For Schillebeeckx, Bishop Robinson's anthropology *implies* theology, and his view of morality *implies* a Christology. This dual implication is manifest in Bishop Robinson's understanding of Christ solely as a moral exemplar. As Schillebeeckx sees it, Bishop Robinson's perspective upholds the idea that 'the profoundest sense of our being is revealed in the man Jesus: he loves until the end … [revealing what it is] to be authentically a human being – that is, a human being living for his fellow human beings'.[14] In his view, Bishop Robinson only articulates a half-truth by making human solidarity the heart of the Christian message – or at least the message of secular Christianity.[15]

12. Ibid., 85–209.
13. Ibid., 88–9.
14. Ibid., 89.
15. Ibid., 90–1.

In response, Schillebeeckx wants to uncover the Catholic significance of Christian secularity, and he uses Bishop Robinson's book to do just that. Schillebeeckx says that what Bishop Robinson teaches us is that 'the best defence of true faith may well lie in a re-stating of traditional orthodoxy in modern terms and a radical renewal of our ideas and practices'.[16] For Schillebeeckx, Bishop Robinson's call for theological renewal means that there must be a reformulation rather than mere reiteration of dogmatic propositions. However, there is a subtle yet important difference between Bishop Robinson and Schillebeeckx as to whether renewal requires either a *replacement* or a *development* of Christian doctrine. In Schillebeeckx's perspective,

> what is new, and profoundly experienced, can obscure earlier truths which remain believable only insofar as they are thoroughly rethought right down to the core of their original formulation and become, as it were, newly discovered. It may appear paradoxical, but the recognition of old truths sometimes demands a more profound conversion than the recognition of attractive, freshly discovered truths which have the advantage of a new and surprising brilliance, although they shock us because they upset our familiar ideas.[17]

In other words, Schillebeeckx thinks that, for Bishop Robinson, 'it is not so much a matter of formulating the faith in an orthodox fashion as of formulating it so that men can understand it'.[18] But for Schillebeeckx, this is to raise the question not of a *replacement*, but rather of the *development* of Christian doctrine.

Following St Thomas Aquinas's account of how we can intelligibly understand that we do not understand the divine mystery,[19] Schillebeeckx argues that words both obstruct and enunciate meaning, but faith finds use for the enunciation that obtains the meaning itself. Schillebeeckx says that the theological implication is that 'orthodoxy is not primarily a question of adherence to the precise conceptual formulation of the articles of faith but of assent to the intent expressed in the

---

16. Ibid., 87.

17. Ibid., 95.

18. Ibid., 104.

19. Thomas Aquinas, Summa Theologiae, http://dhspriory.org/thomas/summa/FP/FP001.html#FPQ1A2THEP1, ST II-II q. 1 a. 2. ad. 2: 'The symbol mentions the things about which faith is, in so far as the act of the believer is terminated in them, as is evident from the manner of speaking about them. Now the act of the believer does not terminate in a proposition [*ad enuntiabile*], but in a thing [*ad rem*]. For as in science we do not form propositions, except in order to have knowledge [*cognitionem*] about things through their means, so is it in faith.' In this vein, St Paul says, 'When we cannot choose words in order to pray properly, the Spirit himself expresses our plea in a way that could never be put into words, and God who knows everything in our hearts knows perfectly well what he means, and that the pleas of the saints expressed by the Spirit are according to the mind of God' (Rom. 8:26–27).

formulation.[20] Following Aquinas, he writes that this intent refers to 'an awareness of direction which views the truth without absorbing it with understanding.[21] Schillebeeckx detects a naive view of theological renewal in Robinson, namely, that theological renewal is a straightforward task of translation that substitutes a contemporary meaning for the old one. In Robinson's view, the exact, appropriate word for the object of faith always *could be otherwise* depending on the epoch in which it is pronounced. Schillebeeckx appreciates Robinson's evangelistically motivated willingness to change a theological image or concept to communicate the gospel. However, Schillebeeckx objects to Robinson's implicit historicist dismissal of 'what we *used* to believe'. For Schillebeeckx, this historicist position invites serious problems of negotiating continuity in the Christian faith amid cultural shifts in understanding, the result of which can be stated as follows: 'all that remains is the language of love', just without the pre-scientific baggage.[22] Against Robinson, Schillebeeckx argues that

> we can only say anything about God within and on the basis of our creative and saving relationship with him; yet we must admit that within this existential relationship God himself can reveal himself to us precisely in his own independent being. Thus we cannot really grasp God conceptually, but nevertheless we can obtain a *knowledgeable perspective* of his independent being, of him as he is in himself.[23]

Thus, in Schillebeeckx's view, Robinson dissolves an important paradox: orthodoxy serves the *act* of faith because of the saving reality of the gospel. Yet, there can be no *act* of faith without an orthodox enunciation of faith's *object*.[24] In other words, orthodoxy preserves the act of faith from being arbitrary by helping us to say what we mean; at the same time, the act of faith keeps orthodoxy from stagnation, helping us to mean what we say.[25] In short, for Schillebeeckx, the exact, appropriate *word* is crucial for the act of faith – the particular word is necessary and cannot be otherwise.[26] However, Schillebeeckx's argument here is not that the word's meaning never idles in a secular age, but rather that, in a secular age, theologians must continue to work to deepen our understanding of that word's meaning.

So far, we have seen how Schillebeeckx engages Bishop Robinson on the crucial issue of theological renewal amid secularization, and how Schillebeeckx takes the

---

20. Schillebeeckx, *God and Man*, 105.

21. Ibid., 105, n. 27.

22. Ibid., 107.

23. Ibid., 127.

24. Ibid., 105.

25. Cf. ST I q. 1 a. 7. ad. 1; E. Schillebeeckx, 'What Is Theology?', *Revelation and Theology*, trans. N. D. Smith, *CW*, vol. 2 (London: Bloomsbury T&T Clark, 2014), 112–14 [174–6].

26. Schillebeeckx, *God and Man*, 106.

discussion away from the *reduction* of theology to anthropology, moving it instead towards the *development* of Christian doctrine.[27] He does so because of his view that development retains and 'frequently makes use of categories derived from an existential experience which belongs to an earlier stage', in order to disclose and renew that understanding for a new generation.[28] In the next section of this chapter, we will transition from this particular engagement to Schillebeeckx's wider theology of secularization.

3. Schillebeeckx's Theology of Secularization

In *God the Future of Man*, Schillebeeckx acknowledges the *phenomenon* of secularization, but he wants to distinguish properly the sociological predictions from the theological distortions in an everyday conception of secularization.[29] He appreciates the sociological association of secularization with modern technological developments in society. He also regards these developments as beneficial insofar as they play an important role 'in the building up of the world and the promotion of the well-being of all peoples'.[30] What concerns Schillebeeckx is how popular conceptions of secularization are 'connected with religion only indirectly insofar as the image that we form of God and the way in which we experience religion are at work within the current image that we form of man and the world'.[31]

For Schillebeeckx, the everyday conception of God and humanity, which crops up alongside conventional interpretations of secularization, unfortunately generates the popular image of the god-of-the-gaps, that is, understanding 'God' as a temporary 'substitute for the powers which man himself lacked'.[32] According to Schillebeeckx, this anthropological reduction of theology has a troubling implication for how we understand *both* God and humanity. The accompanying picture of humanity invites us to view ourselves in terms of 'a situated freedom which, through the collaboration of men, must give itself its own definite character in a task which gives meaning in this world, within a rational sphere of understanding, so that justice, peace and love may prevail among men'.[33]

---

27. Schillebeeckx has a cogent critique of Robinson's dismissal of metaphysics that must be treated in a larger version of this investigation. Interestingly, Schillebeeckx has some important observations that cohere with Cornelio Fabro's intervention in this debate. Schillebeeckx says that Robinson's failure is in not making a proper distinction between 'ultimate reality' and 'a phenomenon as it can be approached by the methods of the natural or special sciences' (Schillebeeckx, *God and Man*, 123).

28. Schillebeeckx, *God and Man*, 72.

29. Schillebeeckx, 'The New Image', *GFM*, 103–7 [172–7].

30. Ibid., 103 [172].

31. Ibid.

32. Ibid., 104 [173].

33. Schillebeeckx, 'Secularization and Christian Belief in God', *GFM*, 33 [55–6].

Indeed, Schillebeeckx says that the anthropological reduction of theology in an everyday sense also includes a picture of humanity as self-made, which has troubling implications for how we, in turn, conceive of the future. Schillebeeckx writes that

> a self-made future therefore should not be equated with a glorified optimism about progress. We ought rather to say that human freedom is so heavily burdened by it that there is real danger, no longer of a flight from the world, but of a flight from the future, and in many different forms – the 'world' has, in fact, become the 'future'.[34]

For Schillebeeckx, secularization does not demand that theologians *retreat* to their private ghetto, but rather proffers an *invitation* for theologians to re-present the Christian faith to a new generation. He argues that the common *theological* mistake is to conflate the god-of-the-gaps image with the essence of religion – such that God ends up competing for the same space as technological advancement.[35] Schillebeeckx says that, for the Christian, 'it is an ideological misconception to call one concrete stage in the development of human history the ultimate point'.[36] Hence, the proper *theological* sense of secularization is

> an attitude which recognizes the presence of God in our human history and which can help to bring about a future of salvation for all men by concern for our fellow-men. It is an attitude in which we, recognizing God in the man Jesus, also recognize him in our fellow-men, who call us to the love which seeks justice for all.[37]

In other words, for Schillebeeckx, a proper theology of secularization holds together the dual emphasis on concrete expressions of love of neighbour and the universal salvation of humanity in history.[38] However, his insight here requires a shift in theological anthropology: since 'transcendence' is often conflated with 'the future', Schillebeeckx says that theologians must re-present God as the future of humanity.[39] According to this view, theologians must highlight 'the divine promise of an ultimate eschatological fulfillment for every man [that] in every moment of our lives proclaims God as the One who is to come ... in the very history that he nonetheless transcends'.[40] In this way, Schillebeeckx argues that faith makes history

---

34. Schillebeeckx, 'The New Image', *GFM*, 106 [177].

35. Ibid., 104–5 [174]. For more, see G. Pattison, *Thinking about God in an Age of Technology* (Oxford: Oxford University Press, 2005).

36. Schillebeeckx, 'The New Image', *GFM*, 113 [186].

37. Ibid., 115 [189].

38. Ibid., 115 [190].

39. Ibid., 109 [181].

40. Ibid., 110 [182–3].

new, and it must be 'clear from the concrete practice of Christian life that God *de facto* manifests himself as the one whose power can bring about the new future'.[41]

By shifting our attention to the concrete expression of love of neighbour, Schillebeeckx's theology of secularization invites us to ask, for instance, about the difference between the church and a humanitarian organization like Greenpeace. In Bishop Robinson's theology, Greenpeace could be a proper substitute for the church depending on the terms we decide to use in a secular age. For Schillebeeckx, however, the church still maintains a positive function for the Christian faith in the form of 'a positive power which continues to exert constant pressure in order to bring about a better world, without humanity itself being sacrificed in the process. The positive content [of the better world desired by humanity] cannot be formulated, but mankind clearly has some negative knowledge of it'.[42] In other words, Schillebeeckx says that there is an unquenchable yet natural desire for future justice, but this desire is deepened through conversion, and it must be cultivated towards hope in the *pastoral* and *prophetic* life of the church: sacramental liturgy and proclamation of the Word.[43] Schillebeeckx draws upon the theological virtues to illustrate his point:

> It is in and through our *active* trust in faith that *God's gift* is realized in history. On the one hand, it is possible to say that the Church, as the community of believers, (1) *participates* in God's activity in this world through her active hope, (2) 'articulates' this activity of God, that is, gives it a *name*, as a testimony to the whole of the world, (3) proclaims the unconscious hope of the world and (4) must play a leading part in humanizing the world, must be in the vanguard in caring for men.[44]

In short, Schillebeeckx argues that 'prayer, the liturgy, the life of the Church as a whole, are extremely meaningful and, for a Christian, indispensable. But we should not forget that *they* refer us to the events of this world as the context in which God comes to us'.[45] Therefore, he says that the church must continue to proclaim the message that 'human existence is *a promise of salvation* which cannot be explained in the light of man's concrete being'.[46] Importantly for Schillebeeckx, the church is the sacrament of world history, but the 'Christian faith is not a flight *from* the world into the Church's liturgy. It aims to enable the world to share in the coming of the kingdom of God, a kingdom of peace, righteousness and love'.[47]

---

41. Ibid., 111 [183–4].
42. Ibid., 116 [191].
43. Ibid., 122–3 [201].
44. Schillebeeckx, 'Secularization and Christian Belief in God', *GFM*, 48 [78]; Cf. E. Schillebeeckx, 'What Is Theology?', *Revelation and Theology*, 71–85 [106–28].
45. Schillebeeckx, 'Secularization and Christian Belief in God', *GFM*, 50 [81].
46. Ibid., 46 [75].
47. Schillebeeckx, 'Secular Worship and Church Liturgy', *GFM*, 61 [102].

To retrace our steps thus far, Schillebeeckx describes secularization as 'facilitated by our own outmoded theology, and above all by our factual experience of Christianity'.[48] Moreover, Schillebeeckx claims that secularization is beneficial because, in popular conceptions of it, it is often a sincere (although one-sided) plea for a better picture of God and humanity. It remains the task of theologians to come forward and clarify *why* this plea is one-sided, and to offer a better *reformulation* of Christian doctrine – otherwise, secularization will undermine Christianity, with its current presentation of a God that competes with the power of technology and a humanity that fashions its own future.[49] In order to seize the opportunity of secularization properly, Schillebeeckx says that theologians must 'listen carefully to what this secularization has to say to us' and must foster a humble attunement to God's self-revelation in Christ through Scripture as saving truth.[50] Indeed, Schillebeeckx affirms that 'the experience of human life, wherever it occurs, is most assuredly a *locus theologicus*, a source for the tenets of faith'. However, 'That human life constituted by Jesus the Christ, nurtured by the people of Israel and the biblical piety of the Old Testament, is the only authorized source of revelation.' Hence, 'As a "source of revelation" the ordinary human experience of life has no authority' other than that which conforms to 'the testimony of apostolic Scripture, [which] is constituted by the human life of Jesus.'[51] In short, Schillebeeckx's theology of secularization includes a strategy to transpose the discourse about Christian secularity into a discourse about Christian humanism.[52]

Conclusion

To conclude, I would like to offer some observations about the way that Schillebeeckx articulates his theological anthropology in the light of his previous comments on secularization and renewal. For Schillebeeckx, the human being is

48. Schillebeeckx, *God and Man*, 94.

49. Ibid., 95.

50. Ibid.

51. Ibid., 141.

52. For more, see M. C. Hilkert, 'Edward Schillebeeckx, OP (1914–): Encountering God in a Secular and Suffering World', *Theology Today* 62, no. 3 (2005): 376–87. See also the expanded version of the article from 1968: E. Schillebeeckx, 'Kritische beschouwingen over het "secularisatie-begrip" in verband met allerlei thema's van het pastoraal concilie', *Pastoraal concilie van de Nederlandse kerkprovincie, V: Vierde plenaire vergadering. Geloofsbeleving, geloofspraktijk en geseculariseerde wereld* (Amersfoort, 1969): 114–39. Also see the following: E. Schillebeeckx, 'Het nieuwe mens- en Godsbeeld in conflict met het religieuze leven', *Tijdschrift voor Theolgie* 7 (1967): 1–27; and E. Schillebeeckx, 'Het nieuwe Godsbeeld, secularisatie en politiek', *Tijdschrift voor Theologie* 8 (1968): 44–65. Many thanks to Christiane Alpers for these references.

open towards, and personally addressed by, the God of salvation.[53] This integral, structural openness towards God has two aspects: a natural and supernatural moment. When speaking of the *natural moment*, Schillebeeckx describes how we discover our immediate relation to God through an indispensable, spontaneous, or reflective self-interpretation among human interactions with the world. Here, Schillebeeckx says that we begin to see the finitude of human freedom as constitutive of our dependence upon God.[54] However, the religious coincides with, but is not exhausted in 'an encounter with one's fellow men and involvement with the world'.[55] Hence, he speaks of a *supernatural moment* as the realm of personal intersubjectivity with God, effected by *grace* elevating, including, perfecting, and authenticating natural desire.[56] Schillebeeckx speaks of grace as intersubjectivity *with the life of God*.[57] He speaks of our natural desire for God and our 'free response to God's gratuitous invitation to mutual love' in terms of intersubjectivity. In this way, Schillebeeckx uses a modern term to speak about sanctifying grace as that direct reciprocity with God, who always takes the initiative towards humanity.[58]

In sum, I have argued that Schillebeeckx offers a distinctive contribution to the radical theology debate from within the Catholic tradition. In the first section, I examined how Schillebeeckx engages with Bishop Robinson regarding the crucial issue of theological renewal amid secularization, and I observed that Schillebeeckx moves the discussion away from the *reduction* of theology to anthropology, instead pushing it towards the *development* of Christian doctrine. In the second section of this chapter, I assessed how this particular engagement with Bishop Robison is inflected in Schillebeeckx's early theology of secularization. My overall argument is that what Schillebeeckx does and claims here still lends itself as an important lesson to contemporary debates about public theology, namely, that because of God's self-communication in Christ, we are addressed personally (in creation and redemption). Thus, Schillebeeckx says, 'In our life of faith, the Absolute is given to us, as a mystery, in *direct* communication, though thematically it is only *indirectly* expressible.'[59] With this reminder, he speaks of

---

53. Schillebeeckx, *God and Man*, 161.

54. Ibid., 163.

55. Ibid., 166.

56. Schillebeeckx, *God and Man*, 183–5. For Schillebeeckx, 'intersubjectivity' means the 'interpersonal relationship of two subjects who are attracted towards each other as subjects' (*God and Man*, 185). And 'theologal' means that which comes from God, as infused gift (*God and Man*, 183). Schillebeeckx draws upon gift and intersubjectivity as two important terms that Aquinas uses: 'Infused virtue is caused in us by God without any action on our part, but not without our consent. This is the sense of the words, "which God works in us without us." As to those things which are done by us, God causes them in us, yet not without action on our part, for He works in every will and in every nature' (ST I-II q. 55 a. 4. ad. 6).

57. Schillebeeckx, *God and Man*, 173.

58. Ibid., 185.

59. Ibid., 181–2, n. 18.

our salvation in terms of irreducible personal intimacy and reciprocity with God.[60] For Schillebeeckx, then, our salvation is a communion that we cannot attain on our own because we cannot furnish the ultimate meaning of life, and yet, 'intimacy with God is the primary task of human life'.[61] Schillebeeckx's early theological position here illuminates the contemporary relevance of his work for public theology, particularly in regard to how he speaks of the church as the Body of Christ and the Sacrament of the World. For Schillebeeckx, 'Secularization is in itself an intra-Christian and intra-ecclesial event, an event within the life of the people of God.'[62] In the end, Schillebeeckx wishes to reclaim the common ground of human flourishing based upon the optimism of grace, because 'the ultimate significance of the secular merges, by virtue of its human character, into the mystery of the order of grace'.[63]

Bibliography

Altizer, T. J. J., *The Gospel of Christian Atheism* (New York: Collins, 1967).

Cavanaugh, W. T., 'Return of the Golden Calf: Economy, Idolatry, and Secularization since Gaudium Et Spes', *Theological Studies* 76, no. 4 (2015): 698–717.

Fletcher, P., *Disciplining the Divine: Toward an (Im)Political Theology* (Farnham: Ashgate, 2009).

Hilkert, M. C., 'Edward Schillebeeckx, Op (1914–): Encountering God in a Secular and Suffering World', *Theology Today* 62, no. 3 (2005): 376–87.

Moody, K. S., *Radical Theology and Emerging Christianity: Deconstruction, Materialism and Religious Practices* (Farnham: Ashgate, 2015).

Pattison, G., *Thinking about God in an Age of Technology* (Oxford: Oxford University Press, 2005).

Robinson, J. A. T., *Honest to God* (London: SCM Press, 1963).

Schillebeeckx, E., 'Het nieuwe mens- en Godsbeeld in conflict met het religieuze leven', *TvT* 7 (1967): 1–27.

Schillebeeckx, E., 'Het nieuwe Godsbeeld, secularisatie en politiek', *TvT* 8 (1968): 44–65.

Schillebeeckx, E., *God and Man*, trans. E. Fitzgerald and P. Tomlinson (London: Sheed & Ward, 1969).

Schillebeeckx, E., 'Kritische beschouwingen over het "secularisatie-begrip" in verband met allerlei thema's van het pastoraal concilie', *Pastoraal concilie van de Nederlandse kerkprovincie, V: Vierde plenaire vergadering. Geloofsbeleving, geloofspraktijk en geseculariseerde wereld* (Amersfoort, 1969): 114–39.

Schillebeeckx, E., *God the Future of Man*, trans. N. D. Smith, *CW*, vol. 3 (London: Bloomsbury T&T Clark, 2014).

E. Schillebeeckx, *Revelation and Theology*, trans. N. D. Smith, *CW*, vol. 2 (London: Bloomsbury T&T Clark, 2014).

60. Ibid., 180.
61. Ibid., 220.
62. Ibid., 224.
63. Ibid., 229.

Towler, R., *The Need for Certainty: A Sociological Study of Conventional Religion* (London: Routledge & Kegan Paul, 1984).

Vahanian, G., *The Death of God: The Culture of Our Post-Christian Era* (New York: George Braziller, 1961).

Van Erp, S., 'The Sacrament of the World: Thinking God's Presence beyond Public Theology', *ET-Studies* 6, no. 1 (2015): 119–34.

Chapter 2

PUBLIC OPPOSITION TO ECCLESIAL INVOLVEMENT IN SECULAR POLITICS: SCHILLEBEECKX'S GRACE-OPTIMISM AS A RESPONSE TO PUBLIC THEOLOGY AND RADICAL ORTHODOXY

Christiane Alpers

Public theology has drawn attention to the contemporary Western-European, post-Christendom context and the new challenges it brings to Christian theology.[1] One such challenge is that Christian contributions to secular political discussions about the common good are no longer accepted by all members of society. Some secularists oppose any religious involvement in politics. Public theologians claim that, consequently, Christian theologians have the new task of convincing everyone of the political benefits Christian insights can provide for the whole society. To this end, they examine how Christian theology can contribute to secular society's understanding of, and strive towards, the common good. Nearly diametrically opposed to this is the Radical Orthodox approach to the contemporary post-Christendom context. Critical of the public theological alliance with a supposedly erroneous secular ontology, Radical Orthodoxy's most prominent author, John Milbank, tries to convince everyone of the political benefits of the Christian vision of *the whole of reality* and its superiority over its secular counterpart.

In this chapter, I highlight that, despite this disparity concerning the best way to counter public opposition to Christian involvement in secular politics, both public theology and Radical Orthodoxy agree that this opposition must be countered. On this shared basis, they merely disagree with regards to the question of how such a countering should delineate Christian political involvement. In mediating between the approaches of public theology and Radical Orthodoxy to post-Christendom societies, I draw on Edward Schillebeeckx's thought in order to argue that Christian theology should not be concerned with how to counter public opposition to Christian involvement in secular politics. Retrieving

1. I would like to thank Mary Catherine Hilkert, O.P. for her insightful comments on earlier versions of this chapter.

Schillebeeckx's emphasis of the gratuitousness of grace as basis for any Christian involvement in politics, my approach is aligned with Radical Orthodoxy insofar as a particularly Christian ontology is preferred over a secular one. However, Schillebeeckx provides a way to adopt a non-triumphalist stance towards secular ontologies because his understanding of gratuity implies that grace does not overcome a lack in nature, but rather perfects an already good nature. This means that Christian theology does not need to repair some supposed shortcomings of secular ontologies. Instead, Christian theology must discern that which is already good in the secular public realm and then perfect this goodness. Consequently, my approach parts ways with both public theology and Radical Orthodoxy insofar as their approaches to politics commence with the detection of a problem that needs to be solved. Christian politics should instead build on the already realized good in society.

My argument proceeds, in the first section of this chapter, by briefly introducing the discussion between public theology and Radical Orthodoxy concerning an adequate Christian theological response to the contemporary Western-European, post-Christendom context. On this basis, I explain in the second section how Schillebeeckx's response to the atheist opposition to ecclesial politics in the 1960s shares Radical Orthodoxy's opposition to the secularization of Christian politics, as well as its advocacy of a retrieved focus on the churches' fundamental relation to God. At the same time, Schillebeeckx refrains from presenting the advantages of a theocentric politics triumphantly over all secular politics. This stance could be suspected of lacking Radical Orthodoxy's audacity to counter the surrounding public mainstream opinion. It could be objected that Schillebeeckx uncritically adopts the secular conviction that it is self-evident that no ontology should be privileged over others. Against this possible objection, I argue, in the third section, that Schillebeeckx's hesitancy to present the superiority of the Christian ontology triumphantly is motivated by his understanding of grace in the Christian world view. Schillebeeckx pays attention to all that which is already graced and good in society, and not to what lacks grace. This view indicates why he can also interpret the public opposition to ecclesial involvement in secular politics not as a problem that needs to be solved, but rather as the mediation of the truly good. One could here object that Schillebeeckx's understanding of Christianity to secular society is naively optimistic or dangerously apolitical. The fourth section of the chapter serves to debunk this objection by demonstrating that, shaped by Schillebeeckx's account of the crucifixion of Jesus, his optimism does not ignore suffering and evil. Moreover, it will be argued how, from the perspective of Schillebeeckx's grace-optimism,[2] Radical Orthodoxy and public theology can both be criticized for a questionable concern about securing a respectable position for the churches in the public realm. The remaining part of the chapter, divided into sections five and six, is then devoted to the argument

2. I adopt this term from M. C. Hilkert, "'Grace-Optimism'": The Spirituality at the Heart of Schillebeeckx's Theology', *Spirituality Today* 43 (1991): 220–39.

that an adequate response to public opposition to ecclesial involvement in secular politics must also find ways to confess publicly past and present ecclesial alliances with evil. To this end, Schillebeeckx's writings, about the importance of lament to God and his notion of the negative contrast experience, are revisited. It will be indicated that contemporary public theological discussions erroneously treat evil as something which needs to be resolved, whereas from a perspective of a Christian ontology of grace, evil can only be overcome by the arrival of a new good.

1. Reacting to the Public Opposition to Ecclesial Involvement in Secular Politics

In this chapter, I refer to public theology as that emerging theological sub-discipline which seeks to determine how the churches as political institutions are to engage other political bodies in a democratic public sphere.[3] In Western-European, post-Christendom societies, this effort encounters the problem that the legitimacy of Christian contributions to public debates about the common good is no longer presupposed.[4] In response to this post-Christendom context, public theologians set themselves the task of justifying this legitimacy.[5] Part of this project of renewing the public trust in, and respect for, the churches is to emphasize the ways in which Christianity has previously contributed to the common good and thus to convince the public of the benignity of Christianity by way of offering such contributions for the contemporary context.[6] What is understood as 'common good' is defined by the society in question.

Radical Orthodoxy offers a contrasting theological response to the contemporary context.[7] The movement's most prominent representative, John Milbank, agrees that, in contemporary societies, the churches have to earn their

---

3. M. Brown, S. Pattison and G. Smith, 'The Possibility of Citizen Theology: Public Theology after Christendom and the Enlightenment', *International Journal of Public Theology* 6 (2012): 183–204 (184); E. Graham, 'Power, Knowledge and Authority in Public Theology', *International Journal of Public Theology* 1 (2007): 42–62 (44); Kim, 'Editorial', 1–4 (1); Kim, *Theology in the Public Sphere: Public Theology as a Catalyst for Open Debate*, 230; W. Storrar, '2007: A Kairos Moment for Public Theology', *International Journal of Public Theology* 1 (2007): 5–25 (16).

4. Graham, *Between a Rock and a Hard Place*, 19, 112, 291.

5. Storrar, 'A Kairos Moment for Public Theology', 5–25 (6); Kim, 'Editorial', 1–4 (2); Graham, *Between a Rock and a Hard Place*, xxiii.

6. Kim, 'Editorial', 147–50 (147); S. Kim, 'Editorial', *International Journal of Public Theology* 4 (2010): 131–4 (133).

7. Radical Orthodoxy has been praised for its rediscovery of Christianity's fundamental publicness and its political commitment to a 'more abundant "worldly" life'. C. Mathewes, *A Theology of Public Life* (Cambridge: Cambridge University Press, 2007), 165.

credence in order to speak publicly about matters of common concern.[8] However, in his view, the necessitated 'demonstration of theology's right to speak' does not imply any meeting of the post-Christian public on its own terms, but rather consists in the offering of a particularly Christian interpretation of the whole of reality as alternative to the prevalent secular ontology.[9] Christianity is to regain the public trust by argumentatively demonstrating that Christian theology is better suited than secular philosophy to make sense of reality and to construct a peaceful common life. This confrontational stance towards their secular surrounding has led public theologians to designate Radical Orthodoxy as countercultural.[10] Public theologians claim that a particularly Christian interpretation of reality risks losing any foothold in the public realm.[11] Moreover, Radical Orthodox authors are criticized for overcoming Christendom at best half-heartedly. Their triumphalist understanding of the Christian faith still advocates a privileged position for Christianity in the public realm, which is most notably discernible in the Radical Orthodox refusal to admit any significant revision of the Christian tradition in response to secular criticisms.[12] It is thus argued that Radical Orthodox theologians insufficiently acknowledge the partiality and possible defectiveness of their own ontology.[13] However, it must be stressed that, despite this disagreement, Radical Orthodox and public theologians agree that public opposition to ecclesial involvement in politics must be countered by Christian theology. In the following section(s), I will present Edward Schillebeeckx as a theologian who would have agreed, on the one hand, with Radical Orthodoxy concerning the superiority of Christian politics over its atheist counterpart. On the other hand, he would have *shared* the conviction of public theology that Christianity should not strive to regain its former privileged position in society.

8. J. Milbank, 'The Body by Love Possessed', *The Future of Love: Essays in Political Theology* (London: SCM Press, 2009), 76. In my exposition of Radical Orthodoxy, I will mainly focus on the work of John Milbank.

9. Milbank, 'The Body by Love Possessed', 81.

10. Graham, *Between a Rock and a Hard Place*, 116.

11. Stronger criticisms would accuse Radical Orthodoxy of advocating the re-establishment of an oppressive Christian imperialism. S. Shakespeare, *Radical Orthodoxy: A Critical Introduction* (London: SPCK, 2007), 150.

12. L. Ayres, 'Book Review: Theology and Social Theory: Beyond Secular Reason', *Scottish Journal of Theology* 45 (1992): 125–6; V. Burrus, 'Radical Orthodoxy and the Heresiological Habit', in *Interpreting the Postmodern: Responses to 'Radical Orthodoxy'*, R. Radford Ruether and M. Gau (eds) (London: T&T Clark, 2006), 36–53 (38, fn 5); D. J. Dunn, 'Radical Sophiology: Fr. Sergej Bulgakov and John Milbank on Augustine', *Studies in East European Thought* 64 (2012): 227–49; Graham, *Between a Rock and a Hard Place*, 108, 117; H. Rayment-Pickard, 'Derrida and Nihilism', in *Deconstructing Radical Orthodoxy: Postmodern Theology, Rhetoric and Truth*, W. J. Hankey and D. Hedley (eds) (Aldershot: Ashgate, 2005), 161–76 (174); Shakespeare, *Radical Orthodoxy*, 150; J. Stout, *Democracy and Tradition* (Princeton: Princeton University Press, 2003), 114–15.

13. Mathewes, *A Theology of Public Life*, 132–3.

2. Responding to the Public Opposition to Ecclesial Involvement in Secular Politics

Edward Schillebeeckx's theology, specifically regarding the discussion concerning Christianity's adequate public positioning vis-à-vis the public opposition to ecclesial involvement in secular politics, is illuminating because he seeks to understand those secularist opponents when examining the connection between ecclesial political failures and modern atheist withdrawal from the churches.[14] In his response to Bishop John Robinson's (a)theology, Schillebeeckx shows his willingness to let the churches' politics be reoriented by public criticism. Schillebeeckx agrees with and further qualifies Bishop John Robinson's interpretation of modern atheism as the positive revelation that the churches' preoccupation with religion had been an obstacle to their political mission.[15] According to Robinson, what is regarded as unnecessary religious embellishment had allegedly mitigated the churches' political message.[16] Freed by modern atheism from this religious baggage, the churches are now being predicted to fail less in responding to their political calling. Schillebeeckx agrees with Robinson that modern atheism is somehow connected to the past political failures of the churches to ameliorate the conditions of human life.[17] However, whereas Robinson understands the preoccupation of the churches with religion as an obstacle in the pursuit of their political calling, Schillebeeckx claims that both modern atheism and the churches' political failures originated in the churches' *insufficient* preoccupation with God.

According to Schillebeeckx, the identification of the essence of Christianity with its political calling, as Robinson's (a)theology suggests, is not only reductionist from an orthodox point of view, but it also inhibits the true political force of Christianity. He concedes that the ancient Christian truth, that God alone is ultimately, in and of Himself loveable, must be recovered.[18] God has to be recognized again as the wellspring of all value that always remains greater than anything which derives from it. Schillebeeckx draws on Aquinas's discussion about the significance of dogma in order to argue that Christian orthodoxy is not primarily about doctrinal correctness, but rather about consciously aiming at reality itself without thereby conceptually encompassing this reality.[19] Aquinas explains that Christian doctrine

---

14. Cf. E. Schillebeeckx, *Church: The Human Story of God*, trans. J. Bowden, *CW*, vol. 10 (London: Bloomsbury T&T Clark, 2014), 162 [163]. Schillebeeckx understands here the privatization of Christianity as people's fundamentally laudable reaction to the oppression and suffering caused by Christian political dominance over non-Christians.

15. E. Schillebeeckx, 'Leven in God en Leven in de Wereld', *God en Mens* (Bilthoven (Holland): Uitgeverij H. Nelissen, 1965), 66–149 (74); trans. *God and Man* (London, Sydney, New York: Sheed & Ward, 1969).

16. Schillebeeckx, 'Leven in God en Leven in de Wereld', 66–149 (68).

17. Ibid., 66–149 (74).

18. Ibid., 66–149 (73).

19. Aquinas, *Summa Theol.* II-II q. 1 a. 2. ad. 2, cited by Schillebeeckx, 'Leven in God en Leven in de Wereld', 66–149 (79; n. 27).

only directly speaks of God Himself if the act of the believer terminates in God and not in the doctrine.[20] In other words, every fixed statement of faith and doctrinal certitude is a necessary aid for the believer who wants to know God. But what makes the believer orthodox is the orientation to, and longing for, God, a disposition that embraces doctrinal belief but does not end there.

Regarding this chapter's discussion, Schillebeeckx agrees with the opponents of Christian involvement in secular politics that Christianity has previously failed to embody its political mission. However, he nuances this criticism by arguing that the ecclesial failure is not that Christians have erroneously spoken about God when they should have spoken about love (or politics). The ecclesial failure consists, rather, in the 'clinging' to traditional utterances about God as having value in and of themselves. Consequently, the public opposition to ecclesial engagement in secular politics should be understood not only as a positive reminder of the churches' political calling, but also as an indication of the human directedness towards, and openness to, an even greater reality than that which the churches could envision in and with their doctrinal propositions *and* political projects. For, a position which simply replaces old doctrinal certainty with political certainty about a realizable common good bears the danger of clinging to the churches' political mission in the same fashion in which the churches have mistakenly clung to doctrinal propositions.

This emphasis on the political benefits of reading the world in its relation to (the Christian) God partly aligns Schillebeeckx with Radical Orthodoxy. However, Schillebeeckx also sides with public theology when he recoils from triumphantly claiming that, if this reading was accepted by all, the whole public would be in a better state. This is not an inconsistency in Schillebeeckx's thought which Radical Orthodoxy would better bring to its logical conclusion. Instead, the partial agreement with both sides of the argument can be illuminated in reference to a more fundamental disagreement of Schillebeeckx's position with both of them. Whereas both public theology and Radical Orthodoxy implicitly agree that theology's main concern should be to resolve any public opposition to ecclesial political involvement, Schillebeeckx does not primarily understand this opposition as a problem to be solved, but rather as the positive revelation both of past and present ecclesial failures, as well as of the good which had continued to be mediated nonetheless. A new ecclesial politics that is responsive to both can thus be critical of the shortcomings of the public opposition to ecclesial involvement in politics without denying that this opposition is most fundamentally good. Nonetheless, Schillebeeckx's conclusion, that subsequent to the emergence of atheist opposition to the Christian faith the churches should not strive to regain their previous privileged position, could be accused for uncritically adopting the modern mainstream conviction that any ontology should admit its own partiality. In order to debunk this objection, I shall argue in the next section how

---

20. Aquinas, *Summa Theol.* II-II q. 1 a..2. ad. 2, http://www.ccel.org/ccel/aquinas/summa.SS_Q1_A2.html (accessed 27 May 2015).

Schillebeeckx's non-triumphalism, as well as his non-reactive approach to politics, are profoundly Christian insofar as they are informed by his understanding of the gratuity of grace.

3. *The Gratuity of Grace as Basis for Non-reactive Ecclesial Politics*

In order to clarify why Schillebeeckx does not argue triumphantly for the superiority of the Christian ontology despite sharing Radical Orthodoxy's conviction that this ontology is politically advantageous, it is important to note that he pauses to stress the gratuitous given-ness of the Christian faith *before* he reflects upon the obligations which this gift implies. To understand the gift of a right relation to God, Schillebeeckx first turns to the gift of Creation, which he calls an unfathomable mystery. He recalls that 'creational grace' is God, who is already complete goodness in Himself, making Himself God for us.[21] The reality that we live in a world that participates freely in God's goodness can evoke joy and thankfulness in a human person. Consequently, Schillebeeckx understands all religion as the response(s) to this creational grace.[22] Human beings begin to worship when they recognize that the whole of Creation exists gratuitously, without any need or purpose, from a source already perfect in itself.

Moreover, this enjoyment of the goodness of Creation gives rise to a human longing to enter into a relationship with the Creator God[23] – it is thus not limited merely to the expression of one's personal thankfulness. However, the longing for such a relationship will be accompanied by the realization that it is impossible; as a creature in this world, the believer is separated infinitely from the Creator, who is not a creature among others but the unfathomable ground of all existence. This is why Schillebeeckx refers to the grace of salvation as a surpassing of the grace of Creation: it is 'salutary grace' by which God expands His being God *for* us into being God *with* us.[24] This salutary grace is as un-necessitated and gratuitous as the first gift of creational grace. This means that Christianity not only celebrates the goodness of Creation, but also the surpassing goodness of being in a personal relationship with the source of all goodness. This view indicates that the atheist refusal to read the world in its relation to God does not necessarily end in a political disaster, as Radical Orthodox theologians tend to argue. Schillebeeckx's understanding of the goodness of creational grace and the utter gratuity of salvific grace would suggest, rather, that, deprived of one's personal relationship with God, a human being lacks a level of joy and fulfilment that lies to some extent beyond political purposes. That this feature does not render Schillebeeckx's theology apolitical will be argued in the following section.

21. Schillebeeckx, 'Leven in God en Leven in de Wereld', 66–149 (131).

22. Ibid., 66–149 (129).

23. Ibid.

24. Ibid., 66–149 (124, 129).

Before doing so, however, it must first be stressed that Schillebeeckx's emphasis on the gratuity of grace sheds new light on the discussion about the public opposition to ecclesial involvement in politics. Seen from this angle, the failure of the churches to maintain an orthodox relationship with God has deprived human beings of an otherwise unattainable level of joy and fulfilment. In this light, the public opposition to ecclesial involvement in secular politics could be understood as due not only to past political failures of the churches, but also to the churches' religious failure to maintain in their members that sense of awe and wonder for the human–divine relationship, which is every human being's greatest joy and deepest longing. The churches have failed to help their members to assent to that relationship of openness, thankfulness, and joy which is true intersubjective communion with God. A perpetuation of this undervaluation of human joy in the gratuitous relationship of humankind with God can be discerned in the reactionary approach to politics that characterizes both Radical Orthodoxy and public theology. Schillebeeckx, to the contrary, focuses on that which is already good and analyses how the churches' politics could perfect it. His emphasis on the purposelessness of grace could be criticized for rendering the churches apolitical, while his overall grace-optimism could be accused of being naive. The following section will counter both objections by highlighting how Schillebeeckx's account of the crucifixion of Jesus shows that a revitalization of the lost joy in the churches' relationship to God enables the churches to unselfishly mediate the good instead of clinging to a delusionary self-identity.

4. Grace-optimism as Liberation from Politically Limiting Self-concern

When public and Radical Orthodox theologians attempt to convince the public of the benefits resulting from Christian involvement in public matters, their efforts bear the danger of being more concerned about the churches' popularity or success in the wider public than about the common good. Milbank might refuse the contrast between self-interest and dedication to the good because he is critical of the secular ethical imperative of uninterested self-sacrifice for the sake of others. He criticizes that such a morality is not oriented towards the furtherance of the good, but rather celebrates self-constraint for its own sake. A Christian ethics must instead presuppose, and be committed towards, the plenitude of the good and embrace death as the consequence of one's orientation towards the good in a fallen world.[25] Because of the Christian belief in the Resurrection, which posits the superior value of the good over evil, such a dedication to the good is then not selfless but assumes that one's own mediation of the good will eternally participate in the good.

Schillebeeckx's account of the crucifixion concurs largely with this argument. However, while Milbank's view conceives of the superiority of the Christian good,

---

25. J. Milbank, 'Can Morality Be Christian?', *The Word Made Strange: Theology, Language, Culture* (Oxford: Blackwell Publishers, 1997), 229.

that is, on the basis of the Resurrection, in an ideal (i.e., non-realized) manner, Schillebeeckx's theology shifts the focus to the concrete mediation of this reality in the here and now. This allows Schillebeeckx to conceive of a disparity between the churches' self-interest in a respectable position in society and their dedication to the common good, without celebrating self-sacrifice for its own sake. Elaborating on the crucifixion of Jesus, Schillebeeckx claims that Christian politics should not aim at popularity or even public acceptance because even Jesus's own life and message has ultimately been rejected by the people.[26] What is crucial, however, is that Jesus did not abandon his message of salvation to the world despite humanity's rejection of that same salvation.[27] Jesus could accept the failure of his message because he had faith and trust in God's power to save humankind nonetheless. This 'nonetheless' is not to be understood as the ideal conviction that the good is more powerful than evil despite all human experiences to the contrary. Rather, it is because of his joyful experience of the divine presence already at hand, despite the approaching crucifixion, that Jesus could accept his political failure. It was Jesus's living communion with God in times of suffering and crucifixion which convinced him that failure will not have the last word. This corresponds with Milbank's call for Christian ethics to be oriented towards resurrection instead of self-sacrifice. However, from this faith in the unfailing superiority of the good, Schillebeeckx draws the conclusion that neither the churches' position in society nor the Christian ontology of the superiority of the good needs to be defended.

In this light, Christianity's past failure, its concern about its doctrinal propositions as an end in themselves, can be read as an erroneous concern about the churches' identity and about their position in, and power over, the world. This means that public theologians' demonstration of the good that Christianity has done, and can do, for the public, in reaction to past political failures of the churches, might be more likely to perpetuate than to solve the problem.[28] Whether the Christian proclamation is accepted or rejected by the public inhabits too prominent a place in public theological considerations. Likewise, the Radical Orthodox 'offering' of a Christian ontology as the attractive solution to contemporary political problems might be too much aimed at the public acceptance of that vision.[29] A renewed Christian politics that evades this failure

---

26. E. Schillebeeckx, *Christ: The Christian Experience in the Modern World*, trans. J. Bowden, *CW*, vol. 7 (London: Bloomsbury T&T Clark, 2014), 819 [823–4].

27. Schillebeeckx, *Christ*, 819–26 [823–31].

28. Kim, 'Editorial', 1–4 (2); Graham, *Between a Rock and a Hard Place*, xxiii.

29. However, it must be added that Radical Orthodox authors do not aim at the straightforward public acceptance of their ontology, but they seek to attract the public by way of scandalous confrontation. Nevertheless, this confrontational strategy is primarily chosen because Radical Orthodox authors believe that this is exactly what the contemporary public needs in order to surpass its present problems. J. Milbank, *The Word Made Strange: Theology, Language, Culture*, 1–3; G. Ward, *The Politics of Discipleship: Becoming Postmaterial Citizens* (Grand Rapids, MI: Baker Academic, 2009), 180.

should not be concerned about how popular its projects are according to public opinion. Instead, the churches should rejoice in the good wherever it appears, an approach that should enable them to accept the possible humiliation and suffering that might follow if their proclamations are rejected. The churches would have to remind themselves that, when they said 'yes' to God's unfathomable offer to enter a relationship with God, they also said 'yes' to a life of uncertainty, to a life which is not in their control, to a life that is single-heartedly directed towards the good irrespective of the most immediate consequences that this orientation might elicit.[30] Schillebeeckx calls Christianity most essentially a giving oneself over to divine acts, a giving that comports with reality.[31] Who a person is does not lie, ultimately, in that person's own power, but rather in God's. This sense of not being in control reaches its apex in the light of the mysteriousness of God. One gives up one's own plans and surrenders to the One who grants mere glimpses of this truth in surprising moments of self-revelation, but whose future revelations cannot be pre-empted.[32] Based on Schillebeeckx's grace-optimism, the churches should not present themselves as if the world depended on their knowledge and mediation of the good. Instead, they must show in their lives that God continuously provides goodness to the world and that it is a grace and joy to mediate this goodness.

Now that it has been explained that public opposition to ecclesial involvement in politics should be interpreted as the positive reminder that the churches' politics is primarily based on the Christian joy in all that is good, it will be argued that such a corrective learning from past failures is not sufficient. A complete response to public opposition to ecclesial involvement in politics must also include a public acknowledgement of the evil with which the churches have, at times, been complicit.

5. Lament as Public Acknowledgement of Inexplicable Evil

Whereas public theology and Radical Orthodoxy have been primarily concerned with the problem of how past ecclesial failures can be strategically corrected, they have not sufficiently attended to the question of whether, and how, past ecclesial alliances with evil should be publicly commented on or expressed. John Milbank highlights the problems any public confession of past ecclesial failures entails. Often someone is held responsible for the full scope of the harm done. John Milbank argues that such an accusation should be avoided because, even if the churches accuse themselves for the suffering inflicted by their past failures, those

---

30. E. Schillebeeckx, 'Dialoog met God en Christelijke Seculariteit', *God en Mens* (Bilthoven, Holland: Uitgeverij H. Nelissen, 1965), 150–66 (156); trans. *God and Man* (London, Sydney, New York: Sheed & Ward, 1969).

31. Schillebeeckx, 'Dialoog met God en Christelijke Seculariteit', 150–66 (156).

32. Ibid., 150–66 (156-7).

held responsible belong – at least partly – to former generations.[33] Milbank argues that such blaming of our ancestors is patronizing insofar as they did not share our perspective. There might be something in the past evil deeds which we cannot understand and which we consequently cannot judge comprehensively from our perspective.

Schillebeeckx, in his critique of the transition from Enlightenment theodicies to later 'anthropocies', clarifies how this unbridgeable rupture between two perspectives on reality is connected to the Christian understanding of evil as pure privation.[34] Schillebeeckx explains that the Enlightenment mistake of accusing God for the evil that occurs in the world had later been transformed into an accusation of the human 'other'.[35] In both cases, evil is regarded as something explainable and as something for which someone else is responsible. Schillebeeckx observes that, prior to Enlightenment theodicies, the intrinsic unintelligibility of evil was respected insofar as God was never directly accused for the suffering undergone by the faithful. Instead, the faithful turned to God in lament about the unintelligibility of evil.[36]

The problem that arises when faced with evil is that, in the abundantly good reality of God, only the instances of all that is good form an interconnected whole.[37] Every instance of goodness is either negatively or positively connected to all other instances. When evil occurs, Christian theology is faced with the problem that, in speaking about the evil, a connection to all that is meaningful and good is drawn linguistically despite the fact that such a connection does not exist in reality. This means that Christians must somehow express that their speech about past suffering only makes sense insofar as that which has occurred is connected to the altogether meaningful reality as its privation. However, they would have to do so acknowledging that there remains a strictly inexpressible core, which is an utterly singular, isolated, and therefore strictly incommunicable evil.[38]

33. J. Milbank, *Being Reconciled: Ontology and Pardon* (Oxon: Routledge, 2003), 52.

34. E. Schillebeeckx, 'Mysterie van ongerechtigheid en mysterie van erbarmen: vragen rond het menselijk leden', *Tijdschrift voor Theologie* 15 (1975): 3–25; trans. 'Mystery of Injustice and the Mystery of Mercy. Questions Concerning Human Suffering', *Stauros Bulletin* 3 (1975): 3–31.

35. Schillebeeckx, 'Mysterie van ongerechtigheid en mysterie van erbarmen', 3–25 (5–8).

36. Ibid., 3–25 (5). This is again related to the Cross where God was silently present and could be called at and prayed to even in the most unintelligible circumstances. E. Schillebeeckx, 'Mysterie van ongerechtigheid en mysterie van erbarmen', 3–25 (18).

37. J. Milbank, *Theology and Social Theory: Beyond Secular Reason* (Oxford: Blackwell Publishing, [1990] 2006), 12; Milbank, *Being Reconciled*, 6; E. Schillebeeckx, 'De "God van Jezus" en de "Jezus van God"', *Concilium* 93 (1974): 100–15 (106–7); trans. 'The "God of Jesus" and the "Jesus of God"', *Concilium* (Am./Engl.) 93 (1974).

38. Schillebeeckx, 'Mysterie van ongerechtigheid en msyerie van erbarmen', 5. This is in agreement with Karen Kilby's argument that theodicies point to a real problem, but that instead of joining their attempts to solve the problem, Christian theology should search for

Schillebeeckx's insight about the importance of ecclesial lament to God could be interpreted to suggest that, in lament, the churches also use words that are drawn from the realm of meaningful reality. However, instead of weaving the evil into the meaningful whole of reality as but one part which is interconnected with all the others, lament uses these words and disconnects them from the whole. Lament 'throws' the words to God, that is, to that which encompasses and lies beyond the interconnected meanings of reality. The words of lament are thus taken out of their usual connected meaning into dialogue with that which remains beyond conceptual grasp. The suffering, for which there are no proper concepts due to its lack of connection to meaningful reality, is verbalized; instead of connecting it with other concepts, however, one confronts the meaningful whole with it. In lament, one is suspended between the fullness of meaning in which one lives and the meaninglessness of the suffering which is experienced.

Moreover, due to the ontological nothingness of evil, the churches cannot regard the new good as a reversal of, or reaction to, the evil that has been instantiated in the past. This would present the new arrival of the good as if it was in a real connection to the past ecclesial failure(s). The churches must instead express their belief that the new instance of goodness participates in the purely good reality of God, which is not in any way connected to the past evil. The churches' public expression of their failure must then consist of the abandonment of their old ontology, for they now know that while everything appeared as meaningfully interconnected, reality, in truth, also contained an evil under the cover of a supposed good. Consequently, the churches must express anew how all that is good forms an interconnected whole, with particular attention to the new good that has arrived.[39]

6. Lament as Expression of the Superior Reality of Grace

How this turning to God in prayerful lament is connected to the present discussion, about Schillebeeckx's reluctance to defend the churches' position in the public realm, can be clarified by his use of the concept of the negative contrast experience. The latter describes experiences of extreme suffering that thwart one's prior experiences of God and of reality as a meaningful whole. Schillebeeckx

---

ways in which it can express things that it cannot make sense of. Karen Kilby, 'Evil and the Limits of Theology', *New Blackfriars* 84 (2003): 13–29.

39. Schillebeeckx may have been more suspicious of any human claim to the vision of the whole due to his engagement with critical theory [see, e.g., W. L. Portier, 'Interpretation and Method', in *The Praxis of the Reign of God: An Introduction to the Theology of Edward Schillebeeckx*, M. C. Hilkert and R. J. Schreiter (eds) (New York: Fordham University Press, 2002), 19–36 (28–9)]. However, the danger of becoming an ideology is reduced if Christians are prepared to change their vision of how all the good is meaningfully interconnected whenever it is disclosed that this ontology was erroneous.

has been repeatedly criticized for not sufficiently explicating the positive and ethical element in these experiences of negative contrast.[40] Barwasser objects that Schillebeeckx unjustifiably privileges the 'no' of protest in these experiences over the unthematic 'yes' that underlies them.[41] It is suggested that Schillebeeckx's idea of the negative contrast experience could be enhanced if those experiences were primarily interpreted as a revelation of the unconditional freedom of human subjects, which allows them to turn any situation into something better. This could be understood as a fundamental theological argument that would help contemporary public theologians to explain why the churches are not bound or paralysed by their past political failures, and why they can react to them in bringing about something new and better. The emphasis would then lie more on the churches' activity than on the supreme reality of the good.

My argument, however, suggests that Schillebeeckx focuses precisely on the negativity in contrast experiences because of his overarching trust in the positivity of reality. The positivity of the churches' freedom from being bound by evil is then the mediation only of one aspect of this ontological positivity. Whereas Barwasser criticizes Schillebeeckx's later theology as remaining on a more descriptive than philosophically critical level,[42] this superficiality can be regarded as an attempt to be as truthful as possible to the whole of reality, instead of hastily confining that which occurs through human attempts at explanation. That Schillebeeckx focused on the 'superficial' negativity in human experiences of suffering, rather than subduing these experiences to a transcendental analysis, corresponds to Schillebeeckx's ontology. For Schillebeeckx, an ethical correction of a past ecclesial failure is a necessary, but incomplete reaction to the suffering that has been inflicted. The irreversible and inexplicable evil which is at the core of the problem cannot be corrected, but nevertheless one should attend to it. Christian theologians can be 'superficially' descriptive because, trusting that reality is ultimately good, they can endure the negativity of any suffering until it naturally ends in the nothingness from which it came.[43] The faithful can patiently wait until the good will reveal itself again, mediated in and through oneself or others. Schillebeeckx illustrates this when commenting on St Augustine's profound sadness experienced at the death of a friend:

> This Christian would not think away the reality of suffering. This is one of the essentially Christian conceptions of suffering; it is not to be reduced to being an

---

40. C. Barwasser, *Theologie der Kultur und Hermeneutik der Glaubenserfahrung: Zur Gottesfrage und Glaubensverantwortung bei Edward Schillebeeckx OP* (Berlin: LIT, 2010), 435; J. Dunn, 'Negative Contrast Experience and Edward Schillebeeckx: Critical Reflections', in *From North to South: Southern Scholars Engaging with Edward Schillebeeckx*, H. Bergin (ed.) (Hindmarsh: ATF Theology, 2013), 65–84.

41. Barwasser, *Theologie der Kultur und Hermeneutik der Glaubenserfahrung*, 436.

42. Ibid., 411–13.

43. Schillebeeckx, *Church*, 136–7 [138–9].

illusion. That is what makes it so impenetrable a grief: not wanting to 'swim' in a great all-embracing divine mystery, in which the I, the person, really disappear as illusion or sleep.[44]

Because the churches trust in the steadfast goodness of God, they can dare not to interweave the past evil into their new ontology in order to render reality in some way manageable. The churches do not necessarily believe that failures can be corrected, but that they are overcome by the arrival of a new instance of goodness. It is thus not so much humankind's abstract freedom which grounds one's hope of a better future, but rather humankind's natural belonging to, and longing for, God. This enables the churches to dare to experience the suffering of the world instead of hastily searching for explanations and solutions. It allows them not to preempt a realizable joy, which is potentially undermined by a fear that true sadness, which so disconcertingly covers all light and hope, will never end. In fact, 'Suffering is destructively *real*, but it does not have the last word.'[45] Consequently, the churches' position in the public realm must not be defended for the sake of the further redemption of the world, for redemption does not depend on the churches' freedom to resist evil. Instead, the churches' freedom to resist evil depends on God's redemption of the world. It is the churches' primary 'task' to enjoy this redemption wherever it is mediated, and thereby to reveal to the world that all of Creation is sustained by a redemption that continues to be graciously offered.

Conclusion

In this chapter, I have argued for a refocusing of the public theological search for a respectable position of the churches against public opposition to ecclesial involvement in secular politics. Public theologians have suggested that, in reaction to this opposition, the churches should emphasize the positive contributions that Christianity has made to public life. Radical Orthodoxy upholds the idea that a Christian reading of reality is better suited than the prevalent secular ontology to cure contemporary political problems. Both responses to the public mistrust of ecclesial involvement in secular politics exhibit an underlying concern about a respectable position of the churches in the public realm that deviates from Edward Schillebeeckx's grace-optimism. The latter's theology has been drawn upon in order to shift the discussion of public theology from its focus on strategic problem-solving to a focus on the grateful enjoyment of the good as it continues to be divinely offered and humanly mediated in various places in the public sphere. This frees the churches from any illegitimate concern about their self-identity, and for a single-hearted dedication to the good.

44. Schillebeeckx, *Christ*, 690 [698].
45. Ibid., 690 [699].

It has been shown that Schillebeeckx's focus on the reality of the good shares many emphases of the Christian ontology which Radical Orthodox authors triumphantly present as solutions to contemporary political problems. Nevertheless, Schillebeeckx likewise shares public theological reservations towards any *triumphalist* presentation of this ontology and admits the possible defectiveness of the Christian theoretical and practical mediation of the good. This is mainly because Schillebeeckx interprets the public opposition to the churches' involvement in politics as a new mediation of the truly good. The public mistrust of ecclesial involvement in politics should consequently be welcomed as an occasion of joy. The churches should celebrate that God continues to provide His goodness to the world even despite the churches' repeated failings. At the same time, the churches should publicly lament about the past evil publicly to God, in order to resist the temptation to explain this evil's unintelligible core, or to resolve it. According to the Christian ontology that confesses that only the good is ultimately real, evil cannot be resolved; it can only be overcome.

In sum, we can learn from Schillebeeckx that, for Christians who put their trust in God, church decline and the feared exclusion of the churches from public life are not reasons to panic. Schillebeeckx describes his alternative view as one of grace-optimism, when he writes that those who are leaving the churches in an honest search for authentic humanism are already searching for God, and that, although they may not find God, God will indeed find those who truly search for God.[46] And even those who might not be actively searching will find no peace in the purely inner-worldly realm, for even one's refusal to enjoy God's offer of the graces of Creation and salvation cannot undo the fact that God personally loves each person and will never leave humankind at rest.[47]

Bibliography

Ayres, L., 'Book Review: Theology and Social Theory: Beyond Secular Reason', *Scottish Journal of Theology* 45 (1992): 125–6.

Barwasser, C., *Theologie der Kultur und Hermeneutik der Glaubenserfahrung: Zur Gottesfrage und Glaubensverantwortung bei Edward Schillebeeckx OP* (Berlin: LIT, 2010).

Brown, M., S. Pattison and G. Smith, 'The Possibility of Citizen Theology: Public Theology after Christendom and the Enlightenment', *International Journal of Public Theology* 6 (2012): 183–204.

Burrus, V., 'Radical Orthodoxy and the Heresiological Habit', in *Interpreting the Postmodern:Responses to 'Radical Orthodoxy'*, R. Radford Ruether and M. Gau (eds) (London: T&T Clark, 2006), 36–53.

Dunn, D. J., 'Radical Sophiology: Fr. Sergej Bulgakov and John Milbank on Augustine', *Studies in East European Thought* 64 (2012): 227–49.

46. Schillebeeckx, 'Leven in God en Leven in de Wereld', 66–149 (115).
47. Ibid., 66–149 (139).

Dunn, J., 'Negative Contrast Experience and Edward Schillebeeckx: Critical Reflections', in *From North to South: Southern Scholars Engaging with Edward Schillebeeckx*, H. Bergin (ed.) (Hindmarsh: ATF Theology, 2013), 65–84.

Graham, E., 'Power, Knowledge and Authority in Public Theology', *International Journal of Public Theology* 1 (2007): 42–62.

Graham, E., *Between a Rock and a Hard Place: Public Theology in a Post-Secular Age* (London: SCM, 2013).

Hilkert, M. C., '"Grace-Optimism": The Spirituality at the Heart of Schillebeeckx's Theology', *Spirituality Today* 43 (1991): 220–39.

Kilby, K., 'Evil and the Limits of Theology', *New Blackfriars* 84 (2003): 13–29.

Kim, S., 'Editorial', *International Journal of Public Theology* 1 (2007): 1–4.

Kim, S., 'Editorial', *International Journal of Public Theology* 1 (2007): 147–50.

Kim, S., 'Editorial', *International Journal of Public Theology* 4 (2010): 131–4.

Kim, S., *Theology in the Public Sphere: Public Theology as a Catalyst for Open Debate* (London: SCM Press, 2011).

Mathewes, C., *A Theology of Public Life* (Cambridge: Cambridge University Press, 2007).

Milbank, J., *Theology and Social Theory: Beyond Secular Reason* (Oxford: Blackwell Publishing, [1990] 2006).

Milbank, J., *The Word Made Strange: Theology, Language, Culture* (Oxford: Blackwell Publishers, 1997).

Milbank, J., 'Beauty and the Soul', *Theological Perspectives on God and Beauty* (London: Trinity Press International, 2003), 1–34.

Milbank, J., *Being Reconciled: Ontology and Pardon* (Oxon: Routledge, 2003).

Milbank, J., *The Future of Love: Essays in Political Theology* (London: SCM Press, 2009).

Portier, W. L., 'Interpretation and Method', in *The Praxis of the Reign of God: An Introduction to the Theology of Edward Schillebeeckx*, M. C. Hilkert and R. J. Schreiter (eds) (New York: Fordham University Press, 2002), 19–36.

Rayment-Pickard, H., 'Derrida and Nihilism', in *Deconstructing Radical Orthodoxy: Postmodern Theology, Rhetoric and Truth*, W. J. Hankey and D. Hedley (eds) (Aldershot: Ashgate, 2005), 161–76.

Schillebeeckx, E., 'Dialoog met God en Christelijke Seculariteit', *God en Mens* [Bilthoven (Holland): Uitgeverij H. Nelissen, 1965], 150–66; [trans. *God and Man* (London, Sydney, New York: Sheed & Ward, 1969)].

Schillebeeckx, E., 'Leven in God en Leven in de Wereld', *God en Mens* [Bilthoven (Holland): Uitgeverij H. Nelissen, 1965], 66–149; [trans. *God and Man* (London, Sydney, New York: Sheed & Ward, 1969)].

Schillebeeckx, E., 'De "God van Jezus" en de "Jezus van God"', *Concilium* 93 (1974): 100–15; trans. 'The "God of Jesus" and the "Jesus of God"', *Concilium* (Am./Engl.) 93 (1974): 110–26.

Schillebeeckx, E., 'Mysterie van ongerechtigheid en mysterie van erbarmen: vragen rond het menselijk leden', *Tijdschrift voor Theologie* 15 (1975): 3–25; trans. 'Mystery of Injustice and the Mystery of Mercy. Questions Concerning Human Suffering', *Stauros Bulletin* 3 (1975): 3–31.

Schillebeeckx, E., *Christ: The Christian Experience in the Modern World*, trans. J. Bowden, *CW*, vol. 7 (London: Bloomsbury T&T Clark, 2014).

Schillebeeckx, E., *Church: The Human Story of God*, trans. J. Bowden, *CW*, vol. 10 (London: Bloomsbury T&T Clark, 2014).

Shakespeare, S., *Radical Orthodoxy: A Critical Introduction* (London: SPCK, 2007).

Storrar, W., '2007: A Kairos Moment for Public Theology', *International Journal of Public Theology* 1 (2007): 5–25.

Stout, J., *Democracy and Tradition* (Princeton: Princeton University Press, 2003).

Ward, G., *The Politics of Discipleship: Becoming Postmaterial Citizens* (Grand Rapids, MI: Baker Academic, 2009).

Chapter 3

A THEOLOGIAN STANDING WITH GOD IN THE WORLD: DEVELOPMENT IN SCHILLEBEECKX'S EPISTEMOLOGY AND IMPLICATIONS FOR FEMINIST THEOLOGY

Megan Loumagne

The theologian is called to stand at the dangerous crossing of the roads – at the point where faith comes into contact with modern thought and the whole of the new philosophical situation, but where no synthesis has as yet been achieved.[1]

Edward Schillebeeckx argues that theology is fundamentally fraught with danger and risk since theologians must always strive to do more than simply repeat church dogma. Refusing to think creatively inevitably renders theology stuck in a paralysis of habitual thought. Instead, Schillebeeckx suggests that theologians must be catalysts helping the church move forward by being the 'antennae with which the church feels modern thought'.[2] This is risky because the theologian who adopts a listening posture to the developments of the contemporary age, and who seeks to synthesize the 'new philosophical situation'[3] with the Christian gospel, runs the risk of being perceived as antagonistic to the Magisterium of the church, which typically serves a conservative function in seeking to protect the deposit of faith and prevent haphazard transitions in the church. Yet, the willingness of theologians to take this risk of thinking creatively is crucial for the continued flourishing of the church, for without some type of synthesis between the Christian faith and contemporary thought, the Christian faith will become increasingly meaningless to humanity. As Schillebeeckx expressed, 'The language of faith and the language of the church become meaningless or empty to the degree that they no longer contain any recognizable reference to real experiences in the everyday

---

1. E. Schillebeeckx, 'What Is Theology?', *Revelation and Theology*, trans. N. D. Smith, *CW*, vol. 2 (London: Bloomsbury T&T Clark, 2014), 106 [163].

2. Schillebeeckx, 'What Is Theology?', 106 [163].

3. Ibid., 106 [163].

world.'[4] The task of the theologian is always evolving as human history develops and the nature of contemporary society also changes. Thus, the theologian has the perpetual responsibility to listen to the world in order to find the places in which God's Spirit is at work, and to seek new ways to express the language of faith in a constantly changing world.

Schillebeeckx, then, emphasizes 'intense presence-in-the-world'[5] as a necessary condition for theology. This approach has gained new relevance since 2013, when Jorge Bergoglio was named pope of the Catholic Church. Bergoglio chose the name Francis as his papal name in honour of St. Francis of Assisi, whom he described as 'the man of poverty, the man of peace, the man who loves and protects creation'.[6] Since the beginning of his papacy, Pope Francis has consistently shown himself to be a shepherd who 'smells like the sheep',[7] and a pastor who is deeply connected to the concerns and sufferings of the people, particularly the poor and marginalized. In his first encyclical, *Evangelii Gaudium*, Francis exhorts the church to take boldly the initiative 'to go out to others, seek those who have fallen away, stand at the crossroads and welcome the outcast'.[8] Here, Francis encourages the church to be outward looking and sensitive to the sufferings of the contemporary age. He also notes that theologians have a crucial role to play in the church by helping 'the judgment of the church to mature',[9] in the light of 'differing currents of thought in philosophy, theology and pastoral practice'.[10] By promoting the notions of a church that embraces the messiness of human history, and theologians who synthesize modern thought with the faith, Pope Francis expresses many of the theological priorities of Edward Schillebeeckx, particularly the notion that human experience can be revelatory of God and is a crucial data source for both pastoral ministry and theological development. The renewed spirit of openness that Pope Francis has ushered into the church, together with his pastoral sensitivity to the daily sufferings of people, presents a timely opportunity for all theologians, and particularly feminist theologians, to retrieve the insights of Edward Schillebeeckx in order to construct new theologies for our time.

While Pope Francis has created more space for theologians in the church, his statements regarding women and gender have been more ambivalent. He has

---

4. E. Schillebeeckx, *Christ: The Christian Experience in the Modern World*, trans. J. Bowden, *CW*, vol. 7 (London: Bloomsbury T&T Clark, 2014), 806 [810].

5. Schillebeeckx, 'What Is Theology?', 107 [165].

6. C. Wooden, 'Pope Francis Explains Why He Chose St. Francis of Assisi's Name', *The Catholic Telegraph*, http://www.thecatholictelegraph.com/pope-francis-explains-why-he-chose-st-francis-of-assisis-name/13243 (accessed 31 May 2015).

7. Pope Francis, *Evangelii Gaudium* §24, http://w2.vatican.va/content/francesco/en/apost_exhortations/documents/papa-francesco_esortazione-ap_20131124_evangelii-gaudium.html (Vatican, 24 November 2013).

8. Pope Francis, *Evangelli Gaudium* §24.

9. Ibid., §40.

10. Ibid.

urged the church to create more spaces for women to speak and to be heard, and he has expressed a desire to see women playing a more prominent role in making decisions in the church.[11] However, he continues to operate within a problematic and antiquated framework for thinking about women that ultimately hinders the important progress that he verbally acknowledges is necessary in the church today. Recall, for example, his continual dependence on the notion of a 'feminine genius'[12] that women possess, a genius which supposedly equips them with special insights into reality. While on the surface this appears to be an idea that is complimentary of women, it is problematic insofar as it presents women as part of a special class of 'others'. If women's limitations and foibles are not equally acknowledged along with men's, a reductive view of women becomes operative, a view that undermines their full membership in the human race, which itself is presented with only a limited range of possibilities. In the concrete life of the church, the special status of women has functioned to cut them off from full participation in its ministry and hierarchy. A more extreme example of Pope Francis's troubling understanding of gender can be seen in his statement that women are 'the strawberry on the cake',[13] which suggests that women are merely decorative, an optional add-on. While it is not entirely clear what Pope Francis meant to communicate with this statement, and it was certainly not meant to be a systematic development of his thoughts on gender, it nevertheless reflects the limitations of his understandings of women and gender, as well as highlights an area of necessary growth in the church.

In this chapter, I argue that the theology of 'intense presence-in-the-world',[14] articulated by Edward Schillebeeckx and supported by Pope Francis both in theory and in practice, must necessarily bear fruit in the church's approach to gender. I focus on the resources that Schillebeeckx's theology and epistemology provide the church in the twenty-first century, as it navigates impasses related to discussions of gender and the role of women in the church. I suggest further that Schillebeeckx provides a theological foundation through which dissenting voices can fulfil a crucial role in the reconsideration and reconstruction of doctrine in the light of historical changes. Because the papacy of Francis has created a greater sense of openness in the church, this is a key moment for feminist theologians to draw from the resources of Schillebeeckx to move towards a more inclusive church.

---

11. H. Roberts, 'Women Theologians Are the "Strawberry on the Cake", says Pope', *The Tablet: The International Catholic News Weekly*, 11 December 2014, http://www.thetablet. co.uk/news/1508/0/-women-theologians-are-the-strawberry-on-the-cake-says-pope (accessed 6 January 2015).

12. Roberts, 'Women Theologians Are the "Strawberry on the Cake", says Pope'.

13. Ibid.

14. Schillebeeckx, 'What Is Theology?', 107 [165].

1. The Authority of Culturally Conditioned Church Dogma

While Schillebeeckx's theology is the fruit of his methodology, the foundation of his methodology is his epistemology, and all of this holds particular relevance for feminist theologians. In regard to Schillebeeckx's epistemology, Daniel P. Thompson has identified three 'epistemological circles'[15] within Schillebeeckx's thought that form the foundation of his methodology, with different circles being featured more prominently at distinct points in Schillebeeckx's career. Indeed, there was a marked development in Schillebeeckx's epistemology and methodology throughout the course of his career. However, this development also reflects continuity, as Mary Catherine Hilkert notes, particularly in regard to the phenomenological emphasis on 'revelation as the encounter between God and humanity which occurs in human history'.[16] In his early work, Schillebeeckx primarily utilizes what Thompson describes as the first 'epistemological circle', which focuses on the necessity of church dogma providing the starting point for theological constructions. In this early phase of his theology, while Schillebeeckx emphasizes that the church's teaching authority is the 'final norm'[17] for the development of theology and the interpretation of Scripture, he also notes that this knowledge is always limited by the existential categories of the time and the perpetual limits of human concepts and language. Schillebeeckx expresses this view when he states that 'the typical intellectual value of our conceptual knowledge of God is therefore situated in a projective act in which we reach out towards God via the conceptual contents'.[18] While church dogma is authoritative and binding, language and concepts are always limited and can never fully capture the reality of God. It is essential to Schillebeeckx's epistemology at this stage to note, 'We cannot grasp God conceptually, although we do know that he is present in the direction that is indicated by the contents of the concept'.[19] Thus, for the early Schillebeeckx, every attempt to do theology or to express theological truth is subject to the authority of the Magisterium, while also being historically conditioned and limited. Humans can never master God or obtain complete knowledge of God; rather, they can make only fragmented attempts to reach out to God, and are always bound to describe God using 'existential categories'.[20]

This first 'epistemological circle' of Schillebeeckx's is useful for feminist theologians in that it provides the groundwork for an ecclesial epistemological humility that promotes dialogue between those who come from different

15. D. P. Thompson, 'Schillebeeckx on the Development of Doctrine', *Theological Studies* 62 (2001): 305.

16. M. C. Hilkert, 'Hermeneutics of History in the Theology of Edward Schillebeeckx', *The Thomist: A Speculative Quarterly Review* 51 (1987): 99.

17. Schillebeeckx, 'What Is Theology?', 82 [123].

18. Schillebeeckx, 'The Concept of "Truth"', *Revelation and Theology*, 199 [20].

19. Schillebeeckx, 'The Concept of "Truth"',199 [20].

20. Ibid., 201 [23].

cultural backgrounds, and who thus have different perspectives or 'existential categories'[21] from which to derive and express truth. If everyone's attempt to name God and to make theological truth claims in the world is 'relativized',[22] or conditioned by one's historical location, then it is essential to the development of a robust understanding of theological truth to hear from those who can offer a different way of conceptualizing truth from one's own. As Hilkert summarizes Schillebeeckx's perspective at this stage, 'The mystery at the heart of reality can and must be approached from different perspectives, none of which is exhaustive or complete.'[23] Thus, even in his early and more dogmatically oriented epistemology – one that exhibits a stronger commitment to the authority of the teaching office of the church as the guarantor of orthodoxy than that found in his later work – Schillebeeckx provides a resource for feminist theology. This way of approaching theological knowledge and the development of dogma presents a challenge to the contemporary situation of the Catholic Magisterium, which has very few women in significant places of authority who can contribute different viewpoints to counterbalance its predominantly male perspective. Schillebeeckx favours a dialogical method of decision-making in the church, as opposed to an overly hierarchical approach. He critiques the latter, evident in the following characterization of its result: 'The laity, above all the women, in it [i.e., the church] are no longer subjects, those who carry on and make church history; they become the objects of the priestly, hierarchical and male proclamation and pastorate.'[24]

In order to promote sufficiently the full humanity and subjectivity of women, and to ensure a nuanced and complex understanding of theological truth as the church moves forward into the twenty-first century, the Magisterium must create more significant spaces to hear from the voices of women. Schillebeeckx's epistemology, even in its early stages, works against an overly hierarchical model of theological development, and it supports the inclusion of women in positions of authority in the church.

2. The Authority of Human History as 'Foreign Prophecy'

Schillebeeckx's second epistemological circle is, as Thompson notes, the 'hermeneutical circle of context, new experiences and reformed context.'[25] In this stage, Schillebeeckx expresses that 'knowledge is mediated by historical tradition, present encounter, and future anticipation.'[26] This is an epistemology rooted in

21. Ibid.

22. Hilkert, 'Hermeneutics of History in the Theology of Edward Schillebeeckx', 100.

23. Ibid., 106.

24. E. Schillebeeckx, *Church: The Human Story of God*, trans. J. Bowden, *CW*, vol. 10 (London: Bloomsbury T&T Clark, 2014), 197 [199].

25. Thompson, 'Schillebeeckx on the Development of Doctrine', 305.

26. Ibid.

the past, grounded in the present, and looking forward with expectation to the eschatological future. While the first epistemological circle is primarily defined by its focus on dogma as the starting point for theology (with an emphasis on the fragmentary nature of conceptual knowledge of God), the second epistemological circle demonstrates Schillebeeckx's theological shift, from dogma as the starting point for theological knowledge to human history as a source of 'foreign prophecy' that reveals the 'familiar voice' of God.[27] This shift can be seen in his approach to Christology. As Thompson notes, for Schillebeeckx, 'the salvific encounter with Jesus is the basis for the explicit language of revelation, Scripture, and confession in the Church.'[28] In *The Interim Report on the Books Jesus and Christ*, which was published in 1980, Schillebeeckx emphasizes that the foundation of the Christian faith is not the dogmas articulated by the Magisterium, but rather the historical experience of Jesus by the first disciples. By making this shift in emphasis, he disturbs the certainty and objectivity of dogmatic statements. He notes that even the creed is 'the groping attempts of Christians, that is, of believers and their leaders, to bear witness to their specific experience of salvation in Jesus. ... The original experience out of which this creed was born is that Jesus of Nazareth, the prophet of the eschatological kingdom, *is* Christ.'[29]

For Schillebeeckx, then, in his second epistemological circle, theological knowledge is always fundamentally anchored in the experience of Christ in the middle of the messiness of human history, where Christ is experienced as the fulfilment of the kingdom of God and the revelation of God's radical love for humanity, which is manifest in the liberation and wholeness of humanity. The creed is, as Thompson notes, the 'translation of Christian experience from one historical context to the next.'[30] Here again one finds Schillebeeckx's ongoing phenomenological focus on theological knowledge as based in an encounter – specifically, the encounter with Christ who is the sacrament of God. While Christ is the image of God, he is also 'the image of what a human being really needs to be, a picture of true and good humanity.'[31] To encounter the risen Christ is to encounter not only divinity, but also humanity fulfilled and freed from all oppression and degradation. As Schillebeeckx notes, 'In the last resort Jesus, whom we may call God's beloved Son, is also a human being just like you or me – except that he is ever more human.'[32] Because Jesus is the fulfilment of the kingdom, he reveals God as permanently committed to the cause of humanity.

27. E. Schillebeeckx, 'Church, Magisterium and Politics', *God the Future of Man*, trans. N. D. Smith, *CW*, vol. 3 (London: Bloomsbury T&T Clark, 2014), 76 [126].

28. Thompson, 'Schillebeeckx on the Development of Doctrine', 306.

29. E. Schillebeeckx, *Interim Report on the Books Jesus and Christ*, trans. J. Bowden, *CW*, vol. 8 (London: Bloomsbury T&T Clark, 2014), 109 [125–6]; original emphasis.

30. Thompson, 'Schillebeeckx on the Development of Doctrine', 309.

31. Ibid., 132.

32. Ibid., 139.

In this epistemological schema, the measuring rod of the orthodoxy of theological statements is not solely their correlation to the 'deposit of faith', but also their connection to the actual liberation and wholeness of humankind. A doctrine cannot be true if it degrades human persons. Schillebeeckx states that 'whatever feature of empirical Christianity contradicts the demands of collective and personal human liberation must therefore be rejected in the name of Christian faith itself'.[33] This stage in Schillebeeckx's epistemology is also where he begins to articulate his notion of negative contrast experiences, or experiences of radical suffering, as particular places of God's revelation in human history.

Schillebeeckx's second epistemological circle is also a useful resource for feminist theologians. In his emphasis on theological knowledge as shaped by the historical encounter with Jesus as the Christ, who is the fulfilment of the kingdom of God, and who brings salvation to humanity that is manifest in the liberation and wholeness of humanity, Schillebeeckx identifies human flourishing – including the flourishing of women – as being of central importance to Christian theological truth. Hilkert notes, 'As a claim about the future and the God who empowers that future, the Christian faith must be "proved true" in the course of human history.'[34] Within this epistemological circle, dogmatic pronouncements or symbolic representations of theological information that dehumanize, diminish, or degrade any human person cannot rightly be considered appropriate reflections of the gospel message. The encounter with Jesus as the sacrament of God's unconditional love of humanity reveals 'God's preference for those who have been diminished and made of no account'.[35] In our time, society is becoming increasingly conscious of the extent to which women's history has been a history of oppression, abuse, dehumanization, infantilization, objectification, and silencing. To propose an epistemology of encounter with the God of liberating love who seeks the wholeness of humanity is to work against the human historical pattern of oppression against women. It promotes the liberation of all who have been subjugated and silenced. Additionally, it holds theology accountable to history. Any theology that diminishes people is a false theology. Thus, Schillebeeckx's second epistemological circle is a particularly valuable resource for feminist theology.

3. The Authority of Negative Contrast Experiences and Orthopraxis

Finally, Schillebeeckx's third epistemological circle, according to Thompson, is the 'critical circle of theory and praxis'.[36] As Thompson notes, in this circle, 'knowledge is mediated by negative contrast experiences, ideology critique, and action on

---

33. E. Schillebeeckx, 'Redemption and Human Emancipation', in *The Schillebeeckx Reader*, R. J. Schreiter (ed.) (New York: Crossroad, 1984), 255.

34. Hilkert, 'Hermeneutics of History in the Theology of Edward Schillebeeckx', 111.

35. Ibid., 138.

36. Thompson, 'Schillebeeckx on the Development of Doctrine', 305.

the behalf of suffering humanity'.[37] It also includes an emphasis on the life of the community of faith in the development of doctrine. This third circle is the most dominant epistemological model used by Schillebeeckx in his later works, and it reflects a more explicitly political turn in his theology. At this point in the development of his writing, as Hilkert notes, Schillebeeckx reflects a growing awareness that 'the language and structures of the living tradition are not only inadequate; they may also be repressive distortions of the true mystery'.[38] Thus, in his later work, Schillebeeckx places a strong emphasis on the importance of 'orthopraxis'[39] as demonstrated in Christian communities for the understanding, and to the development, of orthodoxy.

In this vein, he especially uses the notion of negative contrast experiences, or experiences of radical human suffering, as key sources of theological knowledge. While he maintains throughout his work that revelation can occur in moments of beauty, joy, and human liberation, he notes that it is particularly in the 'contrast experiences'[40] of human suffering that 'the Creator God is revealed "on the underside of the experience" as the source of human hope, protest, and resistance',[41] and 'the power grounding and sustaining humanity in the face of all that is inhuman'.[42] The third epistemological circle is thus the most directly focused on ideological critique, with revelation occurring within Christian communities, and the necessity of the gospel manifesting in human liberation in the light of the excess of suffering in the world.

Schillebeeckx expresses this third epistemological circle in multiple places in his later works, but particularly in *Church: The Human Story of God*, published in English in 1990. Here, he argues that, as Christians, we ought to be 'dissociating ourselves from what an ideological kind of Christianity has done to people up to the present time and still continues to do'.[43] Thus, Schillebeeckx argues that an ideological Christianity contributes to oppression, subverts the message of the gospel, and renders the church a communion that 'obscures its own truth'.[44] He specifically identifies the (strictly) hierarchically structured form of the Catholic Church that resists any democratic elements as a 'historical misunderstanding' that the Magisterium has come to regard as 'divinely willed'.[45] He suggests that this hierarchical structure is a particularly painful area of dissonance between the Catholic faithful and the Magisterium. Because of the growing embrace of democratic ideals in secular culture, this perceived 'monarchical absolutism' in

37. Ibid.
38. Hilkert, 'Hermeneutics of History in the Theology of Edward Schillebeeckx', 118.
39. Thompson, 'Schillebeeckx on the Development of Doctrine', 311.
40. Hilkert, 'Hermeneutics of History in the Theology of Edward Schillebeeckx', 117.
41. Ibid.
42. Ibid.
43. Schillebeeckx, *Church*, 187 [189].
44. Ibid., 212 [214].
45. Ibid., 186 [188].

the church is 'really felt to be intolerable', according to Schillebeeckx.[46] In contrast to this model, he emphasizes the message that was promulgated by the Second Vatican Council, that 'the co-responsibility of all believers for the church on the basis of our baptism in water and the Spirit essentially includes the participation of all believers in decisions relating to church government'.[47] Thus, Schillebeeckx's later work is primarily defined by his growing concern for ideological critique, including critique of the church itself.

Schillebeeckx's emphasis on Christian praxis as essential to theological epistemology can also be seen in *Church: The Human Story of God*. The basis for his argument that Christian praxis is revelatory of theological truth is rooted in his fundamental belief in the Holy Spirit as 'at work throughout the life of the church: generally and specifically in all the people of God and in a specific ministerial way in the official activity of the church leaders'.[48] The Holy Spirit is the source and guarantor of all revelation of truth, and is particularly active in the community of faith and in those who lead it – both those officially part of the hierarchy and 'lay' leaders. Thus, since the life of the community is a primary locus for the work of the Spirit, this life of the community is a special source of revelation. As Schillebeeckx notes, 'The practice of the community is the sphere in which theology is born.'[49] This adds an important nuance to his notion of the centrality of human experience in revelation, which otherwise could run the risk of suggesting an overly individualistic epistemology. In this vein, Hilkert writes, 'The experience which Schillebeeckx describes as a source of revelation is ecclesial, rather than individual, experience.'[50] Christian praxis as central to doctrinal development, then, is another primary focus of Schillebeeckx's later work.

The final element of Schillebeeckx's third epistemological circle is his understanding of negative contrast experiences as especially revelatory of God. His articulation of the centrality of experiences of deep suffering for theological insight is pervasive throughout his later writings. The foundation for this belief, that God is revealed in human suffering, is that God's salvation is manifest in human wholeness and liberation. God intends for humanity to be whole and free. Schillebeeckx thus notes, 'The history of human liberation can become a "disclosure" in which man learns to recognize God as the one who wills the complete liberation of man.'[51] In fact, for humans to understand the meaning of salvation, they must have some experience of liberation.[52] While human liberation

46. Ibid.

47. Ibid., 208 [209].

48. Ibid., 219 [220].

49. E. Schillebeeckx, *The Church with a Human Face*, trans. J. Bowden, *CW*, vol. 9 (London: Bloomsbury T&T Clark, 2014), 10 [12].

50. Hilkert, 'Hermeneutics of History in the Theology of Edward Schillebeeckx', 125.

51. Schillebeeckx, *Christ*, 810 [814].

52. J. O'Meara, 'Salvation: Living Communion with God', in *The Praxis of the Reign of God: An Introduction to the Theology of Edward Schillebeeckx*, M. C. Hilkert and R. J. Schreiter (eds) (New York, Fordham University Press, 2002), 108.

and wholeness reveal God, the more typical experience in human history is of the failure to achieve liberation, and of a scandalous amount of gratuitous suffering. As Schillebeeckx notes, 'Suffering is the alpha and omega of the whole history of mankind; it is the scarlet thread by which this historical fragment is recognizable as human history: history is "an ecumene of suffering".'[53] While human wholeness and flourishing are the marks of the in-breaking kingdom of God, and, as such, are revelatory of God, human suffering also has 'a particular critical and productive epistemological force'.[54] Suffering reveals an implicit and veiled 'awareness of values',[55] specifically the worth of humanity, and it provokes the conscience to resistance and protest. Without minimizing the scandal of human suffering, Schillebeeckx does emphasize that the negative contrast experience can bear both conceptual and practical fruit. Through the experience of suffering, human persons come to a deeper knowledge of the value of humanity, as well as the ways in which the human person 'is kept at this low level precisely by the pressure of existing social structures to which he is subject'.[56] Thus, there exists an intrinsic connection between negative contrast experience and ideological critique. In Schillebeeckx's later work, this focus on the epistemological and practical value of negative contrast experience(s) features prominently.

All three elements of Schillebeeckx's third epistemological circle – the importance of ideological critique, the unity of praxis and theory, and the centrality of negative contrast experiences to theological development – bear profound relevance for feminist theology. Schillebeeckx himself expresses the importance of ideological critique for women when he comments on the exclusion of women from decision-making in the church. This exclusion, he says, renders women 'no longer subjects … who carry on and make church history'; rather, they are 'the objects of the priestly, hierarchical and male proclamation and pastorate'.[57] This persistent objectification of women in the church is a source of scandal, and ideological critique is essential in revealing this injustice. Ideological critique is necessary in order to exhort the church to conversion on this point. Additionally, in *God Is New Each Moment*, Schillebeeckx acknowledges that ideological critique is already occurring within feminist theology. He says, 'Feminist theologians are providing evidence of a fundamental process of emancipation among women. There is a movement which tries to expose the elements that are present in the whole of theology and that discriminate against women.'[58] Thus, Schillebeeckx's late emphasis on the importance of ideological critique – for epistemology and the development of doctrine in the church – provides a rich resource for feminist theologians continuing this process of working towards the full inclusion of women in the church in the contemporary age.

---

53. Schillebeeckx, *Christ*, 718 [725].

54. Ibid., 813 [816].

55. Schillebeeckx, 'Church, Magisterium and Politics', 93 [154].

56. Ibid., 93 [155].

57. Schillebeeckx, *Church*, 197 [199].

58. Schillebeeckx, *God Is New Each Moment*, 77.

In addition, Schillebeeckx's commitment to developing theological knowledge from reflection upon the praxis of the people of God is beneficial to the work of feminist theologians in that this epistemology considers the experiences of all members of the community of faith as potentially revelatory of truth. Since the Holy Spirit is the guarantor of revelation and the source of all truth, and because the Holy Spirit is given to all who are baptized, the experiences of women within the community of faith must hold equal weight with the rest of the baptized in possibly being revelatory of God. However, as Mary Farrell Bednarowski has noted in her book *The Religious Imagination of American Women*, while, statistically speaking, women tend to be highly participatory in religions – even more so than men – their participation has historically been in 'more private ways that have been unacknowledged and undervalued'.[59] This tendency has led to a pervasive sense among religious women in the United States that they are simultaneously insiders and outsiders within the religion. The awkward position of women within many faith communities in the United States has contributed to a common experience of being 'grounded in a deep sense of belonging, familiarity, and commitment and an equally strong sense of alienation and distrust'.[60] If Schillebeeckx is correct in his assertion that the Holy Spirit reveals God through the experiences of all believers within the faith community, then the ambivalent experiences of such a large percentage of the church must be taken into serious consideration as the church moves forward in the twenty-first century. Thus, Schillebeeckx's epistemological emphasis on the value of praxis for the development of doctrinal statements and theological knowledge is a helpful resource for feminist theologians.

Finally, Schillebeeckx's development regarding the value of negative contrast experiences for theological reflection holds particular relevance for feminist theologians. While every human suffers in a variety of ways, the suffering of women is particularly ubiquitous throughout the history of human culture. As Elizabeth Johnson notes,

> While comprising 1/2 of the world's population, women do 3/4 of the world's work; receive 1/10 of the world's salary; own 1/100 of the world's land; form 2/3 of illiterate adults; and together with their dependent children are 3/4 of the world's starving people. In addition, women are raped, beaten, prostituted, and murdered by men to an extent that is not mutual.[61]

---

59. M. Farrell Bednarowski, *The Religious Imagination of American Women* (Indiana: Indiana University Press, 1999), 4. Bednarowski is professor emerita of religious studies at United Theological Seminary of the Twin Cities (Minnesota, USA).

60. Farrell Bednarowski, *The Religious Imagination of American Women*, 19.

61. E. Johnson, 'Forging Theology: A Conversation with Colleagues', in *Things New and Old: Essays on the Theology of Elizabeth A. Johnson*, P. Zagano and T. W. Tilley (eds) (New York: Crossroad, 1999), 91.

In addition, Ann O'Hara Graff notes that the 'deeply troubling fact of violence against women'[62] has been so internalized by women that 'we have become violators of ourselves and others'.[63] She describes the violence as both domestic and social, including 'rape, wife battering, incest, child abuse, [and the fact that] women are the poorest and the most numerous of the poor'.[64] Many women throughout the world are thus very familiar with the experience that Schillebeeckx describes as a negative contrast experience, which evokes the response of 'this cannot go on'.[65] A negative contrast experience also incites the conscience to protest and revolt against the degradation and suffering of humanity. Feminist theologians who seek the emancipation of women from unjust structures of oppression can thus find support in Schillebeeckx's notion of the contrast experience. While this protest is sparked by a negative experience of suffering, the move towards protest and emancipation is essentially positive, as it is an expression of hope. As Schillebeeckx notes, 'The protest prompted by these negative experiences ("this cannot go on") is also the expression of the firm hope that things *can* be done differently, *must* improve, and *will* get better through our commitment.'[66] Thus, Schillebeeckx's exhortation to listen to the voices of those who suffer in the world, and his emphasis on the necessity for all humans – but particularly Christians – to work to relieve that suffering, does not only support the work of feminist theologians to emancipate women; it also reveals this work as crucial to the mission of the church. As he notes, 'On the basis of humane and Christian motives, however, the believer – and especially the theologian – must play a critical but active part in the history of emancipative freedom.'[67] Here, Schillebeeckx promotes an understanding of the role of critical communities within the church as both necessary and beneficial for the church and the world. Dissenting voices that critique any unjust structure – including the church – that threatens the dignity of humanity are significantly contributing to the salvation and liberation of all people because that is the will of God and the heart of the gospel message. This aspect of Schillebeeckx's thought is of great benefit to feminist theologians.

Conclusion

Any praxis which manipulates human freedom and brings about alienation is both wrong and heterodox.[68]

62. A. O'Hara Graff, 'The Struggle to Name Women's Experience', in *In the Embrace of God: Feminist Theological Anthropology* (Maryknoll, NY: Orbis, 1995), 82.

63. O'Hara Graff, 'The Struggle to Name Women's Experience', 82.

64. Ibid.

65. Schillebeeckx, 'Church, Magisterium and Politics', 99 [164].

66. Ibid., 95 [158].

67. E. Schillebeeckx, 'The New Critical Theory and Theological Hermeneutics', *The Understanding of Faith: Interpretation and Criticism*, trans. N. D. Smith, *CW*, vol. 5 (London: Bloomsbury T&T Clark, 2014), 111 [127].

68. Schillebeeckx, 'The New Critical Theory and Theological Hermeneutics', 116 [132].

Spanning the different stages in his work, Schillebeeckx presents many helpful resources to feminist theology in his epistemological commitments that form the foundation of his theological approach. His emphasis on the responsibility of theologians to take the concerns of the contemporary age seriously, and to commit to an 'intense presence-in-the-world',[69] must bear fruit in the church's attitude towards women. As women constitute a significant percentage of those enduring negative contrast experiences in the world, and these negative contrast experiences are significant sources of theological insight, the perspectives of women are of particular import for the church seeking to discover the ways in which God's Spirit is at work in the world. With the new spirit of openness in the church that has been inculcated by Pope Francis, this is a key time for feminist theologians to retrieve the work of Schillebeeckx in contribution to the emancipation of women from unjust practices within the church specifically, but also in the world. Women can provide important critiques of ideology from their experiences of exclusion and silencing that provoke them to exclaim, 'This cannot be!' To protest and revolt against whatever threatens humanity is to follow the example of Jesus, who reveals the kingdom of God as fundamentally concerned with the wholeness of all of humanity. As Hilkert notes, 'In the life-story of Jesus, human suffering is not theoretically resolved, but practically resisted, and ultimately defeated by the power of God.'[70] To follow Jesus as his disciple is to remember and retell the experience of Jesus as the Christ, who presents the eschatological hope of the final fulfilment of humanity in the kingdom of God, and who motivates the praxis of that kingdom here and now.

Bibliography

Farrell Bednarowski, M. F., *The Religious Imagination of American Women* (Indiana: Indiana University Press, 1999).

Hilkert, M. C., 'Hermeneutics of History in the Theology of Edward Schillebeeckx', *The Thomist: A Speculative Quarterly Review* 51 (1987): 97–145.

Johnson, E., 'Forging Theology: A Conversation with Colleagues', in *Things New and Old: Essays on the Theology of Elizabeth A. Johnson*, P. Zagano and T. W. Tilley (eds) (New York: Crossroad, 1999), 91–123.

O'Hara Graff, A., 'The Struggle to Name Women's Experience', in *In the Embrace of God: Feminist Theological Anthropology* (Maryknoll, NY: Orbis, 1995), 71–89.

O'Meara, J., 'Salvation: Living Communion with God', in *The Praxis of the Reign of God: An Introduction to the Theology of Edward Schillebeeckx*, M. C. Hilkert and R. J. Schreiter (eds) (New York: Fordham University Press, 2002), 97–116.

Roberts, H., 'Women Theologians Are the "Strawberry on the Cake", says Pope', *The Tablet: The International Catholic News Weekly*, 11 December 2014.

Schillebeeckx, E., 'Redemption and Human Emancipation', in *The Schillebeeckx Reader*, R. J. Schreiter (ed.) (New York: Crossroad, 1984), 255.

69. Schillebeeckx, 'What Is Theology?', 107 [165].

70. Hilkert, 'Hermeneutics of History in the Theology of Edward Schillebeeckx', 134.

Schillebeeckx, E., *God Is New Each Moment* (New York: Continuum, 2004).

Schillebeeckx, E., *Christ: The Christian Experience in the Modern World*, trans. J. Bowden, *CW*, vol. 7 (London: Bloomsbury T&T Clark, 2014).

Schillebeeckx, E., *Church: The Human Story of God*, trans. J. Bowden, *CW*, vol. 10 (London: Bloomsbury T&T Clark, 2014).

Schillebeeckx, E., *The Church with a Human Face*, trans. J. Bowden, *CW*, vol. 9 (London: Bloomsbury T&T Clark, 2014).

Schillebeeckx, E., *God the Future of Man*, trans. N. D. Smith, *CW*, vol. 3 (London: Bloomsbury T&T Clark, 2014).

Schillebeeckx, E., *Interim Report on the Books Jesus and Christ*, trans. J. Bowden, *CW*, vol. 8 (London: Bloomsbury T&T Clark, 2014).

Schillebeeckx, E., *Revelation and Theology*, trans. N. D. Smith, *CW*, vol. 2 (London: Bloomsbury T&T Clark, 2014).

Schillebeeckx, E., *The Understanding of Faith: Interpretation and Criticism*, trans. N. D. Smith, *CW*, vol. 5 (London: Bloomsbury T&T Clark, 2014).

Thompson, D. P., 'Schillebeeckx on the Development of Doctrine', *Theological Studies* 62 (2001): 303–21.

Wooden, C., 'Pope Francis Explains Why He Chose St. Francis of Assisi's Name', *The Catholic Telegraph*, 18 March 2013, http://www.thecatholictelegraph.com/pope-francis-explains-why-he-chose-st-francis-of-assisis-name/13243 (accessed 31 May 2015).

Chapter 4

DANGEROUS THEOLOGY: EDWARD SCHILLEBEECKX, POPE FRANCIS, AND HOPE FOR CATHOLIC WOMEN

Kate Mroz

Catholic feminist theology is not monolithic, since feminist theologians differ from one another in their perspectives on how reform in the Catholic Church should be pursued. Nevertheless, all theologians who dare to identify as 'feminist' share a certain attitude of bravery in choosing to claim such a controversial word. Edward Schillebeeckx's theology can serve as a resource for Catholic feminist theologians today who encounter tensions within the church and the academy. Comparing the work of Schillebeeckx with some of the recent words and actions of Pope Francis makes us aware that now is an apt time for women to make their voices heard. Schillebeeckx's theology can be used to support movements of renewal in the church, including a robust Catholic feminist theology that encompasses diversity. The words of Schillebeeckx serve as a challenge to not only the exclusion present in the Catholic Church as an institution, but also the exclusion that can occur in liberation movements themselves.

1. Pope Francis and Edward Schillebeeckx: Two 'Living Theologians'

Being a theologian is not an easy or glamorous job. We should not be fooled by the fact that some more well-known and established theologians have authored many books, and occupy large offices on sprawling college campuses. Being a theologian carries with it an enormous responsibility. In the words of Edward Schillebeeckx and Pope Francis, if the theologian's position is too comfortable, then that theologian is not taking his or her vocation seriously.

These words are not meant to discourage current or aspiring theologians. Rather, they are meant to be a source of hope, since the theologian may struggle to balance his or her feelings of love and loyalty towards the Catholic Church with a concern for those who feel marginalized by church teachings that do not speak to their concrete human experience. According to Edward Schillebeeckx, 'The theologian is called to stand at a dangerous crossing of roads,' the point at which faith comes into contact with modern thought. He insisted that living theology is always a step ahead of the official theology of the church, venturing along paths where it is still unprotected by the church's teaching authority.[1] The theologian is not the handmaid of the Magisterium, but is called 'to re-create and verify it [i.e. tradition] against the present-day experience of life and personal reflection on it'.[2] 'An intense presence-in-the-world is a necessary condition for theology'.[3]

Emphasis must be placed not solely on the words of theologians, who are 'the progressive factors in the life of faith', but also on their actions. In addition, the theologian must speak with concern not only for the Catholic community of faith, but for all of humankind. Faith, for Schillebeeckx, is both mystical and political. 'Faith manifests itself not only in prayer, liturgy and ritual but also in ethics'.[4] The theologian must be both a thinker and a doer. 'Not "Lord, Lord, Alleluia," but praxis is decisive'.[5] Although he may not be formally considered a theologian by profession, Pope Francis seems to have demonstrated many of the characteristics of a 'living theologian' in the words and deeds of his papacy thus far.

Schillebeeckx asserts that the church must critique aspects of society which are unjust and not conducive to the salvation of humankind, even though this will be a burdensome task. He proclaims, 'Until the promised eschatological kingdom comes, it will always be difficult to change any actual situation in which man is denied the means of salvation without "dirtying our hands"'.[6] In his encyclical, *Evangelii Gaudium: Apostolic Exhortation on the Proclamation of the Gospel in Today's World*, Pope Francis exclaims, 'I prefer a church which is bruised, hurting, and dirty because it has been out on the streets, rather than a church which is unhealthy from being confined and from clinging to its own security'.[7] The church cannot simply exist in the safety of the privileged centre of society, but must place itself among the most marginalized and destitute.

Pope Francis does not limit his exhortation to care for the poor merely to clergy or even to members of the church. He condemns current economic mechanisms that promote 'unbridled consumerism combined with inequality'[8] and the 'generalized

---

1. E. Schillebeeckx, 'What Is Theology?', *Revelation and Theology*, trans. N. D. Smith, *CW*, vol. 2 (London: Bloomsbury T&T Clark, 2014), 106 [163].

2. Schillebeeckx, 'What Is Theology?', 106 [164].

3. Ibid., 107 [165].

4. E. Schillebeeckx, *On Christian Faith. The Spiritual, Ethical and Political Dimensions* (New York: Crossroad, 1987), 51.

5. Schillebeeckx, *On Christian Faith*, 75.

6. E. Schillebeeckx, 'The New Image of God, Secularization and Man's Future on Earth', in *God the Future of Man*, trans. N. D. Smith, *CW*, vol. 3 (London: Bloomsbury T&T Clark, 2014), 121 [199].

7. Pope Francis, *Evangelii Gaudium*, §49, http://w2.vatican.va/content/francesco/en/apost_exhortations/documents/papa-francesco_esortazione-ap_20131124_evangelii-gaudium.html.

8. Pope Francis, *Evangelii Gaudium*, §60.

practice of wastefulness'.[9] He encourages financial experts and political leaders to ponder the words of John Chrysostom, 'Not to share one's wealth with the poor is to steal from them and to take away their livelihood. It is not our own goods which we hold, but theirs.'[10] Like Schillebeeckx, Pope Francis also affirms that the kingdom of God is not solely a future reality for which we must passively wait. He says of the kingdom, 'It is already present and growing in our midst.'[11] 'Both Christian preaching and life, then, are meant to have an impact on society' right now.[12] This echoes Schillebeeckx's view of the church. He professes that the church is 'not merely a means of salvation. It is Christ's salvation itself, this salvation as visibly realized in the world.'[13]

One may ask at this point, does Pope Francis's praxis match his words? In some ways, we must attest that it does. It can be argued that his actions are just as theologically significant as his words, if not more so. He began his papacy by asking the congregation to give him a blessing. Forsaking an ornate apostolic apartment, he has opted to live in a simple guesthouse at the Vatican. He often forgoes using the Popemobile in favour of a modest car or even public transportation. The bulletproof glass that used to surround the Popemobile to shield the pope from danger has been removed, so that Francis can be closer to the people. In April 2013, an exchange between Pope Francis and a Swiss Guard resulted in Francis bringing the guard a sandwich and commanding him to sit and rest. This story was spread all over the news. On Holy Thursday in 2013, Francis washed the feet of twelve prison inmates. This marked the first time that a pope included females in the rite, and two of the inmates were also Muslim. The following year, he washed the feet of twelve disabled men and women of various ages, ethnicities, and religious confessions.

We must here ask the same question of Schillebeeckx. Did he practice what he preached? We can attest that he shared Francis's spirit of humility to a certain degree. For example, as a theologian and professor of Louvain at the end of the 1940s, Schillebeeckx's remarked that 'theology has to serve if it is to achieve anything'.[14] He lamented the fact that, at that time, students were considered to be in a different category from the professors, who were upheld as superior. Schillebeeckx, convinced that this needed to change, recalled, 'I lived with the students, ate with them, joked with them.'[15] For doing this, he was often the target of criticism. Additionally, in 1981, while teaching in Nijmegen, he was responsible for hiring the first feminist theologian in Europe, Catharina Halkes.

---

9. Ibid., §191.

10. Ibid., §57.

11. Ibid., §181.

12. Ibid., §180.

13. E. Schillebeeckx, *Christ the Sacrament of the Encounter with God*, trans. P. Barret, N. D. Smith, *CW*, vol. I (London: Bloomsbury T&T Clark, 2014), 34 [48].

14. E. Schillebeeckx, *I Am a Happy Theologian Conversations with Francesco Strazzari*, trans. J. Bowden (New York: Crossroad, 1994), 9–10.

15. Schillebeeckx, *I Am a Happy Theologian*, 9–10.

While Pope Francis's actions have endeared many Catholics to him, as well as made him a figure of admiration even among non-Catholics and non-believers, his papacy has also been met with controversy. Conservatives, like Rush Limbaugh, have labelled *Evangelii Gaudium* as 'pure Marxism'. Some bishops, such as Robert Morlino of Madison, Wisconsin, are critical of what Pope Francis has done on Holy Thursday celebrations, insisting that the church must wash the feet of twelve men or not carry out the foot-washing at all, in order for the rite to be a true recreation of what Jesus did at the Last Supper. Francis has not been immune to criticism coming from more liberal,[16] progressive Catholics either. From the standpoint of feminist theology, many are angry that he has not done enough to correct the oppression that women experience in the church, and to promote instead their full flourishing. Some of his words have been perceived as offensive. At the meeting of the International Theological Commission in 2014, he referred to female theologians as 'the strawberry on the cake'.[17] In his first interview with a female journalist, he responded to a question about misogyny in the Catholic Church with a joke about woman being 'taken from the rib'.[18] Yet, the feminist theological perspective on Pope Francis is not entirely negative. Many, at the very least, point to some of his actions and words as a sign of hope and improvement.

Pope Francis has called for the formation of 'a new theology of women'. While it is certainly positive that Pope Francis has asserted that the presence of women must be 'guaranteed in the workplace and in the various other settings where important decisions are made, both in the Church and in social structures',[19] this call is problematic mainly for two reasons. First, he has not specified that this theology needs to be constructed by women. As of now, it appears that he is calling for more of the same: namely, another opportunity for the all-male hierarchy to make claims about who women are and who they should be. Second, it reinforces the notion of gender complementarity, the idea that certain distinct gender roles and characteristics have been given to men and women by God. The 'naturalness' of gender roles is commonly referenced in order to justify the exclusion of women from the priesthood. Francis has reiterated that the question of women priests is not open for discussion.[20]

16. I recognize that the terms 'liberal' and 'conservative' are considered problematic when applied to Catholicism. I am using them for simplicity's sake, but realize that they do need, and deserve, to be critiqued.

17. H. Roberts, 'Women Theologians Are the "Strawberry on the Cake", says Pope', *The Tablet: The International Catholic News Weekly*, 11 December 2014, http://www.thetablet. co.uk/news/1508/0/-women-theologians-are-the-strawberry-on-the-cake-says-pope.

18. *The Guardian*, 'Pope Francis Jokes "Woman Was from a Rib" as He Avoids Vow to Reform the Church', 29 June 2014, http://www.theguardian.com/world/2014/jun/29/pope-francis-woman-from-rib-avoids-pledge-reform-catholic-church (accessed 22 February 2016).

19. Pope Francis, *Evangelii Gaudium*, §103.

20. Ibid., §104.

Francis has not changed church teaching on abortion and artificial contraception, but he does seem to advocate taking a more pastoral, rather than judgemental, approach for dealing with these issues. Schillebeeckx insists that the church is imperfect and must never be exempt from critique stemming from the concrete experience of suffering humanity. He bewails that 'the existing church order has become ossified as an ideology and is an obstacle to what it originally intended to achieve'.[21] Francis appears willing to recognize this, though perhaps not yet to the degree that Schillebeeckx did.

In a candid interview with the Italian Jesuit magazine *La Civilta Cattolica*, in September 2013, Francis warns that the Catholic Church's moral edifice might 'fall like a house of cards' if it does not balance its divisive rules about abortion, gays, and contraception with the greater need to be a presence of love and mercy in the world that fosters the well-being of all people. Responding to those who have reprimanded him for not speaking enough about issues related to abortion, gay marriage, and the use of contraception, Francis insists that we cannot talk about these issues 'all the time', and, when we speak of them, 'we have to talk about them in a context'.[22] Francis follows through with this call in *Evangelii Gaudium*. With regard to abortion, he maintains that 'the Church cannot be expected to change her position on this question'.[23] However, he admits that 'it is also true that we have done little to adequately accompany women in very difficult situations, where abortion appears as a quick solution to their profound anguish, especially when the life developing within them is the result of rape or the situation of extreme poverty'.[24]

It is clear that more work needs to be done in order to address the issue of sexism in the Catholic Church. Nevertheless, the openness of Pope Francis demonstrates that now is a key moment for feminist theologians to draw from the resources of Edward Schillebeeckx to move forward towards a more inclusive church.

2. *Theological Urgency of a More Inclusive Church*

Edward Schillebeeckx avers that Christian redemption, something towards which all of us are supposed to be working, 'is indeed liberation from sin'.[25] However, 'Liberation from sin also has a cultural context. In our time the Christian

21. E. Schillebeeckx, *The Language of Faith: Essays on Jesus, Theology, and the Church*, with an introduction by R. J. Schreiter (Maryknoll, NY: Orbis, 1995), 156.

22. A. Spadano, SJ, 'A Big Heart Open to God: The Exclusive Interview with Pope Francis', *America Magazine: The National Catholic Review* (30 September 2013), http://americamagazine.org/pope-interview.

23. Pope Francis, *Evangelii Gaudium*, §214.

24. Ibid.

25. E. Schillebeeckx, *Church: The Human Story of God*, trans. J. Bowden, CW, vol. 10 (London: Bloomsbury T&T Clark, 2014), 130 [132].

understanding of sin also includes the recognition of systematic disruptions of communication, like sexism, racism, and fascism, and the Western cultural and religious sense of superiority.[26] Sin is not just personal and individual, but social. 'Christian salvation cannot just be the "salvation of the soul"',[27] because 'the praxis of the kingdom of God includes, in addition to interior renewal of life, a renewal and improvement of the structures of the society'.[28] According to Schillebeeckx, 'God's honour is in man's happiness and the raising up of the lowly and the oppressed.'[29]

The church is not exempt from the need for renewal of its institutional structure, as it is not without sin. Schillebeeckx writes, 'Any authority which does not free human beings, which is not expressive of an active, liberating solidarity with human beings, is not a Christian authority.'[30] By excluding women from priestly ministry, the church can be categorized as an authority that does not free women, who are limited in the ways that they can follow the call of God in their lives on the basis of their gender. In addition to this argument for the inclusion of women in the ministry of the Roman Catholic Church, Schillebeeckx also draws attention to the exclusion of women from decision-making processes. He declares that 'the co-responsibility of all believers for the church on the basis of our baptism in water and the Spirit essentially includes the participation of all believers in decisions relating to church government'.[31] This inclusiveness is not a reality. The decisions and doctrines of the church are under the control of a celibate, all-male hierarchy. Regarding church teachings in particular, even those that have a particular bearing on women, sexuality, and married life have largely been, and remain, interpreted by men alone. While women can be consultants during a synod, they do not have a vote. There are no women in the College of Cardinals, even though cardinals do not technically have to be ordained. If, as Schillebeeckx states, justification for the faith lies in its ability to speak to concrete human experience, then we must ask how a celibate male hierarchy can speak to experiences that are not part of their human reality: namely, living on this earth as a female, in a woman's body, and all that this reality entails. Some may argue that men are capable of keeping the well-being of women in mind when making decisions. While this is indeed true, or at least possible, women's voices are still essential. This can be demonstrated by examining the changes that occurred in Schillebeeckx's own thinking after his encounter with the insights of feminist theology.

26. Schillebeeckx, *Church*, 130 [132].

27. E. Schillebeeckx, *Interim Report on the Books Jesus and Christ*, trans. J. Bowden, *CW*, vol. 8 (London: Bloomsbury T&T Clark, 2014), 50 [58].

28. Schillebeeckx, *IR*, 50 [59].

29. Ibid., 53 [63].

30. E. Schillebeeckx, 'Magisterium and Ideology', in *Authority in the Church and the Schillebeeckx Case*, L. Swindler and P. Fransen (eds) (New York: Crossroad, 1982), 12.

31. Schillebeeckx, *Church*, 208 [209].

Schillebeeckx acknowledges that, because of the many books and articles published by feminist theologians, 'I myself have come to think much more feministically.'[32] They made him more conscious of 'the levels at which discrimination is practiced against women in the whole of society and in the whole of the Church.'[33] For example, he points out that 'male domination is clearly expressed in our language about God.'[34] Sometimes it is difficult to notice what diminishes those around us because we have become so accustomed to it. In this vein, Schillebeeckx recalls a conference where he compared the church to a 'decrepit old woman', and that many of the women present felt insulted as a result. Afterward, he vowed never to use this image again. The women's reaction made him more sensitive to how the language we employ affects women.

Perhaps the best example of the evolution of Schillebeeckx's own thought can be found in his Mariology. A stark comparison can be made between Schillebeeckx's first book on Mary and his second one, which was written in collaboration with the feminist theologian Catharina Halkes. In his 1964 book, *Mary, Mother of the Redemption*, Schillebeeckx affirms that Mary was 'a mother and a virgin' who 'prolonged the heavenly gift of her virgin motherhood into a state of celibacy which she freely took upon herself', as 'her single purpose' was 'to belong exclusively to the Redeemer.'[35] He describes Mary's existence as being in a state of 'pure receptivity'. He even goes so far as to say that, because she remained completely open to every divine possibility, Mary's fiat was 'an implicit acceptance of the sacrifice of the cross.'[36] At this early point of his career, a sense of gender complementarity is clearly embedded in Schillebeeckx's theology. He asserts that 'God chose Mary so that this maternal aspect of God's love might be represented in her person. At the deepest level this would seem to be the basic reason why a woman, a mother, should have a role in redemption.'[37] Mary is the 'Mother of the Church and of All Peoples', and Schillebeeckx depicts her as being marked with 'a tenderness, a mildness, even a childlike and loving simplicity'. He calls her, 'the Virgin with the Smile.'[38]

In his later book, *Mary: Yesterday, Today, Tomorrow*, published in 1993, he opens up about the criticism he received for stating that Mary was chosen by God to represent God's maternal aspects.[39] He acknowledges that 'in the future we shall have to look for the theological significance of Mary's femininity more along the

32. E. Schillebeeckx, *God Is New Each Moment* (Edinburgh: T&T Clark, 1983), 75.

33. Schillebeeckx, *God Is New Each Moment*, 75.

34. Ibid., 76.

35. E. Schillebeeckx, *Mary, Mother of the Redemption: The Religious Bases of the Mystery of Mary* (London: Sheed and Ward, 1964), 82.

36. Schillebeeckx, *Mary, Mother of the Redemption*, 86-7.

37. Ibid., 110.

38. Ibid., 111.

39. E. Schillebeeckx and C. Halkes, *Mary: Yesterday, Today, Tomorrow* (New York: Crossroad, 1993).

lines of a sister-ship which brings freedom than a motherhood which binds the child'.[40] Critiquing some of the details of his earlier book on Mary, he writes, 'I would now want to say that it is not Mary but the Holy Spirit which is the source of all life, including that of the Church'.[41] Perhaps surprisingly, Schillebeeckx credits a sermon given by a woman at a celebration of the Eucharist he attended during Advent for influencing his Mariology. In this sermon, the woman pointed out that no one is interested in pictures of the Jewish girl, Miriam, but rather are drawn to 'richly, adorned Madonnas, throned in triumph'. Sadly, the woman continued, 'Christians have almost forgotten that the couple, Mary and Joseph, loved each other and that God wanted a human child as the fruit of love'.[42] Inspired by a woman's preaching, Schillebeeckx realized the need for a new Mariology centred on Jesus that could speak to present-day people. In Catholic liturgy, women are forbidden from giving homilies, yet reflections on the gospel from women's perspectives are desperately needed in the church. Women's experience can not only provide fresh, liberating insights into the meaning of the gospel in today's world, but it can also enable the church to provide better pastoral care to women. Ludmila Javorova, who was ordained a Catholic priest in the underground church in Czechoslovakia in 1970, saw many cases where women were unable to go to confession. She states, 'Some women can't share freely with a man some problems of a personal nature, even with a man of God. This often happens in cases where a woman's husband is a tyrant or very patriarchal, so that the woman loses her ability to trust men in general, thereby missing out on this opportunity for spiritual transformation'.[43]

Schillebeeckx bemoans that, 'Sadly enough, the institutional church has had the inclination to universalize precisely its non-universal, historically inherited peculiar characteristics bound to a certain culture and time, and to impose them uniformly on the entire Catholic world'.[44] According to Schillebeeckx, while dogma can never be revoked, there are, in certain dogmatic formulations, 'representational aspects which are entirely conditioned by the prevailing historical situation and which can consequently be changed at a later period'.[45] Dogma constantly needs to be reinterpreted, and this is most especially true in the light of the experience of Catholic women. Schillebeeckx insists that 'the exclusion of women from the ministry is a purely cultural question, which doesn't make sense now'.[46] He added

40. Schillebeeckx and Halkes, *Mary: Yesterday, Today, Tomorrow*, 22.

41. Ibid., 28.

42. Ibid., 31–2.

43. M. T. Winter, *Out of the Depths: The Story of Ludmila Javarova, Roman Catholic Priest* (New York: Crossroad, 2001), 138.

44. E. Schillebeeckx, 'The Religious and Human Ecumene', in *The Future of Liberation Theology: Essays in Honor of Gustavo Gutierrez*, M. H. Ellis and O. Maduro (eds) (Maryknoll, NY: Orbis, 1989), 186.

45. E. Schillebeeckx, 'The Concept of Truth', *Revelation and Theology*, 203 [26].

46. Schillebeeckx, *I Am a Happy Theologian*, 76.

that the decision to confer the priesthood on women would be 'a great opening for ecumenism', as many other Christian denominations have chosen at that time to move in this direction.[47] Some formerly Catholic women have even switched denominations in order to be ordained, or to be part of a community in which ordination is an open possibility for themselves, or their future daughters and granddaughters.

3. Missiological Urgency of a More Inclusive Church

The clinging of the church to historical contingencies regarding women is damaging the church's credibility in the world. 'Ex-Catholic' is currently the third-largest denomination in the United States. According to the Pew Forum on Religion and Public Life, one in ten adults has left the Catholic Church, which retains only 68 per cent of its members. Substantially more Catholics have left the church due to dissatisfaction with its teachings on abortion (56 per cent), birth control (48 per cent), and how the church treats women (39 per cent) than with the clergy-abuse scandal (27 per cent).[48] The exclusion of women in the church has also detracted from the ability of the sacraments to enhance a committed Christian life in the world. In particular, Schillebeeckx finds troubling the fact that the Eucharist can only be celebrated by priests. Given the shortage of priests, he writes, 'In present circumstances, the celebration of the Eucharist is threatened, reduced to a banal level or even impeded.'[49] The image of the priest that has been created as a result of the sacral view of the church's office has made 'the Christian meaning of community and the Eucharist in contemporary society ridiculous'.[50] Maintaining the centrality of the Eucharist in the Catholic faith, Schillebeeckx proclaims the Eucharist to be a 'right of the Christian community'.[51] He insists that the Christianity community must always be able 'to do everything that is necessary to become a true community'.[52]

Schillebeeckx's theology demonstrates to women that leaving the church need not be their only option. A common problem for feminist theologians is how to seek alternative and liberating ways of living their Catholic faith, while not completely separating themselves from the official church in so doing. A woman's feelings towards the church are often ambiguous. She may have positive memories of growing up Catholic. In a time of difficulty, she may have been comforted and assisted by a Catholic priest. Yet, she may also feel betrayed by the church for

---

47. Ibid., 77.

48. Pew Forum on Religious and Public Life, United States Religious Landscape Survey (2009), http://religions.pewforum.org.

49. Schillebeeckx, *Language of Faith*, 156.

50. Ibid.

51. Ibid., 155.

52. Ibid.

failing to uphold fully her dignity as a human being made in the image of God. She may waver between wanting do what her conscience tells her is right and wanting to obey the formal rules of the church. Challenging church teaching in one's words and actions is a risky endeavour, and the consequences of doing so may be hard to face. Schillebeeckx's theology can serve as a powerful source of encouragement for women who can no longer be silent.

Schillebeeckx's notion of negative contrast experience serves as critical resource for the development of life-giving praxis. A negative contrast experience is an experience of unjust suffering. Still, within this experience of suffering is 'at least a vague consciousness of what human integrity or positive wholeness should entail'.[53] Out of this experience, there comes a call to protest and a rise of praxis that will work towards building a better future. The women who experience subordination do not always want to give up on the church, for in their experience of marginalization, they are still able to envision a more inclusive, egalitarian church. According to Schillebeeckx, most institutions and traditions – like the Catholic Church – were not repressive or oppressive from the start, but later became so often in response to certain cultural or political factors.[54]

Schillebeeckx's ecclesiology, argues Daniel Thompson, 'provides a way for seeing dissenting or alternative communities as part of the nature of the sacramental church itself'.[55] There is room in the church for differences of opinion, for views that are not in complete alignment with the Magisterium. When the Magisterium and believers go divergent ways, it is important to keep in mind Schillebeeckx's words that 'these believers usually do so out of deep concern for the gospel, and for the sake of the church'.[56] Believers cannot be reductively divided into 'orthodox and freethinking'.[57] Christian obedience cannot be defined as passive assent to what is put forth by the hierarchy, but rather must be a 'listening' so as to be involved in 'the moment of grace at a particular time listening in obedience to the suffering of human beings'.[58] From a Christian point of view, truly listening to those who suffer demands a response, which can, in some cases, result in a believer's deviation from the official teaching of the church. In this sense, Schillebeeckx writes, 'In some instances illegality is a higher form of trust in the Spirit of God.'[59] He affirms

---

53. E. Schillebeeckx, *Jesus: An Experiment in Christology*, trans. J. Bowden, *CW*, vol. 6 (London: Bloomsbury T&T Clark, 2014), 583 [622].

54. E. Schillebeeckx, *Christ: The Christian Experience in the Modern World*, trans. J. Bowden, *CW*, vol. 7 (London: Bloomsbury T&T Clark, 2014), 60–1 [73].

55. D. Thompson, 'The Church as Sacrament: Schillebeeckx's Contribution to the Construction of Critical Ecclesiology', *Religious Studies and Theology* 17 (1998): 42.

56. Schillebeeckx, *Church*, 207 [209].

57. Ibid.

58. E. Schillebeeckx, *Ministry: Leadership in the Community of Jesus Christ* (New York: Crossroad, 1981), 103.

59. Schillebeeckx, *Ministry*, 103.

that 'the magisterium is subordinated to the contents of the apostolic tradition'.[60] Therefore, we cannot claim that new praxis does not possess 'an inherent Christian apostolicity' even before it has been sanctioned by the church.[61]

Although he recognizes the very many Christians who are initiating 'an alternative praxis, without waiting for the system to change', he cautions that such praxis may not always be appropriate.[62] 'It would be equally out of keeping with the apostolic spirit to pursue alternative praxis in a triumphalistic way.'[63] Alternative praxis should only be engaged in when there is an 'urgent need'.[64] What constitutes an 'urgent need'? Schillebeeckx does not provide a clear answer. We can surmise, however, given his firm belief that lay women and men who possess 'charisma' should be able to preside over the Eucharist,[65] that, at the very least, situations in which a priest is unavailable, and the Eucharist would thus not take place without breaking the laws of the church, would qualify as an 'urgent need'. However, given his call for Christians to remain always attentive to the situation of humanity at the present time, feminist theology may expand on the definition of urgent need, perhaps to encompass the actions of the Roman Catholic Womenpriest Movement and other acts of disobedience.

One need not look far to see that, in today's world, women are disproportionally the victims of rape and domestic violence. Throughout the course of her life, one in every five women is the victim of sexual assault.[66] Women's bodies are constantly objectified in the media, and many women struggle with body image issues and low self-esteem. According to the National Eating Disorders Association, 80 per cent of women are unhappy with their appearance, and over one-half of teenage girls use unhealthy weight control behaviours, such as skipping meals, fasting, smoking cigarettes, vomiting, and taking laxatives.[67] In today's world, we cannot deny that women are still not regarded as full human beings. Seeing a woman at the pulpit may deliver a powerful message to women that their bodies can image Christ. Some women may only be able to experience the formal sacrament of reconciliation if absolution can be given to them by a woman. Perhaps, most importantly, Schillebeeckx stresses that the hierarchy does not have control over

60. Schillebeeckx, 'Magisterium and Ideology', 12.

61. Schillebeeckx, *The Language of Faith*, 157.

62. Ibid., 158.

63. Ibid.

64. Ibid.

65. Ibid., 151.

66. M. M. Lelwica, 'The Violence of "Perfection": Power, Images, and the Female Body in American Popular Culture', in *The Subjective Eye: Essays in Culture, Religion, and Gender in Honor of Margaret R. Miles*, R. Valantasis (ed.) (Eugene, OR: Pickwick Publications, 2006), 224.

67. National Eating Disorders Association, Facts for Activists, 2005, http://www. nationaleatingdisorders.org/nedaDir/files/documents/handouts/FactsAct.pdf.

the Holy Spirit.[68] No one has the power to stop the Holy Spirit from working in a person's life. A woman priest whom I interviewed as a college student told me that she felt a calling to the priesthood from the time she was ten years old. Regardless of how many times the church's position on women's ordination was repeated to her, the call did not fade. How can we say that responding to the Holy Spirit is not an urgent need?

Above all, Schillebeeckx spoke to the necessity of humility, a characteristic that is crucial to the fruitful reception of feminist theology. The ethical demand for justice and recognition of the other applies even when the other is the source of injustice and violence.[69] Just because the church has been a source of discrimination against women does not mean that feminist theology should make a mockery of the church, or lash out in anger against those who hold more traditionalist views. 'Truth', writes Schillebeeckx, 'is not to be found in a system, but in dialogue'.[70] After all, 'no one has a monopoly of truth'.[71] This includes feminist theology. Respect is not synonymous with total consensus. As womanist theologian Emilie Townes states, 'Refusing to critique is a sign of devaluing and disrespect or worse – ignorance'.[72] Offering true critique requires intense listening. In order to respond to another's arguments, one must become familiar with them. Such familiarity may help us enter the world of another. It may even make us re-evaluate our views, because the other may offer perspectives that we failed to consider. Catholics should strive for a church with enough room for a plurality of views, a church where excommunication is not employed as a tool to squelch critique of the Magisterium, and where those who do not embrace all of the reforms called for by feminist theology are not disparaged as irrational, or as persons who are 'giving in to their own oppression'.[73] Telling people who do not follow all of the Catholic Church's rules to leave, asserts Schillebeecks, is a mistake. The church is an interpretive community.[74]

In today's society, where those who see themselves as religious 'nones' are on the rise, the Catholic Church has a duty to proclaim to all people a loving God who uplifts the broken-hearted and marginalized. Schillebeeckx tells us that '"feeling at home (despite everything)" in a religious or non-religious tradition which one has inherited from the beginning is also a decisive factor in whether or not a person believes in God'.[75] He concedes that we can neither 'demonstrate by rational arguments' that God exists, nor likewise demonstrate that Catholic belief

---

68. Schillebeeckx, *Church*, 225–6 [227].

69. Ibid., 91–2 [94]

70. E. Schillebeeckx, 'Secularization and Christian Belief in God', *GFM*, 40 [66].

71. Schillebeeckx, 'Secularization and Christian Belief in God', 40 [66].

72. E. M. Townes, 'The Womanist Dancing Mind: Speaking to the Expansiveness of Womanist Discourse', in *Deeper Shades of Purple: Womanism in Religion and Society*, S. M. Floyd-Thomas (ed.) (New York: New York University Press, 2006), 240.

73. Townes, 'The Womanist Dancing Mind', 240.

74. Schillebeeckx, *Church*, 43–4 [44–5].

75. Ibid., 79–80 [82].

is better than atheism or other religions.[76] The truth of Christianity is found not in religious arguments or formulas, but in our praxis. For many women, the God depicted in Catholic doctrine and liturgy – a masculine God who's divine will is that only men can be admitted to the ministerial priesthood, who sanctions the firing of unmarried pregnant women from Catholic schools, and who only considers romantic love between a man and a woman as sacred – is not a God to whom they wish to pray. Schillebeeckx claims, 'It is better today not to think that there is a "God" than to adhere to an inhuman God who enslaves men and women.'[77] The name of God has been misused, but it would be wrong 'to place all the blame for this on Rome'.[78] Both the people and the office-bearers are obligated to struggle for change when they have become consciously aware of injustice being done in the name of God, and this includes feminist theologians.

Conclusion: We Cannot Remain Silent

Feminist theology must be more than a radical movement in the church to accommodate the preferences of contemporary Christians. With his strong emphasis on praxis, Schillebeeckx paved the way for a vision of feminist theology as an authentic Christian way of life. Feminist theological praxis cannot stop at a few anecdotes or rituals. It also cannot limit itself to praxis on behalf of women, but must speak out against all forms of injustice. Silence may sometimes be the easier road to take, because it is a way of 'keeping the peace' between opposing viewpoints. However, silence itself speaks volumes. A recent article laments the fact that Pope Francis has yet to denounce openly Gerhard Mueller's condemnation of the Leadership Conference of Women Religious for honouring Fordham University professor and feminist theologian Elizabeth Johnson.[79] Author Michelle Somerville writes that if Pope Francis continues to keep silent, he is, in essence, condoning the 'inquisition-like control' being brought to bear on women religious.[80] Schillebeeckx asserts that, in following Jesus, we must

76. Ibid., 80 [82].

77. Ibid., 32 [32].

78. Ibid., 160.

79. In March 2011, the United States Conference of Catholic Bishops released a twenty-page document in condemnation of Elizabeth Johnson's widely popular book, *Quest for the Living God: Mapping Frontiers in the Theology of God* (New York: The Continuum International Publishing Group Inc, 2007), without even giving Johnson an opportunity to enter into dialogue with them. For a detailed look at this situation, see R. Galliardetz (ed.), *When the Magisterium Intervenes: The Magisterium and Theologians in Today's Church* (Collegeville, MN: Liturgical Press, 2012).

80. M. Somerville, 'Pope Francis I, the Nun-Busters, and Why Catholics Should Buy "Quest For the Living God"', *Huffington Post Religion,* 12 May 2014 (updated 12 July 2014), http://www.huffingtonpost.com/michele-somerville/nunbusters-buy-quest-for-_b_5301458.html.

become 'the disinterested partisan of the oppressed and humiliated', knowing that, in doing so, we run the risk of becoming 'oppressed and done away with … by "this world"'.[81]

All theologians must take these words into consideration. The feminist theologian in the academy treads on very thin ice. There are fears that expressing certain views too publicly can have a negative impact on one's ability to get a job or tenure. Not everyone recognizes feminist theology as a legitimate academic discipline. Doing feminist theology may not make one popular or well-respected in certain places. This holds true not only for women, but also for clergy and lay men, who risk being mocked as 'less masculine' for showing public concern for 'women's issues'. At the same time, the feminist theologian in the academy is privileged. She has the time and energy to focus on issues like women's ordination, whereas women who are impoverished are more interested in the struggle for the basic necessities of life, like food and shelter. Drawing on Schillebeeckx can give theologians the strength and courage to speak loudly, and to put the well-being and happiness of the 'least of these' above their own personal ambitions. Perhaps none of us are able to do this perfectly, but we can at least try to do so to the best of our abilities, given our own socio-economic circumstances.

Bibliography

Galliardetz, R. (ed.), *When the Magisterium Intervenes: The Magisterium and Theologians in Today's Church* (Collegeville, MN: Liturgical Press, 2012).

The Guardian, 'Pope Francis Jokes "Woman Was from a Rib" as He Avoids Vow to Reform the Church', 29 June 2014.

Johnson, E., *Quest for the Living God: Mapping Frontiers in the Theology of God* (New York: The Continuum International Publishing Group Inc, 2007).

Lelwica, M. M., 'The Violence of "Perfection": Power, Images, and the Female Body in American Popular Culture', in *The Subjective Eye: Essays in Culture, Religion, and Gender in Honor of Margaret R. Miles*, R. Valantasis (ed.) (Eugene, OR: Pickwick Publications, 2006), 221–34.

Roberts, H., 'Women Theologians Are the 'Strawberry on the Cake', says Pope', *The Tablet: The International Catholic News Weekly*, 11 December 2014.

Schillebeeckx, E., *Mary, Mother of the Redemption: The Religious Bases of the Mystery of Mary* (London: Sheed and Ward, 1964).

Schillebeeckx, E., *Ministry: Leadership in the Community of Jesus Christ* (New York: Crossroad, 1981).

Schillebeeckx, E., 'Magisterium and Ideology', in *Authority in the Church and the Schillebeeckx Case*, L. Swindler and P. Fransen (eds) (New York: Crossroad, 1982).

Schillebeeckx, E., *God Is New Each Moment* (Edinburgh: T&T Clark, 1983).

Schillebeeckx, E., *On Christian Faith. The Spiritual, Ethical and Political Dimensions* (New York: Crossroad, 1987).

81. E. Schillebeeckx, *IR*, 54 [63].

Schillebeeckx, E., 'The Religious and Human Ecumene', in *The Future of Liberation Theology: Essays in Honor of Gustavo Gutierrez*, M. H. Ellis and O. Maduro (eds) (Maryknoll, NY: Orbis, 1989), 177–88.

Schillebeeckx, E., *I am a Happy Theologian: Conversations with Francesco Strazzari*, trans. J. Bowden (London: SCM Press, 1994).

Schillebeeckx, E., *The Language of Faith: Essays on Jesus, Theology, and the Church*, with an introduction by R. J. Schreiter (Maryknoll, NY: Orbis, 1995).

Schillebeeckx, E., *Christ: The Christian Experience in the Modern World*, trans. John Bowden, *CW*, vol. 7 (London: Bloomsbury T&T Clark, 2014).

Schillebeeckx, E., *Christ the Sacrament of the Encounter with God*, trans. Paul Barret, N. D. Smith, *CW*, vol. I (London: Bloomsbury T&T Clark, 2014).

Schillebeeckx, E., *Church: The Human Story of God*, trans. J. Bowden, *CW*, vol. 10 (London: Bloomsbury T&T Clark, 2014).

Schillebeeckx, E., *God the Future of Man*, trans. N. D. Smith, *CW*, vol. 3 (London: Bloomsbury T&T Clark, 2014).

Schillebeeckx, E., *Interim Report on the Books Jesus and Christ*, trans. J. Bowden, *CW*, vol. 8 (London: Bloomsbury T&T Clark, 2014).

Schillebeeckx, E., *Jesus: An Experiment in Christology*, trans. John Bowden, *CW*, vol. 6 (London: Bloomsbury T&T Clark, 2014).

Schillebeeckx, E., *Revelation and Theology*, trans. N. D. Smith, *CW*, vol. 2 (London: Bloomsbury T&T Clark, 2014).

Schillebeeckx, E., and C. Halkes, *Mary: Yesterday, Today, Tomorrow* (New York: Crossroad, 1993).

Somerville, M., 'Pope Francis I, the Nun-Busters, and Why Catholics Should Buy "Quest for the Living God"', *Huffington Post Religion*, 12 May 2014 (updated 12 July 2014).

Spadano, SJ, A., 'A Big Heart Open to God: The Exclusive Interview with Pope Francis', *America Magazine: The National Catholic Review* (30 September 2013).

Thompson, D., 'The Church as Sacrament: Schillebeeckx's Contribution to the Construction of Critical Ecclesiology', *Religious Studies and Theology* 17 (1998): 33–45.

Townes, E., 'The Womanist Dancing Mind: Speaking to the Expansiveness of Womanist Discourse', in *Deeper Shades of Purple: Womanism in Religion and Society*, S. M. Floyd-Thomas (ed.) (New York: New York University Press, 2006), 236–49.

Winter, M. T., *Out of the Depths: The Story of Ludmila Javarova, Roman Catholic Priest* (New York: Crossroad, 2001).

Part II

FAITHFULNESS TO THE CHRISTIAN TRADITION IN THE PUBLIC SPHERE

Chapter 5

TRADITION HERMENEUTICS: JOSEPH RATZINGER AND EDWARD SCHILLEBEECKX ON THE ROLE OF HISTORICAL-CULTURAL CONTEXT FOR THE UNDERSTANDING OF CHRISTIAN FAITH

Branislav Kuljovsky

In the modern-day Western world, where the traditional and well-respected position of Christianity has been challenged by the tendency to suspect any master narratives claiming the universal truth, questions about the status and role of Christian faith within a changing cultural context arise. It seems that the faith of the Catholic Church, in particular, is becoming increasingly incompatible with the sensibilities of the contemporary world. Various shifts in Western culture are challenging the Christian faith, its beliefs, and structure(s). Besides major sociological shifts, such as de-traditionalization, individualization, and pluralization,[1] perhaps the most visible issues causing polarization between church and society are those appertaining to the realm of ethics.[2] The growing divide between Christian faith and the 'new' ethical sensibilities leads to unforeseeable consequences, especially for Christian institutions, including schools and hospitals.

Consequently, the question arises: how should the church react to this new cultural phenomenon in the West that, for example, in the realm of ethics, is often in opposition to church teaching, at least in its official magisterial documents? Should the church conform to, or at least find a compromise with, what the given cultural consciousness has recognized as authentic and truthful ways of living; or

---

1. Lieven Boeve largely described these trends, as well as their consequences, for the Christian narrative in the Belgian context. Cf. L. Boeve, 'Religion after Detraditionalization: Christian Faith in a Post-Secular Europe', *Irish Theological Quarterly* 70, no. 2 (2005): 99–122; L. Boeve, *Interrupting Tradition* (Leuven: Eerdmans, 2003), 52–5; L. Boeve, *God Interrupts History: Theology in a Time of Upheaval* (New York; London: Continuum, 2007), 21–6.

2. An example of such a split in Western society on the basis of an ethical issue is the question of legal recognition of same-sex marriages. Cf. R. E. Gane, N. P. Miller, and H. P. Swanson (eds), *Homosexuality, Marriage, and the Church* (Berrien Springs, MI: Andrews University Press, 2012), viii–x.

rather, should she raise a voice of protest? The way that one answers such difficult questions depends, among other things, upon the way that one conceives of the complex relationship between Christian faith and culture, especially as this relationship pertains to the development of Christian tradition, its beliefs, and practices. Through an analysis of two prominent twentieth-century theologians, we will analyse the complexities of the interaction between faith and a given historical-cultural context. More specifically, the chapter will discuss how (if at all), within changing historical-cultural frameworks of interpretation, the continuity of faith and its truth claims, revealed by God in Christ, are preserved.

We will proceed through an analysis of the positions of Joseph Ratzinger (b. 1927) and Edward Schillebeeckx (1914–2009) respectively. It is neither accidental nor artificial to juxtapose these two theologians. They share much in common. Both gained fame for their theological work over the past half-century;[3] both played a major and critical role at the Second Vatican Council;[4] both were instrumental to the foundation of the international theological journal *Concilium*;[5] and both

3. For example, Hervé Coutau-Bégarie states that nobody can deny Ratzinger 'the first place within the theological research at the end of the 20th century'. H. Coutau-Bégarie, *Ratzingeriana : bibliographie commentée de Joseph Ratzinger* (Paris: L'homme nouveau, 2012), 10. Upon Ratzinger's resignation, the German chancellor Angela Merkel called him 'one of the most important religious thinkers'. T. Rießinger, *Joseph Ratzinger - Ein brillanter Denker?: Kritische Fragen an den Papst und seine protestantischen Konkurrenten* (Berlin: Lit Verlag, 2013), 1. As for Schillebeeckx, Erik Borgman described him as 'beyond doubt the best known theologian in the Netherlands' in the 1960s and 1970s. E. Borgman, *Edward Schillebeeckx: A Theologian in His History* (London; New York: Continuum, 2003), 1. Stephan van Erp and Maarten van den Bos describe him as 'the most important twentieth century theologian from the Netherlands and Flanders'. M. van den Bos and S. van Erp, *A Happy Theologian: A Hundred Years of Edward Schillebeeckx* (Nijmegen: Valkhof Pers, 2014), 47.

4. Being only thirty-five years old, Ratzinger took part in the Second Vatican Council, first as a personal advisor of Cardinal Joseph Frings, archbishop of Cologne, and towards the end of the first session he was named a *peritus* (an official council theologian). Cf. J. Ratzinger, *Milestones: Memoirs, 1927-1977* (San Francisco, CA: Ignatius, 1998), 121. Even though his opponents blocked Schillebeeckx's appointment to a formal position as conciliar *peritus*, the Dutch bishops appointed him as their own advisor. This still gave him a great influence on the contributions of the Dutch bishops in Rome. Cf. Borgman, *Edward Schillebeeckx*, 320–1. According to Komonchak, both of them belonged to the advocates of theological renewal at the Second Vatican Council and contributed to the *coup d'Église* that oriented the council in a direction quite different from that expressed in the schemas prepared by the curia. Cf. J. A. Komonchak, 'The Church in Crisis: Pope Benedict's Theological Vision', *Commonweal* 132, no. 11 (2005): 12.

5. Hans Küng, Yves Congar, Karl Rahner, Edward Schillebeeckx, and others founded the international journal *Concilium* in 1963 in order to promote the spirit of the council. Although Ratzinger withdrew from his role in *Concilium* at the end of the 1960s, at its

have reflected on the situation of Christian faith in our changing contemporary, Western-European context. Nonetheless, their academic approaches differ, and not simply in regard to the latter point.[6] Their main difference consists in the perspectives from which they appropriate the hermeneutical problem in their understanding of faith, its development, and continuity through historical-cultural interpretations. Therefore, the final section of this chapter will provide a comparative analysis of the two authors, pointing to the commonalities and differences between their respective positions.

1. Joseph Ratzinger on Faith-culture Interaction

In this section, we analyse the perspective of a theologian for whom the question of faith's (un)changeability under the influence of contextual pressures was not simply an abstract theoretical discussion. As Prefect of the Congregation for the Doctrine of the Faith, and later as Pope Benedict XVI, Joseph Ratzinger was charged with discerning, as well as disseminating, the truths of Catholic faith. In what follows, we will present: (a) his justification for the existence of tradition and its relationship to scripture and revelation; (b) his way of conceiving the notion of development within the Christian tradition; (c) his solution to the tension between the continuity and change inherent to the developmental process; and (d) his appraisal of the historical encounter between Greek culture and the Christian faith, and the resultant vision of the ongoing relationship between the Christian faith and culture.

a. Legitimacy of Tradition

In his early writings, Ratzinger deals extensively with the relationship between revelation, scripture, and tradition, and engages with discussions concerning the issue of the material sources of revelation.[7] He argues that the positive sources,

---

inception he served on the board of associate editors and contributed an important essay on collegiality to its first volume. Cf. P. Brand and H. Häring, 'Aggiornamento als wissenschaftliches Projekt: Über Anfänge und Programmatik der Internationalen Zeitschrift für Theologie "CONCILIUM"', in *H. Küng. Neue Horizonte des Glaubens und Denkens. Ein Arbeitsbuch*, H. Häring and K.-J. Kuschel (eds) (München: Piper, 1993), 779–95; Cf. K. Rahner and E. Schillebeeckx, 'General Introduction', *Concilium* 1, no. 1 (1965): 3.

6. A visible sign of their different theological strategies is manifested in their disagreement over the question of extraordinary ministers of the Eucharist, the result of which was an investigation of Schillebeeckx's proposal by Ratzinger, who was at the time Prefect of the Congregation for the Doctrine of the Faith. For Schillebeeckx's impressions from their meeting in Rome, see E. Schillebeeckx, *I Am a Happy Theologian: Conversations with Francesco Strazzari*, trans. J. Bowden (London: SCM Press, 1994), 38–9.

7. Ratzinger elaborates this theme for the first time in his 1955 *Habilitationsschrift* on Bonavetnure, especially in its original first part, which was rejected by one of his correctors,

scripture and tradition, must be brought into relationship with their inner source, revelation (i.e. the living Word of God), from which both scripture and tradition spring.[8] From this basic perspective, he develops a series of theological arguments for the existence of a reality called 'tradition'.

First, tradition stems from the 'non-identity of the two realities, "revelation" and "scripture"'.[9] Revelation always exceeds scripture to the extent that its reality surpasses information about it. For Ratzinger, revelation, rather than being 'a sum of all the revealed contents of faith', always refers to an act in which God shows himself. The second justification of tradition comes from the new understanding of scripture in the New Testament: scripture is identified with the *spirit*, through which the Old Testament *letter* receives its full meaning and the New Testament canon finds 'its true, living (not merely literary) content'.[10] As a result, scripture can no longer have the conclusive and exclusive sense which belonged to it in the Old Testament.[11] In the church's practice, this principle was expressed in the fact that the creed, as a rule of faith, appears as the hermeneutical key to scripture, which must always be interpreted.[12] Finally, tradition also flows from the authoritative, enduring presence of Christ's Spirit in the church, which authorizes the church to interpret the Christ of history in relation to Christ today.[13]

With this last point, we have come to the essence of Ratzinger's notion of tradition. In the same way that the Old Testament was reinterpreted on the basis of the Christ-event and oriented towards that event, the Christ-event itself was reinterpreted on the basis of the *pneuma*, that is, on the basis of the church's present reality. According to this reading, the additional element which distinguishes (later) dogmatic theology (i.e. reinterpretation of the Christ-event from the

Professor Schmaus. The rejected part was published for the first time in 2009. Cf. J. Ratzinger, *Joseph Ratzinger Gesammelte Schriften: Offenbarungsverständnis und Geschichtstheologie Bonaventuras: Habilitationsschrift und Bonaventura-Studien: Band 2*, Gerhard Ludwig Müller (ed.) (Freiburg, Basel, Vienna: Herder, 2009), 53–417.

8. These insights, gained through his reading of Bonaventure, allowed Ratzinger to formulate his thought at the time of the conciliar discussion on revelation. See, for example, his lecture delivered on the eve of the solemn inauguration of the Second Vatican Council to the German-speaking bishops, in J. Wicks, 'Six Texts by Prof. Joseph Ratzinger as Peritus before and during Vatican Council II', *Gregorianum* 89, no. 2 (2008): 269–85.

9. K. Rahner and J. Ratzinger, *Revelation and Tradition*, trans. W. J. O'Hara, Quaestiones Disputatae 17 (New York: Herder and Herder, 1966), 35.

10. Rahner and Ratzinger, *Revelation and Tradition*, 38.

11. Ratzinger is aware that this Pauline dichotomy between *gramma* and *pneuma* does not fully do justice to the understanding of scripture in the Old Testament, where, especially in the book of Jeremiah and Deutero-Isaiah, there appears a longing to go beyond the *gramma* in a new immediacy of the Spirit of God. Nevertheless, he holds firmly the idea that, in the new order of salvation that began with Christ, scripture occupies a different position. Cf. Rahner and Ratzinger, *Revelation and Tradition*, 38–9.

12. Cf. Rahner and Ratzinger, *Revelation and Tradition*, 45.

13. Cf. Rahner and Ratzinger, *Revelation and Tradition*, 45.

church's perspective on the basis of the *pneuma*) from the biblical theology of the New Testament is what is called 'tradition'. For Ratzinger, this implies that *sola scriptura*, as the only guiding principle in Christianity, is indefensible. Scripture is not opposed to tradition, but constitutes one element shaping it.[14] In this earlier vision, however, Ratzinger does not explicitly discuss *to what extent* later historical-cultural frameworks play a role in the church's Spirit-led process of ongoing, consecutive reinterpretations.

b. Tradition, History, and Development

What Ratzinger does emphasize already in 1965 is the principle of continuity. The various consecutive reinterpretations mentioned above are not foreign to one another.[15] However, it is clear that Ratzinger does not understand tradition in a neo-scholastic way, that is, as a static deposit of beliefs and religious practices. He advocates instead a more dynamic understanding of tradition, one that encompasses two elements: the *pneumatological* and the *historical*. Whereas the pneumatological element implies a certain claim of openness to the present through which a growth in tradition may be achieved, the historical element guarantees continuity with the original source.

These two elements of tradition constitute the core of Ratzinger's notion of historical development. In his view, the development of tradition is made possible only in the combination of the elements of identity and change.[16] If there is only identity – that which remains always the same in itself (*Sich-Gleichbleibendes*) – we cannot speak of any development.[17] If an expression of faith is to remain the same, the original articulation must be appropriated anew with historical transformations.[18] 'The timeless is realized for men existing in time only through constantly renewed bonds with time.'[19] By contrast, if development is understood solely as change without continuity, this would imply that one reality succeeds

---

14. Cf. J. Ratzinger, 'Tradition: III. Systematisch', in *Lexikon für Theologie und Kirche*, J. Höfer and K. Rahner (eds), 2. völlig neu bearbeitete Auflage, vol. X (Freiburg: Herder, 1965), 293–9.

15. Cf. Rahner and Ratzinger, *Revelation and Tradition*, 43–5.

16. Cf. J. Ratzinger, *Das Problem der Dogmengeschichte in der Sicht der katholischen Theologie* (Köln, Opladen: Westdeutscher Verlag, 1966), 22. Cf. J. Ratzinger, 'Zur Frage nach der Geschichtlichkeit der Dogmen', in *Martyria, Leiturgia, Diakonia. Festschrift für Hermann Volk Bischof von Mainz zum 65. Geburtstag*, Otto Semmelroth (ed.) (Mainz: Matthias-Grünewald, 1968), 69.

17. Cf. Ratzinger, *Das Problem der Dogmengeschichte in der Sicht der katholischen Theologie*, 9.

18. Cf. Ratzinger, *Das Problem der Dogmengeschichte in der Sicht der katholischen Theologie*, 38.

19. J. Ratzinger, 'The Changeable and Unchangeable in Theology', *Theology Digest* 10, no. 2 (1962): 76.

another.[20] The development undertaken throughout different historical contexts would consist only in the modernization of faith according to the impulses of the present time, something which Ratzinger vehemently opposes.[21] The proclamation of a Christian truth claim must bring the original to the forefront.[22] For this reason, development is also not a question of creating successive interpretive layers on top of the original message because such a procedure ultimately leads to the loss of the original. For Ratzinger, then, development is a process of one identical reality growing within the living faith of the church. This development is not linear because, as a historical appropriation of faith, the original must be preserved in the transformations of changing times.[23] The purpose of this appropriation of revelation is not primarily to know something, but to enter, through the words of the message, a relationship with God.

The historical development of tradition thus possesses a double quality. It can mean an advance in the progressive appropriation and continuous development of the given realities, but it also carries the risk of losing the realities themselves. Throughout history, tradition has indeed developed into distortive forms that later were abandoned and replaced by opposing statements. As a result of this realization, Ratzinger postulates that development must always include a twofold movement: (1) a movement of unfolding, enrichment, and expansion; and (2) a movement of reduction, critique, and simplification. There must then be a process of both acceptance and rejection.

It becomes obvious that a tension is inherent to this vision of the historical development of tradition. On the one hand, behind the focus on the transmission of the unique and original event (identity) stands a claim to the continuity of tradition over time. On the other hand, behind the pneumatological principle, through which a given history enters into tradition (change), stands a claim to the advance of tradition, which, as we said, must be characterized by both expansion and critique/reduction. However, how precisely can these two elements – continuity and change – be coherently upheld together?

c. Continuity and Change of Tradition

In order to clarify the nature of the relationship between continuity and discontinuity, Ratzinger uses the notion of 'the hermeneutics of reform', which he

---

20. Cf. M. G. Steinhauser, 'Cardinal Ratzinger in Dialogue with the Toronto School of Theology: What Was Said in 1986?', *Toronto Journal of Theology* 29, no. 1 (2013): 63.

21. Cf. J. Ratzinger, *Principles of Catholic Theology: Building Stones for a Fundamental Theology* (San Francisco, CA: Ignatius, 1987), 57.

22. Cf. Ratzinger, *Das Problem der Dogmengeschichte in der Sicht der katholischen Theologie*, 44.

23. Cf. Ratzinger, *Das Problem der Dogmengeschichte in der Sicht der katholischen Theologie*, 37; cf. J. Ratzinger, 'Chapter I: Revelation Itself', *Commentary on the Documents of Vatican II*, H. Vorgrimler (ed.), trans. W. Glen-Doepel et al., 2nd edn, vol. III (New York: Crossroad, 1989), 179.

believes to constitute a proper interpretive tool for the Second Vatican Council.[24] The hermeneutics of reform, understood as 'innovation in continuity', attempts to combine both dynamism and fidelity. Ratzinger comments on three major issues that were discussed at the Second Vatican Council – that is, the relationships between faith and modern science, the church and the modern state, and Christian faith and non-Christian religions – and formulates the following conclusion: 'It is clear that in all these sectors, some kind of discontinuity might emerge ... but in which, after the various distinctions between concrete historical situations and their requirements had been made, the continuity of principles proved not to have been abandoned.'[25]

The church's decisions on contingent matters are thus changeable because they refer to a specific reality changeable in itself. In these contingent decisions, we can discern principles – 'undercurrent motivating decisions from within' – that express the permanent aspect.[26] In 1988, Ratzinger names the following as changeable elements of tradition: issues concerning 'technical questions' (e.g. the date of Genesis) or insufficient past reflections.[27] In Ratzinger's view, then, the development of tradition consists in the combination of continuity and discontinuity at different levels. That which is essential remains in continuity, and the practical application of it (in various forms) may be subject to discontinuous change.[28]

However, *what* are these basic decisions of the church that constitute the substance of faith? According to Ratzinger, this is a crucial question in the contemporary context, in which many Christians ask about what changes are permissible in the church. In this vein, Ratzinger talks about the cornerstones of the Christian identity which were established by the catechetical tradition in the course of centuries.[29] These elements, 'the four master components', as Ratzinger calls them,

---

24. Cf. J. Ratzinger, 'Address of His Holiness Benedict XVI to the Roman Curia Offering Them His Christmas Greetings', December 2005, http://www.vatican.va/holy_father/benedict_xvi/speeches/2005/december/documents/hf_ben_xvi_spe_20051222_roman-curia_en.html.

25. Ratzinger, 'Address of His Holiness Benedict XVI to the Roman Curia Offering Them His Christmas Greetings'.

26. Ratzinger, 'Address of His Holiness Benedict XVI to the Roman Curia Offering Them His Christmas Greetings'.

27. Cf. Steinhauser, 'Cardinal Ratzinger in Dialogue with the Toronto School of Theology', 69.

28. Ratzinger consistently preserves the stress on continuity amid all progress throughout his writings. Cf. J. Ratzinger, *The Ratzinger Report: An Exclusive Interview on the State of the Church* (San Francisco, CA: Ignatius, 1985), 35; cf. J. Ratzinger, 'Dogmatic Constitution on Divine Revelation: Origin and Background', *Commentary on the Documents of Vatican II*, H. Vorgrimler (ed.), trans. W. Glen-Doepel et al., 2nd edn, vol. III (New York: Crossroad, 1989), 164–5; cf. J. Ratzinger, *Introduction to Christianity* (San Francisco, CA: Communio, 2004), 110–11.; cf. Ratzinger, *Principles of Catholic Theology*, 379.

29. Cf. Ratzinger, *Principles of Catholic Theology*, 131.

include the Apostles' Creed, the Sacraments, the Ten Commandments, and the Lord's Prayer. In his view, these four components served for centuries as 'a depository and résumé of Catholic teaching', and they are to be taken as 'fixed points in the topics and hermeneutics of Scripture'.[30] They 'precede reflection, for Christianity is not something we devise for ourselves but something we receive as a reality that is antecedent to anything of our own devising'.[31] Thus, although the chosen method for the transmission of faith is to be left to the catechist's decision, the fundamental structure, along with the materials that help to make it manifest, should be respected. Accordingly, Ratzinger stresses the distinction between the 'text' (the content of the faith of the church) and 'the spoken or written commentaries'.[32] In his view, this distinction guarantees the identity of the content of the faith.

To the objection that all human discourse with regard to faith is only an interpretation from a certain historical-cultural perspective, Ratzinger responds that the infinite greatness of the Word of God does not take away from the message of faith its characteristic features.[33] He emphasizes that our conditioning cannot justify relativism. Rather, varying contexts may only reveal new aspects and understandings of the one reality. Interpretations or understandings of texts are limited and therefore can be supplemented, but they cannot be completely opposed to one another.[34]

d. The Unity of Faith and Culture

One of the most significant constitutive elements of the Christian tradition is, according to Ratzinger, its interaction with the philosophical thought of Ancient Greece. He calls this interaction a providential encounter. As a result, Ratzinger upholds the idea that the ongoing unity of faith and reason should ultimately follow the main contours established in the interaction of early Christianity and the philosophy of the Greco-Roman world. In following these contours, the church may facilitate legitimate developments.

Ratzinger believes that the idea of God, as the ontological idea of being, was continuously present in the scriptures,[35] from the story of the burning bush in

---

30. J. Ratzinger, 'Sources and Transmission of the Faith', *International Catholic Review Communio* 10, no. 1 (1983): 29–30.

31. Ratzinger, *Principles of Catholic Theology*, 131.

32. In addition to the question of *what* those basic, unchangeable elements of tradition are, there is the question of *how* (on the basis of what criteria) we can discern them. A set of criteria was outlined by Ratzinger in 1973. See J. Ratzinger, 'Farewell to the Devil?', *Dogma and Preaching: Applying Christian Doctrine to Daily Life* (San Francisco, CA: Ignatius, 2011), 197–205.

33. Cf. Ratzinger, 'Sources and Transmission of the Faith', 34.

34. Cf. Steinhauser, 'Cardinal Ratzinger in Dialogue with the Toronto School of Theology', 66.

35. Cf. Ratzinger, *Introduction to Christianity*, 116–36. Already in his 1959 inaugural lecture in Bonn, Ratzinger started to develop this idea. See J. Ratzinger, *Der Gott des*

Exodus and in the words of Deutero-Isaiah and the Wisdom literature, to the New Testament writings, especially the Gospel of John.[36] Moreover, Ratzinger is convinced that early Christianity decided '*for* the God of the philosophers and *against* the gods of the various religions'.[37] With this choice, Ratzinger does not mean that a decision was made for a strict Hellenistic expression of Christian faith. Rather, it is a decision for the *logos* against any kind of myth, that is, for the truth against custom.[38] For a culture to encounter faith fruitfully it must transcend its own cultural heritage and tendencies. This characteristic of openness is a specific trait of the biblical faith and must, therefore, be a characteristic of the cultures that come into contact with faith. As a result, when Ratzinger claims that the encounter between faith and Greek culture is providential and must, therefore, be a reference point for all further encounters between faith and culture, he does so because he believes that a similar process of self-transcendence was present within the Greek world. This is not to say that all cultures, when encountering Christian faith, must adopt the Hellenistic form of Christianity; rather, they must be linked with Greek thought 'in the form in which it transcended itself'.[39]

In Ratzinger's view, this providential encounter was later interrupted and threatened by Aquinas's distinction between theology and philosophy. In his response to Aristotelian philosophy, a distinction started to emerge between the natural order of inquiry appertaining to philosophy and the supernatural order belonging to theology. Ratzinger views this evolution negatively because, in the nineteenth and twentieth centuries, Aquinas's distinction led to a total opposition between theology and philosophy.[40] Ratzinger argues that if we disavow, or at least forgo, ontology in our theological discourse, the renunciation of the concept of God necessarily follows, as well.

The consequent late-modern separation of Christian faith and culture is, according to Ratzinger, the primary reason for the present-day cultural crisis. The modern culture of the Western world – characterized by the positivist scientific rationality of the Enlightenment – has lost its once constitutive religious roots, the result being that faith in God is excluded from the public sphere and from

---

Glaubens und der Gott der Philosophen (Munich-Zurich: Schnell & Steiner, 1960).

36. For Ratzinger's elaboration of the concept of God in John's Gospel, see J. Ratzinger, 'Faith, Reason and the University Memories and Reflections', *Lecture of the Holy Father presented on the occasion of the meeting with the representatives of science*, Regensburg, 2006, http://www.vatican.va/holy_father/benedict_xvi/speeches/2006/september/documents/hf_ben-xvi_spe_20060912_university-regensburg_en.html.

37. Ratzinger, *Introduction to Christianity*, 137.

38. Religion is understood here in the sense of custom-based mythical religion. Cf. Ratzinger, *Introduction to Christianity*, 138.

39. J. Ratzinger, *Truth and Tolerance: Christian Belief and World Religions* (San Francisco, CA: Ignatius, 2004), 200.

40. J. Ratzinger, *The Nature and Mission of Theology: Essays to Orient Theology in Today's Debates* (San Francisco, CA: Ignatius, 1995), 16–22.

the rational realm. For Ratzinger, various negative, and ultimately destructive, evolutions have resulted from this loss, such as relativism, nihilism, totalitarianism, and absolute liberalism. Modernity's hostility towards religion constitutes the major reason as to why Ratzinger's later writings, concerning the interaction of Christian faith and modern European culture, bear a significantly negative tone.[41] This negativism gained for Ratzinger the label of anti-cultural thinker.[42] However, his 1965 essay, 'The Christian and the Modern World', already presents a more nuanced position. It becomes clear that when he is critical of the world, what he means by the 'world' is precisely 'that behaviour through which man makes a decision *in favor* of this world alone and *against* what is godly and eternal'.[43] The world, understood in this sense, does not constitute a self-contained realm alongside the church. Rather, this world – wilfulness, the tendency to separate from God – exists in the midst of believers. Conversely, to the extent that the world contains elements that come from the centre of Christianity, but which appear in new and challenging forms – for example, the creation of equal opportunities for all peoples, a lightening of the burden of every human being's existence, and/or leading humanity out of its divisions into unity – Ratzinger says that the church should 'admit this' and even 'be grateful'.[44]

2. Edward Schillebeeckx's View on Faith-culture Interaction

In our interpretation of Schillebeeckx's thought, we focus mainly on the so-called second phase of his theological work, a phase which started immediately after the Second Vatican Council and is usually referred to as his 'hermeneutical turn'.[45] Schillebeeckx's embrace of philosophical hermeneutics renders his theology as an important counterpoint to Ratzinger's. In the following subsections, we will present the following: (a) how, according to Schillebeeckx, the theory of hermeneutics challenges our interpretation of Christian faith; (b) how he reflects on continuity in the process of tradition development; and finally (c) his vision of the dialogical relationship between the church and the world.

---

41. J. Ratzinger, *A Turning Point for Europe? The Church in the Modern World – Assessment and Forecast*, trans. B. McNeil (San Francisco, CA: Ignatius, 1994); J. Ratzinger, 'Europe in the Crisis of Cultures', *International Catholic Review Communio* 32, no. 2 (2005): 345–56; J. Ratzinger and M. Pera, *Without Roots: The West, Relativism, Christianity, Islam* (New York: Basic Books, 2006); J. Ratzinger, *Values in a Time of Upheaval* (New York; San Francisco, CA: Crossroad, Ignatius, 2006); J. Habermas and J. Ratzinger, *The Dialectics of Secularization: On Reason and Religion* (San Francisco, CA: Ignatius, 2006).

42. Cf. Boeve, *God Interrupts History*, 5–6.

43. J. Ratzinger, 'The Christian and the Modern World', *Dogma and Preaching* (2011), 169.

44. Ratzinger, *Dogma and Preaching*, 177.

45. Cf. Schillebeeckx, *I Am a Happy Theologian*, x.

a. Challenge of Hermeneutics for Christian Tradition

In the late 1960s, Schillebeeckx developed a new theological perspective within Catholic theology, in respect of the church's recent theological appropriation of history and increased sensibility regarding the concrete situations of people's lives. By taking the hermeneutical problem seriously, he elaborated a new method of interpreting the gospel, one that claims to remain faithful to the Word of God while acknowledging the reality of people's lives. In other words, Schillebeeckx sought to propose a solution through which 'faithfulness to the biblical message in the reinterpretation of faith will continue to be guaranteed'.[46]

In order to understand this solution, we need, in the first place, to elucidate Schillebeeckx's understanding of the hermeneutical problem. In his view, this problem makes us aware that all understanding takes place in a circular movement: 'The answer [to a question] is to some extent determined by the question, which is in turn confirmed, extended or corrected by the answer. A new question then grows out of this understanding, so that the hermeneutical circle continues to develop in a never-ending spiral.'[47] The implications of this conception for truth are as follows: since humans can never escape from this circle and establish perennial truth, there exists no definitive, timeless understanding.[48]

From this perspective, Schillebeeckx holds that, although God's revelation in Jesus was a divine act undertaken freely by God,[49] the Word of God did not come to us in/as a purely divine statement, but rather was given to us 'within the already interpretative response to it of the Old and New Testaments'.[50] God became the subject of a conversation between people, and it was in this way that God's Word was addressed to us. This human dialogue, in which God gave Godself to be understood, was necessarily situated in a certain historical-cultural context. We can even distinguish in the Old and New Testaments various successive 'new contexts', in which an earlier dialogue has been reinterpreted in the light of a

46. E. Schillebeeckx, 'Towards a Catholic Use of Hermeneutics', *God the Future of Man*, trans. N. D. Smith, *CW*, vol. 3 (London: Bloomsbury T&T Clark, 2014), 2 [5]. It is in this book, which originated from a series of lectures delivered in the United States, that Schillebeeckx's hermeneutical turn found its first expression. For a concise and well-written exposition of Schillebeeckx's hermeneutical theory of tradition development, cf. D. Thompson, 'Schillebeeckx on the Development of Doctrine', *Theological Studies* 62, no. 2 (2001): 303–21.

47. Schillebeeckx, 'Catholic Use of Hermeneutics', 4–5 [7–8].

48. The so-called father of the theory of the hermeneutical circle is the German philosopher Martin Heidegger, whom Schillebeeckx directly mentions.

49. See E. Schillebeeckx, 'Theological Interpretation of Faith in 1983', *Essays: Ongoing Theological Quests*, *CW*, vol. 11 (London: Bloomsbury T&T Clark, 2014), 61. Cf. E. Schillebeeckx, 'The Role of History in What Is Called the New Paradigm', in *Paradigm Change in Theology: A Symposium for the Future*, H. Küng and D. Tracy (eds) (Edinburg: Crossroad, 1989), 312.

50. Schillebeeckx, 'Catholic Use of Hermeneutics', 3 [5].

new situation, but in such a way that the content of the earlier dialogue is seen as authoritative in this new interpretation. Hence, we have not only God's words as they were first understood, but also the content of revelation that reaches us in a context enriched by meditation on the faith of the early Christians.[51] A certain tension thus manifests itself in this situation; namely, how the content of revelation expressed and interpreted in a specific historical-cultural situation becomes the norm for our faith today, which is experienced in a totally different historical-cultural context. In Schillebeeckx's view, this situation implies that we can faithfully comprehend the biblical word only through a reinterpretative understanding of the content of faith. In other words, conditioned by our historicity, 'we cannot grasp the biblical text directly "in itself", as though we, as readers or believers, transcended time'.[52]

According to Schillebeeckx, this view has been essential to the Catholic notion of dogma, although it has not been explicitly, or traditionally, referred to as a hermeneutical problem.[53] The contemporary context represents a hermeneutical situation within which, and from which (i.e., certainly not outside it or from above), we can understand in faith the content of revelation.[54]

The traditional distinction, between the unchangeable kernel of dogma (i.e. essential dogmatic affirmation) and its changeable mode of expression, is of no use in the contemporary interpretation of authentic faith because this essence is never given to us as a pure essence, but rather is always conveyed in a historical mode of expression.[55] Thus, we know beforehand that even our contemporary interpretations will become inadequate attempts to express the mystery in a meaningful and objective way. They will become outdated and will have to be demythologized just like the biblical story was itself demythologized.[56] Accordingly, Schillebeeckx asserts that 'truth' is not obtainable separately, but always in correlation to the adopted pattern of reading. 'That is why there are as many different levels of objectivity and of truth as there are scientific models of reading – the concept of truth is multi-dimensional.'[57]

Given our radical historicity, Schillebeeckx states that it is not the literal repetition of the Bible and official magisterial documents that makes us orthodox and faithful to the message of the Bible. Rather, it is the development of dogma, an interpretive contemporary translation of the 'old' material of the faith, which does so.[58] The question is how this translation is to be done without being false to

---

51. Schillebeeckx, 'Catholic Use of Hermeneutics', 3 [5–6].

52. Schillebeeckx, 'Catholic Use of Hermeneutics', 3 [6].

53. Cf. Schillebeeckx, 'Catholic Use of Hermeneutics', 3–4 [6].

54. Cf. Schillebeeckx, 'Catholic Use of Hermeneutics', 4 [7].

55. Cf. Schillebeeckx, 'Catholic Use of Hermeneutics', 8 [12]. Cf. Schillebeeckx, 'The Role of History in What Is Called the New Paradigm', 311.

56. Cf. Schillebeeckx, 'Catholic Use of Hermeneutics', 8 [13].

57. Schillebeeckx, 'Catholic Use of Hermeneutics', 11 [16–17].

58. Cf. Schillebeeckx, 'Catholic Use of Hermeneutics', 14; 16–17 [20; 24].

the gospel. In other words, how can we ensure the continuity of our contemporary interpretive translations with the previous interpretive translations? To put this question in Schillebeeckx's terms: 'In view of the theological pluralism ... what is the criterion which is able to guarantee "orthodoxy" or the correct understanding of faith?'[59]

b. Continuity of Faith in the Development of Tradition

In his *The Understanding of Faith* (1972), Schillebeeckx presents for the first time his three criteria for the orthodox development of Christian faith over and against a heterodox one: the proportional norm, orthopraxis, and the reception by the whole people of God.[60] However, according to Daniel Thompson, it is Schillebeeckx's first criterion that represents the most encompassing explanation of how this process, of the critical translation of experience, should take place. The remaining two criteria are specifications or corollaries thereof.[61] The proportional norm serves two functions: (1) it provides a normative model for an evangelically faithful expression of the contemporary meaning of the Christian message; and (2) it explains how the evangelical identity of meaning has been continuously preserved throughout tradition.[62]

At the beginning of his explanation, Schillebeeckx stresses that any verification of a particular interpretation of faith is impossible on a purely theoretical level. However, he also admits that Christian action (orthopraxis) is likewise inconceivable without an element of theoretical Christian knowledge (orthodoxy). Subsequently, Schillebeeckx goes on to explain how he has come to the criterion of the proportional norm: first, by comparing various *structures* that

59. E. Schillebeeckx, 'Theological Criteria', *The Understanding of Faith: Interpretation and Criticism*, trans. N. D. Smith, *CW*, vol. 5 (London: Bloomsbury T&T Clark, 2014), 51 [56].

60. Cf. Schillebeeckx, 'Theological Criteria', 49–64 [55–72]. Schillebeeckx consistently maintains this proportional understanding of the translation of orthodoxy throughout his later work. Cf. E. Schillebeeckx, 'Theological Interpretation of Faith in 1983', 61–4; cf. Schillebeeckx, 'The Role of History in What Is Called the New Paradigm', 311–14; cf. E. Schillebeeckx, *Church: The Human Story of God*, trans. J. Bowden, *CW*, vol. 10 (London: Bloomsbury T&T Clark, 2014), 38–44 [40–45]. It must be mentioned that although Schillebeeckx presented the proportional norm in 1972 for the first time, he had already discussed the question of tradition development in his earlier writings before the Second Vatican Council. Cf. E. Schillebeeckx, 'The Development of the Apostolic Faith into the Dogma of the Church', *Revelation and Theology*, trans. N. D. Smith, *CW*, vol. 2 (London: Bloomsbury T&T Clark, 2014), 43–61 [63–92].

61. Cf. Thompson, 'Schillebeeckx on the Development of Doctrine', 309. This statement is also confirmed by the fact that in later works (cf. previous footnote) Schillebeeckx elaborates only on this proportional norm.

62. Cf. Schillebeeckx, 'Theological Interpretation of Faith in 1983', 63.

have arisen in the course of history – such structures are intelligible expressions of the Christian experience that arise from combinations of the basic elements of faith[63] and structuring frameworks of particular social and cultural contexts; and second, by noting how such comparisons themselves, in taking the key words of the biblical proclamation as a referential framework, help us to become aware of *structural rules* that preserve their intelligibility as models for every new structuring.[64]

The resultant proportional norm consists in the relationship between the intentionality or act of faith, as inwardly determined by the one mystery of Christ, and the changing referential framework in which that act occurs. The continuity of faith consists, then, in the reproduction of this proportional relationship in different referential (cultural-historical) frameworks. As a result, the constant factor – that is, the evangelical identity of meaning – is found neither at the level of the act or intentionality of faith (the Bible and past Christian tradition) nor at the level of the 'structuring elements' (i.e. the situations, then and now) that express that act. Rather, the constant element, which indicates the direction that every reinterpretation must take, is the relationship between the intentionality of faith and changing structures. As a result, 'The fundamental identity of meaning between successive eras in Christian interpretation of tradition does not refer to corresponding *terms*, for instance between the biblical situation and ours ... but to corresponding *relations* between such terms (message and situation then and now).'[65] The reproduction of this proportional relationship guarantees that the understanding of faith is not frozen in an earlier relationship, but rather addresses the contemporary situation. Only in this relationship and its continual translation can one find Christian identity. As Schillebeeckx puts it, 'Christian identity, that which is one and the same, is not a matter of *equality* but of *proportional equality*.'[66] Consequently, in their differing interpretations of the one gospel, 'particular historical and cultural mediations sometimes *contradict* one another, in the sense that they cannot all be harmonized on the same level'.[67] Schillebeeckx holds that a purely rational, homogeneous continuity of the meaning maintained, for example, by the scholastics or neo-scholastics, or even by the more sophisticated approach of Newman, is a fiction, something that cannot be demonstrated historically. As a result of this vision, Schillebeeckx affirms that the dogmas and creeds, although they are irreversible and cannot be abolished, can become 'thoroughly irrelevant for later generations'.[68]

---

63. It is not completely clear what Schillebeeckx means by the notion of 'basic elements of faith'. He uses it interchangeably with the expressions like 'the biblical kerygma' and 'the data of faith'.

64. Cf. Schillebeeckx, 'Theological Criteria', 53–5 [60–61].

65. Schillebeeckx, 'Theological Interpretation of Faith in 1983', 62.

66. Schillebeeckx, 'Theological Interpretation of Faith in 1983', 63.

67. Schillebeeckx, *Church*, 42 [42]; my emphasis.

68. Schillebeeckx, 'Theological Interpretation of Faith in 1983', 63.

Nevertheless, they remain theologically important because 'they have always expressed and safeguarded the mystery of God and Jesus Christ within a particular socio-cultural system of reference'.[69]

c. Church and the World: Church as Dialogue

In his 1967 essay 'The Church as the Sacrament of Dialogue', Schillebeeckx presents a thorough theological reflection on the relationship between the church and the world. He starts with the assertion that the past mentality of the Catholic Church, characterized (not without a great dose of simplification) by an attitude of *monologue*, was redefined at the Second Vatican Council, in order to accept *dialogue* with the world as a basic principle.[70] In addition, he argues that this new understanding of the church and the world makes it possible for the church to enter into dialogue without abandoning her 'claim to exclusiveness'.[71] He proceeds to explain this idea in greater detail.

A genuine dialogue presupposes that none of the interlocutors can claim in advance the possession of the full truth. Schillebeeckx thinks that such an understanding in this case, of full possession of the truth by the church, is actually in contradiction with the church's true understanding of herself, and he gives three reasons for this. First, even though the church has the task of preserving and guarding the truth, she cannot assert that she is always right simply because 'history provides us with ample evidence to the contrary'.[72] Second, the church has not received any revelation about how she is to undertake the task of humanizing the world. Thus, she must tentatively come up with solutions in a given historical situation, listening to 'the "foreign prophecy" addressed to her from the secular situation, urging her to take decisions which will help to shape the future. These imperatives, or future-making decisions … arise out of negative or "contrast" experiences'.[73] Third, the church's claim to exclusiveness is made relative by the fact that she is still eschatologically oriented; that is, she is still on the way towards the Kingdom of God and not yet identical with it.

From these elaborations, Schillebeeckx concludes that in every new sociocultural situation, the 'Church continually *reinterprets*, in groping fidelity, the unique message of salvation'.[74] As a result, Schillebeeckx states that 'the Church cannot even fulfill her role and present her unique message to the world – the basis of her "claim to exclusiveness" – except in dialogue with the world and human society'.[75] It is in such a way that she achieves her essential character as church.

69. Schillebeeckx, 'Theological Interpretation of Faith in 1983', 63.

70. Cf. E. Schillebeeckx, 'The Church as the Sacrament of Dialogue', *GFM*, 71 [119–20].

71. Schillebeeckx, 'The Church as the Sacrament of Dialogue', 75 [125].

72. Schillebeeckx, 'The Church as the Sacrament of Dialogue', 75 [124].

73. Schillebeeckx, 'The Church as the Sacrament of Dialogue', 83 [136].

74. Schillebeeckx, 'The Church as the Sacrament of Dialogue', 76 [125].

75. Schillebeeckx, 'The Church as the Sacrament of Dialogue', 76 [125].

3. Comparison

On the basis of our exposition, we argue that there is a fundamental similarity between the two positions presented above. This similarity lies in the fact that both positions hold the following: (a) that there is a certain dynamic development of tradition rather than a static repetition of the same formulas throughout history; (b) that although this development necessarily involves a good amount of change and discontinuity, it must be guided by a certain principle of continuity; (c) that the new historical-cultural framework plays a role in this process of development, wherein the same revelation of God in Jesus Christ is always expressed by means of concepts, symbols, and thought-structures of the given context; and (d) that the process of further development or reinterpretation is not to be understood solely on the intellectual, theoretical level, but also requires a certain praxis.

We argue that it is precisely in the ways that they conceive of the intellectual possibility of continuity in tradition development that the positions of Ratzinger and Schillebeeckx differ. Ratzinger views the development of tradition as entailing both identity and change. Whereas change may occur on the level of some practical or technical questions, the main underlying principles remain constant. The fact that we always express the truth in a historical-cultural form does not mean, for Ratzinger, that we can come to different conclusions in different cultural frameworks. We can only conceive of the same reality with better precision; however, the reality, or more precisely the direction pointing to the reality, already expressed in the formulations cannot be contradicted.

It is in regard to this latter point that the thought of Schillebeeckx seems to differ most distinctly from Ratzinger's. According to Schillebeeckx's hermeneutical view of tradition development, there is no direct, unmediated access to the essence of the deposit of faith. All our historical-cultural expressions of the church's identity are but interpretations of the same datum of faith. Although Schillebeeckx attempts to establish a certain principle of continuity in the church's consecutive reinterpretations of faith, continuity cannot be identified on the level of faith's explicit content. We believe the same thing in proportion to the contextual framework by means of which we express our belief. Whenever the context changes, the content of the belief must change accordingly in order for the proportion to remain the same. However, Schillebeeckx's proportional norm does not provide us with any adequate criteria for a faithful reinterpretation of faith. According to Schillebeeckx, we are not able in the present moment to distinguish what in past tradition was merely of cultural import and what appertains particularly to faith's salvific message. Moreover, Schillebeeckx's view seems to imply that the meaning expressed in past interpretations is to a great extent untranslatable from one culture to another. As a result, the difference between the two authors seems to lie in the ways that they view the possibility of intellectually accessing the meaning of the past (re)interpretations of faith. Whereas Ratzinger believes that the meaning conveyed by a subsequent reformulation cannot be in contradiction with the past formulations (at least in its essential principles), Schillebeeckx seems to be sceptical as to whether such an endeavour is actually possible. This is manifested in his admission that a new reinterpretation may be in contradiction with a past one.

We must also highlight that the two authors conceive differently the relationship between the church and the world. Whereas Ratzinger is explicit about the need to criticize the world, Schillebeeckx asserts that the church has not received any unambiguous revelation about how she is to undertake the task of humanizing the world. Ratzinger believes that, even in our different cultural context, we can know the message of the gospel, at least its fundamental characteristics; he is thus able to criticize those cultural elements that contradict these characteristics. Schillebeeckx's notion of the identity of faith, to the contrary, does not presuppose such solid ties to the previous interpretations; the church, in his view, must thus discern her future programme of social engagement on the basis of the general human experiences of contrast. It is clear that Schillebeeckx does not completely disregard the past reinterpretations of faith, since every interpretation implies an object to be interpreted. Nevertheless, his hesitancy to admit that our new reinterpretations of the same salvific mystery of faith must be delineated by the achievements (although provisional) of past interpretations makes his thought prone to 'adaptationist' strategies. In this sense, Ratzinger's position seems to resist such strategies more effectively. However, one should note that Schillebeeckx well articulates the need to bear in mind the provisional nature of all our attempts to formulate the revelation of God. Otherwise, we may unjustly canonize one historical-cultural form of faith that would be lost on those who do not share this cultural framework.

Conclusion

If, at the end of this chapter, we are to formulate an answer to the question asked in the introduction, concerning the church's reaction to the new cultural realities and ways of living that challenge her identity, we must first bear in mind that the intellectual-theological considerations of this question constitute only one aspect of the whole ecclesial undertaking. This undertaking must also take into account the full living organism of the church, including the actual experiences of the faithful. Nevertheless, such an intellectual endeavour is of importance. Our analysis has shown that the thoughts of our authors do not differ exceptionally. Both stress the need to take new cultural phenomena and sensibilities seriously if we want to proclaim the faith authentically. Such phenomena must be deeply studied and analysed in order to realize to what extent they correspond with the intuitions and insights of the Christian faith and its tradition. However, such an enterprise also presupposes an in-depth knowledge of the meaning of the various interpretive understandings of faith. Herein lies, we argue, the major difference between the two theologians. On the level of the explicit content of faith, they differ in their understandings of the possibility to realize a continuous development of tradition. We agree with Ratzinger that, in her reinterpretative formulation(s) of the content and meaning of Christian faith in the present cultural conditions, the church should be directed by the already achieved interpretive advances of the past. She should not make an interpretation that is in contradiction with the sense intended by these statements. Otherwise, she might all too easily exchange her authentic message for the trends of the time.

Bibliography

Boeve, L., *Interrupting Tradition* (Leuven: Eerdmans, 2003).

Boeve, L., 'Religion after Detraditionalization: Christian Faith in a Post-Secular Europe', *Irish Theological Quarterly* 70, no. 2 (2005): 99–122.

Boeve, L., *God Interrupts History: Theology in a Time of Upheaval* (New York, London: Continuum, 2007).

Borgman, E., *Edward Schillebeeckx: A Theologian in His History* (London; New York: Continuum, 2003).

Brand, P., and H. Häring, 'Aggiornamento als wissenschaftliches Projekt: Über Anfänge und Programmatik der Internationalen Zeitschrift für Theologie "CONCILIUM"', in *H. Küng. Neue Horizonte des Glaubens und Denkens. Ein Arbeitsbuch*, H. Häring and K.-J. Kuschel (eds) (München: Piper, 1993), 779–95.

Coutau-Bégarie, H., *Ratzingeriana : bibliographie commentée de Joseph Ratzinger* (Paris: L'homme nouveau, 2012).

Gane, R. E., N. P. Miller, and H. P. Swanson (eds), *Homosexuality, Marriage, and the Church* (Berrien Springs, MI: Andrews University Press, 2012).

Habermas, J., and J. Ratzinger, *The Dialectics of Secularization: On Reason and Religion* (San Francisco, CA: Ignatius, 2006).

Komonchak, J. A., 'The Church in Crisis: Pope Benedict's Theological Vision', *Commonweal* 132, no. 11 (2005): 11–14.

Rahner, K., and E. Schillebeeckx, 'General Introduction', *Concilium* 1, no. 1 (1965): 3–4.

Rahner, K., and J. Ratzinger, *Revelation and Tradition*, trans. W. J. O'Hara (New York: Herder and Herder, 1966), 50–78.

Ratzinger, J., *Der Gott des Glaubens und der Gott der Philosophen* (Munich-Zurich: Schnell & Steiner, 1960).

Ratzinger, J., 'The Changeable and Unchangeable in Theology', *Theology Digest* 10, no. 2 (1962): 71–6.

Ratzinger, J., 'Tradition: III. Systematisch', in *Lexikon für Theologie und Kirche*, J. Höfer and K. Rahner (eds), 2. völlig neu bearbeitete Auflage, vol. X. (Freiburg: Herder, 1965), 293–9.

Ratzinger, J., *Das Problem der Dogmengeschichte in der Sicht der katholischen Theologie* (Köln, Opladen: Westdeutscher Verlag, 1966).

Ratzinger, J., 'Zur Frage nach der Geschichtlichkeit der Dogmen', in *Martyria, Leiturgia, Diakonia. Festschrift für Hermann Volk Bischof von Mainz zum 65. Geburtstag*, Otto Semmelroth (ed.) (Mainz: Matthias-Grünewald, 1968), 59–70.

Ratzinger, J., 'Sources and Transmission of the Faith', *International Catholic Review Communio* 10, no. 1 (1983): 17–34.

Ratzinger, J., *The Ratzinger Report: An Exclusive Interview on the State of the Church* (San Francisco, CA: Ignatius, 1985).

Ratzinger, J., *Principles of Catholic Theology: Building Stones for a Fundamental Theology* (San Francisco, CA: Ignatius, 1987).

Ratzinger, J., 'Chapter I: Revelation Itself', *Commentary on the Documents of Vatican II*, H. Vorgrimler (ed.), trans. W. Glen-Doepel et al., 2nd edn, vol. III (New York: Crossroad, 1989), 170–80.

Ratzinger, J., 'Dogmatic Constitution on Divine Revelation: Origin and Background', in *Commentary on the Documents of Vatican II*, H. Vorgrimler (ed.), trans. W. Glen-Doepel, H. Graef, J. M. Jakubiak, S. Young and E. Young, 2nd edn, vol. III (New York: Crossroad, 1989), 155–98.

Ratzinger, J., *A Turning Point for Europe? The Church in the Modern World—Assessment and Forecast*, trans. B. McNeil (San Francisco, CA: Ignatius, 1994).

Ratzinger, J., *The Nature and Mission of Theology: Essays to Orient Theology in Today's Debates* (San Francisco, CA: Ignatius, 1995).

Ratzinger, J., *Milestones: Memoirs, 1927–1977* (San Francisco, CA: Ignatius, 1998).

Ratzinger, J., *Introduction to Christianity* (San Francisco, CA: Communio, 2004).

Ratzinger, J., *Truth and Tolerance: Christian Belief and World Religions* (San Francisco, CA: Ignatius, 2004).

Ratzinger, J., 'Address of His Holiness Benedict XVI to the Roman Curia Offering Them His Christmas Greetings', December 2005.

Ratzinger, J., 'Europe in the Crisis of Cultures', *International Catholic Review Communio* 32, no. 2 (2005): 345–56.

Ratzinger, J., 'Faith, Reason and the University Memories and Reflections', *Lecture of the Holy Father presented on the occasion of the meeting with the representatives of science*, Regensburg, 2006.

Ratzinger, J., *Values in a Time of Upheaval* (New York; San Francisco, CA: Crossroad, Ignatius, 2006).

Ratzinger, J., *Joseph Ratzinger Gesammelte Schriften: Offenbarungsverständnis und Geschichtstheologie Bonaventuras: Habilitationsschrift und Bonaventura-Studien: Band 2*, G. L. Müller (ed.) (Freiburg, Basel, Vienna: Herder, 2009).

Ratzinger, J., "Farewell to the Devil?', *Dogma and Preaching: Applying Christian Doctrine to Daily Life* (San Francisco, CA: Ignatius Press, 2011), 197–205.

Ratzinger, J., and M. Pera, *Without Roots: The West, Relativism, Christianity, Islam* (New York: Basic Books, 2006).

Rießinger, T., *Joseph Ratzinger - Ein brillanter Denker?: Kritische Fragen an den Papst und seine protestantischen Konkurrenten* (Berlin: Lit Verlag, 2013).

Schillebeeckx, E., 'The Role of History in What Is Called the New Paradigm', in *Paradigm Change in Theology: A Symposium for the Future*, H. Küng and D. Tracy (eds) (Edinburg: Crossroad, 1989), 307–19.

Schillebeeckx, E., *I Am a Happy Theologian: Conversations with Francesco Strazzari*, trans. J. Bowden (London: SCM Press, 1994).

Schillebeeckx, E., *Church: The Human Story of God*, trans. J. Bowden, *CW*, vol. 10 (London: Bloomsbury T&T Clark, 2014).

Schillebeeckx, E., *Essays: Ongoing Theological Quests*, *CW*, vol. 11 (London: Bloomsbury T&T Clark, 2014).

Schillebeeckx, E., *God the Future of Man*, trans. N. D. Smith, *CW*, vol. 3 (London: Bloomsbury T&T Clark, 2014).

Schillebeeckx, E., *Revelation and Theology*, trans. N. D. Smith, *CW*, vol. 2 (London: Bloomsbury T&T Clark, 2014).

Schillebeeckx, E., *The Understanding of Faith: Interpretation and Criticism*, trans. N. D. Smith, *CW*, vol. 5 (London: Bloomsbury T&T Clark, 2014).

Steinhauser, M. G., 'Cardinal Ratzinger in Dialogue with the Toronto School of Theology: What Was Said in 1986?', *Toronto Journal of Theology* 29, no. 1 (2013): 55–84.

Thompson, D., 'Schillebeeckx on the Development of Doctrine', *Theological Studies* 62, no. 2 (2001): 303–21.

Van den Bos, M., and S. van Erp, *A Happy Theologian: A Hundred Years of Edward Schillebeeckx* (Nijmegen: Valkhof Pers, 2014).

Wicks, J., 'Six Texts by Prof. Joseph Ratzinger as Peritus before and during Vatican Council II', *Gregorianum* 89, no. 2 (2008): 269–85.

Chapter 6

METAPHYSICAL THEOLOGY IN HERMENEUTICAL TIMES? LESSONS FROM EDWARD SCHILLEBEECKX

Marijn de Jong

In the contemporary 'late-modern' or 'postmodern' theological scene, 'metaphysics' seems to have become a poisonous term. Following Martin Heidegger's famous critique of the ontotheological constitution of the Western philosophical tradition, various philosophers and theologians have proposed new ways of thinking to 'overcome' metaphysics, or to proceed 'post-metaphysically'. Representative examples of this trend are Emmanuel Levinas's substitution of ethics as *prima philosophia* for metaphysics,[1] Jürgen Habermas's plea for 'post-metaphysical thinking',[2] and Jean-Luc Marion's argument that God should be contemplated 'without' the constraining and idolizing metaphysical discourse about being.[3] Merold Westphal aptly characterizes the situation when he writes the following: 'In postmodern contexts, onto-theology is one of the seven deadly sins.'[4] As several recent publications illustrate, the issue of the viability, or even the (im)possibility, of metaphysics within theology indeed continues to be a much-debated issue in contemporary theology.[5]

---

1. E. Levinas, *Totality and Infinity: An Essay on Exteriority*, trans. A. Lingis (Pittsburgh, PA: Duquesne University Press, 1969).

2. J. Habermas, *Nachmetaphysische Denken: philosophische Aufsätze* (Frankfurt am Main: Suhrkamp, 1988).

3. J.-L. Marion, *God without Being*, trans. T. A. Carlson (Chicago: The University of Chicago Press, 1991).

4. M. Westphal, *Overcoming Onto-theology: Toward a Postmodern Christian Faith* (New York: Fordham University Press, 2001), 13.

5. See, for instance, the following: K. W. Hector, *Theology without Metaphysics: God Language, and the Spirit of Recognition* (Cambridge: Cambridge University Press, 2011); G. Pattison, *God and Being: An Enquiry* (Oxford: Oxford University Press, 2011); E. E. Hall and H. von Sass (eds), *Groundless Gods: The Theological Prospects of Post-Metaphysical Thought* (Eugene, OR: Pickwick Publications, 2014).

In this chapter, I shall challenge the position that theology should proceed without any ontology or metaphysics. Theology has a long history of engaging with philosophy and metaphysics in order to fulfil its task, classically defined as *fides quaerens intellectum*. If theology seeks to continue accounting for the intelligibility and plausibility of Christian faith, it cannot ignore or reject metaphysical discourse altogether. While theology must certainly be attentive to the varied critiques of metaphysics that have been raised over the past century, it remains necessary to reflect on the metaphysical assumptions that are operative in every particular account of God, faith, or religious experience. I shall develop this claim by way of a case study that takes a closer look at the theological oeuvre of Edward Schillebeeckx.

1. Rupture or Continuity?

Given that Schillebeeckx's theological career began in the early part of the twentieth century, it is important to note that his early formation was marked by the Neo-Thomist tradition, which was dominant at that time. Accordingly, his early work on sacramental theology clearly bears the stamp of Thomistic metaphysics.[6] For example, in his book *The Eucharist*, he writes that 'the dogma of creation and the metaphysical realism that is the consequence of this dogma are at the centre of all theological speculation'.[7] Yet, following the Second Vatican Council and the spirit of renewal that this council engendered within the Roman Catholic Church, Schillebeeckx turned towards new currents of thought which brought about a change in his theology, in regard not only to style but also to content.[8] Stated succinctly, he moved away from Neo-Scholasticism with its focus on dogma and towards hermeneutical theory and the phenomenon of religious experience. As a result of this turn, Schillebeeckx eventually became regarded as one of the major representatives of hermeneutical theology.[9] His newly found critical-hermeneutical focus became especially apparent when he published the first two volumes of his Christological trilogy in the 1970s: *Jesus: An Experiment in*

6. See E. Schillebeeckx, *Christ the Sacrament of the Encounter with God*, trans. P. Barret and L. Bright, *CW*, vol. 1 (London: Bloomsbury, 2014). Originally published as *Christus sacrament van de Godsontmoeting* (Bilthoven: Nelissen, 1963).

7. E. Schillebeeckx, *The Eucharist*, trans. N. D. Smith (London: Sheed & Ward, 1968), 147.

8. See R. Schreiter, 'Edward Schillebeeckx', in *The Modern Theologians: An Introduction to Christian Theology in the Twentieth Century*, D. F. Ford (ed.), 2nd edn (Oxford: Blackwell, 1997), 154; F. Schüssler Fiorenza, 'The New Theology and Transcendental Thomism', in *Modern Christian Thought. Vol 2: The Twentieth Century*, J. C. Livingston and F. Schüssler Fiorenza (eds), 2nd edn (Minneapolis: Fortress Press, 2006), 221–4.

9. Schillebeeckx characterizes his own style of theology with the term 'critical hermeneutical'. See, for example, his reflections on his theological approach in *Theologisch Testament. Notarieel nog niet verleden* (Baarn: Nelissen, 1994), 80.

Christology[10] and *Christ: The Christian Experience in the Modern World*.[11] In *Jesus*, Schillebeeckx announces a 'clear break' with the Neo-Scholastic philosophy of Dominicus De Petter, his mentor.[12] Some scholars indeed argue that Schillebeeckx's hermeneutical turn involved the exchange of a 'more neo-Thomist metaphysically grounded theology for a theology rooted in history and language'.[13] According to John Caputo, for instance, this exchange is only logical since 'hermeneutics spells the end of metaphysics'.[14] Yet, other scholars disagree with Schillebeeckx's own assessment of a break in his thinking and instead emphasize the continuity in his thought. For example, Philip Kennedy argues that '[Schillebeeckx] has not in any way or at any time abandoned his most basic epistemological and metaphysical fundamentals' and that the 'inner syntax' of his thought remains the same despite changes in 'outer vocabulary'.[15] Stephan van Erp similarly argues that De Petter's philosophy continues to inform Schillebeeckx's later theology of historical experience.[16]

Building on these insights, I shall offer in this chapter a reading of Schillebeeckx's method that rejects the oppositional image of metaphysics and hermeneutics. I shall put forward the alternative thesis that Schillebeeckx's later hermeneutics of religious experience cannot be understood properly without taking into consideration his earlier metaphysics. A central concern of Schillebeeckx's theology is the universality of his tradition of faith. The leading question throughout his writings is how the early experience of 'salvation from

10. E. Schillebeeckx, *Jesus: An Experiment in Christology*, trans. H. Hoskins and M. Manley, *CW*, vol. 6 (London: Bloomsbury, 2014).

11. E. Schillebeeckx, *Christ: The Christian Experience in the Modern World*, trans. J. Bowden, *CW*, vol. 7 (London: Bloomsbury, 2014).

12. Schillebeeckx, *Jesus*, 580 [618].

13. L. Boeve, 'Experience According to Edward Schillebeeckx: The Driving Force of Faith and Theology', in *Divinising Experience. Essays in the History of Religious Experience from Origen to Ricoeur*, L. Boeve and L. P. Hemming (eds) (Leuven: Peeters, 2004), 199–200.

14. J. D. Caputo, 'Radical Hermeneutics and Religious Truth: The Case of Sheehan and Schillebeeckx', in *Phenomenology of the Truth Proper to Religion*, D. Guerrière (ed.) (Albany: State University of New York, 1990), 149. In Caputo's opinion, however, Schillebeeckx's hermeneutical turn is not radical enough, because it retains what he calls an 'onto-theological centre'.

15. P. Kennedy, 'Continuity Underlying Discontinuity: Schillebeeckx's Philosophical Background', *New Blackfriars* 70 (1989): 264–77 (265).

16. S. van Erp, 'Implicit Faith: Philosophical Theology after Schillebeeckx', in *Edward Schillebeeckx and Contemporary Theology*, L. Boeve, F. Depoortere and S. van Erp (eds) (London: T&T Clark, 2010), 219–20. Other authors have also argued for a line of continuity in Schillebeeckx's work. See, for example, the following: E. Borgman, 'Van cultuurtheologie naar theologie als onderdeel van de cultuur. De toekomst van het theologisch project van Edward Schillebeeckx', *Tijdschrift voor Theologie* 34 (1994): 335–60; and F. Maas, 'Stem en stilte. Waarheid en openbaring bij Schillebeeckx', *Tijdschrift voor Theologie* 50 (2010): 51–72.

God in Jesus Christ' can be experienced anew by other people in different times and different contexts. In grappling with this question, Schillebeeckx seems to rely on the axiom that Thomas Aquinas expressed as follows: '*Omnia cognoscentia cognoscunt implicite Deum in quolibet cognito*' (all knowing beings implicitly know God in everything they know).[17] As we shall see, this dictum will be developed and transformed by Schillebeeckx with the help of hermeneutical and critical theory, yet retains its metaphysical claim. The result is a theological epistemology that entails a dynamic dialectic, or a mutual interdependence, between metaphysics and hermeneutics, between universality and particularity, and between philosophy and theology.

To support this argument, I shall examine four important phases in the development of Schillebeeckx's epistemology, along the following lines in particular: first, his engagement with the philosophy of Dominicus De Petter and the notion of 'implicit faith', which results from this engagement; second, the early hermeneutical investigations in which he explores the possibility of a 'permanence in understanding'; third, the relation between experience and interpretation as developed in the books *Jesus* and *Christ*; and fourth, the notion of the 'contrast experience' within a theology of revelation. Finally, I shall end with a short concluding reflection on Schillebeeckx's contribution to the reconceptualization of the role of metaphysics within theological hermeneutics.

2. Combining Phenomenology and Metaphysics: Implicit Faith

In his 1962 article 'The Concept of "Truth"', Schillebeeckx assesses the contemporary philosophical situation, describing the phenomenological-philosophical reaction to idealism and scholasticism. Phenomenology offers an alternative to abstract conceptuality by drawing attention to *l'expérience vécue* and the historicity of human beings.[18] While Schillebeeckx expresses his sympathy with this renewed focus on the concrete, he also notices that such an approach might make reality and truth fully dependent on the subjective perspective. Looking for a viable third way between rationalism and relativism, he turns to Dominicus De Petter's combination of phenomenology and Thomistic metaphysics. De Petter acknowledges the historical conditions and limitations of human knowing, but, at the same time, he maintains that there is something like reality in itself or absolute truth. He argues that we have a perspectival access to truth: 'From a finite, limited, constantly changing, and historical standpoint, we have a view of absolute truth, although we never have this in our power.'[19]

---

17. T. Aquinas, *De Veritate*, 22, a. 2, ad 1.

18. E. Schillebeeckx, 'The Concept of "Truth"', *Revelation and Theology*, trans. N. D. Smith, *CW* vol. 2 (London: Bloomsbury, 2014), 189–205 [5–29].

19. Schillebeeckx, 'The Concept of "Truth"', 190 [7].

Schillebeeckx took up this perspectival approach to truth in order to propose a theological rethinking of the relation between experience and conceptuality. In the support of this perspectivism, his later hermeneutical focus was already tacitly present. However, Schillebeeckx wrote this article at a time when the Modernist controversy, and the subsequent condemnation of Modernist theology, was still fresh in the minds of theologians.[20] He therefore seeks in this article to distance himself from a complete prioritizing of the subjective experiential dimension of faith, because this may lead to a relativizing of dogmas. In contrast, Schillebeeckx is concerned with maintaining a real, intrinsic connection between conceptuality and experience. He thus deems both conceptuality and experience necessary elements of faith.[21] At this point, De Petter's metaphysics of knowledge provides a solution for explicating the interconnection of these elements.[22] A central aspect of this metaphysics is the notion of 'implicit intuition'. According to De Petter, there is a non-conceptual element in cognition that forms the basis of our conceptual knowledge. The concepts that we use to express our knowledge of reality contain a reference to an implicit and unthematic mode of knowing reality. Through this implicit intuition of reality, we become aware that our concepts are inadequate and limited expressions of this non-conceptual knowledge. Yet, because the non-conceptual moment of knowing is implied within the conceptual moment, there is also an objective dynamism at work within these limited concepts. This objective dynamism provides our concepts, inadequate as they are, with a *real* objectivity. Thus, we do indeed reach absolute truth or reality *in se*, first implicitly, and then, in an imperfect mode, explicitly. Non-conceptual experience and conceptuality, taken together, make up our knowledge of reality.[23]

Schillebeeckx applies this metaphysics of implicit intuition to religious knowledge and theological language. De Petter's concept of implicit intuition is transposed into a concept of implicit faith.[24] The appropriation of this concept

20. For more information on this crisis and its historical background, see J. Mettepenningen, *Nouvelle Théologie - New Theology: Inheritor of Modernism, Precursor of Vatican II* (London: T&T Clark, 2010), 15–29.

21. Schillebeeckx also distinguishes an alternative current in theology, inspired by the philosophers Maurice Blondel and Joseph Maréchal and represented in theology by Karl Rahner. However, he deems their approach unsatisfactory because it resorts to a non-intellectual element in order to explain the relation between concept and reality. For Schillebeeckx's objections against this solution, see the following: Schillebeeckx, 'The Concept of "Truth"',197–8 [17–18], and E. Schillebeeckx, 'The Non-conceptual Intellectual Dimension in our Knowledge of God according to Aquinas', *Revelation and Theology*, trans. N. D. Smith, Collected Works of Edward Schillebeeckx vol. 2 (London: Bloomsbury, 2014), 208–10 [158–62].

22. Schillebeeckx, 'The Concept of "Truth"',192–4 [9–13].

23. Ibid.,198–200 [18–22]. See also D. M. De Petter, 'Impliciete intuïtie', *Tijdschrift voor Philosophie* 1 (1939): 84–105.

24. See Van Erp, 'Implicit Faith', 213–17.

works as follows. Starting phenomenologically, Schillebeeckx asserts that all human knowledge departs from experience of the world. Consequently, God cannot be experienced directly, but must be mediated through worldly experience.[25] Yet, according to Schillebeeckx, in all of our ordinary experience of reality we implicitly co-experience something which surpasses all experience. This becomes evident particularly in the experience of contingency. Contingent reality presents itself to us in the first place as a question. Confronted with the seeming groundlessness, or purposelessness, of reality, however, there is also another perspective opened up: an objective or ontic dynamism towards an absolute and transcendent constitutive ground.[26] This dynamism towards the transcendent ground implicitly accompanies all of our ordinary experiences. Even though it might remain implicit, it nonetheless has a directive force. Schillebeeckx therefore also calls it an 'orientation of a conscious ignorance'.[27]

The implicit experience of transcendence does not remain merely implicit. Rather, it gives rise to reflection and calls for articulation and conceptualization with the help of categories and concepts. Arguing from his embeddedness in the Christian tradition, Schillebeeckx explains that the 'history of salvation' provides specific concepts and ideas to clarify conceptually this implicit experience.[28] To be more precise, the Christian tradition interprets this implicit experience as an experience of God, as an implicit aspect of faith. This implicit experience is made explicit in dogmatic faith formulations. These conceptual formulas imply a real objective reference to God because 'truth is contained not only in the pre-reflexive implicit experience; if grasped in that element, truth is also reached in the reflectively formulated data of faith'.[29] However, Schillebeeckx repeats that it is impossible to express the implicit and pre-reflexive experience of transcendence adequately. The categories and concepts that we use cannot exhaust or grasp God's revelation, which, in the human experience of reality, always remains a veiled manifestation. God remains mystery.[30]

This is, generally speaking, the outline of Schillebeeckx's theological epistemology that he developed in the period preceding the Second Vatican

---

25. E. Schillebeeckx, 'Het niet-godsdienstig humanisme en het godsgeloof', *God en mens. Theologische peilingen deel 2* (Bilthoven: Nelissen, 1965), 49–50, [trans. *God and Man* (London; Sydney; New York: Sheed & Ward, 1969)]; E. Schillebeeckx, 'Faith and Self-Understanding', in *The Word in History. The St. Xavier Symposium*, P. Burke (ed.) (London: Collins, 1968), 46.

26. Schillebeeckx, 'Het niet-godsdienstig humanisme en het godsgeloof', 52–3.

27. E. Schillebeeckx, 'The Search for the Living God', *Essays. Ongoing Theological Quests*, trans. E. Fitzgerald and P. Tomlinson, *CW* vol. 11 (London: Bloomsbury, 2014), 38.

28. Schillebeeckx, 'Faith and Self-Understanding', 50–5.

29. Ibid., 54.

30. On this notion of God as mystery, see also E. Schillebeeckx, 'What Is Theology?', in *Revelation and Theology*, trans. N. D. Smith, Collected Works of Edward Schillebeeckx vol. 2 (London: Bloomsbury, 2014), 89–91 [134–8].

Council. However, inspired by this council's spirit of renewal Schillebeeckx set out to explore new currents of thought. Philip Kennedy recounts the diverse sources on which he began to draw, sources which range from hermeneutics and critical theory to linguistics and historical-critical methods of biblical interpretation.[31] Schillebeeckx's engagement with these sources was fuelled by a 'feverish sense of urgency', caused by 'the unmistakable difficulties of contemporary Christians in a "secularized world"'.[32] As we shall see, while this methodological reorientation brought about important changes in Schillebeeckx's theological method, there also remains a strong line of continuity between his early and later writings.

3. Permanence in Understanding: Early Hermeneutical Investigations

In an article from 1967 entitled 'Towards a Catholic Use of Hermeneutics', Schillebeeckx's engagement with hermeneutical theory bears its first fruit.[33] In this article, he argues that the historicity of human existence and the conditioning role of pre-understanding imply that human understanding necessarily has a circular nature. Every answer to a question becomes a new question; thus, any enduring, timeless understanding (or answer) is impossible. However, according to Schillebeeckx, truth nonetheless transcends its various historical expressions.[34] How is this possible? He argues that the traditional distinction, between an unchangeable 'kernel' of truth and its mutable 'outer elements', no longer provides an adequate solution.[35] There is never a pure kernel because all human understanding is interpretive understanding. Rather, it is precisely *in* the interpretation that we

31. See P. Kennedy, *Schillebeeckx* (Collegeville, MN: The Liturgical Press, 1993), 31–53. To be more precise, Kennedy meticulously lists more than twenty intellectual sources: (1) De Petter's philosophy, (2) French *ressourcement* studies, (3) French and German phenomenology, (4) French personalism and existentialism, (5) Dutch humanism and (6) sociology, (7) philosophical pragmatism, (8) philosophical hermeneutics, (9) historico-, form-, and redaction-critical biblical studies, (10) religious sociology, (11) practical-critical hermeneutics, (12) universal pragmatics, (13) Frankfurt School critical theory, (14) theoretical linguistics, (15) semiotics, (16) philosophies of language and linguistics, (17) secular eschatology, (18) psychology, (19) anthropology, (20) cultural historiography, (21) structuralism, (22) post-structuralism, (23) post-modernism, and (24) the philosophy of Emmanuel Levinas.

32. E. Schillebeeckx, 'The New Image of God, Secularization and Man's Future of Earth', in *God the Future of Man*, trans. N. D. Smith, *CW* vol. 3 (London: Bloomsbury, 2014), 101 [169].

33. E. Schillebeeckx, 'Towards a Catholic Use of Hermeneutics', *GFM*, trans. N. D. Smith, *CW* vol. 3 (London: Bloomsbury, 2014).

34. Schillebeeckx, 'Towards a Catholic Use of Hermeneutics', 1–6 [3–10].

35. As Schillebeeckx notes himself, he did advocate this distinction in his earlier work. Schillebeeckx, 'The Concept of "Truth"', 201–5 [23–9]).

find the 'pure content of faith'. Objectivity and truth are never abstractly given, but rather are always embedded in a contextual tradition of understanding. This tradition not only forms the transcendental condition by which we come to understanding, but also establishes a certain limitation on human understanding. The tradition thus conditions understanding both positively and negatively.[36]

These hermeneutical insights offer a challenge not only to theology, but also to metaphysics. The crisis of faith is also a crisis of metaphysics. However, a complete rejection of metaphysics could turn into an undesirable '*Offenbarungspositivismus*'. This is why Schillebeeckx is reluctant to break completely with metaphysics and instead raises the question whether a 'non-essentialist metaphysics' is possible. Addressing this question leads him to an exploration of the 'conditions for the possibility of theological understanding'.[37] A key issue in this regard concerns the continuity and communicability of a tradition over time. In order to address this issue, he returns to the notion of implicit intuition, but now does so emphasizing the role of existential and historical factors.[38] He begins by arguing that any reinterpretative understanding of a text presupposes a living relation to the reality expressed in the text. This reality itself provides us with a pre-understanding which guides our understanding and praxis. This pre-understanding applies to all understanding, including the understanding of scripture or church councils.[39] In our existential experience of reality, we thus encounter a directive force towards the truth. This directive force is, first and foremost, experienced at an unthematic level of cognition and escapes full, comprehensive, or definitive articulation.[40] Given our diverse contextual traditions of understanding, there is a necessary pluralism in human expressions of this truth. Yet, this view does not imply a simple relativism. Schillebeeckx argues that, despite the flux of history, 'the inviolable aspect of the content of faith is situated in an inexpressible *objective perspective* which is again and again meaningfully suggested from and in a changing historical outline and which makes itself felt *in* every historical outline – the mystery is always giving us to *think*.'[41]

This objective reference to mysterious reality that is un-thematically present in various historical interpretations provides an element of continuity throughout the history of interpretation. Regarding this element, Schillebeeckx considers the term 'trans-historical' too strong and describes it alternatively as an 'implicit permanence' in understanding.[42] The objective directionality of reality that provides for this permanence of understanding seems clearly indebted to his

---

36. Schillebeeckx, 'Towards a Catholic Use of Hermeneutics', 17–19 [26–7].

37. Ibid., 9, n. 20 [15, n. 20].

38. Ibid., 7–8 [12–13].

39. Ibid., 22–3 [33].

40. Ibid., 7–8 [12–13].

41. Ibid., 27 [40]; original emphasis. He refers also to Martin Heidegger's expression, 'that which is "not thought of"' [das Unbedachte], which *gives us to think*, but is itself never thought'. Schillebeeckx, 'Towards a Catholic Use of Hermeneutics', 22 [33].

42. Ibid., 26–7 [38–40].

earlier metaphysics of implicit intuition. Yet, Schillebeeckx not only disassociates himself from 'anti-metaphysical tendencies' in theology,[43] but also refrains from offering a non-essentialist metaphysics that could serve to support a theological hermeneutics. Instead, Schillebeeckx's hermeneutical focus is intensified and developed through an increased focus on the role of experience in faith. This comes clearly to expression in the books *Jesus* and *Christ*. In Schillebeeckx's own view, this removes him even further from his earlier metaphysics. We shall now turn to this phase to examine whether the theological epistemology presented in these works indeed constitutes a break.

4. Radicalizing Hermeneutics: All Experience is Interpretive

In *Jesus*, Schillebeeckx combines hermeneutical theory with insights derived from Critical Theory. This combination leads him to emphasize the inadequacy of theoretical reason apart from praxis, as well as the need for an openness towards the future. A guiding concern throughout this work is how the Christian tradition can confess the universal significance of the particular, historical Jesus event. In his reflections on a so-called universal horizon of understanding, Schillebeeckx focuses on the question of meaning. He argues that, in particular experiences of meaning, it is not universal meaning itself, but rather only the *question* of universal meaning that can be found. Moreover, this question of universal meaning cannot be established merely by way of theoretical reason.[44] In view of these considerations, Schillebeeckx states that he needs to 'break' with his approach of the implicit intuition, because it is based on a theory of participation that assumes a homogenous situation. Confronted with the contemporary, pluralistic society, he believes that the idea of participation must be replaced by an idea of anticipation within an unfolding history. Any particular theoretical formulation of such anticipation must be tested as a hypothesis against human historical experiences, to which Schillebeeckx has given pride of place.[45]

Schillebeeckx subsequently returns to the experience of contingency. In the contingent human person, he finds a constitutive reference to a transcendent reality. Yet, and more strongly than before, he now emphasizes that this reference is not only revealing, but also concealing. To express this ambiguity, he uses the expression 'mediated immediacy'. For (historical) human beings, any perspective on transcendence takes place *in* the world, *in* history, and *in* encounters with fellow humans, and it always points towards the future.[46] To retain this openness to the future, and to emphasize the current incompleteness, Schillebeeckx prefers to speak of *anticipation* rather than of participation. This shift in language and the

43. Ibid., 28 [41].
44. Schillebeeckx, *Jesus*, 559–73 [595–612].
45. Ibid., 580–1 [618–19].
46. Ibid., 594 [632].

emphasis on particularity and incompleteness clearly show that Schillebeeckx feels compelled to change his methodology.

The central role that is ascribed to historical experience in *Jesus* is taken up again in the *Christ* book. Schillebeeckx argues here that revelation is intrinsically connected with experience.[47] In order to explain religious experience, he provides a general structure of experience that attends specifically to the relation between experience and interpretation. The central assertion is that there is no 'immediate experience'; all experience is interpreted experience. Yet, this assertion should not obscure the fact that experience has both objective and subjective elements. Schillebeeckx therefore introduces an analytical distinction between (1) encounter with the world or event, (2) thinking or reflection, and (3) language or expression. In concrete human experience, these three elements are always dialectically interwoven and cannot be neatly separated.[48] Schillebeeckx nevertheless uses this analytical distinction to avoid a reduction of experience to pure subjectivity. Despite the fact that we only experience interpretively, there is something 'given' at work in experience. The experienced reality offers something that escapes human manipulation. Reality, then, transcends our perspectival experience.[49] Mary Catherine Hilkert notes that this element of 'givenness' in experience forms an abiding insight for Schillebeeckx, and she attributes it to his phenomenological background.[50]

The joint role of subjectivity and objectivity in experience is further explained by distinguishing between 'inner experiential interpretative elements' and 'outer reflective interpretative elements'. On the one hand, experiential interpretive elements have their ground and origin 'directly in what is experienced' and make this experience 'somewhat transparent'. On the other hand, reflective interpretive

---

47. See also E. Schillebeeckx, 'Experience and Faith', *Essays: Ongoing Theological Quests*, trans. M. Manley, *CW*, vol. 11 (London: Bloomsbury, 2014), 1–34. Because of the central role that Schillebeeckx ascribes to experience, his theology has also been called a 'theology of experience'. See, for instance, E. Schillebeeckx, 'Theologie der Erfahrung – Sackgasse oder Weg zum Glauben? Ein Gespräch mit Prof. Edward Schillebeeckx', *Herder Korrespondenz* 32 (1978): 391–7.

48. Schillebeeckx, *Christ*, 34–5 [49].

49. Ibid., 17–18 [31–3]. It is interesting to note Graham Ward's more recent investigation of 'what is prior to interpretation and the impact it has on the way we think and behave'. G. Ward, *Unbelievable: Why We Believe and Why We Don't* (London: I.B. Tauris, 2014).

50. 'One of Schillebeeckx's perduring convictions, drawn from his phenomenological background and crucial to his theology of revelation, emerges at this point: experience contains a dimension of "givenness" that comes from beyond the subject. While there is no uninterpreted experience, neither can experience be reduced to the subjective construct, or creation, of the interpreter. Reality remains independent of the perceiver, something which we cannot manipulate or change.' M. C. Hilkert, 'Experience and Revelation', in *The Praxis of the Reign of God: An Introduction to the Theology of Edward Schillebeeckx*, M. C. Hilkert and R. Schreiter (eds), 2nd ed. (New York: Fordham University Press, 2002), 64.

elements are given to us from outside this experience, for example by the cultural or religious tradition(s) to which we belong. The result is an ongoing and reciprocal interrelation between experience and interpretation. Interpretation is necessary to experience and can deepen, but never exhaust experience.[51] In the notion of 'inner experiential interpretative elements', we recognize again the metaphysical principle of objective directionality. Yet, Schillebeeckx neither consciously makes this connection nor reflects on the metaphysical assumptions underlying his assertion that something 'given' is at work in experience. Nevertheless, this view of the 'given' is featured again, and more prominently, in his understanding of revelation. The contours of his notion of revelation are announced in *Christ*, and the concept is developed further in *Church: The Human Story of God*.[52]

5. Givenness Becomes Revelation: The Contrast Experience

Schillebeeckx's search for a universal horizon of understanding is essentially an attempt to account for the universality of divine revelation. Since he holds that all human-divine encounters happen in the world of historical experience, the universality of revelation must have a grounding in the very structure of human experience. Schillebeeckx finds such a universal element in the experience of contingency. In our attempts to grasp and understand reality, we also encounter resistance to our designs and models from reality itself. This refractory dimension of reality forms the hermeneutical principle both for the disclosure of reality and for the revelation of God.[53] Schillebeeckx develops this insight through his notion of the 'contrast experience'.[54] This concept can be explained as follows. In our lives, we continually encounter suffering and failures. These negative experiences show the finitude of humanity and the impossibility of absolute knowledge.[55] However, the same negative experiences also contain a positive element. Negative experience itself calls for a 'no' to inhumanity and suffering, based on a trust and hope that the world can be changed. This hope and trust originate in reality, which, like a 'hidden magnet', orders and directs our knowing and acting.[56] The phrase 'hidden magnet' seems to be a clear reference to what we earlier discussed, under the heading of 'objective directionality'. But Schillebeeckx does not explicitly use this notion to explain how a positive horizon can appear within a situation of suffering.

---

51. Schillebeeckx, *Christ*, 18–19 [33–4].

52. E. Schillebeeckx, *Church: The Human Story of God*, trans. J. Bowden, *CW*, vol. 10 (London: Bloomsbury, 2014). Originally published as *Mensen als verhaal van God* (Baarn: Nelissen, 1989).

53. Schillebeeckx, *Christ*, 20 [34–5].

54. Ibid., 5–6 [6]. Another text in which Schillebeeckx succinctly summarizes the main characteristics of the contrast experience is *Theologisch Testament*, 128–32.

55. Schillebeeckx, *Christ*, 21 [35].

56. Ibid., 21 [35].

Religious people may recognize God in this confluence of negativity and positivity. Yet, Schillebeeckx is very much aware that this experience is not necessarily interpreted religiously.[57] He nevertheless argues that it provides a perspective within our historical horizon of experience that enables us to discuss transcendent meaning.[58] In *Church*, he speaks of the contrast experience as a 'basic, pre-religious experience'.[59] He elucidates this idea by discussing the notion of absolute limit. The absolute limit is not experienced immediately, but is always co-experienced in experiences of relative boundaries. It should therefore not be understood as something like Friedrich Schleiermacher's '*schlechthinniges Abhängigkeitsgefühl*'.[60] Moreover, it is always experienced and articulated with the help of interpretive frameworks, either religious or atheistic. On the one hand, a different interpretation makes the experience of radical contingency a truly different experience. The Christian recognizing God in this experience thus, in some way, inhabits a different world.[61] On the other hand, there is also a familiarity in religious and non-religious experiences of radical contingency. While cultural and religious interpretive frameworks are necessary, they are not all-determining. Schillebeeckx uses the expression 'universally human', or 'pre-linguistic' moment of experience, in order to explain this familiarity.[62] The phrase 'implicit intuition' is not used, but the parallels with this concept are quite obvious. The prelinguistic moment of experience not only explains the possibility of a universal experience, but also safeguards the *semper maior* of reality and especially of God. This becomes particularly manifest in his description of revelation in *Church*:

> 'Revelation' can be understood at two different levels of language. On the one hand revelation is essentially that which cannot be named, the inexpressible which lies beyond all conceptual knowledge and is the basis of experience of faith – of the praxis of faith and the thought of faith. On the other hand revelation is also the Unnameable caught in reflection: the conceptualized, as it were 'comprehended', manifestation of the not directly comprehendible foundation of faith. At its deepest, revelation is the non-reflective, pre-theoretical givenness – or more correctly, the self-giving – of that which is always already the basis of the process of faith, that which is constitutive for faith and makes it possible.[63]

57. Ibid., 36 [50].
58. Ibid., 34 [48].
59. Ibid., 5–6 [5–6].
60. Ibid., 75–6 [77–8].
61. Ibid., 36 [50]. See also 77–8 [79–80].
62. Schillebeeckx, *Church*, 78 [80].
63. Schillebeeckx, *Mensen als verhaal van God*, 46–7. I provided my own translation here because the English version (*Church* 26–7 [27–8]) is inaccurate. Whereas the Dutch version purports to say that an imperfect degree of 'expressibility' is possible, according to the English version revelation is said to be entirely inexpressible.

This quotation clearly shows that Schillebeeckx maintains a distinction in his later work between the implicit and the explicit level that was developed in his early work. Moreover, the implicit level is deemed more original than, and prior to, the explicit level. He emphasizes, however, that, in actual experience, we never have the two levels apart from each other, but rather always in dialectical interrelation.[64]

Finally, it is important to note something which Schillebeeckx continually stresses in his reflections on revelation, namely, its donative character. Revelation occurs to us as a gift *via the medium of human experience in the world*. As we experience interpretively, we can name this offer-from-God, but we can never completely catch the inexpressible from a reflective standpoint. The unthematic, or prelinguistic, moment guides and norms our interpretations of faith: 'The offer-from-God of course provides its own *direction* of interpretation, as the normative basis of our non-arbitrary interpretations of faith.'[65] Without this gift, our interpretations of faith would become pure projections. Even though this prelinguistic, experiential moment is never available without interpretation, Schillebeeckx stresses that we should take seriously the object of experience and revelation and the directive interpretive force that it exerts.[66]

Assessing Schillebeeckx's later theology of revelation, it becomes manifest that his critical-hermeneutical approach remains dependent on an earlier metaphysical framework. The notion of 'implicit intuition' or 'implicit' faith makes a surprising comeback in these later writings. Without De Petter's epistemology and Schillebeeckx's theological appropriation of this epistemology, it seems difficult to comprehend the notion of the 'contrast experience'. In the first place, Schillebeeckx continues to rely on the idea of objective directionality to account for the emergence of a positive horizon within the world of suffering. Moreover, in order to account for the universality of the contrast experience, he resorts again to the notion of an implicit level of experience and revelation. This implicit element of experience also contains the objective directionality that is necessary to avoid a complete subjectivization of experience, as well as to retain the primacy and normativity of revelation. However, while Schillebeeckx clearly assumes a metaphysical framework for his theological epistemology, he merely alludes to his older concepts and does not consider these metaphysical presuppositions explicitly and critically. To give an example, he only states that the contrast experience falls within the domain that is traditionally called 'natural theology', without elaborating any contours of such a natural theology.[67]

---

64. The view expressed here by Schillebeeckx bears a striking resemblance to Karl Rahner's theology of revelation, which distinguishes between a transcendental and a categorical level of revelation. See, for instance, K. Rahner, *Foundations of Christian Faith: An Introduction to the Idea of Christianity*, trans. W. V. Dych (New York: Crossroad, 1978), 137–75.

65. Schillebeeckx, *Church*, 37 [38].

66. Ibid., 37 [38].

67. Ibid., 5–6 [6].

Conclusion

In this chapter, I have traced the development of Schillebeeckx's theological epistemology. I have shown that, his hermeneutical turn notwithstanding, metaphysics continues to play a fundamental role in his theological epistemology. Contrary to Caputo's bold claim, Schillebeeckx's case shows that hermeneutics does not necessarily spell the end of metaphysics. As we have seen, his hermeneutics of experience requires an equally important metaphysics of experience. There is a clear ontological thread in Schillebeeckx's work, from the theory of implicit faith, through the objective directionality of experience, and to the contrast experience. It must be granted, however, that Schillebeeckx refrained from consciously developing the metaphysical elements of his theological hermeneutics. The question arises, therefore, whether we can 'go with Schillebeeckx beyond Schillebeeckx' and explicate the implicit metaphysics underlying his hermeneutics. In this final section, I shall offer some concluding reflections that could mark a starting point for thinking about what he called a 'non-essentialist metaphysics' in support of a theological *fides quaerens intellectum*. I will do so by laying out three possible connections with other thinkers, namely, Charles Taylor, William Desmond, and Paul Ricoeur.

In his reflections on the relation between experience and interpretation, Schillebeeckx constantly seeks to maintain a balance between the subjective and the objective poles. His hermeneutical turn intensifies the attention to the conditioning role of historicity and context, yet without eliminating the equally important element of objective directionality. This directional influence of reality in our interpretive experience requires a specific ontological understanding of reality. It requires a metaphysical realism that understands reality not only as independent of the human subject, but also as offering itself to human subjectivity. For Schillebeeckx, this objective initiative or directionality is disclosed primarily in our experience of the contingency of reality. It is precisely when we encounter suffering, death, sorrow, finitude, and so forth that we come to realize that we human subjects do not ultimately control and determine reality. Reality is a mystery which gives us to think. The metaphysical realism assumed by Schillebeeckx has become suspect ever since Immanuel Kant's transcendental critique of metaphysics. However, realism seems to be making a comeback more recently within philosophy. Charles Taylor is an example in this case.[68] In *A Secular Age*,[69] he develops an argument for a 'fullness in terms of openness

---

68. Markus Gabriel is another example of this resurgence of interest in metaphysical realism. See his book *Fields of Sense: A New Realist Ontology* (Edinburgh: Edinburgh University Press, 2014).

69. See C. Taylor, *A Secular Age* (Cambridge, MA: The Belknap Press of Harvard University Press, 2007).

to transcendence' that presupposes some form of ontological realism.[70] More recently, Taylor has also criticized 'mediational' epistemology, proposing a realist epistemology. He argues that, through our bodies, we have a direct and common access to the world, which is prior to our reflection and conceptualization, yet also enables us to speak – and disagree – about reality.[71] Given the central role of metaphysical realism in Schillebeeckx's theology, it would be worthwhile to bring him into conversation with contemporary philosophical voices that advocate such an ontological realism.

The second area that may develop Schillebeeckx's thought concerns the topic of natural theology. For Schillebeeckx, a hermeneutics of the contingency of reality does not merely involve a decentring of the subject and a disclosure of the mysterious nature of reality. This experience of contingency may also involve a revelation of God. Thus, in the contrast experience a situation of negativity is broken open by a positive dimension. Following Schillebeeckx's own suggestion, a natural theology could be developed around this notion of the contrast experience. Philip Kennedy has noted that 'a doctrine of creation still undergirds Schillebeeckx's more recent religious epistemology'.[72] Developing such a natural theology should therefore involve a constructive dialogue between philosophy and theology, specifically drawing on Schillebeeckx's theology of creation. One philosopher supporting such a mutual engagement between philosophy and theology is William Desmond. His argument for the porosity of being leads him to advocate a similar porosity between philosophy and religion or theology.[73] Desmond's work could therefore be an impetus for bringing Schillebeeckx's theology of creation into dialogue with his metaphysics of knowledge, without the fear of a theological contamination of philosophical discourse.

Third, I want to conclude with a suggestion, and challenge, concerning Schillebeeckx's rather sharp opposition between the notion of participation and the notion of anticipation. Although I understand his concern to avoid premature closures and to retain an openness towards the future, I do not think that a participatory metaphysics must necessarily become a self-enclosed system that ignores otherness, difference, or future surprises. Moreover, the notion of anticipation itself also raises another question, namely whether something such as revelation can be anticipated if there is not already some sort of preconception present. If we are to hear, recognize, and make sense of God's revelation, it cannot be completely strange and foreign to us. For there to be revelation, then, there must

70. G. Vanheeswijck, 'Does History Matter? Charles Taylor on the Transcendental Validity of Social Imaginaries', *History and Theory* 54 (2015): 69–85.

71. See C. Taylor, 'Retrieving Realism', in *Mind, Reason and Being-in-the World: The McDowell-Dreyfus Debate*, J. K. Schear (ed.) (Oxford: Routledge 2013), 61–90. Taylor's newer book (co-authored with Hubert Dreyfus), *Retrieving Realism* (Cambridge, MA: Harvard University Press, 2015), offers a more detailed account of his argument.

72. P. Kennedy, 'God and Creation', *The Praxis of the Reign of God*, 52.

73. W. Desmond, *God and the Between* (London: Blackwell, 2008).

be some sort of *Anknüpfungspunkt* between human beings and God. This seems to call for a metaphysics of participation that thematizes this relation. To be sure, the notion of anticipation remains important insofar as it indicates the provisional and incomplete nature of this relationality. Yet, it should be a complement to, rather than a replacement of, the notion of participation. To explore a more modest participatory metaphysics, Paul Ricoeur's idea of a 'broken ontology' (*ontologie brisée*) might be relevant.[74] His insights may help to develop a metaphysics which seeks to be mindful of human limitations, yet nonetheless attempts to account for a universal element in the rich variety of human experiences. Such an account seems indispensable for anyone who holds on to the universal dimension of the Christian message of faith.

Bibliography

Boeve, L., 'Experience according to Edward Schillebeeckx: The Driving Force of Faith and Theology', in *Divinising Experience: Essays in the History of Religious Experience from Origen to Ricoeur*, L. Boeve and L. P. Hemming (eds) (Leuven: Peeters, 2004).

Borgman, E., 'Van cultuurtheologie naar theologie als onderdeel van de cultuur. De toekomst van het theologisch project van Edward Schillebeeckx', *Tijdschrift voor Theologie* 34 (1994): 335–60.

Caputo, J. D., 'Radical Hermeneutics and Religious Truth: The Case of Sheehan and Schillebeeckx', in *Phenomenology of the Truth Proper to Religion*, D. Guerrière (ed.) (Albany: State University of New York, 1990), 146–74.

De Petter, D. M., 'Impliciete intuïtie', *Tijdschrift voor Philosophie* 1 (1939): 84–105.

Desmond, W., *God and the Between* (London: Blackwell, 2008).

Gabriel, M., *Fields of Sense: A New Realist Ontology* (Edinburgh: Edinburgh University Press, 2014).

Habermas, J., *Nachmetaphysische Denken: philosophische Aufsätze* (Frankfurt am Main: Suhrkamp, 1988).

Hall, E. E., and H. von Sass (eds), *Groundless Gods: The Theological Prospects of Post Metaphysical Thought* (Eugene, OR: Pickwick Publications, 2014).

Hector, K. W., *Theology without Metaphysics. God Language, and the Spirit of Recognition* (Cambridge: Cambridge University Press, 2011).

Hilkert, M. C., 'Experience and Revelation', in *The Praxis of the Reign of God: An Introduction to the Theology of Edward Schillebeeckx*, M. C. Hilkert and R. Schreiter (eds), 2nd edn (New York: Fordham University Press, 2002), 59–78.

Kennedy, P., 'Continuity Underlying Discontinuity: Schillebeeckx's Philosophical Background', *New Blackfriars* 70 (1989): 264–77.

Kennedy, P., *Schillebeeckx* (Collegeville, MN: The Liturgical Press, 1993).

Kennedy, P., 'God and Creation', in *The Praxis of the Reign of God: An Introduction to the Theology of Edward Schillebeeckx*, M. C. Hilkert and R. Schreiter (eds), 2nd edn (New York: Fordham University Press, 2002), 37–58.

74. See P. Ricoeur, *Oneself as Another*, trans. K. Blamey (Chicago: The University of Chicago Press, 1992).

Levinas, E., *Totality and Infinity: An Essay on Exteriority*, trans. A. Lingis (Pittsburgh, PA: Duquesne University Press, 1969).

Maas, F., 'Stem en stilte. Waarheid en openbaring bij Schillebeeckx', *Tijdschrift voor Theologie* 50 (2010): 51–72.

Marion, J.-L., *God without Being*, trans. T. A. Carlson (Chicago: The University of Chicago Press, 1991).

Mettepenningen, J., *Nouvelle Théologie – New Theology: Inheritor of Modernism, Precursor of Vatican II* (London: T&T Clark, 2010), 15–29.

Pattison, G., *God and Being: An Enquiry* (Oxford: Oxford University Press, 2011).

Rahner, K., *Foundations of Christian Faith: An Introduction to the Idea of Christianity*, trans. W. V. Dych (New York: Crossroad, 1978).

Ricoeur, P., *Oneself as Another*, trans. K. Blamey (Chicago: The University of Chicago Press, 1992).

Schillebeeckx, E., 'Het niet-godsdienstig humanisme en het godsgeloof', *God en mens. Theologische peilingen deel 2* (Bilthoven: Nelissen, 1965), 49–50, [trans. *God and Man* (London; Sydney; New York: Sheed & Ward, 1969)].

Schillebeeckx, E., *The Eucharist*, trans. N. D. Smith (London: Sheed & Ward, 1968).

Schillebeeckx, E., 'Faith and Self-Understanding', in *The Word in History: The St. Xavier Symposium*, P. Burke (ed.) (London: Collins, 1968).

Schillebeeckx, E., 'Theologie der Erfahrung – Sackgasse oder Weg zum Glauben? Ein Gespräch mit Prof. Edward Schillebeeckx', *Herder Korrespondenz* 32 (1978): 391–7.

Schillebeeckx, E., *Mensen als verhaal van God* (Baarn: Nelissen, 1989).

Schillebeeckx, E., *Theologisch Testament. Notarieel nog niet verleden* (Baarn: Nelissen, 1994).

Schillebeeckx, E., *Christ the Sacrament of the Encounter with God*, trans. P. Barret and L. Bright, *CW*, vol. 1 (London: Bloomsbury, 2014). Originally published as *Christus sacrament van de Godsontmoeting* (Bilthoven: Nelissen, 1963).

Schillebeeckx, E., *Christ: The Christian Experience in the Modern World*, trans. J. Bowden, *CW*, vol. 7 (London: Bloomsbury, 2014).

Schillebeeckx, E., *Church: The Human Story of God*, trans. J. Bowden, *CW*, vol. 10 (London: Bloomsbury, 2014).

Schillebeeckx, E., *Essays: Ongoing Theological Quests*, trans. E. Fitzgerald and P. Tomlinson, *CW*, vol. 11 (London: Bloomsbury, 2014).

Schillebeeckx, E., *God the Future of Man*, trans. N. D. Smith, *CW*, vol. 3 (London: Bloomsbury, 2014).

Schillebeeckx, E., *Jesus: An Experiment in Christology*, trans. H. Hoskins and M. Manley, *CW*, vol. 6 (London: Bloomsbury, 2014).

Schillebeeckx, E., *Revelation and Theology*, trans. N. D. Smith, *CW*, vol. 2 (London: Bloomsbury, 2014).

Schreiter, R., 'Edward Schillebeeckx', in *The Modern Theologians: An Introduction to Christian Theology in the Twentieth Century*, D. F. Ford (ed.), 2nd edn (Oxford: Blackwell, 1997), 152–61.

Schüssler Fiorenza, F., 'The New Theology and Transcendental Thomism', in *Modern Christian Thought. Vol 2: The Twentieth Century*, J. C. Livingston and F. Schüssler Fiorenza (eds), 2nd edn (Minneapolis: Fortress Press, 2006).

Taylor, C., *A Secular Age* (Cambridge, MA: The Belknap Press of Harvard University Press, 2007).

Taylor, C., 'Retrieving Realism', in *Mind, Reason and Being-in-the World: The McDowell-Dreyfus Debate*, J. K. Schear (ed.) (Oxford: Routledge, 2013), 61–90.

Taylor, C., and H. Dreyfus, *Retrieving Realism* (Cambridge, MA: Harvard University Press, 2015).

Van Erp, S., 'Implicit Faith: Philosophical Theology after Schillebeeckx', in *Edward Schillebeeckx and Contemporary Theology*, L. Boeve, F. Depoortere, and S. van Erp (eds) (London: T&T Clark, 2010), 209–23.

Vanheeswijck, G., 'Does History Matter? Charles Taylor on the Transcendental Validity of Social Imaginaries', *History and Theory* 54 (2015): 69–85.

Ward, G., *Unbelievable: Why We Believe and Why We Don't* (London: I.B. Tauris, 2014).

Westphal, M., *Overcoming Onto-Theology: Toward a Postmodern Christian Faith* (New York: Fordham University Press, 2001).

Chapter 7

RE-EXAMINING EDWARD SCHILLEBEECKX'S ANTHROPOLOGICAL CONSTANTS: AN ONTOLOGICAL PERSPECTIVE

Daniel Minch

The reception of Edward Schillebeeckx's work over the course of the past thirty years has been mixed, in the sense that some commentators have not always clearly understood both the conclusions and starting points of Schillebeeckx's theology. To some extent, Schillebeeckx himself has caused much of the confusion. His works, although detailed, voluminous, and, I would argue, remarkably consistent throughout the years, are still quite 'unsystematic' in their presentation. We sometimes encounter the opinion that Schillebeeckx, in being such a 'hermeneutical' thinker, was mainly concerned with contemporary and worldly political realities. The implication here is that both 'hermeneutical' and 'contextual' are watchwords for theological lines of thought that only take the immediate present into account, without consideration for the 'cosmological' import of statements about God, the church, and especially Jesus. We also see this assessment in criticisms of Christologies 'from below' that emphasize that the humanity of Jesus is more accurately described by the term 'Jesusology', rather than Christology.[1] Hermeneutical-contextual theologies are even said to operate in a way that is anti-metaphysical, since they are tied to contingent notions of truth – which emerge and are linguistically mediated – and in history, eschewing older language of 'nature' and 'supernature'.

The most extreme form of this criticism holds that such theologies are matters more of sociology or anthropological studies, rather than investigations concerning the revelation of God. Such assertions, however, ignore the contexts in which contextual and hermeneutical approaches arose, as well as the fact that they have arisen in response to the perceived inability of traditional formulations to adequately embody the Christian faith in the (post)modern world. While Schillebeeckx has often been charged with similar accusations, a careful reading of

1. L. Scheffczyk, 'Christology in the Context of Experience: On the Interpretation of Christ by Edward Schillebeeckx', *The Thomist* 48, no. 3 (1984): 402.

his work – or really even a broad reading of his works over time – reveals neither any traces of an anti-metaphysical stance nor any attempts to mitigate the universal significance of Jesus as the ultimate self-revelation of God to human beings. What we find instead is a different notion of what 'metaphysics' means, namely, that Schillebeeckx designates categories of ontological significance, which is really a post-Heideggerian way of speaking about 'metaphysics' that does not ruffle the feathers of the more philosophically inclined. At the same time, this line of thought indeed operates with a different concept of the 'meta-' involved here than do many older, nineteenth-century thought patterns. In this chapter, I will present a unified reading of Schillebeeckx's hermeneutical 'anthropology' and demonstrate its dependence on an ontological foundation. This involves re-evaluating what hermeneutics is as a methodology and what kind of theology it produces. The result is a theological view of the human being that begins, or departs, from embodiment in the world and in a specific narrative tradition, and from there *finds* its ultimate ground in the transcendent God, rather than presumptively beginning with the transcendent and dictating what historical humanity can and should be. This brief study will mark out the boundaries of Schillebeeckx's hermeneutics, in terms of his 'anthropological constants' and the search for a universal element in humanity.

1. Schillebeeckx's Hermeneutical Anthropology

Anthropology is a critical evaluation of what it is that makes up human beings, and the idea of a philosophical or theological anthropology is already founded on the possibility of a universal 'human nature'. In earlier times, this 'positive' view of human nature was filled out with particular characteristics of what the ideal human should be and how it should act in the world. Premodern societies looked backwards to the past for these values and for the ideal portrait of humanity, and then projected these onto the present and the future. Human beings should strive to be like their ancestors, and the goal is a return to an idealized state located in the past, or a 'conservative utopia'.[2] A fundamental but gradual shift has occurred in the transition from premodern to modern perspectives, a process that Schillebeeckx identifies with the secularization that began sometime around the thirteenth century.[3] This shift has involved a move away from pregiven, positively defined notions of 'human nature', towards more voluntaristic visions of what this term can mean. The reason for the shift has been the actualization of humanity's potential ability to create the world, that is, to shape and structure both our natural environment and our societies. The long and slow transition to thinking of society as a human process and product, rather than as a pregiven, divine order,

---

2. E. Schillebeeckx, *Christ: The Christian Experience in the Modern World*, trans. J. Bowden, *CW*, vol. 7 (London: Bloomsbury T&T Clark, 2014), 652–4 [662–3].

3. E. Schillebeeckx, 'Secularization and Christian Belief in God', *God the Future of Man*, trans. N. D. Smith, *CW*, vol. 3 (London: Bloomsbury T&T Clark, 2014), 31–7 [54–61].

has also given rise to the realization that human beings – both individuals and societies – have specific potential to be other than what they already are. We must here also distinguish between a form of this idea that has been associated with the modern master narratives of progress, and a more nuanced and contextual one. The former is really quite close to a premodern, 'pregiven' vision of nature, wherein the ideological values of the master narrative determine ahead of time what the human being should be and how it should evolve. We can see an example of the modern master narrative of progress clearly in the evolutionary process of a communist society, where the goal for humanity is to achieve the universal proletariat as the universal subject of history. This type of ideological view of human nature is the reverse image of the premodern one, since the characteristics of the ideal *humanum* are still pregiven and considered to be a priori values that aim at a particular goal. However, the ideal *humanum* is found not in the past, but in the future. The focus in such societies, then, is on realizing an anticipated, necessary future. In essence, such an appeal, to either a forward- or backward-looking anthropology, is an ideological attempt to dictate what humanity *will* be without observing or accounting for what it can or *should* become based on the reality of the present context.

Schillebeeckx's later anthropology comes after not only his early grounding in positive and speculative theology, but also serious critical engagement with historical research, hermeneutic theory, and critical theory. From the outset, Schillebeeckx is careful to avoid the idea that one particular view of humanity, based on sociological or cultural observations, will engender one normative and universalizable portrait of humanity suitable for Christian theology. Schillebeeckx also avoids beginning with a purely transcendental approach. Rather, he takes a phenomenological approach and begins from the point of embodiment.[4] 'In his very essence', notes Schillebeeckx, 'man [sic] is a narrative, a historical event rather than a pre-determined fact.'[5] He goes on to sketch seven 'anthropological constants', which constitute a system of coordinates that are related directly to humanity's embodiment in the world. These are meant to be broad, but essentially universal elements of human experience that point the way towards a more human future, one that is consonant with Christian salvation, but not necessarily coterminous with it. By the publication of Schillebeeckx's second *Jesus* volume in 1977, he had come a long way from the position of his inaugural lecture at Nijmegen in 1958. In his inaugural address, 'The Search for the Living God', he asserts that salvation, at least as it is realized within lived history, is consonant with human attempts at the 'humanization' of the world, arguing that Christian values have become

---

4. In this regard, he follows the work of Maurice Merleau-Ponty. See P. Kennedy, *Schillebeeckx*, Outstanding Christian Thinkers (Collegeville, MN: The Liturgical Press, 1993), 42.

5. E. Schillebeeckx, 'Questions on Christian Salvation of and for Man', in *Toward Vatican III: The Work That Needs to Be Done*, D. Tracy with H. Küng and J. B. Metz (eds) (New York: Gill and MacMillan, 1978), 30. Hereafter: 'Questions'.

'secularized' and have so penetrated Western culture that they now find expression in human efforts.[6] Such a strong position had already faded prior to the opening of the Second Vatican Council, and, although he never stopped believing in the importance of praxis and Christian action in the world, he no longer assumed broad or easy continuity between Christian salvation and secular efforts.[7]

Schillebeeckx takes the phenomenological route in terms of looking for what may be considered 'universally human', arriving at 'constants' that cross cultures, national boundaries, and contextual limitations. This does not mean, however, that the position that these constants are built upon does not rest on more fundamental philosophical principles. In fact, a careful, 'archeological' excavation of the foundations of Schillebeeckx's thought reveals the rich way that he drew on the philosophical sources available to him. Schillebeeckx has, with his 'system of coordinates of man and his salvation', left a corner of this foundation uncovered, and it is just enough to begin the excavation. From here, we can see that Schillebeeckx has actually made the so-called transcendental move much earlier in his work than he would let on, and that the true universal element of his theology is not unavailable. The key to this move and its theological fruits lies in Schillebeeckx's turn to hermeneutics and his subsequent methodological shift, including his engagement with Critical Theory. As far as I can tell, Schillebeeckx transitions from speaking about seven (or eight) constants to referring primarily to one around 1978; nevertheless, this development has been in his work since at least his turn to hermeneutics expressed in 'Towards a Catholic Use of Hermeneutics' in 1967.[8] Part of what has made Schillebeeckx such an important thinker has, in fact, been

---

6. E. Schillebeeckx, 'The Search for the Living God', *Essays: Ongoing Theological Quests*, *CW*, vol. 11 (London: Bloomsbury T&T Clark, 2014), 35–8. See, for example, p. 36: 'What was formerly Christian charity is now known as social justice.'

7. I would directly dispute the alleged 'optimism' of Schillebeeckx with regard to modernity and contemporary culture. His writings simply do not support facile optimism or an uncritical 'overlap' between Christian salvation and human efforts; instead, they reveal a thoroughly Christian hope informed by eschatology. See especially 'God, Society and Human Salvation', in *Faith and Society/Foi et Société/ Geloof en maatschappij: Acta Congressus Internationalis Theologici Lovaniensis 1976*, BETL 47, M. Caudron (ed.) (Gembloux, Belgium: Éditions J. Duculot, 1978), 87–99.

8. See E. Schillebeeckx, 'Ik geloof in God, Schepper van hemel en aarde', *Tijdschrift voor geestelijk leven*, 34 (1978): 5–23 [trans. 'I Believe in God, Creator of Heaven and Earth', *God among Us: The Gospel Proclaimed*, trans. J. Bowden (New York: Crossroad, 1983), 91–102]. See note 35 below. Finally, see E. Schillebeeckx, 'Towards a Catholic Use of Hermeneutics', *GFM*, *CW*, vol. 3 (London: Bloomsbury T&T Clark, 2014), 1–29 [2–44]. This essay originally appeared as 'Naar een katholiek gebruik van de hermeneutiek', *Geloof bij kenterend getij. Peilingen in een seculariserend Christendom*, H. van der Linde and H. Fiolet (eds) (Roermond: Maaseik, 1967), 78–116. It was later collected in E. Schillebeeckx, *Geloofsverstaan: Interpretatie en kritiek*, Theologisch Peilingen vol. 5 (Bloemendaal: Nelissen, 1972), 11–40.

his commitment to hermeneutics while keeping in mind that this is '*not proposing a method*; [it is] describing *what is the case*'.[9] In other words, the hermeneutical worldview – taken over by Schillebeeckx from Gadamer and Heidegger – does not merely judge between competing interpretations of the world, a posteriori. It is a thoroughgoing examination of the very foundations of being itself, and therefore is an attempt to present an ontological position.

2. The Possibility of Hermeneutics

The very possibility of hermeneutics is founded on the constitution of the human subject as an *experiencing subject*. The so-called 'linguistic turn' in philosophy provides a picture of the linguistic constitution of being. Understanding is not simply *of language*, but it actually occurs *by means of language*.[10] There is no mediation without medium, and, therefore, no content can be given without form, which as the form of expression is also co-constitutive of the meaning that is expressed.[11] Truth is co-constituted by the context in which a statement arises, in both its form and its expression, because of the radical way in which 'form' has an impact on content.[12] This is also true for the experiencing human subject, who is formed by the active process of understanding the world, in and by means of language. This, however, calls for an expanded definition of 'language'.

'Language' does not merely mean spoken languages, written texts, or some combination of discrete signs that phonetically or pictorially represent *words*. A 'language' is an open, porous set of images, patterns, themes, as well as the written and spoken word that human beings use to organize their perception of reality (and which conversely influences how their reality can be organized). The human subject must understand both *from what is given*, as well as *what is given*. The difference between these understandings can be stated as follows: understanding *from* what is given is the default mode of understanding in the world. We are initially given language, and 'no one is sovereign over his or her own speech. As

9. H.-G. Gadamer, 'Hermeneutics and Historicism (1965)', in *Truth and Method*, trans. J. Weinsheimer and D. G. Marshall, 2nd edn (New York/London: Continuum, 2011), 512.

10. G. Ebeling, *Introduction to a Theological Theory of Language*, trans. R. A. Wilson (London: Collins, 1973), 119, 126. Cf. E. Betti, 'Hermeneutics as the General Methodology of the *Geisteswissenschaften*', in *The Hermeneutic Tradition: From Ast to Ricoeur*, G. L. Ormiston and A. D. Schrift (eds) (Albany, NY: SUNY Press, 1990), 178.

11. This point is in contrast to the mistaken view of hermeneutics taken by Scheffczyk in 'Christology in the Context of Experience'. See especially pp. 404–5, 407.

12. L. Boeve, 'Orthodoxy, History and Theology: Recontextualisation and Its Descriptive and Programmatic Features', in *Orthodoxy, Liberalism, and Adaptation: Essays on Ways of Worldmaking in Times of Change from Biblical, Historical and Systematic Perspectives*, Studies in Theology and Religion vol. 15, B. Becking (ed.) (Leiden/Boston, MA: Brill, 2011), 186.

a beginning, we can say that the speaker appeals to a language which he or she did not invent, but which was already given to the speaker.'[13] This constitutes a way of 'being experienced' in a particular linguistic tradition. One adopts the language (i.e. the structures of meaning) given over by the context and utilizes this as a means for organizing and understanding the world. Understanding *what* it is that is already given, however, is a process of examining our prejudices, that is, our linguistic – and, by extension, our socio-temporal – situatedness and what it predisposes us to believe. The hermeneutical moment of self-examination of our own prejudgements about reality is of fundamental importance to human existence, and continued extension in the world. Hermeneutics presumes a 'fore-conception of completeness', the expectation of a meaningful whole that rests on the prejudices of a particular language.[14] This preconceived wholeness is important, because it conditions the hermeneutic movement: the whole is expected and known from its parts, while the parts are reinterpreted in the light of the whole.[15] A historically affected critical-consciousness is necessary to discern where these inherited and constructed prejudices do not accord with reality and to correct them. The whole of a subject's interpretive theory allows for the anticipation of experiences, which in turn changes and shapes the nature of that whole.

Experience provides the substance of human understanding, wherein the human subject must process what has been perceived in an active way. Pregiven language and the previously constituted horizon for expectation establish a boundary against which new experiences are to be measured. This is a theory of knowledge that is based essentially on experience and perception. There is no knowledge outside of experience, since all thinking, following Kant, is an experiential process of judgement, and even pure contemplation occurs in the mind in linguistic categories and is an inner *experience of thought*. The hermeneutical horizon of experience, including the movement that it entails, takes the form of 'question and answer'.[16] In the case of historical events, the meaning of an event is sought through interpretation. To seek to understand an event is to ask a question about its meaning.[17] The question is produced in and from the particular point of view of the interpreter, who stands in a specific historical tradition, and who uses traditional language to form an expectation-horizon. Contact with the actual answer never conforms perfectly to the expectation, since each experience is in some way unique. Even repeated actions take on the character of 'repeating', and are thus different from one-off occurrences.

13. E. Schillebeeckx, 'The Magisterium and Ideology', in *Authority in the Church*, ANL vol. 26, P. F. Fransen (ed.) (Leuven: Leuven University Press, 1983), 8.

14. Cf. Gadamer, *Truth and Method*, 364.

15. E. Schillebeeckx, 'Theologie der Erfahrung – Sackgasse oder Weg zum Glauben?', *Herderkorrespondenz* 92 (1978): 393.

16. Gadamer, *Truth and Method*, 363. Cf. Schillebeeckx, 'Catholic Use of Hermeneutics', *GFM*, 19 [28]; Schillebeeckx, 'I Believe in God', 100.

17. Gadamer, *Truth and Method*, 367.

The relation of the subject and object in this schema of experience follows the phenomenological insight that, in interpretation, there is an intrinsic connection between subject and object, rather than a fundamental separation and autonomy.[18] Our intention here is not to develop fully Schillebeeckx's theory of experience, but it must be sketched at least in part in order to reach the centre of his ontological framework.[19] Schillebeeckx assigns great importance to the interpretive theory that the subject uses in understanding.[20] According to this theory, a lived experience, which must be interpreted, is referred to as the *interpretandum*.[21] A subject's understanding of the *interpretandum* is made up of interpretive elements, the *interpretaments*, or the 'concrete images, concepts and narratives' used to give expression to the lived experience.[22] Schillebeeckx resists collapsing the subject-object relationship in any way by maintaining the independence of both that which ob-jects itself and the interpreting subject; yet, the relationship is not a smooth or clear dualism. There is also an intrinsic link between the two, since what appears as an ob-ject is always already within the theoretical model of those who perceive it. Schillebeeckx points out that, since Kant 'the insight has grown that a theory or model has a certain primacy

18. See Kennedy, *Schillebeeckx*, 42: 'The upshot of adopting a phenomenological perspective is that the notions of pure objectivity and pure subjectivity are rendered nonsensical: there can no more be an object without a subject than there can be a subject without an object, just as there can no more be a known without a knower than there can be a knower without a known. According to Husserl, subject and object are indivisible: an object only comes to be within experience in virtue of a subjective interpretation. ... The experienced object comes to be within experience insofar as experiencing essentially involved the interpretation of certain material to permit a particular object to appear to consciousness within experience'. Cf. Schillebeeckx, *Church: The Human Story of God*, *CW*, vol. 9 (London: Bloomsbury T&T Clark, 2014), 65–6 [67].

19. For a more complete view of Schillebeeckx on experience, see L. Boeve, 'Experience According to Edward Schillebeeckx: The Driving Force of Faith and Theology', in *Divinising Experience: Essays in the History of Religious Experience from Origen to Ricoeur*, L. Boeve and L. P. Hemming (eds) (Leuven: Peeters Press, 2004), 206–7.

20. Boeve, 'Experience', 207; E. Schillebeeckx, *Theologisch geloofsverstaan anno 1983* (Baarn: Nelissen, 1983), 26.

21. Boeve, 'Experience', 202–3, 206. See Schillebeeckx, *Christ*, 39 [53]: 'There is no neutral given in experience, for alternative interpretations influence the very way in which we experience the world.'

22. Boeve, 'Experience', 207. These terms are explained in Schillebeeckx, *Jesus: An Experiment in Christology*, *CW*, vol. 6 (London: Bloomsbury T&T Clark, 2014), 645 [746]. While *interpretandum* is a cumbersome term, I will primarily use it in conjunction with 'lived element' of experience, since there is no ready alternative, and it is inappropriate to refer to something like a 'pure' or 'raw' experience. Schillebeeckx himself acknowledges this in *Interim Report on the Books Jesus and Christ*, trans. J. Bowden, *CW*, vol. 8 (London: Bloomsbury T&T Clark, 2014), 15 [18]: 'Naively trusting in so-called immediate experiences seems to me, therefore, to be a form of neo-empiricism.'

above the experience; at least in this sense, that, on the one hand, there are no experiences without at least an implicit theory and, on the other hand, that theories cannot be derived from experiences by means of induction, but are the human spirit's own creative initiative.'[23]

Pure, unmediated experience is 'illusory, because all experiences, even mundane experiences, are theoretically mediated.'[24] This priority is not absolute, however, and refers to the basic need for a theory to exist for an experience to be interpreted.

To live in the present while oriented towards the future presupposes neither the elimination of all prejudices nor the unqualified confirmation of our expectations. Rather, the very 'process of understanding is accomplished precisely in the possible *correction* of our preunderstanding.'[25] Schillebeeckx articulates this point in his early essays on hermeneutics, and he recognizes the intrinsic importance of 'that which is "not thought of", which *gives to us to think*, but is itself never thought of.'[26] In *Church: The Human Story of God* (1989), he works this idea into his theology of revelation, which follows the same structure of human experience: '*In* such an experience, what we ourselves had never thought of and never produced occurs to us as a gift.'[27] This describes revelation, both secular and religious, but it also describes experience in general, since 'reality is always more than and different from what we imagine [i.e. "anticipate"] it to be.'[28] Therefore, the object, as that which ob-jects itself in experience, retains a certain priority, as well. This priority is one of the object's 'own direction of interpretation' (een eigen interpretatie*richting*), which has a real content such that the meaning of an object is taken up as an offer, but is still interpreted within the sphere of the *interpretaments*.[29] The object demands an interpretive response, which can take the form of non-recognition, misunderstanding, or interpreted understanding. An interpretive experience that is open to the otherness of the object must be a product of hermeneutical-critical consciousness, where the expectation-horizon 'cracks' under the pressure of a new experience, and must be reconstituted to account for what has just occurred. In this way, there is always a back-and-forth movement between the shifting grounds of the subject's expectation-horizon and new events. The alternative is that the object will not be taken for what it truly is, but rather will be fit or forced into predetermined categories, will be ideologically cut down to size, and, practically

23. Schillebeeckx, *IR*, 14–15 [17]. Cf. Schillebeeckx, 'Catholic Use of Hermeneutics', *GFM*, 19 [28]: 'Our continued openness to new possibilities is expressed in this question [that we ask of a text]. It does not in any sense mean that we obliterate our whole preunderstanding and allow the other (that is, the text) to pre-empt our consciousness.'

24. Schillebeeckx, 'Theologie der Erfahrung', 392; my translation.

25. Schillebeeckx, 'Catholic Use of Hermeneutics', *GFM*, 18 [26]; original emphasis.

26. Ibid., 22 [33].

27. Schillebeeckx, *Church*, 21 [22]; original emphasis. Cf. *Christ*, 32–3 [47].

28. Ibid., 32 [47].

29. Ibid., 37 [38]; original emphasis.

speaking, the theoretical framework will not change. Schillebeeckx states it plainly: 'Our plans are frustrated by the unruliness of reality. There is something in reality that is not planned by humans, that is not made and also cannot be projected by humans. I believe that here lies the anthropological basis for revelation.'[30]

3. Finitude, or the Absolute Limit as the Precondition for Experience

The hermeneutical movement between part and whole, which is also the movement between past horizon and present experience, is centred in and around the experiencing subject. There is an interplay of negative contrast and positive extension that constitutes human experience: the moment of non-recognition or negative recoil is where our expectation-horizon fails and where we must work to understand the reality with which we are met. This moment is inseparable from the positive reconstitution of our interpretation-horizon, as perceptions are formed to include the object in question. Again, even a response of 'non-understanding' is a form of perception, and we now know 'object X' as something that is not well understood. What allows for this structure of question-answer, or call-and-reply, is only well articulated by Schillebeeckx in his final *Jesus* volume, despite the fact that the fundamental insight runs throughout much of his earlier work. At its base, ontological finitude is the precondition for all knowledge, all experience, all revelation, and the foundation of the experiencing human subject. Schillebeeckx calls this the 'absolute limit' (*absolute grens*), and this can be demonstrated as the root of all of the anthropological constants that he enumerates in his earlier work. Experience provides the link between the phenomenological and the ontological structures of Schillebeeckx's theology, and it allows us access to the deepest foundations of being, the point where we can make a 'transcendental' move in the search for what is 'universally human'.

'The absolute limit', remarks Schillebeeckx, 'is thus the basic condition of our whole human existence.'[31] The experience of this 'absolute limit' is extrapolated from experiences of our various relative limits, or those places where we come up against a reality that is other than what we have imagined or expected.[32] This makes it a mediated experience in and of itself, but through it we 'experience that we are neither lords nor masters of ourselves, [and] far less of nature and of history.'[33] Technically, we reach this barrier in each and every experience, since the process of understanding itself requires that our previous interpretive framework 'cracks' in response to objective stimuli. 'We ourselves are this limit,' Schillebeeckx contends, whether we view ourselves as created beings in relation to an infinite

---

30. Schillebeeckx, 'Theologie der Erfahrung', 393–4; my translation.
31. Schillebeeckx, *Church*, 77 [79].
32. Ibid., 76 [78].
33. Ibid.

God or not.[34] Attempts to do away with this limit through claims to total mastery of nature, or 'absolute openness to the future', are both equally ideological.[35] Because we are finite beings, this limit, along with our experience of it, constitute a universal human foundation that grounds the possibility of all experience by providing a relief against which new experiences can occur. Finitude can be interpreted in many different ways, but its facticity remains. The projection of wholeness is a direct expression of the absolute limit because it is through testing this projection against the challenge(s) of experience that we run up against our relative limits in understanding, prompting the subject to create a new vision of wholeness. This is the basic hermeneutical-epistemological interplay of positive grasping and negative contrast.

4. Seven 'Anthropological Constants'

The anthropological constants that are elaborated by Schillebeeckx in several places all circle around the ontological finitude of the human subject, albeit without ever quite coming to the point.[36] His desire to find a universal point of entry into human experience is tempered by his engagement with hermeneutics and critical theory, since he is painfully aware of the problems inherent in ideologically informed 'universals'.[37] The purpose of giving a 'system of coordinates' is to furnish ways of speaking kataphatically about humanity and human values, particularly in terms of social culture. There is a great deal of sensitivity given to the fact that any concrete norms for human life must be filled in with due regard for the context. Each of the seven anthropological constants is, upon further investigation, somehow reducible to, and built on, the one ontological basis: finitude, the absolute limit. We will enumerate the seven constants and their respective relationships to finitude here.

The first constant is, in some ways, the most obviously related to finitude: human corporeality. The human being 'both is and has a body', and this embodiment

34. Ibid., 76 [79].

35. Ibid., 77 [79]; 'I Believe in God', 92: '[Human beings] do not want to accept their finitude or contingency; they hanker after that which is not finitude, after immortality and omniscience, so that they can be like God.'

36. These are seen in Schillebeeckx, *Christ*, 725–37 [731–43] and in his 1978 contribution to the volume, *Toward Vatican III*, 'Questions on Christian Salvation of and for Man', 27–44. I will follow the latter here because of some additional material that was added to the beginning and end of the section, material which is interesting and relevant to our current discussion. In 1976, he enumerated the first five constants in a slightly different form. See 'God, Society and Human Salvation', 89–90. Cf. M. Merleau-Ponty, 'What Is Phenomenology?', in *The Merleau-Ponty Reader*, T. Toadvine and L. Lawlor (eds) (Evanston, IL: Northwestern University Press, 2007), 60–1.

37. Schillebeeckx, 'Questions', 30–1.

ties humanity to ecology in a particular way.[38] Specifically, we see this in the human need to create a 'meta-cosmos' to inhabit within the world as it is given, making that world more hospitable to humanity. Embodiment means that human existence is finite, both in time – as beings oriented towards death – and in the fact of physical limitations. Second, the nature of humanity, as both *being* and *having* a body, speaks to the very rootedness of the human condition in ontology, 'since the thinker never thinks from *any* starting point but the one *that he is*'.[39] The double-sided movement, between inner and outer, perception and understanding, is modelled on embodiment. The interior life of the human subject is not the whole of life, and the exterior manifestation of the human subject is more than just the expression of the inner life. In fact, inner consciousness, that which *has* a body, is affected and enriched by what comes from beyond itself, although this is not reducible to mere epiphenomena, and, as such, the person is more than just a body. The interior-exterior movement between mind and world mirrors the hermeneutical movement of experience.

The second and third constants are closely related to one another, since they are both fundamentally about the intersubjectivity of human beings. First, the existence of human beings is always *coexistence*, which follows from the previous constant insofar as we can refer to ecology. This second point goes further, however, because it is about the coexistence of human beings with one another, such that the human face is always an image *for* others. Intersubjectivity is also subject to essential limitations, since an encounter with the other is always a moment of contrast and a realization that what I encounter is not merely another part of my own subjectivity.[40] Schillebeeckx also points out the basic fact that no one 'can enter into a relation of real encounter with all people' due to our embodiment and, therefore, also our finitude.[41] The third constant follows closely on the second: the human relation to institutional and social structures. This is a more extended view of human intersubjectivity that includes structural forms of interactions because humans are understood as fundamentally social beings.[42] What it really contributes to an adequate understanding of human subjectivity is the realization that social relations are not merely tacked on to our identity as experiencing subjects, as if through addition, but are really already a synthetic dimension of our identity.[43] This is an affirmation of the phenomenological insight into the intrinsic relation between subject and object, as well as an expression of the hermeneutic-linguistic character of being.[44] Ontological finitude is what makes the encounter with an

---

38. Ibid., 31.

39. Merleau-Ponty, 'What Is Phenomenology?', 66; my emphasis.

40. Schillebeeckx, 'Questions', 34.

41. Ibid.

42. Ibid., 34–5.

43. Ibid.

44. The empirical sciences have, to some degree, supported this interrelatedness, particularly in a 2009 study on the linguistic 'prosody', or melody, of infants' cries. This

'other' possible at all. Without contrast, there is no recognition and no process of understanding; no hermeneutical movement can occur without some degree of otherness and contrast, and this depends on finitude. This constant, with its resting on human finitude, delivers a fundamental critique of the Hobbesian view of social anthropology and its contemporary political heritage: libertarianism. No person is a solitary subject who only chooses to enter into relationships that are beneficial, or which provide security in exchange for reduced autonomy. The network of social relations is a structural given that, of course, changes over time, but is an essential part of being and becoming human; no one *becomes* human in a vacuum.

The fourth constant is the time-space element of both the person and culture. The facticity of temporal existence is a direct condition of finitude at the ontological and ontic levels, and it is indeed impossible to remove the socio-temporal context even with optimal norms, values, or social structures.[45] Here, death is the ultimate 'limit situation' through which humanity's relative limits are experienced, since even this is not a 'direct experience' of the absolute limit, but a mediated form of it.[46] The impossibility of escaping the limitations of space and time also makes humanity subject to suffering. Through suffering, and especially unwarranted suffering, existence is 'also experienced as a *hermeneutical* enterprise', such that we are both able to understand and unmask critically what is oppressive in our social existence; we both illuminate existence as well as engage in its critical renewal.[47] Furthermore, the individual, society, and even history are all contingent and not purely autonomous or grounded in themselves.[48] The real threat to human existence is not its finitude, but its refusal of that finitude in favour of the will to absolute mastery over self, society, and history; in short, this is to fail to understand death and finitude as a feature of human existence rather than as a flaw to be overcome.[49]

Fifth, the intrinsic relation between theory and praxis is put forward as a constant, referring to the fact that human beings always act from a specific standpoint. In order to be able to act at all, we need a place, a specific spatial-

---

study shows a correlation between the melody of an infant's cry and the mother tongue of the parents. This conditions the infants to perceive and understand the surrounding language even before birth. See B. Mampe, et al., 'Newborns' Cry Melody Is Shaped by Their Native Language', *Current Biology* 19, no. 23 (2009): 1994–7.

45. Schillebeeckx, 'Questions', 35.

46. Ibid.

47. Ibid., 36; E. Schillebeeckx, 'Theological Criteria', *The Understanding of Faith: Interpretation and Criticism*, trans. N. D. Smith, *CW*, vol. 5 (London: Bloomsbury T&T Clark, 2014), 59–60 [66–7].

48. E. Schillebeeckx, 'The New Critical Theory and Theological Hermeneutics', *UF*, *CW*, vol. 5 (London: Bloomsbury T&T Clark, 2014), 117 [133].

49. Schillebeeckx, 'Questions', 36; 'I Believe in God', 92. Cf. L. Boeve, *God Interrupts History: Theology in a Time of Upheaval* (New York/London: Continuum, 2007), 174.

temporal situation at which point a certain interpretive theory exists, and where we stand in a certain relationship to particular traditions.[50] Theory always implicitly or explicitly precedes praxis, although this says nothing about the truth content of either theory or praxis, since a worldview can be well-practised, but untrue and unjust (and vice versa).[51] Again, the hermeneutical movement is invoked here, wherein the finite subject first acts from its theory and then must reform its theory in the light of experience.

The basic orientation of the finite subject towards the next experience leads to the sixth constant, which Schillebeeckx calls the 'para-religious' consciousness of humanity.[52] He has partially derived this constant from Ernst Bloch's 'secular' eschatology and utopian consciousness, or the vision of what the future will or should look like. In many cases, this is expressed as an attempt to escape finitude and contingency, or at least many of its symptoms, such as suffering and death.[53] This 'utopian' impulse is built on the principle of 'wholeness' given in the hermeneutical movement and the implicit trust that the subject has in its own vision of the meaning of reality. Elsewhere, Schillebeeckx himself affirms that the vision of wholeness and the meaning of reality is an anthropological constant, giving us a seventh, but more basic 'constant' that is only one step removed from the absolute limit.[54] The basic trust (*Basisvertrauen*) that life has and will have meaning, can only be seen in the interplay of negative and positive elements of life, or in the contrast experiences that reveal not only the human expectation of goodness, but also the orientation towards praxis that drives us to create a more human world.[55] Faith in the presence of meaning, or at least the ability to make sense of what is given, is the basis of hope for the future.[56]

Schillebeeckx explicitly delineates a final constant in the irreducible synthesis of the other six, although we can think of this the second-to-last coordinate in the light of this analysis. Each of these constants is linked to the others, and their coexistence and codependence underpins human culture as an autonomous reality apart from any 'proofs' for the existence of God.[57] What the synthesis tells us is that the creation of concrete norms for human societies will result in a *necessary* pluralism, precisely because they are built on the absolute limit. No experience is ever exactly the same because we are finite and exist in time and space, and this gives rise to a plurality of interpretation, even within a single person's experience. *Pluralism* becomes the default mode of being human. Consequently, it should also be thought of as an eighth anthropological constant that we would do well

---

50. Schillebeeckx, 'Theologie der Erfahrung', 394.
51. Schillebeeckx, 'Questions', 37.
52. Ibid., 38.
53. Ibid.
54. Schillebeeckx, 'Theologie der Erfahrung', 393.
55. Ibid.
56. Schillebeeckx, 'Questions', 38; cf. Schillebeeckx, 'I Believe in God', 98.
57. Schillebeeckx, 'Questions', 39.

to remember in our political life.[58] In this sense, Schillebeeckx is echoing Origen, who long ago sought to explain the unequal state of humans in the world, but could only conceive of it as stemming from a flaw in the human will. Schillebeeckx still locates most unwarranted suffering in the realm of human sin, but *pluralism* itself, built on the absolute limit, is not a flaw in creation, but its very *possibility*. The point of the system of coordinates is to act as a guide – but not a recipe – for forming 'a modern, livable humanity'.[59]

Schillebeeckx has already pointed to an irreducible theological pluralism in an essay from 1969.[60] The days of a common Christian worldview and philosophical framework are over, and even unrecoverable now that there is truly a 'global church'. The differentiation of the sciences and pluralization of philosophical standpoints, as well as the rise of contextual theologies and philosophies 'from the margins', have all contributed to this, but so has the fact that bishops in former European colonies now come from the indigenous populations and are not sent as 'missionary' bishops to foreign lands. Further, the 'modern sciences' are no longer 'determined in any way by philosophy', meaning that a ruling Aristotelian framework no longer guides what 'science' is or can be.[61] Certainly there are 'philosophies of science' implicit in every scientific methodology and experiment. The essential finitude of human beings, and therefore the limited scope of one person's experience, precipitates a plurality of perspectives, because all people, and indeed all theologians, have a different starting place in time, in society, and in history.[62] By acknowledging this as a fact, and by opening myself to the limitations of my own perspective, it is possible to take in the perspective of the other as complementary to my own view of reality. By way of an example, theology has long been broken down into four traditional areas (practical, systematic, historical, and biblical). Today, these main areas now consist of various sub-disciplines, each requiring years of specialized training and indoctrination into the 'language' of the field. The fragmentation of theology and its sub-disciplines means that there will likely never be another Karl Rahner, Edward Schillebeeckx, or Joseph Ratzinger. In terms of synthesizing the results of multiple areas of theological expertise, no one can 'do it all' anymore, due (in part) to the sheer volume of data and the amount of requisite specialized training. Thus, the default mode of the theologian should be collaborative and synoptic: the willingness to listen and work with others to present a more coherent theological view. But this pluralism is not confined to theology. It is really 'an aspect of the historical reality of man [*sic*] and cannot be overcome'.[63] An essential pluralism of viewpoints is an additional anthropological constant, resulting precisely from the ontological finitude of the subject. The

58. Ibid., 40.
59. Ibid.
60. Schillebeeckx, 'Theological Criteria', *UF*, 41–68 [45–77].
61. Ibid., 45 [50].
62. Ibid., 46 [51].
63. Ibid., 48 [54].

religious person should take this as a challenge and a praxical task to be met by faith, rather than despair. There is, after all, no absolute pluralism, and 'translation' and communication are always at least theoretically possible within the sphere of lived humanity.[64] The essential commonality of 'being human' also evinces the possibility of translation, so plurality is never absolute; yet, at the same time, it is never entirely overcome because the process of interpretation through experience is never finished in history.

Conclusion: *The Transcendental Movement – One Ontological Constant*

Finitude, Schillebeeckx explains elsewhere, is 'really the definition of all secularity' that cannot be totally secularized.[65] Finitude allows humanity to be creative, and reflection on this creativity gives rise to the insight that we are neither merely locked up in our finitude, nor absolutely free to create and make the universe in every respect, as though we were the masters of reality.[66] God's creative freedom is seen in the fact that salvation is an experiential concept that cannot be made into a purely immanent and easily understandable concept.[67] God's Rule, in and through the new and salvific relationship of humanity to God, is perhaps for this reason always expressed in parables and metaphors that broadly approximate what it is and will be.[68] Because we continue in time as finite subjects in and through great traditions of experience, this relationship is always shifting and changing, and must always be maintained and renewed as we respond to God's call. Creative activity on the part of the People of God is certainly always a response, but it is a response in and from our situated freedom and mediated through our categories. Maurice Blanchot once expressed that all understanding is predicated on misunderstanding, and to the extent that no experience can be directly repeated, this is true. Each individual process of 'coming to understand' something new – and God is ever ancient but ever new – requires that we first are not able to understand it, and then that we forge a new, flawed, and provisional expression of what has been revealed to us. Epistemology is a 'negative epistemology' that is based on contrast.

This is the root of experience, including our experience of God. The limit is always on our side, confirming Schillebeeckx's phrase, 'mediated immediacy', as the mode of God's presence.[69] God is infinite, and infinitely present to us as created persons, who can only experience God in the places where we reach our real, ontological limits. These are the places where we run up against what was not

---

64. Ibid., 49 [55].

65. Schillebeeckx, 'I Believe in God', 101.

66. Ibid.; cf. Schillebeeckx, *Church*, 78–80 [80–3].

67. Schillebeeckx, 'Questions', 41.

68. E. Schillebeeckx, 'I Believe in the Man Jesus: The Christ, the Only Beloved Son, our Lord', in *God among Us: The Gospel Proclaimed* (New York: Crossroad, 1983), 107.

69. Schillebeeckx, 'I Believe in the Man Jesus', 110; Schillebeeckx, *Church*, 77 [79].

produced by us, but comes to us from the other. An experience of divine revelation challenges our narrative structures, which we use to interpret the world, to change. Sometimes these structures must change radically in response to what has been shown to us: namely, something new and unexpected. Thanks to the clues given to us through tradition, this 'new' element can still be named, if only provisionally as salvation coming from God.

In conjunction with this notion of salvation and this ontological foundation presented by Schillebeeckx, the Christian idea of politics must reach further than pragmatism or *Realpolitik*; it must at least begin to reach for the realization of present-day salvation for humanity. The epistemic force of suffering necessitates that Christians respond to the suffering other, since all understanding of reality through a projection of total meaning, especially a religious one, must also include a critical element in our attempts to avoid ideological manipulation. The Christian understanding of reality must serve humanity in both a specifically Christian and humanly universal way.[70] This makes Christian political involvements different from those driven by purposive knowledge of science and technology, as exemplified today in our contemporary economic systems. The need for Christian salvation to be political is seen precisely in the fact that it must also be salvific for those who interpret reality differently, while keeping in mind that the total meaning of reality, or final salvation, is eschatological and ultimately rests in God's hands. The specific motivation of Christian practice and the expectation of salvation cannot be universalized to the point of broad secularization, even if its effects are broadly felt beyond the Christian community.[71] To do so would constitute an attempt to 'secularize' finitude to the point of cutting off God's relationship to creation, deleting the eschatological piece of the praxical equation.

Christian praxis, therefore, must come from a specifically Christian tradition to avoid falling under 'purposive' interest that either narrows the field of what is possible or does away with finitude altogether, and returning us to a closed master narrative. Schillebeeckx gives us a glimpse of how the human being functions through the 'anthropological constants', while also showing that these constants are not perfectly absolute. They are also built on something prior, namely human finitude, as the ontological precondition for being-in-the-world in an active manner. A century of anthropological and sociological examinations of society, after largely unfettered belief in specific Western visions of 'humanity' – that is, the mutually exclusive, positive views of humanity of which Schillebeeckx is so wary – has skewed the way that we think of what is 'universal'. The foundation that he espouses does not automatically disqualify all of our positive models and values – it qualifies them by placing them in a constant state of movement, flux, and uncertainty. It is only from our finitude, that is, our specific, yet fluid and uncertain stance in the world and in tradition, that we are empowered to act in an eschatologically responsible way in pursuit of the Rule of God.

---

70. Schillebeeckx, 'Questions', 42–3.
71. Schillebeeckx, 'I Believe in God', 101.

Bibliography

Betti, E., 'Hermeneutics as the General Methodology of the *Geisteswissenschaften*', in *The Hermeneutic Tradition: From Ast to Ricoeur*, G. L. Ormiston and A. D. Schrift (eds) (Albany, NY: SUNY Press, 1990), 159–97.

Boeve, L., 'Experience According to Edward Schillebeeckx: The Driving Force of Faith and Theology', in *Divinising Experience: Essays in the History of Religious Experience from Origen to Ricoeur*, L. Boeve and L. P. Hemming (eds) (Leuven: Peeters Press, 2004), 199–225.

Boeve, L., *God Interrupts History: Theology in a Time of Upheaval* (New York/London: Continuum, 2007).

Boeve, L., 'Orthodoxy, History and Theology: Recontextualisation and its Descriptive and Programmatic Features', in *Orthodoxy, Liberalism, and Adaptation: Essays on Ways of Worldmaking in Times of Change from Biblical, Historical and Systematic Perspectives*, Studies in Theology and Religion vol. 15, B. Becking (ed.) (Leiden/Boston, MA: Brill, 2011), 185–204.

Ebeling, G., *Introduction to a Theological Theory of Language*, trans. R. A. Wilson (London: Collins, 1973).

Gadamer, H.-G., *Truth and Method*, trans. J. Weinsheimer and D. G. Marshall, 2nd edn (New York/London: Continuum, 2011).

Kennedy, P., *Schillebeeckx*, Outstanding Christian Thinkers (Collegeville, MN: The Liturgical Press, 1993).

Mampe, B., A. D. Friederici, A. Christophe, K. Wermke, 'Newborns' Cry Melody Is Shaped by Their Native Language', *Current Biology* 19, no. 23 (2009): 1994–7.

Merleau-Ponty, M., 'What Is Phenomenology?', in *The Merleau-Ponty Reader*, T. Toadvine and L. Lawlor (eds) (Evanston, IL: Northwestern University Press, 2007), 55–68.

Scheffczyk, L., 'Christology in the Context of Experience: On the Interpretation of Christ by Edward Schillebeeckx', *The Thomist* 48, no. 3 (1984), 383–408.

Schillebeeckx, E., 'Naar een katholiek gebruik van de hermeneutiek', in *Geloof bij kenterend getij. Peilingen in een seculariserend Christendom*, H. van der Linde and H. Fiolet (eds) (Roermond: Maaseik, 1967), 78–116.

Schillebeeckx, E., *Geloofsverstaan: Interpretatie en kritiek*, Theologisch Peilingen vol. 5 (Bloemendaal: Nelissen, 1972), 11–40.

Schillebeeckx, E., 'God, Society and Human Salvation', in *Faith and Society/Foi et Société/ Geloof en maatschappij: Acta Congressus Internationalis Theologici Lovaniensis 1976*, BETL 47, M. Caudron (ed.) (Gembloux, Belgium: Éditions J. Duculot, 1978), 87–99.

Schillebeeckx, E., 'Questions on Christian Salvation of and for Man', in *Toward Vatican III: The Work That Needs to Be Done*, D. Tracy, with H. Küng and J. B. Metz (eds) (New York: Gill and MacMillan, 1978), 27–44.

Schillebeeckx, E., 'Theologie der Erfahrung – Sackgasse oder Weg zum Glauben?', *Herder Korrespondenz* 92 (1978): 391–7.

Schillebeeckx, E., 'I Believe in the Man Jesus: The Christ, the Only Beloved Son, Our Lord', in *God Among Us: The Gospel Proclaimed*, trans, J. Bowden (New York: Crossroad, 1983), 103–115.

Schillebeeckx, E., 'Ik geloof in God, Schepper van hemel en aarde', *Tijdschrift voor geestelijk leven* 34 (1978): 5–23 [trans. J. Bowden, 'I Believe in God, Creator of Heaven and Earth', *God among Us: The Gospel Proclaimed* (New York: Crossroad, 1983), 91–102].

Schillebeeckx, E., 'The Magisterium and Ideology', in *Authority in the Church*, ANL vol. 26, P. F. Fransen (ed.) (Leuven: Leuven University Press, 1983), 5–17.

Schillebeeckx, E., *Theologisch geloofsverstaan anno 1983* (Baarn: Nelissen, 1983).

Schillebeeckx, E., *Christ: The Christian Experience in the Modern World*, trans. J. Bowden, *CW*, vol. 7 (London: Bloomsbury T&T Clark, 2014).

Schillebeeckx, E., *Church: The Human Story of God*, trans. J. Bowden, *CW*, vol. 10 (London: Bloomsbury T&T Clark, 2014).

Schillebeeckx, E., *Essays: Ongoing Theological Quests*, *CW*, vol. 11 (London: Bloomsbury T&T Clark, 2014).

Schillebeeckx, E., *God the Future of Man*, trans. N. D. Smith, *CW*, vol. 3 (London: Bloomsbury T&T Clark, 2014).

Schillebeeckx, E., *Interim Report on the Books Jesus and Christ*, trans. J. Bowden, *CW*, vol. 8 (London: Bloomsbury T&T Clark, 2014).

Schillebeeckx, E., *Jesus: An Experiment in Christology*, trans. J. Bowden, *CW*, vol. 6 (London: Bloomsbury T&T Clark, 2014).

Schillebeeckx, E., *The Understanding of Faith: Interpretation and Criticism*, trans. N. D. Smith, *CW*, vol. 5 (London: Bloomsbury T&T Clark, 2014).

Chapter 8

FORGING A WAY THROUGH CREATION: 'GOD OR THE WORLD?' OR 'GOD AND THE WORLD?'

Rhona Lewis

On the western shore of North America, at the Scripps Institution of Oceanography, there is a small public museum. Its displays reflect 'a conception of earth history ... reliably grounded in dozens of independent sources of evidence ... that tells a complex story of the earth spread over hundreds and even millions of years'.[1] Martin Rudwick, a historian of science, describes how, not many miles away, and 'just off the interstate that leads inland towards Texas', there is another small museum, the Institute of Creation Research. In this latter institute, there is, among other displays, 'a mural photograph of the Grand Canyon ... accompanied by the claim that the mile-thick pile of rocks exposed in its walls had all been deposited, and the canyon then excavated through them, only a few millennia ago and within the geological twinkle of an eye'.[2] In this second museum, another display features an 'ingenious reconstruction of Noah's Ark, complete with pairs of animals in a receding vista of stalls' with extraordinarily realistic sound effects. Rudwick and his colleagues from the University of California (San Diego) took graduate students in science studies 'to both these museums ... to try to understand how our modern world can contain such radically divergent interpretations of the natural world around us'.[3] Most of the students 'unhesitatingly identified the Scripps museum as "Science" and the Creation museum as "Religion"', assuming an 'intrinsic and perennial conflict between the two'.[4]

Both museums seek to explain how the natural world around us has come to be, one in terms of a scientific account of the history of the earth, the other

---

1. M. Rudwick, 'Geology and Genesis: A Historical Perspective on the Interaction of Two Historical Sciences', lecture presented in the *Herbert H. Reynolds Lectureship in the History and Philosophy of Science* (Baylor University, Baylor, Texas, 1 March 2005), http://www.baylor.edu/content/services/document.php/30846.pdf, 1.

2. Rudwick, 'Geology and Genesis', 1.

3. Ibid., 1–2.

4. Ibid.

in terms of an interpretation of Holy Scripture. Sometimes religion claims to provide an explanation of the natural universe either overtly, as in creationism, or, less directly, by resorting to a 'God of the Gaps' approach, which affirms the supernatural intervention by God to account for unexplained natural phenomena. There is a popular perception that this approach is characteristic of religion in general. Edward Schillebeeckx, in writing about his Christian creation faith, emphatically refutes an understanding of creation faith as providing an explanation in quasi-scientific terms of why things are as they are in the world. He writes, 'Jewish-Christian creation faith does not give us any explanation of our world and our humanity; it does make us ask quite different questions from those we would ask if we wrongly understood creation as an explanation.'[5] What, according to Schillebeeckx, are the consequences of the Christian confession of belief in God, Creator of heaven and earth? Does belief in God the Creator have implications for understanding humanity and the world? Are belief in God and a true understanding of humanity intrinsically linked? Does a focus on God necessarily include a focus on humanity? In what follows, I examine elements of Schillebeeckx's grounding in Thomist creation faith and to where this grounding leads him theologically.

1. *The Basis and Development of Creation Faith in Schillebeeckx's Theology*

After his novitiate, the foundation of Schillebeeckx's studies as a young Dominican included three years of philosophical study, the typical formation curriculum of the Roman Catholic Church at the time. The philosophy curriculum of the 1930s consisted of a 'systematic reading of Aquinas' theology with the help of commentaries on Aquinas'.[6] Exceptionally, the *philosophicum* at Ghent included courses taught by Dominicus De Petter on modern and contemporary philosophy: 'a complement to the ideas of Aquinas'.[7] Schillebeeckx 'fell in love with philosophy',[8] medieval and modern, and it became a lifelong interest. Despite the range of the philosophy that Schillebeeckx was reading, the philosophical foundation for his theology was fed, above all, by one major source: the metaphysics of Aquinas He was steeping himself in Aquinas's metaphysics, and, although the historical analysis of Aquinas had begun in the nineteenth century (as Bernard McGinn points out[9]), it was not until Schillebeeckx studied under Marie-Dominique

---

5. E. Schillebeeckx, *God among Us: The Gospel Proclaimed*, trans. J. Bowden (New York: Crossroad, 1983), 94.

6. P. Kennedy, *Schillebeeckx* (London: Geoffrey Chapman, 1993), 18.

7. Kennedy, *Schillebeeckx*, 18–19.

8. E. Schillebeeckx, *I Am a Happy Theologian: Conversations with Francesco Strazzari*, trans. J. Bowden (London: SCM Press, 1994), 5.

9. See B. McGinn, *Thomas Aquinas's Summa Theologiae* (Princeton and Oxford: Princeton University Press, 2014), 188–9.

Chenu in 1946–7 that he encountered an approach to Thomist theology that investigated its significance for contemporary thinking. In 1974, however, and particularly in the first volume of his Christological trilogy, Schillebeeckx 'refers to having made a break with his earlier philosophical heritage'.[10] Does this mean that he saw as redundant the metaphysical formulations of creation faith which he shared with Aquinas?

Commenting on Schillebeeckx's theological shifts, Philip Kennedy argues from a philosophical base that there is 'continuity underlying the discontinuity'; as he succinctly puts it, Schillebeeckx's 'philosophical groundwork has changed its outer vocabulary while retaining its inner syntax'.[11] From a theological basis I would argue that from the point of departure of Christian faith in God the Creator, Schillebeeckx's post-1963 theology is in the main, a way of speaking about the consequences of the metaphysical tenets of Christian creation faith, tenets which he holds in common with Thomas Aquinas. Brian Davies writes that 'the notion of creation pervades [Aquinas's] writings',[12] and Kennedy memorably states that 'the idea of creation is the oxygen and lifeblood of Edward Schillebeeckx's theology'.[13] Schillebeeckx's later theology deals with God's immanence, which springs from the very nature of God's transcendence. His theology is inseparably both 'top-down' and 'bottom-up'.

2. Knowledge of God and Creation in Christian Theology

How am I using the terms 'top-down' and bottom-up'? In Old Testament imagery, the two places where human beings most closely experience God are the sanctuary and the heavens. The sanctuary is perhaps more commonly named as the place where human beings experience God although it becomes, by virtue of being the locus of human encounter with God, a place of 'heaven', as it were. The heavens are where God 'dwells'. 'Heaven' and 'sky' are the same word in Hebrew, *shamayim*.[14] In turn, the mountaintop is depicted as the place where human beings draw near to heaven and venture to approach the transcendent God. 'Mountain' in Hebrew is *har*.[15] I am, therefore, using the word 'top' as a shorthand way of denoting God in his

10. P. Kennedy, 'Continuity Underlying Discontinuity: Schillebeeckx's Philosophical Background', *New Blackfriars* 70 (1989): 264.

11. Kennedy, 'Continuity Underlying Discontinuity', 265.

12. B. Davies, *The Thought of Thomas Aquinas* (Oxford: Clarendon Press, 2009), 33.

13. P. Kennedy, 'God and Creation', in *The Praxis of the Reign of God: An Introduction to the Theology of Edward Schillebeeckx*, M. C. Hilkert and R. J. Schreiter (eds) (New York: Fordham University Press, 2002), 37.

14. G. Bartelmus, *Theological Dictionary of Old Testament*, vol. 15, G. J. Botterweck, H. Ringgren, and H.-J. Fabry (eds.), D. E. Green and D. W. Stott (trans.) (Grand Rapids, MI: Eerdmans, 2006), 204–36.

15. S. Talmon, *Theological Dictionary of Old Testament* vol. 3, G. J. Botterweck and H. Ringgren (eds.), D. E. Green (trans.) (Grand Rapids, MI: Eerdmans, 1975), 427–47.

transcendent divinity. Hence, God is the focus of attention for 'top-down' theology, which considers the attributes and action of the divine. From God, such theology moves, or may move, down, so to speak, to the earth in order to consider creation and, in particular, human beings. When, however, theology mainly considers questions from creation, such as attempts to describe human nature, and speaks of God's immanent presence in creation and human life, it is perceived as bottom-up theology. It explores such questions as 'What is humanity's place in creation and its responsibility towards creation, that is, under God's guidance?' It seeks to find, and to test, what forms right-living might take, according to God's will, and in any given cultural context once the world is seen and understood as being created by God. At its best, bottom-up theology takes for granted what top-down theology focuses on.

Yet, how is top-down theology able to consider the divinity of God in the first place? Thomas Aquinas maintains that the only way that God can be known (insofar as human beings can know God) is through creation. It is through the effects of creation, both in nature and in the workings of God's grace in human experience, that God is manifested:

> Even though we cannot know the real definition (*quid est*) of God, nonetheless, in the science of sacred doctrine we use His effects, whether effects of nature or effects of grace, in place of a definition in regard to the things that are considered about God in this doctrine – just as in the other philosophical sciences, too, something is demonstrated about a cause through its effect, where the effect takes the place of a definition of the cause.[16]

According to Aquinas, then, top-down theology cannot be done without initially reflecting on the effects of God's creation, contemplating from the bottom of the mountain and using a bottom-up method. Therefore, when Aquinas writes theologically about God, he is working in a top-down manner, but is able to do so because he has reached to the top of the mountain by means of a bottom-up path or method. Philip Kennedy avers that 'Schillebeeckx's entire theological corpus is one vast digression from this fundamental point and an extended variation of Aquinas' theme'.[17] Schillebeeckx 'transposes' Aquinas's point by saying that 'the divine discloses itself in relation to human experiences of creatureliness (or contingency)'.[18] In his later work, it is the basic human experience of resistance to suffering that Schillebeeckx regards as the pre-religious condition for 'a cognitive experience of God'.[19]

The two foci, or approaches, of top-down and bottom-up theology are clearly shown in the Christological debates of the first three centuries of Christianity.[20]

---

16. T. Aquinas, *Summa Theologiae* I, q.1, a.7. ad.1, cited by Kennedy, *Schillebeeckx*, 36.

17. Kennedy, *Schillebeeckx*, 36.

18. Ibid.

19. Ibid., 128.

20. See H. E. W. Turner, *Jesus the Christ* (London: Mowbray, 1976), 37–8.

The church in Alexandria, on the one hand, demonstrated a top-down approach, laying heavier emphasis on Jesus's divinity. The church in Antioch, on the other hand, used a bottom-up approach, focusing more on the humanity of Jesus. Schillebeeckx refers to these early articulations of the divine and the human in Jesus when he writes the following:

> Christians learnt to express the content of what 'God' is and the content of what 'man' is, in a stammering way, through the life of Jesus. Within its own later and different framework of thought the Council of Chalcedon had the same intention as the Apostles' Creed when it said: 'One and the same, Jesus Christ, is truly man and truly God.'[21]

A key point, however, is that the order in which aspects of a theological question are considered is not necessarily identical with the intrinsic importance attached to them. As Schillebeeckx observes, it is not the number of pages that one devotes to an issue that necessarily measures its importance.[22] In contemplating the divine and the human in the person of Jesus, the theologian may consider each to be of equal importance yet he/she has to start by talking about one or the other. To focus on one of the two, the divine or the human, need not preclude or diminish the importance of the other. Rather, it might be intended as a way of speaking about each as having equal importance.

3. God's Freedom from Creation

What I am considering here, then, is the focus, rather than the method, of Schillebeeckx's theology. In order to discover whether, and to what degree, Schillebeeckx's theology is of the 'mountaintop' or of the 'earth beneath', I will examine the element of creation in his theology. Is his theology top-down (i.e. a reflection on God as Creator), or is his focus bottom-up, asking questions about what is it to be a human creature? If his theology is both, what is the relation between the two? I am selecting two basic tenets of Aquinas's creation faith that are also intrinsic to Schillebeeckx's creation faith: namely, that (i) God does not have to create, and (ii) God's action in creation is ongoing.[23] I proceed to look at how Schillebeeckx developed the corollaries, or consequences, of these tenets. In the *Summa Theologiae*, Aquinas, in a top-down way, first articulates metaphysical theological tenets about the Creator. The way in which he begins influences

21. Schillebeeckx, *God among Us*, 109.

22. E. Schillebeeckx, *Interim Report on the Books Jesus and Christ*, trans. J. Bowden, *CW*, vol. 8 (London: Bloomsbury T&T Clark, 2014), 93 [105].

23. I have made this initial selection of two tenets from the work of Fergus Kerr and find strong support for them in Rudi te Velde's writing, as well.

how he then goes on to talk about creation. As David Burrell remarks about creation theology in general, 'Creation not only comes first, as it were, in our God's transactions with the world; it is also true that the way we understand that founding relation will affect our attempts to articulate any further interaction.'[24] In particular, I want to look at how Schillebeeckx embraces this top-down theology and see what he does with it. Is it the seed-bed of his bottom-up theology?

The first tenet can be delineated as follows: God the Creator does not have to create; he creates his creation freely and is neither internally nor externally coerced. Fergus Kerr writes, 'Thomas repeatedly attacks the idea that God had to create the world, in particular to complete or complement his own being. Thomas wants to show creation grounded in the eternal, immanent activity of God.'[25] 'The existence of the world, and of humanity, adds nothing to God, in the sense that it makes no difference to God.'[26] Rudi te Velde elaborates this point, as well, in the following manner: 'Creation is an utterly free act on the part of God. The notion of divine beatitude even points to the perfect self-sufficiency of God, enjoying himself in utter bliss without being in need of anything else.'[27] At first glance, the fact of God's self-sufficiency could be seen as implying that this is a deist God, remote and unconcerned about his creation.[28] Rather, what it means is that God acts 'by no other act than the pure act that he is as *ipsum esse* for no other act is capable of such a singular effect.'[29] Expanding on this idea, Aquinas writes that, 'By postulating a procession of love [in the Trinity] it is shown that God did not produce creatures in virtue of any neediness on his part nor because of any alien cause extrinsic to him, but on account of love of his own goodness.'[30] Kerr describes this tenet as a radically non-anthropocentric doctrine; in the terms that I am using, it is thus radically top-down.

Schillebeeckx, for his part, stresses the fact that God's creative action is undertaken freely. He states this explicitly when he writes, 'God *freely* creates men and women,'

24. D. B. Burrell, 'Act of Creation with Its Theological Consequences', *Aquinas on Doctrine: A Critical Introduction*, T. G. Weinandy et al. (eds) (London: T&T Clark, 2004), 27.

25. F. Kerr, *Thomas Aquinas: A Very Short Introduction* (Oxford: Oxford University Press, 2009), 51.

26. Kerr, *Thomas Aquinas*, 54.

27. R. te Velde, *Aquinas on God: The Divine Science of the Summa Theologiae* (Aldershot: Ashgate, 2006), 71.

28. Te Velde writes that Aquinas's God 'cannot [even] be labelled in a clear and unambiguous sense as a "theistic" God'. He argues that, 'instead of an abstract transcendence, over against the immanence of the world, Aquinas offers us a speculative notion of excessive transcendence'. R. te Velde, 'God and the Language of Participation', in *Divine Transcendence and Immanence in the Work of Thomas Aquinas*, H. Goris, H. Rikhof and H. Schoot (eds) (Leuven-Walpole, MA: Peeters, 2009), 19–20.

29. T. G. Weinandy, *Does God Suffer?* (Notre Dame, IN: University of Notre Dame Press, 2000), 132–3.

30. T. Aquinas, *ST* 1.32.1, cited by F. Kerr, *After Aquinas: Versions of Thomism* (Oxford et al.: Blackwell Publishing, 2002), 39.

and he refers to God's freedom in his creative action as '*sovereign*'.[31] Schillebeeckx shares with Aquinas the belief in the radical freedom of God's creative action and grounds within it, to use Burrell's terminology, 'a free human response to the One from whom all that is comes forth'.[32] On the basis of his belief in the contingency of creation, Schillebeeckx develops his ideas of the contingency of both the natural/non-human elements of the universe and human free will. When Aquinas speaks of God as Creator, and interprets the movements of nature and human acts of free choice, he does so using the abstract categories of Aristotelian causation in his task of 'faith seeking understanding of itself'.[33] Frederick Christian Bauerschmidt emphasizes the Thomist point that the dependence of the human creature on God does not preclude freedom, that 'creatures are not simply "occasions" for God's exercise of causality, but are genuine causes'.[34] He writes, 'This dependence of creatures on the primary causality of God does not vitiate the causal capacity of creatures, and Aquinas takes Aristotle to have given a compelling account of this capacity in his metaphysics of act and potency'.[35] Kathryn Tanner, however, in assessing the different kinds of language to express the relation between God's non-necessary choice to create and his creation, emphasizes Aquinas's preference for the language of personalistic imagery rather than natural causation. She writes, 'Aquinas thinks that personalistic imagery is better able to display [the non-necessity of God's creative action] since natural causes (that work immediately) are necessarily productive (unless hindered or defective)'.[36] Schillebeeckx may well have felt more at home with Aquinas's language of personalistic imagery rather than his analysis of causation because the former courts no danger of confusing God with a scientific agent or process.

The task of the natural sciences is to observe, explain, and predict natural phenomena in whatever ways that they manifest. In the pre-scientific age, mishaps of nature were often attributed to God, whether as divine punishments inflicted on sinful human beings or, at the very least, as part of God's plan. For example, the disciples of Jesus ask of the man born blind, 'Who sinned, he or his parents?' to which Jesus answers, 'Neither he nor his parents sinned but [he was born blind] in order that the works of God might be made visible in him'.[37] Even in the scientific age, Schillebeeckx gives the example of a pope, at the beginning of the nineteenth century, who 'condemned the practice of inoculation against smallpox, an illness which at that time was interpreted as a divine punishment ... because of a mistaken conception of [the theology of] creation as explanation'.[38]

---

31. Schillebeeckx, *God among Us*, 104; my emphasis.

32. Burrell, 'Act of Creation with Its Theological Consequences', 31.

33. Kerr, *Thomas Aquinas*, 38.

34. F. C. Bauerschmidt, *Thomas Aquinas: Faith, Reason, and Following Christ* (Oxford: Oxford University Press, 2013), 50.

35. Bauerschmidt, *Thomas Aquinas*, 50.

36. K. Tanner, 'Creation ex Nihilo as a Mixed Metaphor', *Modern Theology* 29 (2013): 151.

37. Jn 9:3.

38. Schillebeeckx, *God among Us*, 96.

4. Human Freedom and Human Finitude as Divine Gifts

The contingency of human actions involves questions about human free choice and fatalism. Schillebeeckx argues forcefully against fatalism, predeterminism, and the avoidance of human responsibility by drawing out the implications of the potency and contingency of human free will. He goes so far as to say that, to use God in a fatalistic way – that is, as an explanation of how things and events in the world have come to pass[39] – would mean both of the following: that any attempt to change things or situations would be blasphemous, and that 'human beings and our whole world [are turned] into a puppet-show in which God alone holds the strings in his hands behind the screen: human history as a large-scale Muppet show!'[40]

Crucially, moreover, the contingency of nature and the contingency of human free will are intertwined. The natural world and human beings are, and should be, symbiotic. God creates 'man as the principle of his own human action, who thus himself has to develop the world and its future and bring them into being within contingent situations'.[41] Nature is not only contingent, but, as a creation, has limits. Schillebeeckx writes, 'I would say that within all contingency, one concern for humanity is: For what sort of humanity are we ultimately making a choice? … We have learnt, from irresponsible behaviour, the specific implications of this finitude of nature. … Development is not unlimited, as we have learnt to our shame and to our hurt.'[42]

Contingency strikes a deep chord with Schillebeeckx, and he fully develops the idea in applying it not merely to the fact of creation, but also to the workings of the natural world and to human action within it. In the bleakness of the aftermath of the Second World War, Schillebeeckx found himself face-to-face with existentialism during a year spent in Paris. This encounter was facilitated predominantly by the writings of Sartre and Camus, with their twofold emphasis on the human person's freedom to choose while standing in an absurd and meaningless world. Schillebeeckx is acutely aware of the reality and power of human freedom. However, on the basis of his Christian creation faith, he argues that the believer's and the non-believer's experience of contingency are related but distinct.[43] For the full-blooded existentialist, the sense or experience of the contingency of life tells him/her that there is nothing 'out there' or after death. Yet, for the Christian, the

---

39. Examples of this might include saying that smallpox is a punishment from God, or that war is inevitable because of the way God has made human beings.

40. E. Schillebeeckx, *Church: The Human Story of God*, trans. J. Bowden, *CW*, vol. 10 (London: Bloomsbury T&T Clark, 2014), 227 [230].

41. Schillebeeckx, *God among Us*, 95.

42. Ibid., 99.

43. Regarding this latter point, see M. Poulsom, *The Dialectics of Creation: Creation and the Creator in Edward Schillebeeckx and David Burrell* (London: Bloomsbury T&T Clark, 2014), 65.

experience of contingency leads to a sense of finitude, the counterpart of which is a sense of the absolute sustaining presence of God the Creator, however dire the immediate circumstances may be.[44] Schillebeeckx also affirms that the contingency of human deeds represents a freedom that is God-given for God's purposes; contingency should thus be seen as liberating rather than as a 'condemnation to be free'.[45] Schillebeeckx writes that God 'creates man to develop in freedom his own human future, to realize it in contingent human situations by virtue of his finite human free will which can choose between different alternatives, even between good and evil'.[46] Schillebeeckx understands human freedom as a gift from God, to be deployed in the praxis of the reign of God.

For both Aquinas and Schillebeeckx, God is Creator and therefore the cause of 'there being anything not-God'. God is the ultimate cause of all that exists in creation. Te Velde writes, 'In traditional manuals of Thomistic metaphysics, creatures are often spoken of in terms of being "finite beings."'[47] Finite beings are understood to be finite 'insofar as they do not have in themselves the ground of their existence, but depend on something else, the infinite being, as their cause'.[48] Te Velde then goes on to examine how, for Aquinas, being a creature 'certainly entails more than that it is not its own ground of existence'.[49] It entails 'embodying, in a particular way, the universal value of being by which it is constituted in a likeness with absolute being'.[50] This idea, in turn, brings te Velde to a discussion of Aquinas's notion of participation. Schillebeeckx, however, follows the concept of finitude in another direction. From the fact that human beings do not have in themselves the ground of their existence, he moves his focus to the daily, concrete conditions that constitute the finitude of human life. He probes *what* human finitude *means* and describes it as 'coming and going, mortality, failure, mistakes and ignorance' and even 'the burden of subjection'.[51] For Schillebeeckx, then, it is possible for human creatures to fail and make mistakes without sinning, despite the fact that many, or perhaps the majority, of our mistakes and failures stem from sin. In the event that there is no sin involved, creaturely, intrinsically finite human life in the intrinsically finite world is, in the words of Genesis, 'very good'.[52] However, the characteristic features of finitude can sound like a flaw rather than a limit; they are thus often cast in a negative light and lumped together with all that is a consequence of sin in the world. When this occurs, the whole of creation tends to be seen as fallen, spoilt,

44. Poulsom, *Dialectics of Creation*, 138.

45. J.-P. Sartre, *L'Etre et le Néant: Essai d'ontologie phénoménologique* (Paris: Gallimard, 1943), 484.

46. Schillebeeckx, *God among Us*, 95.

47. Te Velde, *Aquinas on God*, 139–40.

48. Ibid.

49. Ibid.

50. Ibid.

51. Schillebeeckx, *God among Us*, 92–3.

52. Gen. 1:31.

and no longer intrinsically good. Schillebeeckx refutes this lapsarian view when he writes, 'Humanity and the world are not the result of a fall, an apostasy from God, nor are they a failure, much less a testing ground in expectation of better times.'[53]

As Schillebeeckx puts it, 'The basic mistake of many misconceptions about creation lies in the fact that finitude is felt to be a flaw, a hurt which as such should not really have been one of the features of this world.'[54] In contrast to these kinds of misconceptions, Schillebeeckx avers that, in a Christian perspective, the limits of our human condition are not something to be escaped from, or transcended, by means of a spiritual escapism that is dualistic. He argues that the desire to escape finitude is not only a refusal to accept finite creaturehood, but also, according to Genesis, the 'primal human sin'.[55] Schillebeeckx argues, rather, that the conditions of human finitude are the very material of the human task. God, as both Creator-Spirit and incarnate Word in Jesus, works with the grain of his creation and not against it. Creation is not something to be escaped from or disdained. As Robert Sokolowski writes, in reference to the Council of Chalcedon, 'God does not destroy the natural necessities of things he becomes involved with, even in the intimate union of the incarnation.'[56]

5. Creation as God's Continuous Act of Salvation

The second tenet of Aquinas's creation faith that I will here examine is that creation is not a punctiliar, one-off act, but rather an ongoing action of God. Kerr expresses Aquinas's view in the following manner: 'Creating the world is an on-going event, so to speak, that God does – but like all God's doings, according to the principle of divine simpleness, creating as God's doing is also God's being.'[57] Te Velde writes, 'One may say that Christian belief in creation prerequires the truth of the proposition that all things depend on God as on their cause, but this clearly does not exhaust its full and complete meaning.'[58] He goes on to discuss the 'triadic structure of the causality of creation', namely, the 'three conceptually different aspects of the one single act of creation': these are the 'producing' of the world, the 'ordering' of the world, and the providential 'guidance' of the world. 'Creation is not like the past origin of a thing's physical existence; it is the permanent condition of any form of existence in the world.'[59] In his post-1960s theology, Schillebeeckx gives attention to the view that the creature is permanently within the embrace

---

53. Schillebeeckx, *God among Us*, 93.

54. Ibid., 92.

55. Schillebeeckx, *Interim Report*, 98 [112].

56. R. Sokolowski, *God of Faith and Reason* (Washington, DC: Catholic University of America Press, 1995), 34-6, cited by Burrell, *Act of Creation*, 27.

57. Kerr, *Thomas Aquinas* (referring to *ST* 1.45.3), 54.

58. Te Velde, *Aquinas on God*, 124.

59. Ibid., 125–6.

of the Creator. He writes, 'The world and man are totally other than God, but within the presence of the creator God. Therefore this other-than-God can never emigrate from the divine act of creation.'[60] Marguerite Abdul-Masih sheds light on this view and tenet, particularly in terms of the relationship between God's transcendence and immanence, in the following passage: 'God is wholly other, a transcendent reality radically different from the reality of the human. God is also the creator and thus both intimate and immanent. Crucially, Schillebeeckx does not regard the transcendence and immanence of God as antithetical; rather, he argues that precisely because God is transcendent, God is immanent.'[61]

Rosemary Radford Ruether makes a similar argument in an article in which she states that God in God's transcendence is one and the same as God in God's immanence. She articulates this position against the following associations regarding God's transcendence and immanence: the association of transcendence with a 'male' kind of God, who is cerebral, distant, and disembodied; and the association of immanence with a 'female' kind of God, who is sensitive, close, and bodily. She explains – using an insight that she acquired from Dorothee Sölle's writings – that because God, in His transcendence, is 'radically free from our systems of sin and lies, [God] is closer to us than we are to ourselves.'[62] Ruether writes that the two understandings 'are ultimately one': namely, that the God who is transcendent in the power of his creative action is one and the same as the God who is immanent in his liberating presence, 'in, through and under us to break free of the oppressive realities of sin and lies.'[63] She thus weaves together the interaction of God's transcendence and immanence with the interaction between creation and salvation. This is precisely what Schillebeeckx does in his understanding of the constant presence of the Creator God, what he calls the absolute presence of God, as being in direct proportion to his abiding presence as Saviour. Creation and salvation are not two separate acts, or actions, of God, and they are not to be understood as two separate narratives. God is always present for humanity in the very action of sustaining our existence, in both good times and bad: 'God is with us and in us [though not in a pantheistic or panentheistic sense], even in our failures, our suffering and our death, just as much as he is in and with all our positive experiences and experiences of meaning. It also means that he is present in forgiveness for the sinner.'[64]

Schillebeeckx ties this belief, in the unity of God's creative action and salvific presence, to the lives and aspirations of believers and humanity in general. From the 1930s onwards, he had been averse to Christian faith being reduced

---

60. Schillebeeckx, *God among Us*, 93.

61. M. Abdul-Masih, *Edward Schillebeeckx and Hans Frei: A Conversation on Method and Christology* (Waterloo, ON: Wilfrid Laurier University Press, 2001), 61.

62. R. Radford Ruether, 'The God of Possibilities: Immanence and Transcendence Rethought', *Concilium* 2000/4 (2000): 48–9.

63. Radford Ruether, 'The God of Possibilities', 48–9.

64. Schillebeeckx, *God among Us*, 94.

to 'a collection of soulless truths',[65] arguing that 'faith in God the creator is not simply a question of another interpretation or theory'.[66] To crystallize his view, Schillebeeckx considers that perhaps the best way to describe salvation is by using the summary of Irenaeus: '"The glory of God is the happiness of living humankind; but the happiness of humankind is the living God." That is how Irenaeus rightly summed up the Christian gospel. The accent on the salvation and happiness of human beings present in the gospel and Christianity finds its mystery only in the living God.'[67]

In this maxim of Irenaeus as interpreted by Schillebeeckx, God and human beings belong together in a dynamic of glory and happiness. While human happiness and flourishing may not be fulfilled completely on this side of eternity, it is nevertheless to be striven for by human beings. They do so, with and in God's saving presence, by struggling for 'more justice in the world, committing themselves to a new earth and an environment in which human beings can live fuller lives'.[68] Schillebeeckx's theology demands attention be paid to the concrete world because of its view (and firm belief) that the God-Creator is also humanity's saving presence, liberating human persons for the praxis of the reign of God.

Conclusion

I have aimed to delineate a connection in Schillebeeckx's theology, between tenets of metaphysical theology that he holds in common with Aquinas and his own developments of those tenets, with a particular focus on human beings and their task in creation, in the daily life of the world. It might seem in Schillebeeckx's later work that he has abandoned classical theism and the Thomist tradition. I would propose, however, that the Thomist metaphysical truths of Christian creation remained fundamental to Schillebeeckx's own Christian creation faith. These metaphysical truths influenced and shaped his thinking and writing concerning the concrete realities of being a human being in the world. Aquinas and Schillebeeckx both say that it is only through the effects of God's creation that God can be known, and Schillebeeckx made his own the top-down tenets of Aquinas's creation faith. He found, however, that top-down theology is but one-half – a vital half – of two distinct and related halves. Until the late 1960s, he describes his theology as 'following the lines of open Thomism'.[69] Thereafter, he deliberately started to work in a bottom-up way, exploring what it means to be human in the light of

---

65. E. Borgman, *Edward Schillebeeckx: A Theologian in His History*, trans. J. Bowden (London: Bloomsbury T&T Clark, 2006), 23.

66. Schillebeeckx, *God among Us*, 100.

67. E. Schillebeeckx, *For the Sake of the Gospel*, trans. J. Bowden (New York: Crossroad, 1989), 58.

68. Schillebeeckx, *God among Us*, 100.

69. Schillebeeckx, *I Am a Happy Theologian*, x.

God's creative activity, and seeing the contemporary situation 'as an intrinsic and determinative element for understanding God's revelation'.[70] This was not because he was in any way suggesting that a Thomist focus on the divine in theology is of lesser importance. Rather, he discovered that the created had been neglected in favour of contemplating what the Creator might want of creatures and creation regardless of context. At different stages of his career, Schillebeeckx may have concentrated more on one question than the other – the divine nature, on the one hand, and human nature, on the other – but never on one question in isolation from the other. Creator and creation are indissolubly linked. The creation is both inseparable and distinct from the Creator.

What, therefore, can we learn from Schillebeeckx? What does he show us? First, he can help us to see that what is important in theology, and the order in which it is done, are not identical. The Creator is an essential focus of theology, and a 'Creator' requires that a creation exists. Theology, therefore, must also reflect on creation if it is not to suffer amputation. Second, Schillebeeckx shows us that a bottom-up theology which asks, 'What is it to be human, as creatures of God?' is, at the same time, a way of complementing top-down theology. Without the second, the first is incomplete. It is thus possible to be a top-down theologian while using a bottom-up focus. In the end, for Schillebeeckx, the top-down and bottom-up approaches are two sides of the same coin. They are neither opposed nor in competition with each other. Whichever side of the coin a theologian focuses on, whether on God's transcendence or immanence, what matters is the destination to which that theology leads. Is it making the world a better place in terms of enabling all human beings to flourish and find meaning in their lives? Does theology show that God-given human freedom, expressed in the worldly praxis of the reign of God, brings happiness? To put it another way, is theology showing the way to happiness for human beings, which is God's glory?

In my introduction, I referenced the account given by Rudwick, of the visits by his graduate students to the Scripps Institution of Oceanography and the Institute of Creation Research, which shows an alleged conflict between 'Science' and 'Religion' to which many subscribe. What would Schillebeeckx's reaction have been, faced with these two institutes? How, as a theologian, does he approach the issue of science and religion? He writes, 'I studied the war between evolutionist and creationists.'[71] His conviction is that religion and science are two spheres that are not in conflict, and which must both be taken equally seriously. It is not a question of one or the other. So far as Schillebeeckx is concerned, science and theology are both ways of engaging with life and the world. For him, Christian creation faith does not provide scientific explanations, but it does lead to our asking fundamental questions about God's purposes for us, about the implications of our human limits and the scope of our human freedom. It is the task of 'scholars and scientists' to give

---

70. Schillebeeckx, *Interim Report*, 3 [3].
71. Schillebeeckx, *I Am a Happy Theologian*, 47.

us 'information about the internal constitution of man, the world and society'.[72] Theology may seem to be a 'top-down' pursuit, and the eyes of science may seem to be earthbound, but the key issue is, 'Where does each lead us?' Schillebeeckx writes that the sciences 'strive for healing, making whole or "salvation" of human beings and their society'.[73] Theologians talk about God, on the basis of human and Christian experience, in order to point to 'the glory of God in the happiness of living humankind; and that happiness itself is the living God'.[74] Christianity sees 'co-humanity as a dimension with religious depth'.[75] Fragile, vulnerable human beings are 'not left in isolation but [are] supported by the absolute presence of the Creator God. And this presence remains an inexhaustible source which can never be secularized'.[76] Overall, therefore, I would suggest that Schillebeeckx is a theologian who focuses on both the divine and the earthly. He talks about God in order to engage with the world, the world which is God's creation. In doing so, he uncovers the arena where the Creator and the human creature can forge their relation into a relationship, in order to bring about the happiness that comes with the reign of God.

Bibliography

Abdul-Masih, M., *Edward Schillebeeckx and Hans Frei: A Conversation on Method and Christology* (Waterloo, ON: Wilfrid Laurier University Press, 2001).

Bartelmus, G., 'Heaven', in *Theological Dictionary of Old Testament*, vol. 15, eds. G. J. Botterweck, H. Ringgren, and H.-J. Fabry, trans. D. E. Green and D. W. Stott (Grand Rapids, MI: Eerdmans 2006), 204–36.

Bauerschmidt, F. C., *Thomas Aquinas: Faith, Reason, and Following Christ* (Oxford: Oxford University Press, 2013).

Borgman, E., *Edward Schillebeeckx: A Theologian in His History*, trans. J. Bowden (London: Bloomsbury T&T Clark, 2006).

Burrell, D. B., D. A. Keating and J. P. Yocum, 'Act of Creation with Its Theological Consequences', in *Aquinas on Doctrine: A Critical Introduction*, T. G. Weinandy (ed) (London: T&T Clark, 2004), 27–44.

Davies, B., *The Thought of Thomas Aquinas* (Oxford, Clarendon Press, 2009).

Kennedy, P., 'Continuity Underlying Discontinuity: Schillebeeckx's Philosophical Background', *New Blackfriars* 70 (1989): 264–77.

Kennedy, P., 'God and Creation', in *The Praxis of the Reign of God: An Introduction to the Theology of Edward Schillebeeckx*, M. C. Hilkert and R. J. Schreiter (eds) (New York, Fordham University Press, 2002), 37–58.

Kennedy, P., *Schillebeeckx* (London: Geoffrey Chapman, 1993).

Kerr, F., *After Aquinas: Versions of Thomism* (Oxford et al.: Blackwell Publishing, 2002).

72. Schillebeeckx, *God among Us*, 96.

73. Ibid., 100.

74. Schillebeeckx, *For the Sake of the Gospel*, 58.

75. Schillebeeckx, *God among Us*, 101.

76. Ibid.

Kerr, F., *Thomas Aquinas: A Very Short Introduction* (Oxford: Oxford University Press, 2009).

McGinn, B., *Thomas Aquinas's Summa Theologiae* (Princeton and Oxford: Princeton University Press, 2014).

Poulsom, M., *The Dialectics of Creation: Creation and the Creator in Edward Schillebeeckx and David Burrell* (London: Bloomsbury T&T Clark, 2014).

Radford Ruether, R., 'The God of Possibilities: Immanence and Transcendence Rethought', *Concilium* 2000/4 (2000): 45–54.

Rudwick, M., 'Geology and Genesis: A Historical Perspective on the Interaction of Two Historical Sciences', lecture presented in the *Herbert H. Reynolds Lectureship in the History and Philosophy of Science* (Baylor University, Baylor, TX, March 1, 2005).

Sartre, J.-P., *L'Etre et le Néant: Essai d'ontologie phénoménologique* (Paris: Gallimard, 1943).

Schillebeeckx, E., *Church: The Human Story of God*, trans. J. Bowden, *CW*, vol. 10 (London: Bloomsbury T&T Clark, 2014).

Schillebeeckx, E., *For the Sake of the Gospel*, trans. J. Bowden (New York: Crossroad, 1989).

Schillebeeckx, E., *God among Us: The Gospel Proclaimed*, trans. J. Bowden (New York: Crossroad, 1983).

Schillebeeckx, E., *I Am a Happy Theologian: Conversations with Francesco Strazzari*, trans. J. Bowden (London: SCM Press, 1994).

Schillebeeckx, E., *Interim Report on the Books Jesus and Christ*, trans. J. Bowden, *CW*, vol. 8 (London: Bloomsbury T&T Clark, 2014).

Sokolowski, R., *God of Faith and Reason* (Washington, DC: Catholic University of America Press, 1995).

Talmon, S., 'Mountain', in *Theological Dictionary of Old Testament* vol. 3, eds. G. J. Botterweck and H. Ringgren, trans. D. E. Green (Grand Rapids, MI: Eerdmans, 1975), 427–47.

Tanner, K., 'Creation ex Nihilo as Mixed Metaphor', *Modern Theology* 29 (2013): 138–55.

Te Velde, R., *Aquinas on God: The Divine Science of the Summa Theologiae* (Aldershot: Ashgate, 2006).

Te Velde, R., 'God and the Language of Participation', in *Divine Transcendence and Immanence in the Work of Thomas Aquinas*, H. Goris, H. Rikhof and H. Schoot (eds) (Leuven-Walpole, MA: Peeters, 2009), 19–36.

Turner, H. E. W., *Jesus the Christ* (London: Mowbray, 1976).

Weinandy, T. G., *Does God Suffer?* (Notre Dame, IN: University of Notre Dame Press, 2000).

Chapter 9

REFLECTIONS ON THE CONTRAST EXPERIENCE'S METHODOLOGICAL UNDERCURRENT

Thijs Caspers

Looking at Schillebeeckx's theology, one could say that the '(negative) contrast experience' is one of the central themes of his work. In his *Theologisch testament*, Schillebeeckx emphasizes the importance of this personal experience that protests against injustice and opts for humane life: 'The backbone of my thoughts, as well as of this book, is based on what I have been calling with greater clarity these last decades a radical foundational experience.'[1]

The centrality of the contrast experience provides Schillebeeckx's theology with an inductive entrance that gives his theology a profoundly human face. It is people's protest against injustices, and their yearning for a 'new earth' that is constantly breaking through in the contrast experience, which fuels Schillebeeckx's theological endeavours.[2] Although his writings are generally dense and complex,

---

1. The original Dutch quotation is as follows: 'Als achtergrond van mijn denken, alsook van heel dit boek ligt er wat ik de laatste decenniën geleidelijk met grotere helderheid ben gaan noemen een radicale grondervaring.' E. Schillebeeckx, *Theologisch testament, notarieel nog niet* verleden (Baarn: Nelissen 1994), 128. *Theologisch testament* is an edited and rewritten Dutch version of *Sono Un Teologo Felice. Colloqui con Francesco Strazzari* (Bologna: EDB, 1993). The English edition, *I Am a Happy Theologian: Conversations with Francesco Strazzari*, trans. J. Bowden (London: SCM Press, 1994), is a translation of the Italian original; therefore, I provided my own English translation of the Dutch. The text on the contrast experience in *Theologisch testament* partly corresponds with Schillebeeckx, *Church. The Human Story of God*, 5–6 [5–6].

2. Schillebeeckx describes the contrast experience in the following way: '[As] the human experience of suffering and evil, of oppression and unhappiness, [that] is the basis and source of a fundamental "no" that men and woman say to their actual situation of being-in-this-world. ... A positive element in this fundamental experience of contrast, [and] the second element in this basic experience, is ... human indignation. ... [The] human inability to give in to the situation offers an illuminating perspective. It discloses an openness to another situation which has the right to our affirmative "yes"'.Schillebeeckx, *Church*, 5–6 [5–6]).

the emphasis on human experience keeps his theology closely connected to the struggles of everyday life.

With this being said, the contrast experience also contains an intrinsic ambivalence: is it solely a 'human experience', or a 'human experience of *something else*' that breaks through from the outside. This ambiguity can be traced back to Schillebeeckx's own writings. On the one hand, Schillebeeckx characterizes the contrast experience as a 'basic human experience' or a 'pre-religious experience', as if it were an anthropological concept by 'those who believe in God fill[ed] out … in religious terms'.[3] On the other hand, however, he insists that 'eschatological faith [cannot] be taken over by a principle within man himself'.[4] Part of this ambivalence is related to the dynamics of critical theory, from which Schillebeeckx derives the important cornerstones for his contrast experience. In critical theory, there is a tendency to deny or limit the referential dimension of human experience, and to problematize the idea that human experience can point towards a transcendent, meaningful whole. At the same time, however, this theory provides the emancipative orientation to the future that Schillebeeckx is looking for when exploring new theological horizons in the aftermath of the Second Vatican Council (1962–5).

In this chapter, I will explore the undercurrent of the contrast experience by focusing on the dynamics of critical theory. First, it positions the contrast experience in Schillebeeckx's methodological development, as well as clarifies the theological and methodological landscape from which Schillebeeckx develops his concept of contrast experience. Second, the possible pitfalls, or reductive dangers, related to the dynamics of the critical theory are explored. Third, it investigates the possibilities that are offered by the dynamics of critical theory. This third part also addresses the question as to whether possible reductive tendencies, as introduced in the second part, can be overcome.

1. Methodological Embedding of the Contrast Experience

In 1968, and shortly after the Second Vatican Council, Schillebeeckx introduced the concept of the contrast experience in his article 'The Magisterium and the World of Politics', which appeared in *Concilium*.[5] At the time, Schillebeeckx stood at a crossroads of profound methodological changes that would have a deep impact on his theology. In a way, the contrast experience is the result, or outcome, of a 'philosophical turnabout' in Schillebeeckx's theology: 'an exchange of an aprioristic epistemology for an *a posteriori* theory', to quote Philip Kennedy.[6]

---

3. Schillebeeckx, *Church*, 6 [6].

4. Schillebeeckx, *God the Future of Man*, 120 [197].

5. E. Schillebeeckx, 'The Magisterium and the World of Politics', *Concilium* (Am.) vol. 36 (1968): 19–39; *Concilium* (Engl.) 4 (1968) nr. 6: 12–21.

6. P. Kennedy, *Schillebeeckx* (Collegeville, MN: The Liturgical Press, 1993), 127.

Until the late 1950s, Schillebeeckx shared the conviction of his fellow Dominican and mentor, De Petter (1905–71), that 'human beings [could] enjoy a positive knowledge of God in conscious ignorance'.[7] For Schillebeeckx, it was evident that human beings have no adequate conceptual notion of who or what God is. However, they do have an 'implicit intuition' of the meaningful whole. According to the view of De Petter, 'An individual's intellect involves an intuition-moment which makes contact with extra-mental reality. More than that, [De Petter] contended that the intuitive factor establishes a cognitive awareness of the *total* meaning of reality'.[8] When Schillebeeckx was asked in 1968 – the year that he introduced the contrast experience as a concept in his work – whether he still believed 'in the epistemology, in the gnoseology of Father De Petter?', he answered the question by saying that 'De Petter's epistemology no longer enjoyed any importance in his thought at the time'. He went on, stating that he 'wishes to retain De Petter's metaphysical ontological thought, but to give it an existential basis'.[9] It is precisely this existential basis that becomes paramount in Schillebeeckx's theologizing from the 1960s forward. Instead of a purely epistemological approach, he starts to favour a theological approach that is grounded in the experience and the praxis of everyday life, and which contains a strong ethical component.

In this regard, two questions arise. First, what caused this methodological shift in Schillebeeckx's theology? And second, what element attracted Schillebeeckx to critical theory, of which he started to make extensive use in his theological explorations?

To understand what caused the methodological shift in Schillebeeckx's works, one should, in the first place, be aware of the dramatic changes within the Roman Catholic Church itself during the short, but significant pontificate of Pope John XXIII (1958–63). It was this pope that initiated a council that would completely alter the pre-conditions of theology. Whereas the encyclical, *Humani generis* (1950), of Pope John's predecessor, Pius XII (1939–58), infused a climate of fear within the church – and brought the theological developments of the representatives of the so-called *nouvelle théologie* (including Schillebeeckx's mentors, De Petter and Chenu) to a virtual standstill – the impact of the Second Vatican Council resulted in just the opposite: the church would open itself towards the modern world in a way very much in line with the *nouvelle théologie*.[10] Consequently, theologians such as Schillebeeckx felt free to apply new methods

---

7. Kennedy, *Schillebeeckx*, 127.

8. Kennedy, *Schillebeeckx*, 125. For an overview of the influence of De Petter on Schillebeeckx, see also E. Borgman, *Edward Schillebeeckx: A Theologian in His History*, trans. J. Bowden (London: Bloomsbury T&T Clark, 2006), 37–51. Orig. E. Borgman, *Edward Schillebeeckx: een theoloog in zijn geschiedenis* (Baarn: Nelissen, 1999).

9. Kennedy, *Schillebeeckx*, 126.

10. Borgman, *Edward Schillebeeckx*, 122–39. In *I Am a Happy Theologian*, Schillebeeckx writes about the relief he felt in being 'liberated from suspicion' after the Second Vatican Council. According to Schillebeeckx, 'The spirit of Humani generis (1950), Pius XII's encyclical which condemned Le Saulchoir and La Fourvière [the Dominican studium and

and ideas in theological reflection, thus profoundly changing the face of Roman Catholic theology. As Schillebeeckx's biographer Erik Borgman writes, the council 'represented a fundamental breakthrough' for Schillebeeckx, in such a way that he had the feeling that he 'should make a new theological start'.[11] In his memoirs, Schillebeeckx describes the changes that took place within his own theology: 'My theology [under influence of the council] could no longer be said to be 'scholastic' or "neo-scholastic". ... I found strong support among those in the Netherlands who at the time had been encouraging the study of psychology and sociology, in a word the human sciences. That was a great change for me.'[12]

A second impulse for this methodological change can be located in the aftermath of the council. In his article 'The New Image of God, Secularization and Man's Future on Earth', Schillebeeckx states the following:

> I feel that two experiences brought me to a new stage. On the one hand, I became directly acquainted with the 'secularized world' of the United States and, at the personal level, with those who are called 'death of God' theologians. On the other hand, I had a discussion, lasting a whole afternoon, with about forty French university chaplains.[13]

Encounters like these had a deep impact on Schillebeeckx because of the challenges that secularizing society entailed for his view of contemporary theology. Kennedy writes that 'during and after [Schillebeeckx's] visits to North America in 1966, and again in 1967, he became profoundly unsettled by what he interpreted as a pervasive crisis of faith taking place among people living in secularized pluralistic cultures such as the United States'.[14] This new context demanded a different, more future-oriented approach with a solid experiential basis, according to Schillebeeckx.[15]

Consequently, the methodological changes within the works of Schillebeeckx can be related to two developments. On the one hand, the climate within the Catholic Church changed, and, with that, so too did the possibilities for its theologians. The openness towards contemporary culture initiated by the Second Vatican Council resulted in the unrestrained use of philosophical, sociological,

Jesuit faculty that were the torch bearers of *nouvelle théologie*] ... had been weighing heavily on us'. Schillebeeckx, *I Am a Happy Theologian*, 16.

11. Borgman, *Edward Schillebeeckx*, 366–7.

12. Schillebeeckx, *I Am a Happy Theologian*, 14.

13. Schillebeeckx, 'The New Image of God', 101 [169].

14. Kennedy, *Schillebeeckx*, 43.

15. Elizabeth Tillar states: 'The new picture of humanity and the futuristic orientation of society that Schillebeeckx encountered in European and American secularism precipitated his realization that the older language of faith was obsolete; it emerged from bygone experiences that are no longer fully intelligible in the contemporary world.' E. K.Tillar, 'The Influence of Social Critical Theory on Edward Schillebeeckx's Theology of Suffering for Others', *The Heythrop Journal* 42/2 (2001): 150.

and psychological methodologies in theology; this had been impossible in the era prior to the council, when Neo-Scholasticism was the absolute norm. On the other hand, Schillebeeckx's visits to the United States and his encounters with pluralized and secularized society made him realize that he had to revise his theological approach. This realization resulted in his moving away from a solely aprioristic epistemological stance, and towards an 'a posteriori theory' that strongly emphasized the primacy of human experience as a source from which to derive new theological insights.

With these two developments in mind, this chapter will now proceed to investigate the following question: What was it in critical theory that attracted Schillebeeckx? As indicated above, by the end of the 1960s, Schillebeeckx became increasingly aware of the fact that his theology was in need of an 'existential basis'. Critical theory provided the philosophical framework needed to make that possible. On the one hand, Schillebeeckx adopted the theoretical idea of 'critical negativity' developed by the founders of the so-called 'Frankfurter school', Theodor Adorno (1903–69) in particular. He 'borrowed from Critical Theory "the principle of correlation of critical resistance" to ideologies and inhumane systems and integrated that philosophical principle into his theology so as to interpret suffering for others in a meaningful way – as a critical element in the healing of systems that cause suffering'.[16] On the other hand, he added to this the insight of 'new' critical theory, as developed in particular by the second-generation exponent of this school, Jürgen Habermas (*1929–), who argued for a 'unification of theory and praxis'. Schillebeeckx utilized this idea, translating it as 'orthopraxis',[17] which holds that theory involves ethics: 'Critical theory is not based exclusively on scientific analysis. It depends in the first place on a fundamental ethical option in favour of emancipation and freedom.'[18] This ethical option finds its starting point in the historical, experiential praxis of everyday life, as Schillebeeckx indicates when he writes, 'There is only one source of ethical norms, namely, the *historical reality* of the value of the inviolable human person with all its bodily and social implications. That is why we cannot attribute validity to abstract norms *as such*' (emphasis mine).[19]

As Kennedy ascertains, Schillebeeckx is 'selective in the ideas he culls from the [Critical] Theory'.[20] Nonetheless, critical negativity, the emancipative (future-oriented) drive, and the primacy of praxis can be seen as essential ingredients that will culminate in Schillebeeckx's notion of the contrast experience. It is this theory, then, that provides 'a frame of reference in which experiences of

---

16. Tillar, 'The Influence of Social Critical Theory', 152.

17. Ibid., 163.

18. E. Schillebeeckx, 'The New Critical Theory and Theological Hermeneutics', *The Understanding of Faith: Interpretation and Criticism*, trans. N. D. Smith, *CW*, vol. 5 (London: Bloomsbury T&T Clark, 2014), 109–10 [125].

19. Schillebeeckx, 'The Magisterium', 27.

20. Kennedy, *Schillebeeckx*, 49.

apparently meaningless suffering are construed as potentially valuable insofar as they afford opportunities for insight into reality and for action to improve the human condition'.[21]

2. Philosophical and Psychological Reduction

This section shall now attempt to clarify how the philosophical undercurrent from which critical theory derives has a tendency to enclose experience in the experiential sphere itself, disconnecting it from that which is experienced. As Schillebeeckx himself points out, 'The origin of the term "critical theory" and all that is meant by it is to be found in the critical movement of the enlightenment, which initiated a "criticism of ideology" in many different spheres'.[22] The characteristics of the Enlightenment are clearly described by one of its best-known exponents, Immanuel Kant: 'Enlightenment, [Kant] argued, is man's emergence from his self-imposed immaturity. Immaturity is the inability to use one's understanding without guidance from another. This immaturity is self-imposed when its cause lies not in lack of understanding, but in lack of resolve and courage to use it without guidance from another'.[23] This view results in the idea that the individual should – in order to be true to himself/herself – act and think autonomously. According to Michael Gillespie,

> To be modern is to be self-liberating and self-making, and thus not merely to be *in* history or tradition but to *make* history. To be modern consequently means not merely to define one's being in terms of time but also to define time in terms of one's being, to understand time as the product of human freedom in interaction with the natural world. Being modern at its core is thus something titanic, something Promethian.[24]

Being human is no longer a gift, but a project. This Promethian nature of the Enlightenment shines through in the presuppositions of critical theory, as described by Schillebeeckx in the following passage:

> At the basis of critical theory there is a certain working hypothesis or presupposition, namely that, since mankind has become one social whole, we are able, as free, responsible human beings, to make history ourselves. In

---

21. E. K. Tillar, 'Dark Light: Wrestling with the Angel at the Edge of History', in *Edward Schillebeeckx and Contemporary Theology*, L. Boeve, F. Depoortere and S. van Erp (eds) (London: T&T Clark, 2010), 145.

22. Schillebeeckx, 'The New Critical Theory', 89 [102].

23. M. A. Gillespie, *The Theological Origins of Modernity* (Chicago; London: The University of Chicago Press, 2008), 258.

24. Gillespie, *The Theological Origins of Modernity*, 2.

other words, at the level of reason and freedom, we can control the structures which determine our being. This hypothesis is not imposed as a necessity on the analysis of society, nor is the point of departure for this analysis a particular religious, ethical or humanist image of man which might in turn impose on us the task of making our history freely and responsibly ourselves. The point of departure is an empirically deduced theory.[25]

Thus is the claim at least of Jürgen Habermas.[26] For him, this means that humanity is capable of shaping his own history, consequently his future, and thereby himself. In a way, one could say that the human person is a constant *creatio ex nihilo*: he/she is not dependent on any form of tradition or culture whatsoever. On the basis of this person's own will to change the situation, and through the power developed by modern science and technology, he/she is able to create the society, and ultimately the world, that he/she wants.

To identify the latent dangers that this entails for the contrast experience, this investigation will now look at the different notions of 'the self' as identified by Charles Taylor. He detects a change in the notion of the human 'self' with the coming of the modern era. He argues, 'A crucial condition … was a new sense of the self and its place in the cosmos: not open and porous and vulnerable to a world of spirits and powers, but what I want to call "buffered".'[27] Whereas in premodern times, the 'porous self' understood itself as permeable and part of a greater whole that influenced and defined it, the modern 'buffered self' leaves no room for ontology and primarily sees the human subject as the source of all meaning. This leads to a disenchanted world, as Taylor points out in the following passage:

> If thoughts and meanings are only in minds, then there can be no 'charged' objects, and the causal relations between things cannot be in any way dependent on their meanings, which must be projected on them from our minds. In other words, the physical world, outside the mind, must proceed by causal laws which in no way turn on the moral meanings thing have for us.[28]

The idea that contemporary humanity operates with a 'buffered self' generates a two-sided problem. First, experience can only be seen as something self-enclosed, rather than as something embedded in, and referring to, a reality outside of itself (i.e. a meaningful, 'charged' world). It is humanity that not only produces meaning, but also, in the way described by Habermas, makes its own history. It ultimately does not need to look beyond itself, because the autonomous 'buffered

25. Schillebeeckx, 'The New Critical Theory', 100 [114–15].

26. Schillbeeeckx refers mainly to J. Habermas, *Theorie und Praxis: Sozialphilosophische Studien* (Neuwied am Rhein: Luchterhand, 1963).

27. C. Taylor, *A Secular Age* (Cambridge, MA: The Belknap Press of Harvard University Press, 2007), 27.

28. Taylor, *A Secular Age*, 35.

self', collectively as well as individual, is the source of all meaning and does not rely on 'a particular religious, ethical or humanist image of man' whatsoever. This inevitably leads to a sense of isolation: experience ends up being locked up in itself. In this anthropocentric framework, any transcendent horizon will appear as an option, a matter of interpretation that is ultimately superfluous. Thus, the contrast experience ends up being one possible experience among others, an experience which those who believe in God may fill out in religious terms, that is, if they wish to do so.[29] This is clearly not what Schillebeeckx means when he speaks of the Contrast Experience as the 'backbone of my thoughts'.

Second, through the 'buffered self', not only does the referential dimension of experience(s) disappear, but experience itself also becomes immune to the possibility of transcendence breaking through. This generates exactly the philosophical pitfall which Schillebeeckx tries to avoid by using the concept of 'contrast experience'. Prior to the council, it was the philosophical framework of Neo-Scholasticism that placed grace on top of nature and avoided any 'sacramental reintegration of nature and the supernatural' – such a reintegration was advocated, for example, in the first half of the twentieth century by the proponents of the *nouvelle théologie*, who sought to conceive of reality as always already graced and charged by divine meaning and presence.[30] In an unexpected way, the same division reproduces itself within the framework of critical theory: the experiential sphere is buffered to the point of impenetrability, that is, to anything coming from the outside.

When experiences of contrast are solely seen as human experiences detached from any transcendent horizon, or impenetrable to anything breaking through from the outside, they run the risk of ending up as (i) mere psychological experiences instead of (ii) implicit expressions of, and contact points with, the anticipatory message intrinsic to the Christian faith. This latter view is exactly what Schillebeeckx thought they ultimately were.

3. Towards 'Practical Apophatism'

Schillebeeckx's encounter with secularized, pluralistic culture in the United States and Europe made him aware of the fact that he had to re-evaluate his theological method. The 'aprioristic epistemology' developed by his mentor, De Petter, no longer seemed applicable and meaningful within contemporary society. At the end of the 1960s, a sociological evaluation of modern society drew Schillebeeckx towards critical theory. This theory not only matched with the characteristics and orientation of modern society, but also provided a framework to develop a new theological approach.

29. Cf. Schillebeeckx, *Church*, 6 [6].

30. See H. Boersma, *Nouvelle Théologie and Sacramental Ontology: A Return to Mystery* (Oxford: Oxford University Press, 2009).

So what changes did Schillebeeckx discern within society? And why did he choose to make use of critical theory in addressing these changes? To answer these questions with more clarity, it will be fruitful to analyse Schillebeeckx's article 'The New Image of God, Secularization and Man's Future'.[31] In this text, written in 1968, he points at a fundamental change in humanity's orientation. Schillebeeckx says that

> formerly, man was orientated primarily towards the past, but now he looks resolutely towards the future. This revolution which has come about in man's attitude towards the world – instead of professing his belief in the primacy of the past … he is now actively engaged in claiming primacy for the future – may be called the exponent of the whole process of change.[32]

Schillebeeckx emphasizes that modern humanity no longer has a 'pre-scientific and pre-industrial attitude', but instead looks at the world through a lens that is shaped by the 'natural sciences' and 'technology'. They are 'thrusting man towards the future'.[33]

In this situation, theology has to find and articulate a 'new concept of God' that is in accordance with contemporary culture. This new concept is 'partly determined as to its explicit content and ideas by present-day culture'; otherwise it would not be plausible within modern society. Regarding this point, Schillebeeckx states the following:

> In … a [modern] cultural framework, the God of those who believe in him will obviously reveal himself as the 'One who is to come', the God who is *our* future. This, of course, brings about a radical change – the God whom we formerly, in the light of an earlier view of man and the world, called the 'wholly Other' now manifests himself as the 'wholly New', the One who is *our future*, who creates the future of mankind anew.[34]

The impact of this new concept of God as the 'wholly New' should not be underestimated. In a way, it asks for a different approach and method. It is exactly here that the method of critical theory comes into play. In particular, the emancipative and future-oriented characteristics of this theory match with the demands and orientation of present-day humanity. As previously noted, within critical theory, it is the human being that is capable of changing the structures of society, and with that, his future. Schillebeeckx is, as Kennedy points out, selective in the elements that he culls from critical theory. On the one hand, he uses its

---

31. Schillebeeckx, 'The New Image of God', 101–25 [168–203].

32. Ibid., 103 [172].

33. Ibid., 103–4 [172–3].

34. Ibid., 109 [181]. See also K. A. McManus, *Unbroken Communion: The Place and Meaning of Suffering in the Theology of Edward Schillebeeckx* (New York: Rowan & Littlefield, 2003), 25–6.

directedness towards the future, but, on the other hand, he is reticent in giving too much priority to the idea that humanity is capable of shaping its future single-handedly. In contradistinction to the anthropocentric approach of critical theory, Schillebeeckx prefers the interplay between God and man:

> The new concept of God – that is, faith in the One who is to come, in the 'wholly New One' who provides *us* here and now with the possibility of making human events into a history of salvation through an inward creation which makes us 'new creatures' dead to sin, thus radically transforms our commitment to make a world more worthy of man, but at the same time it reduces to only relative value every result which has so far been achieved.[35]

It is God 'who provides us with the possibilities', and who enables us to transform our history into a history of salvation. Although salvation is established in our world through our acts, it is not man-made. It is God who 'comes first' as the 'wholly New' and engages Godself with human history, enabling human beings to act in history in connection with the Lord.

The different features that Schillebeeckx culls from critical theory can be seen as valuable cornerstones which provide him with the framework for theology that he is looking for after the Second Vatican Council. But what about the possible risks of philosophical and psychological reduction that come with the increasing importance of human experience? It seems that Schillebeeckx himself was aware of possible ways to misunderstand his theology in the 1970s. At the end of this decade, he wrote the *Interim Report*, a small but important book that tries to clarify some of the theological and philosophical presuppositions from which he wrote *Jesus: An Experiment in Theology* (Dutch original 1974) and *Christ: The Christian Experience in the Modern World* (Dutch original 1977).[36] At the beginning of *Interim Report*, he elaborates on the relation between revelation and human experience. Schillebeeckx states, in a highly nuanced passage, the following: 'The self-revelation of God does not manifest itself *from* our experiences but *in* them, as an inner reference to what the experience and the interpretative language of faith have called into being. In the faith-inspired response to experience, the fact of being addressed by God ultimately becomes clear, at least humanly speaking.'[37]

Here, Schillebeeckx manages to combine the 'self-revelation of God' with human experience in such a way that our human response is truly a *response*. By articulating this nuanced interplay between God and humanity, Schillebeeckx avoids and

---

35. Schillebeeckx, 'The New Image of God', 113 [186].

36. E. Schillebeeckx, *Interim Report on the Books Jesus and Christ*, trans. John Bowden, *CW*, vol. 8 (London: Bloomsbury T&T Clark, 2014); E. Schillebeeckx, *Jesus: An Experiment in Christology*, trans. H. Hoskins and M. Manley, *CW*, vol. 6 (London: Bloomsbury, 2014); E. Schillebeeckx, *Christ: The Christian Experience in the Modern World*, trans. J. Bowden, *CW* vol. 7 (London: Bloomsbury, 2014).

37. Schillebeeckx, *Interim Report*, 11 [12].

explicitly contradicts the idea that the autonomous individual is the source of all meaning. On the contrary, the 'experiential basis' is of great importance, but it is God who 'comes first', and it is the human person who understands and answers this call in humanly confined way. Although this response is shaped within our experiential sphere, it is not a product that ultimately originates in our experience, that is, in the psychological sense.

From the moment that Schillebeeckx introduces the contrast experience in his works, he has firmly rejected the idea that faith can originate solely from experience. According to Schillebeeckx, there are no principles – the contrast experiences included – that make God and his grace superfluous. Contradicting those who think that contemporary secularization proves Christianity obsolete, Schillebeeckx remarks, 'How it would be possible for this critical function of eschatological faith to be taken over by a principle within man himself which leaves his redemption in grace out of account, one which might arise from a social and cultural secularization, in which the supplementary functions of religion are discontinued, I simply cannot see.'[38]

To explore the interplay between God and humanity more thoroughly – and with that the transcendent and experiential sphere – it might prove useful to turn towards negative theology. When Schillebeeckx, in *The Understanding of Faith*, discusses what theology might learn from critical theory, he briefly mentions the 'theologia negativa'.[39] However, he does not extensively elaborate on this 'negative' option. In this case, appearances can be deceiving, for this 'negative option' is far more important than one might expect. Kennedy emphasizes a significant shift in Schillebeeckx's theology by describing his theological development and the eminent role of negative theology, when he argues the following:

> In the early works, the positive factor, the implicit intuition, or the non-conceptual aspect of knowledge, sustains the negative feature of conceptuality, passing through it, so to speak, to refer to God. In these terms, God is known negatively only by way of a conceptual analogy. In the later writings, however, the implicit intuition is transposed into the notion of a positive hope that arises in suffering, and the negativity of conceptuality assumes the form of the negativity inherent in experiential suffering. In both the early and later works the actual cognitive contact with God is achieved in an implicit, inexpressible dimension of faith.[40]

---

38. Schillebeeckx, 'The New Image of God', 120 [197].

39. Schillebeeckx writes: 'What theologians have learnt form critical theory is to be more cautious in their use of such terms as "value," "meaning" and "peace." These concepts seem positive enough, but their content has been indirectly or negatively deduced, with the result that theologians are reminded of the most distinctive characteristic of their science, namely that it is a *theologia negativa*.' Schillebeeckx, 'The New Critical Theory and Theological Hermeneutics', 128 [147].

40. Kennedy, *Schillebeeckx*, 129.

The thread that links Schillebeeckx's early and late theology is this negative undercurrent. That is why Kennedy speaks of a gradual transformation within the theology of Schillebeeckx, from 'conceptual to practical apophatism'.[41]

In human experience, specifically in the contrast experience, this 'practical apophatism' is articulated most clearly. It is the place par excellence where God – seen as the 'wholly New' – breaks through from the future into our everyday lives. In an unforeseen manner, transcendence comes to the fore in human hope: in people's resistance towards injustices, and in their demand for a better and *humane* world. Therefore, 'God is found and known above all in the midst of actions that seek to surmount and suppress suffering'.[42]

Our 'yes' anticipates a future that is not yet known to us, but is received as a gift. God's grace guides and transforms human endeavours in a way that surpasses our own abilities and expectations, because in the end, all theory, as well as all praxis, cannot explain or justify the 'excess of suffering and evil' that infests our human history. As Schillebeeckx states, 'There is a barbarous "too much" that defies every explanation and interpretation'.[43] Although there are numerous emancipative moments in our world, moments that express our disagreement and resistance towards injustices, nonetheless these victories are limited and finite. 'For millions of men, who have been excluded, today or in the past, an eventual decisive emancipation will come too late.'[44] It is the mystery of mercy that reveals itself in experiences of contrast, and which shows time after time that it is stronger than all injustice. This is the basis of the hope that those who were not saved will ultimately be included in God's coming salvation.

Here, grace is not added to nature, but rather is intertwined with it; all of reality is, in some sense, graced by God. Consequently, salvation is *given* to us and is not man-made; although, it is secretly present in our deepest, most foundational experiences and hopes. God's promise of salvation 'shines through' in our affirmative, contingent, and historically situated 'yes', as the answer to the question of whether another, better world is possible. That is why Schillebeeckx argues, 'Salvation has to be made a reality in every human dimension on earth. That is what the biblical image of "a new heaven and earth" points to and that is the perspective of liberation.'[45]

---

41. Ibid.

42. Ibid., 131.

43. E. Schillebeeckx, 'Mystery of Injustice and the Mystery of Mercy, Questions concerning Human Suffering', *Stauros Bulletin* 3 (1975): 10.

44. Schillebeeckx, 'Mystery of Injustice', 12.

45. See E. Schillebeeckx, H. Oosterhuis and P. Hoogeveen, *God Is New Each Moment. Edward Schillebeeckx in Conversation with Huub Oosterhuis en Piet Hoogeveen* (New York: Seabury Press, 1983), 37.

Conclusion

Critical theory enabled Schillebeeckx to reinvent his methodological approach in the aftermath of the Second Vatican Council, and to make the shift from an 'aprioristic epistemology' towards an 'a posteriori theory'. However, this alliance with critical theory has its latent dangers. As the concept of the 'buffered self' makes clear, a one-sided emphasis on human experience might lead to a philosophical and psychological stance that detaches the experiential basis from any transcendent horizon. Schillebeeckx manages to avoid these pitfalls by selectively culling the elements from critical theory that he needs. For example, he utilizes its experiential basis and the emancipative drive for a better future, but nevertheless keeps human experience oriented towards a transcendent horizon from which God as the 'wholly New' is constantly breaking through. It is in experiences of contrast in particular that God's self-revelation shines through in our hopes and orients humans towards the future. This future is not produced by human will and power, but is received as a gift and a promise that makes action possible. From our human, confined perspective, this grace can only be made visible via the 'theologia negativa': in experiences of contrast, maybe best described as 'apophatic practices'. Within this horizon, Schillebeeckx's intuition, that 'eschatological faith [cannot] be taken over by a principle within man himself',[46] makes perfect sense. It is the experiential sphere that is the birthplace of a never-ending grace *given* by God, because in the end, only the 'wholly New' can carry the weight of our turbulent human history.

Bibliography

Boersma, H., *Nouvelle Théologie and Sacramental Ontology: A Return to Mystery* (Oxford: Oxford University Press, 2009).

Borgman, E., *Edward Schillebeeckx: een theoloog in zijn geschiedenis* (Baarn: Nelissen, 1999).

Borgman, E., *Edward Schillebeeckx: A Theologian in His History*, trans. J. Bowden (London: Bloomsbury T&T Clark, 2006).

Gillespie, M. A., *The Theological Origins of Modernity* (Chicago; London: The University of Chicago Press, 2008).

Habermas, J., *Theorie und Praxis: Sozialphilosophische Studien* (Neuwied am Rhein: Luchterhand, 1963).

Kennedy, P., *Schillebeeckx* (Collegeville, MN: The Liturgical Press, 1993).

McManus, K. A., *Unbroken Communion: The Place and Meaning of Suffering in the Theology of Edward Schillebeeckx* (New York: Rowan & Littlefield, 2003).

Schillebeeckx, E., 'The Magisterium and the World of Politics', *Concilium* (Am.) vol. 36 (1968): 19–39, Concilium (Engl.) 4 (1968) nr. 6: 12–21.

46. Schillebeeckx, 'The New Image of God', 120 [197].

Schillebeeckx, E., 'Mystery of Injustice and the Mystery of Mercy, Questions concerning Human Suffering', *Stauros Bulletin* 3 (1975): 3–31.

Schillebeeckx, E., H. Oosterhuis, and P. Hoogeveen, *God Is New Each Moment: Edward Schillebeeckx in Conversation with Huub Oosterhuis en Piet Hoogeveen* (New York: Seabury Press, 1983).

Schillebeeckx, E., *Sono Un Teologo Felice. Colloqui con Francesco Strazzari* (Bologna: EDB, 1993).

Schillebeeckx, E., *I Am a Happy Theologian: Conversations with Francesco Strazzari*, trans. J. Bowden (London: SCM Press, 1994).

Schillebeeckx, E., *Theologisch testament, notarieel nog niet verleden* (Baarn: Nelissen 1994).

Schillebeeckx, E., *Christ: The Christian Experience in the Modern World*, trans. J. Bowden, *CW*, vol. 7 (London: Bloomsbury, 2014).

Schillebeeckx, E., *Church. The Human Story of God*, trans. J. Bowden, *CW*, vol. 10 (London: Bloomsbury, 2014).

Schillebeeckx, E., *God the Future of Man*, trans. N. D. Smith, *CW*, vol. 3 (London: Bloomsbury, 2014).

Schillebeeckx, E., *Interim Report on the Books Jesus and Christ*, trans. J. Bowden, *CW*, vol. 8 (London: Bloomsbury T&T Clark, 2014).

Schillebeeckx, E., *Jesus: An Experiment in Christology*, trans. H. Hoskins and M. Manley, *CW*, vol. 6 (London: Bloomsbury, 2014).

Schillebeeckx, E., *The Understanding of Faith: Interpretation and Criticism*, trans. N. D. Smith, *CW*, vol. 5 (London: Bloomsbury T&T Clark, 2014).

Taylor, C., *A Secular Age* (Cambridge, MA: The Belknap Press of Harvard University Press, 2007).

Tillar, E. K., 'The Influence of Social Critical Theory on Edward Schillebeeckx's Theology of Suffering for Others', *The Heythrop Journal* 42/2 (2001): 148–72.

Tillar, E. K., 'Dark Light: Wrestling with the Angel at the Edge of History', *Edward Schillebeeckx and Contemporary Theology*, L. Boeve, F. Depoortere, and S. van Erp (eds) (London: T&T Clark, 2010), 142–60.

Part III

THEOLOGICAL CRITIQUE OF THE PUBLIC SPHERE

Chapter 10

THE GOOD NEWS ABOUT CLIMATE CHANGE

Jan Jorrit Hasselaar

On 15 February 2014, the Dutch newspaper *Trouw* recounted a conversation on climate change between sociologist Zygmunt Bauman and his daughter, the architect Irena Bauman.[1] In this interview, Zygmunt Bauman calls climate change, 'the invisible present in each great debate'. Irena asks her father if one should respond to climate change with optimism. He answers by affirming that it is wrong to divide the world into optimists and pessimists, and he says that there is a third possibility: a hopeful one. This remark by Bauman is interesting because it points to an important distinction between hope and optimism, which are often confused with each other. A similar distinction is made by the Roman Catholic theologian Edward Schillebeeckx (1914–2009), particularly between optimism, pessimism, and hope. Generally speaking, while people believe that they know what 'optimism', 'pessimism', and 'hope' mean, popular misconceptions regarding these terms abound. A nuanced understanding of the differences between them thus demands further clarification. Following Bauman's suggestion, in this chapter, I will explore the notion of hope in the context of climate change, using the work of Edward Schillebeeckx, as well as that of the renowned Jewish rabbi Jonathan Sacks.

The words 'optimism' and 'pessimism' find their origin in Latin. They are, respectively, *optimum* and *pessimum*. The word *optimum* is the superlative of *bonum* (good) and means '(morally) best/most favourable'. The word *pessimum* is the superlative of *malum* (bad) and means '(morally) worst/least favourable'. In his book *God among Us*, Edward Schillebeeckx recognizes these two, in their 'pure' form, as views of history and human society.[2] Schillebeeckx argues that these two views present history not as contingent, but as evolving with intrinsic necessity according to a 'predetermined blueprint'. According to Schillebeeckx, a

---

1. F. van Rootselaar, 'De mens kan niet wereldwijd denken', *Trouw*, 15 February 2014, http://www.trouw.nl/tr/nl/5009/Archief/article/detail/3597612/2014/02/15/De-mens-kan-niet-wereldwijd-denken.dhtml (accessed 25 January 2016).

2. E. Schillebeeckx, *God among Us: The Gospel Proclaimed*, trans. J. Bowden (New York: Crossroad, 1983), 98.

pessimistic view considers change as evil because it is a deviation from a certain good period in the past; the best that one can hope for is minimal deviation. In stark contrast, an optimistic view conceives of progress – even extensive deviation – ultimately as good. Schillebeeckx presents a theology of creation, or creation faith, as an alternative view, one which holds that we are not alone (or on our own) in this world. This alternative perspective stimulates the continual renewal of hope.[3] 'Creation faith therefore has its own critical and productive force over against pessimistic and optimistic, and ultimately unrealistic, views of history and society.'[4] Schillebeeckx calls this creation faith 'good news'.[5] What does this good news mean in the context of climate change?

In this chapter, and keeping in mind the words of Zygmunt Bauman regarding hope, I will explore Schillebeeckx's creation faith as a stimulus of hope. Schillebeeckx's creation faith will be considered in dialogue with a theory of society by rabbi Jonathan Sacks. This dialogue about hope will be undertaken in relation to climate change. The aim of the present chapter is ultimately to examine a theological contribution of hope to climate change.

1. Negative Contrast Experiences

During his lifetime, Edward Schillebeeckx tried to identify concrete challenges, in the real world and from life experiences, which could act as a starting point for Christian ethics. In his own words, this starting point, or foundation, is not a pre-existing order,

> but [rather is] *man who has already been damaged*: disorder, both in his own heart and in society. The *humanum*, threatened and in fact already damaged, leads specifically and historically to ethical demand and the ethical imperative, and thus to confrontation with quite definite, negative experiences of contrast. Therefore ethical invitation or demand is not an abstract norm but, historically, an event *which presents a challenge*: our concrete history itself, man in need, mankind in need.[6]

Here, we see that Schillebeeckx uses the term 'negative experiences of contrast' to describe those experiences that threaten the *humanum*. In other contexts, he calls these the 'radical experiences of contrast'.[7] Schillebeeckx identified several of these

---

3. Schillebeeckx, *God among Us*, 98.

4. Ibid.

5. Ibid., 91.

6. E. Schillebeeckx, *Christ: The Christian Experience in the Modern World*, trans. J. Bowden, *CW*, vol. 7 (London: Bloomsbury T&T Clark, 2014), 649 [659].

7. E. Schillebeeckx, *Essays: Ongoing Theological Quests*, *CW*, vol. 11 (London: Bloomsbury T&T Clark, 2014), 154 [128] = "Theological Quests" [from *Theologisch testament*, 69–137].

radical experiences of contrast, for example, the two world wars, concentration camps, and homelessness in developing countries.[8] Since the 1970s and 1980s, it has been difficult to shake off the impression that the *humanum* is threatened by several ecological issues. These issues are often surrounded by an atmosphere of fear and apocalyptic language (or even apocalypse itself). Although these issues have emerged more recently, they are not completely absent in the writings of Schillebeeckx. For example, in the epilogue of his book *Church*, Schillebeeckx reflects on environmental issues and even refers in this context to the notion of 'ecological contrast experiences' derived from the term 'contrast experiences'.[9] The theme of negative contrast experiences pervades Schillebeeckx's theology. However, 'Schillebeeckx acknowledges that the ecological and cosmic dimension of his work needs to be developed more fully and has remarked that his theology of creation provides the basis for that'.[10] Before we consider climate change in particular and discuss Schillebeeckx's theology of creation, let us examine Schillebeeckx's notion of the negative contrast experience.

Schillebeeckx states that the negative contrast experience is 'a pre-religious experience and thus a basic experience accessible to all human beings, namely that of a "no" to the world as it is'.[11] At the same time, this 'no' to the world as it is discloses an openness to another situation which has the right to our affirmative 'yes'.[12] Schillebeeckx calls this the 'open yes'. This 'open yes' is nurtured, established, and sustained by fragmentary, but real experiences of meaning and happiness on both small and large scales. According to Schillebeeckx, the 'open yes' serves as a rational basis, not only for solidarity between believers and non-believers, but also for common commitment to a better world with a human face.[13] But, in talking about ecological issues, Schillebeeckx widens the focus of negative contrast experiences by no longer solely concentrating on the threatened *humanum* but also on threatened nature. He mentions issues like the pollution of the environment and the exhaustion of the natural resources. In the epilogue of *Church*, Schillebeeckx criticizes humanity for its tendency to forget that it shares one creation with inorganic and organic creatures.[14] He talks about 'the catastrophe to the environment' and even uses the notion 'the modern ecological experiences of contrast', caused (at least in part) by technology and economic progress.[15]

8. E. Schillebeeckx, 'The Magisterium and the World of Politics', *Concilium* 4 (1968): 21–40.

9. Schillebeeckx, *Church: The Human Story of God*, 237 [239].

10. M. C. Hilkert, 'The Threatened Hunamun as *Imago Dei*: Anthropology and Christian Ethics', in *Edward Schillebeeckx and Contemporary Theology*, L. Boeve, F. Depoortere, and S. van Erp (eds) (London; New York: T&T Clark International, 2010), 136, n. 18.

11. Schillebeeckx, *Church*, 5 [5].

12. Ibid., 6 [6].

13. Ibid.

14. Ibid., 234 [236].

15. Ibid., 237 [239].

Before I proceed, it is important to be more precise when dealing with environmental issues if one is to make a constructive theological contribution. Not all of the environmental problems facing the world today constitute a 'catastrophe'. Of course, during past decades, the rising impact of exploitative economic activity on the environment has become clearer. However, the economist Deirdre McCloskey is also right in showing examples of how the environment has improved over the last 150 years. McCloskey therefore questions the logic that economic growth inevitably hurts the environment. She supports her assertion by referring to improvements like water quality and air quality.[16] These are indeed good examples of improvements stemming from the relation between economic activity and the environment. For example, Dutch environmental policy in recent decades has shown how environmental pressure declines while the economy grows.

> In the 1980s and 1990s, the Netherlands was a frontrunner in its approach to environmental issues. This was born of necessity. Compared with other countries, in the Netherlands, an unusually high concentration of environmentally harmful activities took place, and continues to take place, per square kilometre. Huge progress has been made in many areas. Issues such as smog, surface water pollution and acid rain have been largely solved.[17]

Schillebeeckx suggests, rather than argues, that there are 'modern ecological experiences of contrast' caused by technology and economic progress. At the same time, he says that technology is not wrong in itself, but that it can also serve 'the authentic values of true, good and truly happy humanity'.[18] Perhaps one can say, using Schillebeeckx's terms, that, in many cases, a strong 'No, it can't go on like this' has already helped to solve several of the ecological issues. However, Maarten Hajer, director of the Netherlands Environmental Assessment Agency (PBL), points out that the Dutch Fourth National Environmental Policy Plan (NMP4) indicates that, despite positive developments and policy successes, a number of persistent environmental problems will continue to exist in the long term.[19] NMP4 mentions examples like biodiversity loss and climate change.[20] In the following section, I will limit my analysis to the example of climate change.

16. D. N. McCloskey, *The Bourgeois Virtues: Ethics for an Age of Commerce* (Chicago; London: The University of Chicago Press, 2006), 17.

17. N. Hoogervorst, M. Hajer, F. Dietz, J. Timmerhuis and S. Kruitwagen, *Changing Track, Changing Tack: Dutch Ideas for a Robust Environmental Policy for the 21st Century* (The Hague: PBL Netherlands Environmental Assessment Agency, 2013), 5.

18. Schillebeeckx, *Church*, 237 [240].

19. M. Hajer, *The Energetic Society: In Search of a Governance Philosophy for a Clean Economy* (The Hague: PBL Netherlands Environmental Assessment Agency, 2011), 14.

20. Ministerie van Volkshuisvesting, Ruimtelijke Ordening en Milieubeheer, *Een wereld en een wil: werken aan duurzaamheid, Nationaal Milieubeleidsplan 4* (Den Haag, 2001), 15.

2. Climate Change

Steve Rayner and Gwyn Prins define earlier environmental issues, for example, the damage to the ozone layer from chlorofluorcarbons (CFCs) and acid rain, as tame problems.[21] Tame problems are complicated, but they exist with defined and achievable end-states. Climate change, however, is perceived as a different kind of problem than these earlier environmental issues. 'The reason has to do with wicked uncertainty. Wicked uncertainty occurs when the problem is too complex and/or too uncertain to resolve by focusing on a single object and the outcomes from taking action, including doing nothing, are unknowable. Climate change is not a conventional environmental problem that can simply be solved by reducing CO_2 emissions!'[22]

A growing number of scholars, and even religious leaders like Pope Francis – particularly in his encyclical *Laudato Si* – and Ecumenical Patriarch Bartholomew, argue that climate change is not only a technical issue, but also involves questions of ethics, identity, and world view. Dutch theologian Erik Borgman considers climate change as a social question.[23] In the words of Harvard leadership experts Ron Heifetz and Marty Linsky, one can call climate change an 'adaptive challenge', opposed to a more technical problem.[24] One dimension of such an adaptive challenge is a societal transformation. Considering climate change as a social question or an adaptive challenge means that it is not external to human beings. It is, in fact, about the way that we have organized our society and the images that we live by. Within the field of transition management, this type of process of change is considered as profound, because it involves both individual and societal transitions.[25] In the case of climate change, then, the decisive question is the question of Schillebeeckx: 'What image of human beings do we opt for?'[26]

From Schillebeeckx's writings, it becomes clear that he believes that we should opt for 'a cosmic community in solidarity'.[27] However, we do not know in advance what exactly we are opting for, because human beings are simply unaware of what

21. G. Prins and S. Rayner, *The Wrong Trousers: Radically Rethinking Climate Policy* (Oxford: Institute for Science, Innovation and Society, 2007), v.

22. G. C. van Kooten, *Climate Change, Climate Science and Economics: Prospects for an Alternative Energy Future* (Dordrecht et al.: Springer, 2013), 270.

23. E. Borgman, *Overlopen naar de barbaren: Het publieke belang van religie en christendom* (Kampen: Uitgeverij Klement, 2009), 156.

24. R. Heifetz, A. Grashow and M. Linksy, *The Practice of Adaptive Leadership: Tools and Tactics for Changing Your Organization and the World* (Boston: Harvard Business Press, 2009), 29.

25. J. Grin, J. Rotmans and J. Schot, *Transitions to Sustainable Development: New Directions in the Study of Long Term Transformative Change* (New York; Abingdon: Routledge, 2010), 3.

26. Schillebeeckx, *Church*, 237 [240].

27. Ibid.

the consequences of a particular development will be. For example, an idea of dramatic climate change was not what humanity sought when starting to use fuel fossils. In any case, we cannot go back to where it began. Moreover, we can neither undo the past nor necessarily regret it. The breathtaking numbers of uncertainties surrounding climate change make it a difficult problem indeed, a problem that is even hard or impossible to define at this point. This may contribute to an atmosphere of fear and apocalypse.

3. Another Story to be told

On 27 February 2014, business leaders of companies like Allianz and Lloyd Banking wrote a letter to the *Financial Times* calling on Westminster 'to think about how it will manage the growing risk of widespread flooding'.[28] According to the article in the *Financial Times*, the business leaders drew a direct link between the widespread flooding in Somerset and the Thames Valley, on the one hand, and climate change, on the other. However, a closer examination of the letter shows that it is worded more carefully. The business leaders argue that 'the type of extreme weather that we are currently experiencing is in line with climate change predictions, which also warn that such events will become more frequent'.[29]

Scientifically, it is indeed more suitable to talk about prediction when treating the relationship between single weather events and climate change, as opposed to attributing such events simply and directly to climate change.[30] At the same time, however, the perceived (direct) link between flooding and climate change might say something about the power of the idea of climate change on a popular scale. Most of the time, climate change is surrounded by an atmosphere of fear and even apocalypse. According to the French philosopher Pascal Bruckner, this is an atmosphere of alarmism and human guilt to nature; one can take, for example, the notion of 'footprint'.[31] Bruckner, however, highlights another story that can be told using the same facts and the same sequence of events. Alongside of fear and apocalypse, there is also something else, namely 'that history also surprises us with its good sides. ... In the sequence of causes and effects, something new and better can appear'.[32] In the words of Schillebeeckx, one might call this 'fact[,] that history also surprises us with good sides', a general human feeling. In his terms,

---

28. J. Pickard, 'Businesses seek urgent action on climate change after floods', *Financial Times*, 27 February 2014, http://static1.1.sqspcdn.com/static/f/270724/24444431/1393609533200/ FT+letter+-+Flooding+emphasises+need+to+address+climate+change.pdf?token=k2tuh PxHngEf%2FOdx0MFrXtiwuhw%3D (accessed 29 January 2016).

29. Ibid.

30. Van Kooten, *Climate Change, Climate Science and Economics*, 240–1.

31. P. Bruckner, *The Fanaticism of the Apocalypse: Save the Earth, Punish Human Beings* (Cambridge; Malden: Polity Press, 2013), 2.

32. Bruckner, *The Fanaticism of the Apocalypse*, 44.

it is an 'open yes' within the context of a radical contrast experience. However, if the 'contrast experience' and the 'open yes' are both pre-religious, is there still an added value of the Christian tradition in (and for) the public sphere?

Schillebeeckx argues that the history of religion affirms and deepens this perception of reality. For Christians, the 'open yes' takes on a more precise direction because they believe that there is a divine mystery at the heart of the human experience. Schillebeeckx argues that a theology of creation opens up a perspective of hope within concrete experiences. The 'open yes' is something of a sigh of mercy, of compassion, which is hidden in the deepest depths of reality, 'and in it believers hear the name of God. That is how the Christian story goes'.[33] For Christians, the 'open yes' is not an incidental occasion, but a well-founded hope. It is based on liberative experiences in the past. In *Church*, Schillebeeckx mentions experiences like the exodus from Egypt and liberating experiences in the life of Jesus. 'Here we can see that talking in the language of faith about the actions of God in history has an experiential basis in a very particular human activity in the world and in history'.[34] According to Schillebeeckx, the 'open yes' gets a more lively relief by the acknowledged divine dimension because the 'yes' can then be interpreted as revealing, 'sometimes and very short', the face of a mild and merciful mystery. This mystery invites us, after all of our resistance against our situation, to surrender ourselves to its depths. 'There is more between heaven and earth than what our human theory and praxis can do on their own account'.[35] With the 'open yes', a new perspective can come to us. In the contrast experiences, there is an echo of hope.[36] Schillebeeckx derives this echo of hope from the perspective of creation faith. Therefore, let us now turn to discuss this perspective.

4. Creation Faith

Schillebeeckx describes that, within the Jewish-Christian tradition, a concept of creation has developed over a long history of experience. He explains that this concept of creation is never an explanation of our world, our humanity, or the origin of the world. It is, rather, good news, which says something about God, humanity, and the world in their relationship(s) to one another. Schillebeeckx states that this news is not alien to human experience. It is like a voice that can be heard from the familiar world of the own experience, from nature and history.[37] This shows that, for Schillebeeckx, creation faith can never be solely a matter of propositional beliefs, but also is attached to a particular way of life in the world. Schillebeeckx argues that creation faith is about the absolute presence of God in

33. Schillebeeckx, *Church*, 6 [6].
34. Ibid.
35. Schillebeeckx, 'Theological Quests', 158 [132].
36. Ibid., 156 [130].
37. Schillebeeckx, *God among Us*, 91.

this world; amid all the suffering and failure, God remains in and with the finite. At the same time, it is only possible to talk about God in an indirect way. Nature and the world may not be absolutized or divinized. Schillebeeckx is opposed to a creation faith that saves human beings from their finitude and everything that the finitude involves. 'God is with and in us, even in our failures, our suffering and our death, just as much as he is in and with all our positive experiences and experiences of meaning.'[38] Schillebeeckx stresses that the absolute presence of God in this finite world stimulates the continual renewal of hope.[39] The question remains, what does this stimulation of the continual renewal of hope accomplish?

When we look at Schillebeeckx's proposals regarding the protection of creation, we see that, above all else, he advocates self-restraint and a more sober lifestyle.[40] At the same time, in the epilogue of *Church*, he raises further thoughts about creation. For example, he discusses the following: constructive and caring creativity; the integrity of all creation (i.e. as an echo of the conciliar process); creation as a cosmic community in solidarity; and redemption in Jesus Christ, which also supports a more cosmic, contemplative, and ludic relationship to the world of animals and nature. The following section will try to deepen these lines. Before doing so, however, let us make a last remark. Schillebeeckx argues that when people recognize a negative experience of contrast they will respond spontaneously.[41] This seems to be perhaps too positive, at least in the case of a complex social question or problem. A critical question will be raised about this notion of spontaneous response later in this chapter. It is striking that, when Schillebeeckx refers to the concept of creation faith, he does not refer to the Christian tradition, but rather to the Jewish-Christian tradition.[42] This reference corresponds to important developments within the Roman Catholic Church, namely regarding its view of the relationship between Judaism and Christianity.

5. Judaism and Christianity

The Second Vatican Council was an effort of *aggiornamento*, bringing the church up-to-date in a manner of speaking. In 1965, during this council, the Catholic Church published a declaration entitled *Nostra Aetate*, which is about its relationships with non-Christian faiths.[43] In 1975, this declaration was elaborated in the text *Vatican Guidelines and Suggestions for Implementing the Conciliar Declaration Nostra Aetate (n. 4)*, which was drafted under the presidency of the

---

38. Ibid., 94.

39. Ibid., 98.

40. Schillebeeckx, *Church*, 236 [238].

41. Hilkert, 'The Threatened Hunamun as Imago Dei', 131.

42. Schillebeeckx, *God among Us*, 91.

43. Pope Paul VI, *Declaration on the Relation of the Church to non-Christian Religions: Nostra Aetate*, 28 October 1965, http://www.cin.org/v2non.html.

Dutch cardinal Willebrands. These guidelines distinguish three areas in which conversation with Judaism can be fruitful for the church: (1) the use of scripture; (2) liturgy; and (3) ethical and social questions. In 1999, the Dutch Roman Catholic bishops wrote a letter in which they added a fourth area: hope.

> Catholics have come increasingly to realize that we share a common messianic mission to make the earth inhabitable. ... Slavery and death [do not] have the last word but liberation and life in God's presence is our common conviction. ... Jews and Christians live from one and the same hope. With this hope as a solid basis, modern man does not necessarily have to experience the future as an ominous void.[44]

In the light of these parallels, we shall now develop the notion of hope in conversation with rabbi Jonathan Sacks.

Rabbi Jonathan Sacks is one of the most important voices in the modern world in terms of representing Judaism, in particular, and religion more generally. He is former chief rabbi of the United Hebrew Congregations of the Commonwealth (1991–2013) and currently serves as a professor at several distinguished institutions.[45] Like Schillebeeckx, Jonathan Sacks has an interest in civil and political society as a specifically religious concern. In addition, and central to Sacks's writings, there is a notion similar to what Schillebeeckx calls 'creation faith'. Sacks endeavours to recover faith in the idea that we are not alone in this world.[46] In an interview, he noted the following: 'There are, I believe, three fundamental concepts that are better understood by Judaism than by any secular philosophy with which I am familiar: human freedom, human dignity and hope.'[47] Hope plays a central role in the writings of Sacks.[48] He defines 'hope' as God being 'mindful of our aspirations, with us in our fumbling efforts, that He has given us the means to save us from ourselves; that we are not wrong to dream, wish and work for a better world'.[49] But Sacks does not wish merely to define hope, because it is not simply a notion or the application of a timeless value to a particular human situation; hope

---

44. The Roman Catholic Bishops of the Netherlands, *Living with One and the Same Hope on the Meaning of the Meeting with Judaism for Catholics* (1999).

45. Jonathan Sacks is currently professor of Judaic thought at New York University and University Professor of Jewish Thought at Yeshiva University. He has also been appointed as professor of law, ethics and the Bible at King's College London.

46. J. Sacks, *Future Tense: Jews, Judaism, and Israel in the Twenty-First Century* (New York; Toronto: Schocken Books, 2009), 2.

47. H. Tirosh-Samuelson and A. W. Hughes (eds), *Jonathan Sacks, Universalizing Particularity* (Leiden; Boston: Brill, 2013), 117.

48. J. Sacks, *The Dignity of Difference: How to Avoid the Clash of Civilizations* (London; New York: Continuum, 2002), 206–7; Sacks, *Future Tense*, 231–52.

49. Sacks, *The Dignity of Difference*, 207.

is also not about the application of the common notion of stewardship.[50] In the biblical context, stewardship is often derived from Genesis 1 and 2. Schillebeeckx leans heavily on these chapters when dealing with environmental issues.[51] Sacks similarly deals with these texts when talking about the environment.[52] But there is also another clear line in Sacks's work that is based on the interpretation of the Exodus story as a metanarrative of hope for Western civilization. This interpretation might provide some novel insights into the case of climate change as social question. The following section will focus on Sacks's theory of society,[53] which he sometimes calls 'the politics of hope'.[54]

6. Exodus

In Sacks's political theory of society, the central concept is 'covenant'.[55] A covenant is a way of organizing society. It is, moreover, a bond of identity: 'It is part of who I am'.[56] Sacks writes, 'The politics of covenant is about faith and hope, the faith that together we can build a gracious future and the hope that history can be redeemed from tragedy'.[57] The logic of covenantal politics is based on three key words: *mishpat*, *tzedek*, and *chessed*.[58] *Mishpat* can be understood, roughly, as justice-as-reciprocity. It is the principle of the golden rule: 'Treat others as you would like others to treat you.' According to Sacks, *mishpat* is the minimum of a just society.[59] *Tzedek*, or *tzedakah*, is usually translated as 'charity', but in fact means social or distributive justice. Finally, there is *chessed*, which is the most distinct key word and the driving force of the covenant.[60] *Chessed* is one of the key devices in the *Torah*.[61] It is usually translated as 'kindness', but it means covenantal love. According to Sacks, *chessed* is a loyalty which one owes to those members who are family. However, in a covenantal society, all citizens are considered as

50. M. Hulme, *Why We Disagree about Climate Change: Understanding Controversy, Inaction and Opportunity* (Cambridge: Cambridge University Press, 2009), 148.

51. Schillebeeckx, *Church*, 238, 243 [241, 246].

52. Sacks, *The Dignity of Difference*, 161–79.

53. J. Sacks, *A Letter in the Scroll, Understanding Our Jewish Identity and Exploring the Legacy of the World's Oldest Religion* (New York: Free Press, 2000), 125.

54. J. Sacks, *The Politics of Hope* (London: Jonathan Cape, 1997), 260.

55. Sacks, *The Politics of Hope*, 61.

56. Sacks, *The Politics of Hope*, 61.

57. J. Sacks, *The Great Partnership: God, Science and the Search for Meaning* (London: Hodder & Stoughton, 2011), 134.

58. Sacks, *A Letter in the Scroll*, 125.

59. Ibid.

60. Sacks, *The Politics of Hope*, 63.

61. J. Sacks, *To Heal a Fractured World: The Ethics of Responsibility* (New York: Schocken Books, 2005), 52.

children of one God. *Chessed* presents the idea that a good social order can never be constructed on rights and obligations alone. It additionally calls for engagement.

In the Torah, justice is the foundation of society, but *chessed* is prior to justice and even to society itself. *Chessed* is the personal, unquantifiable. It is the face-to-face relationship (an idea elucidated, for example, in the work of Jewish philosopher Emmanuel Levinas). Sacks also connects *chessed* with the 'I-Thou dimension of society, the compassion and humanity that can never be formalized as law but instead belong to the quality of relationships, to the idea that the poor, the widow, the orphan and the stranger are my brothers and sisters'.[62] Thus, in this covenant, all people of society are seen as being brothers and sisters. But it seems that one can extend this covenant even further. Sacks refers to Martin Buber when he mentions the I-and-Thou relationship.[63] It is important to note that, within his poem *I and Thou*, Martin Buber indicates that the combination of I-Thou is not limited to the sphere of human beings, but also includes the relationship of humanity and nature.[64] The covenant, then, seems to bear in itself the potential to include non-humans as well.

According to Sacks, covenantal politics is based on storytelling, not on abstract theory.[65] Every covenant involves a narrative. In the case of the Hebrew Bible, the story of the Exodus is of prime importance. In Sacks's view, this story is about individual and societal transformation(s). In the narrative, God leads a group of Israelite slaves, the members of whom seek their freedom through great effort and by changing the images that they live by (at individual and communal levels). Slavery is just one of the clearest manifestations of individual and societal transformation; it is an affront to human dignity that is very present in human consciousness today. Climate change also involves the dimensions of individual and societal transformation; in other words, meeting this challenge today – and being liberated from its potential bondage – will require transformation at both the personal and societal levels, with a major shift in the images by which we all live. Therefore, the Exodus narrative might 'function' as a prism through which we can approach the context of climate change. The next section will focus on one element of the Exodus story that is crucial for our discussion, namely the Sabbath.

7. Sabbath

Above, this chapter questioned Schillebeeckx's logic that, when people recognize a negative experience of contrast, they will respond spontaneously and immediately. In some cases, people may indeed be able to respond spontaneously and

---

62. Sacks, *A Letter in the Scroll*, 128.

63. J. Sacks, *The Home We Build Together: Recreating Society* (London; New York: Continuum, 2007), 174.

64. M. Buber, *I and Thou*, trans. R. G. Smith (London: Bloomsbury, 2013), 5.

65. Sacks, *The Great Partnership*, 134.

immediately. In the case of climate change, however, people need to learn how to take responsibility for this social question, and this takes time. In order to explain the time needed for societal transformations, Sacks refers to the twelfth-century Jewish thinker Moses Maimonides and his work, *The Guide of the Perplexed* (part III, chapter 32). Maimonides writes that it is 'impossible to go from one extreme to another'. It takes time to change the human heart and images. Regarding the story of the Exodus, for example, it is impossible for the Israelites suddenly to discontinue everything that they have been accustomed to in Egypt.

> Here, Maimonides states a truth he saw as fundamental to Judaism. ... God never intervenes to change human nature. To do so would be to compromise human free will. That is something God, on principle, never does. ... He could not force the pace of the moral development of mankind without destroying the very thing He had created. This self limitation ... was God's greatest act of love. He gave humanity the freedom to grow. But that inevitably meant that change in the affairs of mankind would be slow.[66]

Sacks appropriates Maimonides's assertion that God wanted humans to abolish slavery, but by their own choice, and thus he argues that the process takes time. According to Sacks, the Sabbath is the key to the politics of Exodus, and its presence looms large in this book.[67] The Sabbath is not only a religious institution, but 'also and essentially a political institution'.[68] The Sabbath enacts the Promised Land while the Israelites are journeying through the desert. Sacks therefore calls the Sabbath, 'Utopia Now'.[69] The Sabbath, in some sense, is the revelation of the end at the beginning. According to Sacks, God wants the people to catch glimpses of the destination so that they will not lose their way in the wilderness of time. After the ordeal in Egypt, Israelites were no longer allowed to see themselves as slaves. They might be reduced to a condition of slavery for a period of time, but this would not constitute their identity.

Sacks emphasizes that the Hebrew Bible sees the Sabbath as the education of a people in two fundamental truths. In the first place, the Sabbath was, and remains, an ongoing tutorial in freedom, equality, and human dignity. In the second place, it is also an environmental tutorial. On Sabbath, God's people are reminded that they are creation and not creators. On that day, human beings have to renounce their mastery over animals and creation. The Sabbath thus stimulates respect for nature. What the Sabbath does for humans and animals, the Sabbatical and Jubilee years do for the land itself: they give a period of rest.[70] The Sabbath day is especially about relations of *chessed*. The Sabbath sets forth a view that is not human-centred, but God-centred.

---

66. J. Sacks, *Covenant & Conversation, Exodus: The Book of Redemption* (Jerusalem; London: Maggid Books, 2010), 99.

67. Sacks, *Covenant & Conversation*, 16–17.

68. Sacks, *A Letter in the Scroll*, 136.

69. Sacks, *Covenant & Conversation*, 16.

70. Sacks, *The Dignity of Difference*, 167.

This day creates space for experiencing relations of *chessed* between humans and non-humans and stimulates the extension of the covenant to non-humans.[71]

The theme of the Sabbath also resonates with the work of Schillebeeckx.[72] However, Sacks's understanding of the Sabbath deepens Schillebeeckx's notion of the 'open yes', by providing an interpretation of Exodus as a metanarrative for dealing with adaptive challenges. The remaining questions include the following: what does this metanarrative mean, as retold in the context of climate change? Does it present some good news?

8. Recreating Society through Public Love

Climate change as a social question involves individual and societal transition(s). It is about identity and changing the images that we live by. Sacks's covenantal politics relates to these questions. The metanarrative of this politics is the story of the Exodus, and the covenant therein established is a bond of identity. The driving force of this bond is not a contract or the law, but *chessed*, or covenantal love. This love creates the possibility for experiencing nature not as an object, but as a subject. In experiencing nature as subject, the images that we live by will change. In the metanarrative of this covenantal politics, we hear of how slaves – that is, persons objectified – became free subjects through an arduous journey of forty years. The dimension of *chessed* resonates with what the social scientist Jeffrey C. Alexander calls 'the civil sphere',[73] precisely because both are extended towards 'outsiders'. The civil sphere is a space for searching and where promises may be articulated. Promises can be redeemed when outsiders, vulnerable, and/or marginalized members of civil society demand the expansion, or development, of the images organizing society.[74] At the beginning of the twentieth century, for example, we could not have imagined the development of civil society regarding the roles of women, racial minorities, gays, and lesbians. Their positions in society were, and often still are, the subject of complex social debates. In his book *Politics of Nature*, Bruno Latour refers to these social questions as examples of extending democracy. He describes the various ecological issues facing humanity today as an obligation to internalize the environment.[75] Latour pleas for extending democracy to the 'voices' of non-humans: 'To limit the discussion to humans, their interests, their subjectivities, and their rights, will appear as strange a few years from now as having denied the right to vote of slaves, poor people, or women.'[76] He adds that we

---

71. A more detailed consideration of the extension of the covenant to all humanity (i.e. in an intra-generational and intergenerational sense) would surpass the scope of this chapter.

72. Schillebeeckx, *Church*, 240–1 [242–3].

73. J. C. Alexander, *The Civil Sphere* (New York: Oxford University Press, 2006), 549–53.

74. Alexander, *The Civil Sphere*, 549–53.

75. B. Latour, *Politics of Nature: How to Bring the Sciences into Democracy*, trans. C. Porter (Cambridge; London: Harvard University Press, 2004), 58.

76. Latour, *Politics of Nature*, 69.

still do not have the slightest idea of what the consequences of such an extension may look like.[77] In line with Sacks's theory, Latour also stresses that it is not possible to find quickly remedies that extend democracy to non-humans. He affirms that we have to slow down and try to see another reading of reality.[78] Changing the images that one lives by perhaps takes '40 years in the desert'. However, we have the impression that humanity is already on the way in this regard. Climate change and its uncertainties put additional pressure on present situations. For example, how do we deal with rising sea levels, shifts in the discharges of river systems, salinization, and so forth? For the low-lying delta of the Netherlands, finding answers to such questions is a matter of high importance.

The search for answers to these questions must not be deferred to the future, but should shape contemporary research. For instance, one should consider the Dutch consortium Ecoshape, which is comprised of private partners, government agencies, and think tanks. They have undertaken research and reflection on ecological matters, but have done so by including nature as a stakeholder: 'building with nature' instead of 'building in nature'. "'Building with nature forces us to take a step back, rethink the problem and analyze the natural and social systems involved. ... Compared with traditional approaches, this calls for ... three fundamental changes: to think, act and interact differently.'"[79]

Conclusion

Climate change is often associated with pessimism and less frequently with optimism. Irena Bauman asked her father how one should respond to climate change, and we recall Zygmunt Bauman's answer that there is a third possibility, a hopeful one. In this chapter, I have explored this third possibility. I defined climate change as a social question, which means that climate change is not external to human beings. It is about the way that we have organized our society and the images that we live by. A decisive question is then about identity. In this chapter, I have tried to explore a hopeful response to climate change from the Jewish-Christian heritage of Western civilization, in particular from the writings of Edward Schillebeeckx and Jonathan Sacks. In their works, it is creation faith, the idea that we are not alone in this world, which plays a central role as stimulus of hope. If hope means that we are not alone in this world, then hope is not a vague term, but rather an unremitting challenge with implications for how we think about the world, human life, and questions in public and personal life. This chapter is an effort to contribute to the public issue of climate change by taking Schillebeeckx's theology of creation

77. Ibid., 82.

78. Ibid., 3.

79. H. de Vriend and M. van Koningsveld, *EcoShape, Building with Nature: Thinking, Acting and Interacting Differently* (Alphen a/d Rijn: Drukkerij Holland, 2012), http://www.ecoshape.nl/files/paginas/ECOSHAPE_BwN_WEB.pdf, 11.

as a starting point for a hopeful response in the present context. At the heart of Schillebeeckx's experience of contrast lies the 'no' that gives rise to the 'open yes' of resistance to that which threatens the *humanum* and nature. This 'open yes' is accessible to all human beings and based on shared experiences and responses. However, this 'open yes' is deepened in conversation with Jonathan Sacks and his interpretation of the Exodus narrative. In the context of climate change, these together provide a distinctive, critical, productive, and inspiring alternative to pessimism and optimism in their 'pure' forms. It is distinctive because it focuses on a theory of society instead of the common protagonists in the context of climate change, namely the market and the state. Furthermore, this alternative is critical because it does not present a utopian vision for all set in the distant future, or even require a major technical breakthrough. It does present a transitional pathway by which images and the human heart may gradually change. One could imagine a redemption of small steps: act by act, day by day. The way from here to there, like the journey of the Israelites through the wilderness, takes time. It is also critical because it argues for institutions like the Sabbath to stimulate the conversion of hearts and minds by reorienting one's focus relationally. This alternative is productive because it is about creating new individual and social life. The driving, recreating force of this alternative is the notion of *chessed*, as a creative and public form of love that will help to build society in such a way that non-humans may be integrated, as well. This love recreates human beings and institutions. The notion of *chessed* carries the promise of recreating the images that we live by, as well as of constructing a new and common subjectivity of humans and non-humans. This alternative shows how the centrality of love may influence public and economic powers to include outsiders into the considerations of civil society. Finally, it is inspiring because, in generating responses to climate change, it presents and offers us a powerful story and framework of thought.

By exploring this alternative, I have attempted to contribute to the development of the ecological and cosmic dimension of Schillebeeckx's work via his theology of creation. The alternative of hope here formulated can stimulate and deepen efforts – at schools, universities, businesses, and in societies at large – to build new partnerships and contribute to concepts like 'building with nature'. Is there good news about climate change? Yes, there is, but this good news is maintained especially by love, which cannot be taken for granted, and which can easily be crowded out, as economists say. Therefore, love has to be carefully nurtured and sustained by public institutions like schools, festivals, and especially the Sabbath. There is good news about climate change, but it is fragile, and there is much work to do, like rethinking the public or political function of the Sabbath.

Bibliography

Alexander, J. C., *The Civil Sphere* (New York: Oxford University Press, 2006).
Borgman, E., *Overlopen naar de barbaren: Het publieke belang van religie en christendom* (Kampen: Uitgeverij Klement, 2009).

Bruckner, P., *The Fanaticism of the Apocalypse: Save the Earth, Punish Human Beings* (Cambridge/Malden: Polity Press, 2013).

Buber, M., *I and Thou*, trans. R. G. Smith (London: Bloomsbury, 2013) (German original: *Ich und Du*, 1937).

De Vriend, H., and M. van Koningsveld, *EcoShape, Building with Nature: Thinking, Acting and Interacting Differently* (Alphen a/d Rijn: Drukkerij Holland, 2012).

Grin, J., J. Rotmans, and J. Schot, *Transitions to Sustainable Development: New Directions in the Study of Long Term Transformative Change* (New York/Abingdon: Routledge, 2010).

Hajer, M., *The Energetic Society: In Search of a Governance Philosophy for a Clean Economy* (The Hague: PBL Netherlands Environmental Assessment Agency, 2011).

Heifetz, R., A. Grashow, and M. Linksy, *The Practice of Adaptive Leadership: Tools and Tactics for Changing Your Organization and the World* (Boston: Harvard Business Press, 2009).

Hilkert, M. C., 'The Threatened Hunamun as *Imago Dei*: Anthropology and Christian Ethics', in *Edward Schillebeeckx and Contemporary Theology*, L. Boeve, F. Depoortere and S. van Erp (eds) (London; New York: T&T Clark International, 2010), 127–41.

Hoogervorst, N., M. Hajer, F. Dietz, J. Timmerhuis, and S. Kruitwagen, *Changing Track, Changing Tack: Dutch Ideas for a Robust Environmental Policy for the 21st Century* (The Hague: PBL Netherlands Environmental Assessment Agency, 2013).

Hulme, M., *Why We Disagree about Climate Change: Understanding Controversy, Inaction and Opportunity* (Cambridge: Cambridge University Press, 2009).

Latour, B., *Politics of Nature: How to Bring the Sciences into Democracy*, trans. C. Porter (Cambridge; London: Harvard University Press, 2004).

McCloskey, D. N., *The Bourgeois Virtues: Ethics for an Age of Commerce* (Chicago; London: The University of Chicago Press, 2006).

Pickard, J., 'Businesses seek urgent action on climate change after floods', *Financial Times*, 27 February 2014.

Pope Paul VI., *Declaration on the Relation of the Church to Non-Christian Religions: Nostra Aetate*, 28 October 1965.

Prins, G., and S. Rayner, *The Wrong Trousers: Radically Rethinking Climate Policy* (Oxford: Institute for Science, Innovation and Society, 2007).

Sacks, J., *The Politics of Hope* (London: Jonathan Cape, 1997).

Sacks, J., *A Letter in the Scroll, Understanding Our Jewish Identity and Exploring the Legacy of the World's Oldest Religion* (New York: Free Press, 2000).

Sacks, J., *The Dignity of Difference, How to Avoid the Clash of Civilizations* (London; New York: Continuum, 2002).

Sacks, J., *To Heal a Fractured World: The Ethics of Responsibility* (New York: Schocken Books, 2005).

Sacks, J., *The Home We Build Together: Recreating Society* (London/New York: Continuum, 2007).

Sacks, J., *Future Tense: Jews, Judaism, and Israel in the Twenty First Century* (New York; Toronto: Schocken Books, 2009).

Sacks, J., *Covenant & Conversation, Exodus: The Book of Redemption* (Jerusalem; London: Maggid Books, 2010).

Sacks, J., *The Great Partnership: God, Science and the Search for Meaning* (London: Hodder & Stoughton, 2011).

Schillebeeckx, E., 'The Magisterium and the World of Politics', *Concilium* 4 (1968): 21–40.

Schillebeeckx, E., *God among Us: The Gospel Proclaimed*, trans. J. Bowden (New York: Crossroad, 1983).

Schillebeeckx, E., *Christ: The Christian Experience in the Modern World*, trans. J. Bowden, *CW*, vol. 7 (London: Bloomsbury T&T Clark, 2014).

Schillebeeckx, E., *Church: The Human Story of God*, trans. J. Bowden, *CW*, vol. 10 (London: Bloomsbury T&T Clark, 2014).

Schillebeeckx, E., *Essays: Ongoing Theological Quests*, *CW*, vol. 11 (London: Bloomsbury T&T Clark, 2014).

Tirosh-Samuelson, H., and A. W. Hughes (eds), *Jonathan Sacks, Universalizing Particularity* (Leiden; Boston: Brill, 2013).

Van Kooten, G. C., *Climate Change, Climate Science and Economics: Prospects for an Alternative Energy Future* (Dordrecht; Heidelberg; New York; London: Springer, 2013).

Chapter 11

DEVELOPMENT AMID SIN: SCHILLEBEECKX AND
NEWMAN FOR TODAY

Christopher Cimorelli

It is tempting to believe that the subject of doctrinal development is passé after the Second Vatican Council, or perhaps that it bears little upon the field of public theology, since it appears to be a discourse relevant solely within the *Ecclesia Romanum*. This chapter will attempt to show, however, the critical importance of (revisiting) this subject in, and for, the contemporary context. It will do so by investigating the works of two influential theologians, who never abdicated the responsibility to connect meaningfully traditional religion with the contemporary context and its obstacles to faith. They are, namely, John Henry Newman (1801–90) and Edward Schillebeeckx (1914–2009).

To do so, our investigation will, concretely, be carried out in three sections. First, this chapter will introduce the views of Newman and Schillebeeckx regarding doctrinal development, looking in particular at the 'theological' solutions they offered to the challenge of, and problems raised by, historical consciousness when applied to revealed religion. Second, it will highlight the ways in which their views resist falling into an ideological stance regarding ecclesial speech and doctrinal truth claims, and it will cite their acute awareness of human finitude and sin as the reasons for such resistance. Only with such an awareness, even and especially concerning the subject of doctrinal statements in correspondence with divine truth(s), can they articulate views in which the true eschatological dimensions of human existence are brought to the fore. In this vein, the views of both thinkers remain relevant for the contemporary Roman Catholic Church, which has seen some troubling 'developments' in its own view of tradition-development after the Second Vatican Council. In a concluding reflection, this chapter will argue that the views of Newman and Schillebeeckx are able to contribute significantly to the modern social imaginary,[1] which seems ill-equipped, in the light of constrained

---

1. I will define this term in section 3 of this chapter. See C. Taylor, *Modern Social Imaginaries* (Durham and London: Duke University Press, 2004), 23–4.

notions of the human person and progress, to deal with challenges which may imperil the very survival of our species.

1. Newman and Schillebeeckx on the Development of Doctrine

Given the goals and limits of this chapter, this section will *introduce* the views of Newman and Schillebeeckx on development, and particularly on doctrinal development, which can be defined as follows: the ongoing explication of religious truth claims concerning the infinite, revealing God, yet made by finite, sinful humanity in and through the church gifted with the Holy Spirit. The elements of human finitude and sin, in particular, are crucial to keep in mind if one is to avoid an overly progressive, evolutionary view of the development of doctrine. Such a progressive view may lose sight of the eschatological dimension inherent in any response to God, and thus may undermine praxis in the present, leading to extreme views either favouring past accomplishments, on the one hand, or an illusory, paradigmatic future, on the other.

Remarkably, the views of Newman and Schillebeeckx regarding development are similar,[2] and this holds true even when taking into account some of Schillebeeckx's later considerations of the subject.[3] Newman's most famous treatment – his *An Essay on the Development of Christian Doctrine*, published originally in 1845 and significantly edited and reorganized in 1878 – has been called the *locus classicus* for the issue,[4] inspiring a century of controversy and debate regarding the way(s) in which church tradition develops in history, changing yet remaining in continuity with itself. Newman held a somewhat Romantic view of development,[5] in which the Incarnation led to a divine impression on the first believers – and especially

2. A. Nichols, *From Newman to Congar: The Idea of Doctrinal Development from the Victorians to the Second Vatican Council* (Edinburgh: T&T Clark, 1990), 247. See also E. Schillebeeckx, 'The Development of the Apostolic Faith into the Dogma of the Church', *Revelation and Theology*, trans. N. D. Smith, *CW*, vol. 2 (London: Bloomsbury, 2014), 46–8 [68–71]. This work by Schillebeeckx was translated from the original collection of essays: *Openbaring en Theologie*, Theologische Peilingen, I (Bilthoven: H. Nelissen, 1964). For more on the origin of this Dutch work, see pp. 182–3 below.

3. For example, see (in chronological order) the following works by Schillebeeckx: 'Theological Interpretation of Faith in 1983', *Essays: Ongoing Theological Quests*, trans. E. Fitzgerald and P. Tomlinson, *CW*, vol. 11 (London: Bloomsbury, 2014), 51–68; *Church: The Human Story of God*, trans. J. Bowden, *CW*, vol. 10 (London: Bloomsbury, 2014); 'Discontinuities in Christian Dogmas' (1994), *Essays*, 85–109.

4. Y. Congar, *Tradition and Traditions: An Historical and a Theological Essay*, trans. M. Naseby and T. Rainborough (London: Burns & Oates, 1966), 211.

5. Stephen Prickett has treated this theme – looking particularly at Newman in chapters 6 and 7 – in his work *Romanticism and Religion: The Tradition of Coleridge and Wordsworth in the Victorian Church* (London: Cambridge University Press, 1976). Prickett has also

on the Apostles – an impression which exists in the minds of believers, who help to realize this 'Christian Idea' in their concrete lives.[6] The idea becomes manifest not merely in the lives of individual believers, but in the corporate, communal reality of the church, eventually finding expression in society at large. One aspect of such development is the explication of doctrines regarding divine revelation, usually when a particular contextual controversy demands the church's response.[7] Development is a native component of living ideas, and the development of the Christian Idea was evident to Newman from his study of the past, so much so that he described it as a 'fact'.[8] While historical studies could lead to practical certainty regarding the fact that development had occurred, they could not, in Newman's eyes, yield certainty regarding the continuity of that development.[9] Newman therefore sought a principle of continuity, which he determined was the tradition of the church, safeguarded – when need be – by an infallible teaching authority, ultimately under the bishop of Rome.[10]

Schillebeeckx's most concise and focused treatment regarding doctrinal development occurred in an early theological entry on the subject. This entry was first published in the *Theologisch Woordenboek* in 1952,[11] later included in his work *Openbaring en Theologie* (1964),[12] and eventually translated into English in the volume *Revelation and Theology*, in 1967. While this entry is critical for understanding Schillebeeckx's view of doctrinal development, it was, perhaps unfortunately, written in his early life and thus well before his shifts in theological emphasis after the Second Vatican Council. However, Schillebeeckx did author

---

written on the broader topic of European Romanticism, in his work *European Romanticism: A Reader* (London: Continuum, 2010).

6. J. H. Newman, *An Essay on the Development of Christian Doctrine* (London: Longmans, Green, and Co., 1909), 33–40, 55–9. All citations will be from this edition (i.e. a republication of the 1878 version). Hereafter cited: *Essay*. For Newman's earlier version, see J. H. Newman, *An Essay on the Development of Christian Doctrine* (London: James Toovey, 1845).

7. Newman, *Essay*, 58.

8. Newman, *Essay*, 55–7, 75. See also p. 3.

9. M. Chapman, 'Temporal and Spatial Catholicism: Tensions in Historicism in the Oxford Movement', in *The Shaping of Tradition: Context and Normativity*, C. Dickinson (ed.) (Leuven: Peeters, 2013), 25–6.

10. Newman, *Essay*, 75–92 (esp. 86–7). For a slightly more nuanced perspective, particularly regarding the role of the Roman See, cf. Schillebeeckx, 'Discontinuities in Christian Dogmas', 89. Schillebeeckx here explains that the pope's infallibility is a result of his exercise of the 'Petrine office', his individual bishopric representing an 'addition' to that office.

11. E. Schillebeeckx, 'Dogma-ontwikkeling', in *Theologisch Woordenboek* I, H. Brink, O.P. (ed.) (Roermond en Maaseik: J. J. Romen & Zonen, 1952), 1087–107. See also E. Schillebeeckx, 'Scholasticism and Theology', *Revelation and Theology*, 169–70 [259].

12. E. Schillebeeckx, 'De ontwikkeling van het Apostolisch Geloof tot Kerkelijk Dogma', in Openbaring en Theologie (Bilthoven: H. Nelissen, 1964), 50–67.

some later works that not only approach the subject of doctrinal development, but also seriously consider – contra the judgement of Aidan Nichols[13] – 'the role of the Church's public doctrine in his account of Christian believing'.[14] These works will be examined in more detail in section 2 of this chapter.

Schillebeeckx's entry from 1952 appears specifically in the fourth chapter of *Revelation and Theology*, 'The Development of the Apostolic Faith into the Dogma of the Church'.[15] Here, he provides an overview of the subject of development, as well as his own synthesis in the light of previous views.[16] Schillebeeckx begins the essay by undertaking a brief historical survey of the problem, or question, of doctrinal development, as it was understood in previous eras of Christianity, starting with the Patristic church. However, the subject, as it is popularly known, truly emerges only in the Modern period,[17] in which three types of 'solutions' are typically offered. The first solution is called the 'historical' type, which attempts to establish the continuity of development through historical research; however,

---

13. For this judgement, see A. Nichols, *From Newman to Congar*, 269–74. Schillebeeckx may have veered away from classical metaphysical approaches in his later works – especially regarding a hierarchical view that he interpreted as removing the church from the realm of history (see chapter 4 of Schillebeeckx, *Church*, 196–205, 211–12, 214–26 [198–207, 213, 216–28]) – but that does not mean he was operating without any kind of a metaphysical view (if such is even possible), or that traditional formulations of faith were forgotten. He was instead attempting to reflect rationally on Christian truths, which were promulgated during times with clearer metaphysical frameworks, in order to help their meaning continue to be experienced in the present. Regarding the vital importance of vehicles of tradition and the ongoing study of the past for present action, Schillebeeckx writes, 'But that does not mean that the historical, socio-cultural vehicles of tradition must necessarily be denigrated. On the contrary, as the only possible vehicles of the manifested substance of faith they have a *positive function* for the very reason that the transcultural component of the gospel is only to be found *in* the particularity of cultural hermeneutic structures. Those who denigrate historical transmission in all its relative particularisations – that is, relate them exclusively to the situation at that time – rob Jesus' history of its significance for our present-day history. It is *in* historical transmission that the *Christian constants* emerge, not as it were "abstracted *from*" concrete history. ... Hence the hermeneutic problem of Christian identity throughout the ages can be solved only by comparing the various cultural forms of religious experience and religious interpretation, in which the substance of the gospel is articulated in diverse ways'. Schillebeeckx, 'Theological Interpretation of Faith in 1983', 58–9. See also. p. 66; Schillebeeckx, 'Discontinuities in Christian Dogmas', 96–102.

14. Nichols, *From Newman to Congar*, 272.

15. Schillebeeckx, 'The Development of the Apostolic Faith into the Dogma of the Church', 43–61 [63–93].

16. For a more in-depth summary of Schillebeeckx's position in this essay, see Nichols, *From Newman to Congar*, 236–47.

17. Schillebeeckx, 'The Development of the Apostolic Faith into the Dogma of the Church', 47 [70].

this type is lacking in that historical evidence itself is often not sufficient enough to yield certainty and a definitive conclusion regarding continuity.[18] The second solution he calls the 'logical' type, in which logical, discursive reasoning is made 'the principle both of the unchangeable character of dogma and of its development'.[19] This view is lacking because it overly attributes theological development to logical reasoning alone, failing to account for how 'Christian reasoning plays an *instrumental* part within the greater complex of the development of tradition';[20] in other words, such reasoning, while significant, is only one element of the life of faith.[21] The third solution is the 'theological' type, which combines elements of the previous two types in order to account more adequately for the experience of faith as leading to development. Schillebeeckx identifies Newman as the major figure in articulating this theological type, and he writes that 'The appearance of Christ aroused in the apostles' consciousness of faith a comprehensive intuition of the essence of christianity [*sic*]. There are, in addition to explicit aspects, also implicit orientations and unexpressed elements in this initial "impression" or "idea", which constitute a knowledge that is experienced rather than consciously thought out.'[22]

By supporting this notion of an original 'consciousness' or 'intuition', Newman and others were able to maintain that later doctrinal developments truly belong to the original deposit of faith, but that they required the passage of time, the controversies of history, and the development of human consciousness to come to the fore.[23] For Newman, the principle of doctrinal development is reason, or reasoning (both implicit and explicit), and the 'principle of continuous development' is the church's authority.[24]

Schillebeeckx, while clearly finding himself in accordance with the 'theological' type, nevertheless attempts to provide his own contribution towards a synthesis

18. Ibid.

19. Ibid., 47–8 [70–72].

20. Ibid., 49 [73].

21. Schillebeeckx additionally points out that 'a development of faith can only have a strictly supernatural principle', which is not required when logic alone is the principle of development. Schillebeeckx, 'The Development of the Apostolic Faith into the Dogma of the Church', 49 [73]. These insights of Schillebeeckx are significant because they lead him to argue that it is more accurate to speak of the development of tradition than of doctrine alone, an idea which was affirmed at the Second Vatican Council. See Schillebeeckx, 'The Development of the Apostolic Faith into the Dogma of the Church', 49, 54 [74, 81]. See also *Dei Verbum* 8.

22. Schillebeeckx, 'The Development of the Apostolic Faith into the Dogma of the Church', 51 [76].

23. Newman, *Essay*, 36–40, 53, 59–60; Schillebeeckx, 'The Development of the Apostolic Faith into the Dogma of the Church', 60–1 [912]; Schillebeeckx, 'Discontinuities in Christian Dogmas', 93–102.

24. Schillebeeckx, 'The Development of the Apostolic Faith into the Dogma of the Church', 51–2 [76–8].

by speaking of the function of the 'light of faith' (*lumen fidei*), understood as an inner instinct that is implanted by God in the faithful, prompting them to believe. Schillebeeckx is here reflecting on the light of faith as it was primarily articulated by Thomas Aquinas,[25] but he applies this notion to the question of development in particular. It is through this light that the inner lives of believers are adapted for 'the supernatural dimension of the mystery of revelation',[26] enabling them to understand more concerning revelation than could otherwise be gleaned through logic or history alone. While this light of faith comes from God, 'its meaning and content ... come from objective, public revelation' that is proclaimed by the church.[27] The light of faith moreover helps believers to judge correctly regarding whether something 'new' authentically belongs to the deposit of faith.[28] Given its source in God, the light of faith is infallible in its operation.[29] However, 'The *individual* light of faith cannot function as the principle of the continuity of the development of the church's dogma' because the light of faith 'is, so to speak, lost in the concrete human psychology, within which many different forms of resistance, prejudices, social influences, and so on can give a new interpretation to and even neutralise the pure effects of' this light[30] – one is here seeing Schillebeeckx's germinal concern with experience. This is not to say that the individual's judgement is always erroneous due to prejudice, but rather that an individual reaction, or judgement, cannot be known 'with absolute certainty' as 'the result of the light of faith or not.'[31] The individual's judgement, therefore, should be referred to the

25. Schillebeeckx provides several references for Aquinas's treatment of this notion. See Schillebeeckx, 'The Development of the Apostolic Faith into the Dogma of the Church', 55 [82–3], n. 34–5. For example, see the following from Aquinas: *Summa Theologiae* II-II, q. 2, a. 9, ad. 3; *Super Evangelium secundum Johannem* c. 6, lect. 5; *Quodlibeta Disputata* II, q. 4, a. 1, ad. 1; *Quattuor Sententiarum P. Lombardi* III, d. 23, q. 2, a. 1, ad. 4.

26. Schillebeeckx, 'The Development of the Apostolic Faith into the Dogma of the Church', 55 [83].

27. Ibid.

28. Ibid., 55–6 [83–5].

29. Ibid., 56 [84].

30. Ibid., [78]. This sentiment about prejudices in every age was shared by Newman. In the context of writing about judging which developments are authentic, Newman writes, 'But it is difficult to say who is exactly in this position. Considering that Christians, from the nature of the case, live under the bias of the doctrines, and in the very midst of the facts, and during the process of the controversies, which are to be the subject of criticism, since they are exposed to the prejudices of birth, education, place, personal attachment, engagements, and party, it can hardly be maintained that in matter of fact a true development carries with it always its own certainty even to the learned, or that history, past or present, is secure from the possibility of a variety of interpretations.' Newman, *Essay*, 76.

31. Schillebeeckx, 'The Development of the Apostolic Faith into the Dogma of the Church', 57–8 [86–7].

ecclesial body, where 'the growth of the church's faith is still a communal work'.[32] The multifaceted participation of the faithful leads to the dynamism and ongoing development of tradition, one aspect of which is the development of doctrines (or even dogmas), which concretely and formally takes place when theological speculation is refined over a period of time, until the teaching authority of the church makes an official declaration regarding a truth claim.[33] Schillebeeckx describes this long process as one of convergence, in which 'the light of faith makes itself more and more strongly felt' over time, until what has long been experienced in the church is able to find concrete, explicit form.[34]

Both Newman and Schillebeeckx articulated a solution in accordance with the 'theological' type, in which ongoing, faithful development finds ultimate security in the infallible teaching authority of the church;[35] such development, while finding concrete expression in doctrines, is indicative of complex, multifaceted participation on the part of the pilgrim people of God, at both the implicit and explicit levels. Moreover, both thinkers were keen to emphasize the finitude of individuals, and even of particular contexts. Finitude necessitates the ongoing (intellectual) activity of the faithful in every time period, activity which helps to maintain the continuity of the deposit of faith. In other words, as believers intellectually, even critically, reflect on the received mysteries of faith in the light (and hope) of future communion with God, they facilitate the process by which the gospel may meaningfully speak to the present context.[36] It is finitude and

---

32. Ibid., 58 [87].

33. Schillebeeckx argues that history shows that these declarations also bear 'witness to the fact that the church's teaching office solemnly declares a truth of faith to be a dogma only when the collective reaction of the believing community points clearly and explicitly in that direction and the community of theologians puts forward convincing arguments'. Schillebeeckx, 'The Development of the Apostolic Faith into the Dogma of the Church', 59 [89–90]. The process of development is therefore one in which the whole body of believers is involved.

34. Schillebeeckx, 'The Development of the Apostolic Faith into the Dogma of the Church', 59 [89]: 'The collective reaction of the whole of the church as a believing community, on a basis of the never-ceasing dynamic force of the light of faith, which is, in a confused manner, operative among all the members of the church, is infallible not only as a matter of principle but also in fact.'

35. Schillebeeckx, 'The Development of the Apostolic Faith into the Dogma of the Church', 59–60 [90–1]; Newman, *Essay*, 88–9.

36. While this idea may seem more evident for a hermeneutical thinker like Schillebeeckx, see Newman, *Essay*, 31, 40. See also 'Letter to Flanagan, 1868', in *The Theological Papers of John Henry Newman on Biblical Inspiration and Infallibility*, J. D. Holmes (ed.) (Oxford: Clarendon, 1979), 157–8. This latter source was an unpublished (i.e. until 1979) exchange between one Fr. John Stanislas Flanagan and John Henry Newman (through Ignatius Ryder, a member of Newman's oratory community), in which Newman provides a clear summary and clarification of his view regarding development. For more on this letter, see C. Cimorelli,

particularity that provide for the creative mimesis of the trans-historical church, the people of God.

2. Finitude, Sin and Theories of the Development of Doctrine

With the discussion of finitude and particularity, however, one is also dealing with the question of sin and its consequences, which tend to refer to the misuse of human free will relative to the will of the infinite God; this constitutes an 'offense', or 'error', in some sense. The Greek form of the word, 'sin' (i.e. *hamartía*), and the Hebrew equivalent (*chata*), together carry the connotation of 'missing a goal', or mark.[37] What is not clear at this point is how this question is related to the topic of development.[38] This section will attempt to shed light on this subject by first emphasizing the inadequate treatment of sin in the Roman Catholic view of development, as well as the consequences of such neglect. Second, it will turn again to the views of Newman and Schillebeeckx – in fact, to their own 'later' reflections on development – in order to highlight their shared commitment to account adequately for development in the light of finitude *and* amid a world indubitably marred by sin.

Theories of the development of dogma according to the Roman Catholic perspective largely – at least overtly[39] – tend to avoid sin, or perhaps only treat it indirectly.[40] There are a number of logical factors behind this tendency. For example,

'The Possible Advantage of Doctrinal Growth: Revisiting Newman's Understanding of Development', *Newman Studies Journal* 11, no. 1 (Spring 2014): 32–44.

37. See, for example, the following: *Perseus Digital Library*, 'ἁμαρτία', http://www.perseus. tufts.edu/hopper/morph?l=a%28martia&la=greek (accessed 27 May 2015); Thayer and Smith (eds), 'Hamartia', *The NAS New Testament Greek Lexicon*, http://www.biblestudytools. com/lexicons/greek/nas/hamartia.html (accessed 27 May 2015); W. L. Holladay (ed.), 'חָטָא', in *A Concise Hebrew and Aramaic Lexicon of the Old Testament* (Leiden: Brill, 2000), 100.

38. The fact of a relationship in this regard should not be surprising, at least from a biblical perspective. To be clear, with the subject, and question, of doctrinal development, one is, in some sense, dealing with the knowledge of good and evil (see Gen. 2–3).

39. It is important to note that an argument can be made that sin perhaps *too strongly* marks the Catholic understanding of tradition-development, especially since the conclusion of the Second Vatican Council. This argument will not be pursued at this time, but it is worthy of further investigation, especially regarding the possible implications for delineating a post-conciliar theological anthropology.

40. For more on the Roman Catholic view of doctrinal development and infallibility, see the following: F. Cardinal Seper, Congregation for the Doctrine of the Faith, *Mysterium Ecclesiae*, 2–5 ('Declaration in Defense of the Catholic Doctrine Against Certain Errors of the Present Day'), http://www.vatican.va/roman_curia/congregations/cfaith/documents/ rc_con_cfaith_doc_19730705_mysterium-ecclesiae_en.html (accessed June 2013); A. Dulles, *Magisterium: Teacher and Guardian of the Faith* (Naples, FL: Sapientia Press, 2007);

such theories may be attempting to delineate between fallible and infallible speech on the part of the church,[41] rather than addressing the more fundamental issue of the possibility of infallibility for finite, sinful humanity in the first place. In addition, development has been conceived as being tied to the abiding presence and assistance of the Holy Spirit in the church,[42] so it is problematic to discuss sin when dealing with such operation on the part of the Spirit. Finally – and this is something that Newman extensively dealt with – there is the idea that sin, in the form of heterodoxy or theological imprecision, instigates the process by which doctrine emerges. In this vein, doctrines both correct erroneous views and further clarify the church's understanding of the deposit of faith.[43] The end result of these factors is the articulation of theories of development that are overly progressive, and which posit the ever-increasing understanding of the deposit of faith and penetration into the heart of the gospel over time, in anticipation of the second coming of Christ.[44]

Such a progressive, asymptotic view of tradition-development was partially accepted at the Second Vatican Council,[45] most notably in *Dei Verbum* 8.[46] This

F. A. Sullivan, *Magisterium: Teaching Authority in the Catholic Church* (Eugene, OR: Wipf & Stock Publishers, 2002). Regarding the 'scope' of infallibility, see Dulles, *Magisterium*, 59 ff. For an indication of the 'avoidance', or neglect, of sin, one might conduct a word search for the terms 'sin' and 'finite' (and their cognates) in A. Nichols's impressive work, *From Newman to Congar*, in which a host of theories of doctrinal development are explored; such a search reveals few matches.

41. See *Mysterium Ecclesiae* 2, 5.

42. See, for example, *Dei Verbum* 8. See also note 46 below.

43. For example, see Newman, *Essay*, 58, 273–322. Regarding the function of doctrinal promulgations, as answering questions and excluding error(s), see *Mysterium Ecclesiae*, 5; International Theological Commission, 'Interpretation of Dogma' (1989), B.II.2, http://www.vatican.va/roman_curia/congregations/cfaith/cti_documents/rc_cti_1989_interpretazione-dogmi_en.html (accessed 27 May 2015). Hereafter cited as: ITC, 'Interpretation of Dogma' (1989).

44 See, for example, *Gaudium et Spes* 62, *Lumen Gentium* 12, and *Dei Verbum* 8.

45. For more on this topic, see C. Cimorelli and D. Minch, 'Views of Doctrine: Historical Consciousness, Asymptotic Notional Clarity, and the Challenge of Hermeneutics as Ontology', *Louvain Studies* 37, no. 4 (2013): 327–63.

46. The critical passage is the following: 'This tradition which comes from the Apostles develop [*sic*] in the Church with the help of the Holy Spirit. For there is a growth in the understanding of the realities and the words which have been handed down. This happens through the contemplation and study made by believers, who treasure these things in their hearts (see Luke, 2:19, 51) through a penetrating understanding of the spiritual realities which they experience, and through the preaching of those who have received through Episcopal succession the sure gift of truth. For as the centuries succeed one another, the Church constantly moves forward toward the fullness of divine truth until the words of God reach their complete fulfillment in her [*in ipsa consummentur*].' *Dei Verbum* 8, http://www.

text did, nevertheless, attempt to acknowledge the many factors of development, including (i) the 'contemplation and study made by believers', (ii) the 'penetrating understanding of the spiritual realities' experienced by believers, and (iii) 'the preaching' of the bishops. According to historical theologian Mark Schoof, this order was theologically important, emphasizing the secondary, and ultimately pastoral, function of the hierarchy in the process of development.[47] In several post-conciliar ecclesial texts treating the subject of development, however, there have been attempts seemingly to invert this process, reorienting the focus, with respect to the dynamism of tradition, on the promulgation of doctrine by the Magisterium.[48] In addition, there has been what may be called 'creeping infallibility' attributed to a variety of church teachings, seeming to subdue, or prematurely curtail, any serious reflection and conscientious engagement with, for example, the church's ethical directives.[49] These post-conciliar 'developments' indicate that a potentially rigid view of tradition-development remains a risk in the contemporary context. They moreover signify the church's perpetual temptation to fall into the sin of idolatry regarding its own speech, and the complacency which invariably follows. It is important to remark, however, that a notable exception to this trend is the most recent document of the International Theological Commission, 'Sensus Fidei in the Life of the Church' (2014).[50] This section will now return to the views of Newman and Schillebeeckx, which anticipated these risks.

When dealing with a notion of doctrinal development, it is imperative to recall that Newman's *Essay* was a *theory* on the development of Christian doctrine and tradition, what he called 'an hypothesis to account for a difficulty'.[51] Newman was therefore clear that his theory was not in any way exhaustive of the historical evidence, but was in fact targeted at removing an impediment to belief.[52] Consequently, one can argue that any theory of doctrinal development, attempting

vatican.va/archive/hist_councils/ii_vatican_council/documents/vat-ii_const_19651118_dei-verbum_en.html (accessed 27 May 2015).

47. M. Schoof, *A Survey of Catholic Theology 1800–1970*, trans. N. D. Smith (Eugene, OR: Wipf & Stock Publishers, 1970), 251–8.

48. See the following three documents: *Mysterium Ecclesiae*, 2, 5; John Paul II, *Fides et Ratio* 11, 66, http://www.vatican.va/holy_father/john_paul_ii/encyclicals/documents/hf_jp-ii_enc_15101998_fides-et-ratio_en.html (accessed November 2013); ITC, 'Interpretation of Dogma' (1989), C.III.5–6.

49. Schillebeeckx, 'Discontinuities in Christian Dogmas', 102–9.

50. See ITC, '*Sensus Fidei* in the Life of the Church' (2014), nos. 39, 75, 82, 89, 93, 99, 116, http://www.vatican.va/roman_curia/congregations/cfaith/cti_documents/rc_cti_20140610_sensus-fidei_en.html (accessed 5 March 2015). This document attempts, among other things, to delineate the connections between the 'sense of faith' of the whole church, participation in the sacraments, and the development of tradition.

51. Newman, *Essay*, 30.

52. Ibid., 30–2. There is a parallel here to Schillebeeckx's abiding concern for a reasonable/intelligible (i.e. meaningful) faith.

to deal with the 'problem' and challenges of history, must remain provisional, that is, open itself to development, lest it become ideology. This does not mean that the synthesis achieved by Newman, refined by major theological figures of the twentieth century – Schillebeeckx among them – and largely accepted at the Second Vatican Council must be scrapped in favour of some completely new model;[53] rather, the theory must be 'open' to the insights of later contexts and their ever-shifting epistemological horizons.

An overly progressive view of doctrinal development, or one that focuses too intently on the propositional 'results' of the developmental process, and not enough on the ongoing factors that facilitate development, risks upholding the idea of a body of ecclesial speech that lies outside of history.[54] This is precisely the risk that Newman, who was intently aware of human finitude and the limits of ecclesial speech, tried to avoid, both in his *Essay* and in a letter written more than twenty years after the *Essay*'s original publication.[55] In this letter, Newman speaks of the deposit of faith as a 'divine philosophy' that is to be lived and practised by believers.[56] He describes doctrinal formulas and explicated tradition of the church as a *memoria technica*, that is, as a technical vocabulary, which functions as the material content for concrete engagement on the part of believers in the present.[57] Those who treat the content of tradition – that is, the fruits of past Christians who engaged their contexts and its questions – as 'the beginning and end of their study' Newman describes as 'formalists, pedants, bigots, and will be as little made philosophers by their verbal knowledge, as boys can swim because they have corks'.[58] The ongoing growth of the *memoria technica* over time does not lead to superior future Christians. The explicated tradition becomes, rather, an 'advantage' that may or may not be employed in presently living in relationship to the sacred philosophy of Christianity. In addition, Newman qualifies the gift of infallibility, as the temporary illumination of the pope or of a council 'so far forth and in such portion of it as the occasion requires'.[59] The implication here is that it is only through the serious engagement of a particularly trying situation that the 'operation of supernatural grace'[60] can occur in this manner. Finally, all the development that the church sees in the course of history leads to what the apostles were in themselves, or 'living, present treasur[ies] of the mind of the

53. See Schoof, *A Survey of Catholic Theology*, 40; G. H. McCarren, 'Are Newman's "Tests" or "Notes" of Genuine Doctrinal Development Useful Today?' *Newman Studies Journal* 1, no. 2 (Fall 2004): 51.

54. Schillebeeckx, *Church*, 211–12 [213]; Schillebeeckx, 'Discontinuities in Christian Dogmas', 98.

55. See note 36 above.

56. Newman, 'Letter to Flanagan, 1868', 158.

57. Ibid., 157.

58. Ibid.

59. Ibid., 159.

60. Ibid.

Spirit of Christ'.[61] Newman therefore articulated a view of development which upheld, on the one hand, the assistance of the Holy Spirit in keeping the church on track through history and towards its fulfilment in Christ. On the other hand, his conception placed central importance on the need for the ongoing practice of the faithful in response to *present* challenges and amid uncertainty. Newman was keenly aware of finitude and the tendency to fall complacent in glorifying past achievements, and he thus sought to enunciate a view in which previously explicated achievements were the materials for present action in pursuit of future hope. In other words, he knew that certain views of tradition fell into the errors, and sins, of idolatry and sloth. Newman's view, on the contrary, allows for notional progress regarding the explicit understanding of revelation on the part of the corporate *ecclesia*, but it does not fall into the errors of traditionalist fideism or blind adoption of present or utopian concepts; it is, rather, to be described as an eschatological view, and one which resists linear reduction.

Schillebeeckx, in his work treating development after the Second Vatican Council, demonstrates an acute awareness of finitude, subjectivity, sin, and suffering. Applied to the question of doctrinal development, he attempts to articulate a view that upholds the value of past forms of ecclesial speech while not falling into ideology regarding finite conceptions, even those conceptions uttered by the institutional church.[62] It is precisely because past doctrines are meaningful and have salvific relevance that believers are called to reinterpret them in the contemporary context, so that their meaning can continue to be experienced.[63] It is in the process of reinterpretation that the present context – or perhaps elements of the present – becomes part of the Christian tradition.[64] Historically, this is observable when identifying contextual elements that have influenced particular developments within the church, one example being the way that feudal political structures found expression in church organization and hierarchy.[65] Another example, this time from the realm of doctrine, includes the way in which the salvation of non-Christians was treated at the Council of Florence in the mid-fifteenth century and at the Second Vatican Council.[66] The former council declared that 'none of those who are outside of the Catholic Church, not only pagans … can become sharers of eternal life'.[67] The latter council included a dogmatic constitution and declaration which upheld, respectively, that salvation

---

61. Ibid., 158.

62. For example, see Schillebeeckx, 'Theological Interpretation of Faith in 1983', 64–7.

63. Ibid., 65.

64. Ibid., 64. 'Interpretation creates new tradition, handing down a living religious tradition to future generations with creative piety.'

65. Schillebeeckx, *Church*, 185 [187], 214–19 [216–20].

66. Schillebeeckx, 'Discontinuities in Christian Dogmas', 97–8.

67. Pope Eugene IV, 'Bull of Union with the Copts and the Ethiopians Cantate Domino, February 4, 1442', in Enchiridion symbolorum definitionum et declarationum de rebus fidei et morum; *Compendium of Creeds, Definitions, and Declarations on Matters of Faith*

is possible for those who 'do not know the Gospel of Christ or His Church' and that other religions possess 'rays' of truth which the Catholic Church does not reject.[68] Schillebeeckx affirms that, while these conciliar statements appear to be in contradiction with one another, they both concern truths that were expressed according to the particularities of their contexts.[69] Therefore, the study of the past, including the emergence of doctrines in particular contexts, is necessary for understanding them today.[70] This analysis leads Schillebeeckx to say that, while the language of past doctrines is not alterable, doctrines themselves are relative in light of the overall tradition,[71] which will only be fulfilled with the eschaton.

When doctrine is treated ideologically, and the 'dialectical relation between past, present and to be accomplished future'[72] – referring to the hermeneutical task of theology in service to the gospel – is restricted, theory becomes ideology and is divorced from praxis. Schillebeeckx's view is of prime importance in our contemporary context, which features even greater consciousness of historicity and particularity, meaning that a theory which is unable to adapt to and integrate the insights from the praxis and experience of believers will be recognized for what it is (i.e. ideology) and cease to be meaningful.[73] Because the subject of development ultimately concerns the dynamism of tradition, a great deal is at stake. In accordance with what was said of Newman above, Schillebeeckx affirms that

and Morals, 43rd edn, H. Denzinger and P. Hünermann (eds) (San Francisco, CA: Ignatius Press, 2010), 348–9 (no. 1351).

68. See, respectively, *Lumen Gentium* 16 and *Nostra Aetate* 2, in Austin Flannery (ed.), *Vatican Council II: Constitutions, Decrees, Declarations, The Basic Sixteen Documents* (Northport, NY: Costello Publishing, 1996).

69. Schillebeeckx, 'Discontinuities in Christian Dogmas', 98–9. To be clear, Schillebeeckx affirms that the proclamations of these councils should not be set in direct opposition to one another because the objects of the councils differed, as did their contexts and horizons. Their promulgations, then, should be seen as 'perspectival' judgements. According to this logic, one might say that the teachings of the earlier council were saying something primarily about the church and salvation, while those of the latter council were saying something primarily about non-Christians.

70. Schillebeeckx, 'Discontinuities in Christian Dogmas', 101. 'Personally I would venture to say that, no matter how true dogmas may be in the historical context in which they were formulated, they may become totally irrelevant in another historical context. A dogmatic pronouncement is only valid in terms of the question it is supposed to answer and the language game in which the questions and answers are articulated.' See also E. Schillebeeckx, 'Theological Interpretations of Faith in 1983', *Essays*, 58–9.

71. Schillebeeckx, 'Theological Interpretation of Faith in 1983', 61–4 (esp. 63). Cf. K. Rahner, 'The Development of Dogma', *Theological Investigations*, vol. I, trans. C. Ernst (London: Darton, Longman and Todd, 1965), 41–7.

72. Schillebeeckx, 'Theological Interpretation of Faith in 1983', 55.

73. Ibid., 59–62. The idea of 'meaning' in the past may have been taken for granted. Cf. Nichols, *From Newman to Congar*, 269.

one must not forget that, together with the affirmations of the *Ecclesia indefectibilis* and *Ecclesia sancta*, is also the affirmation of the *Ecclesia semper purificanda* (the church which must always purify itself).[74] He writes, 'The indefectibility of the church is therefore not a static, as it were fixed, essentialist property of the church which could by-pass the constantly precarious, existential faith of the church in obedience to God's promise. The promised indefectibility becomes effective only in the faith, trust and constant self-correction of the church.'[75]

Conclusion

In his work *Modern Social Imaginaries*, Charles Taylor discusses the way(s) in which theories of social order move over time, from the notional realm of the elite into societies at large, transforming the 'social imaginary', which he defines as follows: 'the ways people imagine their social existence, how they fit together with others, how things go on between them and their fellows, the expectations that are normally met, and the deeper normative notions and images that underlie these expectations'.[76] In this work, he pays particular attention to the rise of the dominant social imaginary in the West,[77] which was the fruit of Enlightenment and democratic revolutionary principles. Taylor is keen to note, however, that imaginaries are not static aspects of the social consciousness, moving only from theory into reality; rather, they develop and are influenced by social practices.[78] In other words, imaginaries are dynamic, constantly developing. Our current Western imaginary does not provide an account of, or adequately factor in, the ideas of human finitude and sin relative to an infinite Creator, and I suspect that this is where Christianity can have the greatest impact for developing the modern social imaginary.[79]

74. Schillebeeckx, *Church*, 193–5 [195–6].

75. Ibid., 194–5 [196]. It is apropos here to note one of Newman's oft-quoted statements from *Essay* regarding the nature of 'great' ideas: 'In a higher world it is otherwise, but here below to live is to change, and to be perfect is to have changed often.' Newman, *Essay*, 40.

76. Taylor, *Modern Social Imaginaries*, 23. Regarding this idea, Taylor writes, 'I adopt the term imaginary (i) because my focus is on the way ordinary people "imagine" their social surroundings, and this is often not expressed in theoretical terms, but is carried in images, stories, and legends. It is also the case that (ii) theory is often the possession of a small minority, whereas what is interesting in the social imaginary is that it is shared by large groups of people, if not the whole society'. Taylor, *Modern Social Imaginaries*, 23.

77. See chapter 1 in Taylor, 'The Modern Moral Order', *Modern Social Imaginaries*, 3–22.

78. Taylor, *Modern Social Imaginaries*, 29–30.

79. Cf. Taylor, 'A Catholic Modernity?', in *A Catholic Modernity? Charles Taylor's Marianist Award Lecture*, J. L. Heft (ed.) (Oxford: Oxford University Press, 1999), 13–37 (esp. 35).

In the first two sections of this chapter, I attempted to show how Newman and Schillebeeckx articulated 'theological' solutions to the problem of development that were highly conscious of finitude and sin; this is remarkable given the modern, and abiding, temptation to try and remove ecclesial speech from the realm of history. For followers of Christianity, human finitude and sin are much more than notions that help them to make sense of the world in theory, or that help to support a house of metaphysical and dogmatic cards, so to speak. They are, rather, fundamentally important *experiences* that accompany the life of faith, which is experienced eschatologically: present action nourished by connection to past revelation and tradition in the light of future hope and communion with God. Human finitude, frailty, and sinfulness are not marks of *abject* failure, but rather are experienced facts, and they do not excuse action and responsibility in the present.[80] On the contrary, the experience of finitude implies the ongoing possibility of change and development, while the experience of sin (i.e. *hamartia*) indicates the possibility of changing for the better, of reorienting one's self on actual good when one has missed the mark (i.e. to try again). If anything, responsibility is *increased* in this view.

The world is currently facing significant challenges that may be critical for the existence of our species, challenges of the ecological, political, and religious varieties (to name just a few types). In the West, there seem to be several standpoints with which to treat such challenges: (i) false nostalgia for the selectively remembered past; (ii) paralyzing cynicism caught in the present; or (iii) blind faith in technological progress that will deliver a future image.[81] These standpoints fail precisely because they do not adequately treat human persons as finite, eschatological beings caught up in past and future traditions.

Christianity, therefore, has much to offer the contemporary Western context, specifically regarding how collective action is possible amid sometimes devastating failure: through a living tradition, an honest anthropology, and a humble relationship with the living, infinite God. The Catholic Church has something particularly important to say here, in the light of its dynamic view of, and emphasis on, tradition, as well as its conviction that sin has not utterly undermined human agency. Yet, it must be wary of idolizing its own speech, or allowing its understanding of tradition to recede from the particular, potentially to the point of meaninglessness. One way in which it can avoid this pitfall, and thus speak meaningfully to the present context – including its own members –

---

80. See Schillebeeckx, *Church*, 75–8 [77-80].

81. This third standpoint has been discussed in the vein of 'progress traps' in a recent documentary [i.e. the BBC documentary, *Surviving Progress* (2011)]. A progress trap is something into which a person 'falls' when he or she unflinchingly puts faith in technological progress, as that which will save humanity, without considering how technological progress has played a part in the current dilemmas that now face humanity. To put it simply, a progress trap involves belief in technology without an adequate consideration of the manner in which humans tend to wield it.

about the gospel, is by beginning with the experiences of finitude and sin over any metaphysical account of them. The former are everywhere present and can act as a spur towards understanding traditional accounts of the human condition, on the one hand, and individual and collective action even in their presence, on the other. What makes the contributions of Newman and Schillebeeckx regarding development so enduring, and meaningful, is that their conceptions of the dynamism of tradition depart from and *do not forget* experience, thus fading into abstraction. Experience, then, can lead to the ongoing engagement with traditions that speak meaningfully to the present. When this occurs, creative participation on the part of the whole church provides for the development, continuity, and transmission of those traditions. The West would do well to recall its own rich intellectual history in this regard.

Bibliography

Aquinas, T., *Quattuor Sententiarum P. Lombardi.*

Aquinas, T., *Quodlibeta Disputata.*

Aquinas, T., *Summa Theologiae.* Complete English edn (Westminster, MD: Christian Classics, 1981).

Aquinas, T., *Super Evangelium secundum Johannem.*

Chapman, M., 'Temporal and Spatial Catholicism: Tensions in Historicism in the Oxford Movement', in *The Shaping of Tradition: Context and Normativity*, C. Dickinson (ed.) (Leuven: Peeters, 2013).

Cimorelli, C., 'The Possible Advantage of Doctrinal Growth: Revisiting Newman's Understanding of Development', *Newman Studies Journal* 11, no. 1 (Spring 2014): 32–44.

Cimorelli, C., and D. Minch, 'Views of Doctrine: Historical Consciousness, Asymptotic Notional Clarity, and the Challenge of Hermeneutics as Ontology', *Louvain Studies* 37, no. 4 (2013): 327–63.

Congar, Y., *Tradition and Traditions: An Historical and a Theological Essay*, trans. M. Naseby and T. Rainborough (London: Burns & Oates, 1966).

Dulles, A., *Magisterium: Teacher and Guardian of the Faith* (Naples, FL: Sapientia Press, 2007).

Flannery, A. (ed.), *Vatican Council II: Constitutions, Decrees, Declarations, the Basic Sixteen Documents* (Northport, NY: Costello Publishing, 1996).

Holladay, W. L. (ed.), 'אׁמֶת', in *A Concise Hebrew and Aramaic Lexicon of the Old Testament* (Leiden: Brill, 2000), 100.

McCarren, G. H., 'Are Newman's "Tests" or "Notes" of Genuine Doctrinal Development Useful Today?' *Newman Studies Journal* 1, no. 2 (Fall 2004): 48–61.

Newman, J. H., *An Essay on the Development of Christian Doctrine* (London: James Toovey, 1845).

Newman, J. H., *An Essay on the Development of Christian Doctrine* (London: Longmans, Green, and Co., 1909).

Newman, J. H., 'Letter to Flanagan, 1868', in *The Theological Papers of John Henry Newman on Biblical Inspiration and Infallibility*, J. D. Holmes (ed.) (Oxford: Clarendon, 1979).

Nichols, A., *From Newman to Congar: The Idea of Doctrinal Development from the Victorians to the Second Vatican Council* (Edinburgh: T&T Clark, 1990).

Pope Eugene IV, 'Bull of Union with the Copts and the Ethiopians Cantate Domino, February 4, 1442', in Enchiridion symbolorum definitionum et declarationum de rebus fidei et morum; *Compendium of Creeds, Definitions, and Declarations on Matters of Faith and Morals*, 43rd edn, H. Denzinger and P. Hünermann (eds) (San Francisco, CA: Ignatius Press, 2010), 348–9 (no. 1351).

Prickett, S., *Romanticism and Religion: The Tradition of Coleridge and Wordsworth in the Victorian Church* (London: Cambridge University Press, 1976).

Prickett, S., *European Romanticism: A Reader* (London: Continuum, 2010).

Schillebeeckx, E., 'Dogma-ontwikkeling', in *Theologisch Woordenboek* I, H. Brink, O.P. (ed.) (Roermond en Maaseik: J. J. Romen & Zonen, 1952), 1087–107.

Schillebeeckx, E., 'De ontwikkeling van het Apostolisch Geloof tot Kerkelijk Dogma', in *Openbaring en Theologie* (Bilthoven: H. Nelissen, 1964), 50–67.

Schillebeeckx, E., *Church. The Human Story of God*, trans. J. Bowden, *CW*, vol. 10 (London: Bloomsbury, 2014).

Schillebeeckx, E., *Essays: Ongoing Theological Quests*, trans. E. Fitzgerald and P. Tomlinson, *CW*, vol. 11 (London: Bloomsbury, 2014).

Schillebeeckx, E., *Revelation and Theology*, trans. N. D. Smith, *CW*, vol. 2 (London: Bloomsbury, 2014).

Schoof, M., *A Survey of Catholic Theology 1800–1970*, trans. N. D. Smith (Eugene, OR: Wipf & Stock Publishers, 1970).

Sullivan, F. A., *Magisterium: Teaching Authority in the Catholic Church* (Eugene, OR: Wipf & Stock Publishers, 2002).

Taylor, C., 'A Catholic Modernity?', in *A Catholic Modernity? Charles Taylor's Marianist Award Lecture*, J. L. Heft (ed.) (Oxford: Oxford University Press, 1999), 13–37 (esp. 35).

Taylor, C., *Modern Social Imaginaries* (Durham and London: Duke University Press, 2004).

Chapter 12

EXPERIENCE AND CRITICAL REFLECTION IN RELIGION: SCHILLEBEECKX'S THEOLOGY AND EVOLUTIONARY STUDIES OF RELIGION

Tom Uytterhoeven

Evolutionary studies of religion, which we define in this chapter as the scientific study of religion that regards religion as a product of evolutionary processes, is one of the youngest branches of religious studies.[1] Although evolutionary studies of religion assume that the meaning of religion should be studied on the intuitive level of consciousness, Schillebeeckx's analysis of religious experience demonstrates that we need to take reflective thinking into account if we truly want to understand religion. In general, evolutionary studies of religion discard reflective thinking as irrelevant to the study of religion, assuming that unconscious evolutionary processes determine the meaning of religious aspects of human life. According to Edward Schillebeeckx, however, religious experience, like all human experience, is inherently interpreted experience. Moreover, Schillebeeckx argues that reflective thinking is one of the main driving factors in the development of a religious tradition. When we connect these different perspectives, bringing evolutionary studies of religion, with its deep historical perspective on culture, into dialogue with theology, with its focus on critical interpretation, we learn to see religious meaning as the result of a combined process of discovery and construction, on both the conscious and unconscious levels.

This chapter will first discuss evolutionary studies of religion, describing how this branch of religious studies approaches its subject and pointing to an implied bias of this approach. Second, we will address this bias on the basis of Schillebeeckx's theological analysis of the relation between experience and interpretation. Third, we will argue that Schillebeeckx's views, of the relation between theology and the natural sciences, as well as the role of interpretation in religious experience, can help theology to move beyond tacit, or even explicit, conflict with evolutionary studies of religion. In conclusion, this chapter will advocate for a theology that

---

1. For a recent introduction, see R. Trigg and J. Barrett (eds), *The Roots of Religion: Exploring the Cognitive Science of Religion* (Farnham: Ashgate, 2014).

acknowledges the evolutionary origins of religion without, however, endorsing a reduction of religious meaning to evolutionary processes.

1. Evolutionary Studies of Religion and Retro-Reductionism

An example of evolutionary studies of religion can be found in the work of the anthropologist Pascal Boyer, who integrates cultural anthropology with cognitive science in his study of religion.[2] He proposes that religion is the result of a process of cultural evolution, ultimately depending on the evolved mental abilities of human beings. Natural selection favours individuals that react promptly to possible threats. For example, those who assumed that weeds were moving because a lion tried to hide behind them survived and procreated more successfully. Those, however, who thought it was just the wind perhaps did not survive to regret their mistake. This helps to explain why we, the descendants of generations of hen-hearted individuals still startle when we glimpse a sudden movement from the corner of our eyes; although, more often than not, it is just the wind, or perhaps a cat. Boyer theorizes that religious beliefs are based on the illusory, but natural and inborn, tendency to posit agency where there is none, leading humans to deduce from this tendency the existence of supernatural agents where in fact only natural causes are at work. Unconscious cultural processes, analogous to the processes of biological mutation and natural selection, have formed these 'raw materials' into the religions that we now know.[3] The hidden assumption behind these conclusions is that the evolutionary origin of religions determines the current nature of religions, a position that we will call 'retro-reductionism'.[4]

2. P. Boyer, *Religion Explained: The Human Instincts That Fashion Gods, Spirits and Ancestors* [London: Vintage (Random House), 2001]. New atheists Richard Dawkins and Daniel Dennett both refer to Boyer's work in their criticisms of religion as an irrational phenomenon that should be replaced by rational alternatives. R. Dawkins, *The God Delusion* (London: Black Swan, 2007); first published as ibidem (London: Bantam Press, 2006); D. C. Dennett, *Breaking the Spell: Religion as a Natural Phenomenon* (New York: Viking, 2006).

3. For more detailed accounts, see the following: W. Burkert, *Creation of the Sacred: Tracks of Biology in Early Religions* (Cambridge, MA: Harvard University Press, 1996); J. R. Feierman (ed.), *The Biology of Religious Behavior: The Evolutionary Origins of Faith and Religion* (Santa Barbara, CA, et al.: Praeger, 2009); R. Hinde, *Why Gods Persist: A Scientific Approach to Religion* (New York: Routledge, 1999); L. A. Kirkpatrick, *Attachment, Evolution, and the Psychology of Religion* (New York: The Guilford Press, 2005); J. Schloss and M. Murray (eds), *The Believing Primate: Scientific, Philosophical, and Theological Reflections on the Origin of Religion* (Oxford: Oxford University Press, 2009).

4. J. F. Haught develops a similar notion of science as preoccupied with the past, a notion which he refers to as 'the archeological vision'. J. F. Haught, *Resting on the Future: Catholic Theology for an Unfinished Universe* (New York: Bloomsbury, 2015), 23.

Retro-reductionism works in three steps. In the first step, a distinction is made between intuitive, unreflective aspects of religion and conscious, reflective ones, with only the former deemed important for learning about the nature of religion. We will discuss this step further below. Second, an evolutionary explanation for these intuitive religious beliefs and/or religious behaviours is proposed. Such an explanation more often than not turns to functionalism, that is, to the question of who or what benefits from having these beliefs or by performing this behaviour.[5] Third, evolutionary studies of religion, even when they purport to be neutral about the truth of religion, suggest that religion (a religious belief, a religious ritual, a religious narrative) does not mean what theology says that it means, but rather what science says that it means.[6]

I will focus here on the first step of retro-reductionism. Cognitive scientist Justin Barrett offers a good example when he makes a distinction between 'non-reflective' and 'reflective' beliefs. While reflective beliefs are the result of conscious deliberation, non-reflective beliefs 'are those that come automatically, require no careful rumination, and seem to arise instantaneously and sometimes even "against better judgment"'.[7] These non-reflective beliefs form the backbone of religious beliefs, determining which reflective beliefs are possible, and replacing these when there is too much pressure to allow for reflection.[8] Another example can be found in A. Norenzayan's monograph, *Big Gods*.[9] Norenzayan explicitly rejects the possibility of reflective theists in his discussion of different types of atheism.[10] He argues that 'analytic atheism' is the result of reflective thinking. It is telling that he does not consider the possibility of 'analytic theism' (i.e. theism as a result of reflective thinking), for example, through theology. Instead, he operates with the following distinction: intuitive thinkers are theists, while analytic thinkers are atheists, adding to this that analytic thinking encourages disbelief, while intuitive thinking encourages religious belief. Moreover, Norenzayan dismisses theological concepts as 'unconventional'.[11] These two examples show how retro-reductionism excludes reflective thinking from religion, allowing it at best a marginal role in the development of religious traditions. However, as we shall see in the following section, this implies that evolutionary studies of religion, when they accept the

---

5. For an overview of different approaches in evolutionary studies of culture, see K. N. Laland and G. R. Brown, *Sense & Nonsense: Evolutionary Perspectives on Human Behaviour*, 2nd edn (Oxford: Oxford University Press, 2011). For a discussion of functionalism in biology, see Hinde, *Why Gods Persist,* 107.

6. Cf., for example, Burkert, *Creation of the Sacred.*

7. J. L. Barrett, *Why Would Anyone Believe in God?* (Walnut Creek: Altamira Press, 2004), 2.

8. Barrett, *Why Would Anyone Believe in God?*, 16–17.

9. A. Norenzayan, *Big Gods: How Religion Transformed Cooperation and Conflict* (Princeton: Princeton University Press, 2013).

10. Norenzayan, *Big Gods*, 181–3.

11. Norenzayan, *Big Gods*, 183.

premise that reflective thinking is irrelevant to understanding religion, fail to understand the complex reality of their very object of study. Moreover, this implies that retro-reductionism is a hindrance to any potential dialogue between theology and evolutionary studies of religion.

2. The Intertwinement of Experience and Interpretation

Although an exhaustive analysis of Schillebeeckx's work on experience is beyond the scope of this chapter, the following discussion will nevertheless allow us to identify the problem which retro-reductionism presents, not only for evolutionary studies of religion, but also for the possibility of a constructive conversation between evolutionary studies of religion and theology. This problem is, namely, that religious experience and reflective thinking cannot, as retro-reductionism assumes, be conceived separately. Instead, they are deeply intertwined.

To interpret, or identify, a given experience as religious had become nearly self-evident during Edward Schillebeeckx's lifetime;[12] his work, however, sought to look at the relationship between experience and interpretation at a more fundamental level. Schillebeeckx argues that because an experience always generates the need for its interpretation, interpretation (i.e. addressing this need or lack) is actually an inherent part of experience itself. In other words, interpretation is not something added to experience, but rather an inner moment of experience.[13] While this is the case for individual, instantaneous experiences as such, it applies even more to a tradition of experiences, in particular to the Christian tradition, which depends on a history of interpretations, or on an interpreted history. This is what Schillebeeckx calls an 'experience with experiences'.[14] Schillebeeckx describes how humans are cultural creatures, and deduces from this notion that religious

12. See E. Schillebeeckx, 'Het kritische statuut van de theologie', De toekomst van de kerk: Verslag van het wereldcongres 'Concilium' te Brussel 12–17 September 1970 (Amersfoort, Bussum: De Horstink/Paul Brand, 1960), 60; E. Schillebeeckx, 'Secularization and Christian Belief in God', *GFM*, *CW*, vol. 3 (London: Bloomsbury T&T Clark, 2014), 40 [66]; E. Schillebeeckx, *Tussentijds verhaal over twee Jezusboeken, Bloemendaal* (Baarn: Nelissen, 1978), 15 [Schillebeeckx, E., *Interim Report on the Books Jesus and Christ*, trans. J. Bowden, *CW*, vol. 8 (London: Bloomsbury T&T Clark, 2014)]. See also E. Schillebeeckx, *Mensen als verhaal van God* (Baarn: Nelissen, 1989), 24–6 [Schillebeeckx, E., *Church: The Human Story of God*, trans. J. Bowden, *CW*, vol. 10 (London: Bloomsbury T&T Clark, 2014)], where he discusses how humanity's 'veto against the world as it is' can lead to both an agnostic and religious 'open yes'.

13. Schillebeeckx, *Tussentijds verhaal*, 21. Schillebeeckx goes on to identify interpretation with the construction of theories. Schillebeeckx, *Tussentijds verhaal*, 24–6.

14. Schillebeeckx, *Tussentijds verhaal*, 16–17; 44. The expression 'experience with experiences', includes the aspect of interpretation and, therefore, could be read as an intimate intertwinement of interpretation and experience.

faith is always lived within a cultural context, modelled on a cultural context, and assimilated through a given cultural context.[15] He argues that the constant tension between inherited tradition and the present cultural context, as well as the desire to seek a new balance between these two poles, both drive the course of Christian tradition through history.[16] This implies that interpretation is also intrinsically part of revelation[17] and of salvation history.[18] Schillebeeckx argues that human experiences are always interpreted experiences ('geïnterpreteerde ervaringen'), some of which can be identified as religious experiences through the support of religious traditions, which, in turn, are the effect of earlier interpretations of experiences. It is important to note that Schillebeeckx explicitly rejects the notion of religious experience (revelatory experience) as being a product of the mind;[19] as we have seen before, this is the position upheld by Pascal Boyer. Moreover, we argued that retro-reductionism leads evolutionary studies of religion to start from the assumption that our interpretations of experiences, which lead to the emergence of religious beliefs, lack rationality because they are intuitive, inborn interpretations that even overrule rational reflection and interpretation. This view implies that humans are biological beings, that their communication with the natural world is determined by processes of mutation and natural selection, and that their rationality is a hard-won faculty against their inborn tendencies to *project* meaning onto nature.

The crux of the matter seems to be Schillebeeckx's insistence that experience is never authoritative, meaningful experience – that is, the kind of experience that, from a scientist's perspective, could be the evolutionary origin of a religion; or, the kind of experience that, from a theologian's perspective, could be revelatory – if it is not intrinsically interpreted experience, which means that religious experience as such includes a rational, critical element.[20] Schillebeeckx pictures humans as cultural beings, communicating with (learning from, acting upon) the natural world through the prevalent culture. This suggests not only that there are limits to what human beings can think and do – we can never step outside of culture to reach the world in a 'pure' manner (i.e. there is no 'what-you-see-is-what-you-get' for our species) – but, foremost, that humanity has possibilities which no other species on Earth has, including the ability to *discover* meaning in nature.

15. Schillebeeckx, *Mensen als verhaal van God*, 52; 36.

16. Schillebeeckx, *Mensen als verhaal van God*, 52–63.

17. Schillebeeckx, *Tussentijds verhaal*, 19.

18. Schillebeeckx, *Mensen als verhaal van God*, 26.

19. Schillebeeckx, *Mensen als verhaal van God*, 31; 46–7. Schillebeeckx explicitly argues for the God-given character of revelation. See also E. Schillebeeckx, 'Towards a Catholic Use of Hermeneutics', *GFM*, 28 [42], in which he explains the interplay between God and the human creature in discerning revelation.

20. See Schillebeeckx, *Mensen als verhaal van God*, 40. Moreover, according to Schillebeeckx, the complex of experience and interpretation does not only affect the individual, but also the communal level of understanding.

We have established that, according to Schillebeeckx, interpretation and critical reflection are inherent to religious experience. From this view, and from a theological perspective, we deduced that religious meaning is discovered, rather than, as a retro-reductionist position implies, constructed. We will now turn to the question of whether it is possible to bridge the gap between these two positions.

3. The Relation between Science and Theology

In order to analyse the relation between theology and the natural sciences, we now turn to Ian Barbour's influential work on the models which represent different approaches to this relationship.[21] We shall see that Schillebeeckx advocates for a qualified dialogue between theology and science, a view which corresponds with one of the possibilities articulated by Barbour.

Overall, Barbour identifies four possible approaches to, or conceptions of, the relation between religion and science: (a) conflict, (b) independence, (c) dialogue, and (d) integration. The model of conflict assumes that religion and science are competing fields of knowledge. It is important to note Barbour's conclusion here: when we talk about conflict between religion and science, we are inaccurate, since the conflict actually occurs between religion (or theism, in Barbour's terminology) and 'a metaphysics of materialism'.[22] Barbour sees the model of independence as a strategy to avoid conflict between religion and science by stressing their differences, on both the methodological and epistemological levels. He evaluates the independence model as insufficient because it would undermine the possibility of actual dialogue between and religion science.[23] The model of dialogue entails actively pursuing the possibilities for interaction between religion and science. Similar to the independence model, the model of dialogue aims at avoiding conflict, but nevertheless sees a closer relationship between religion and science. In brief, one could argue that dialogue forms a middle ground between independence, discussed above, and integration. In the model of integration, the lines demarcating science and theology are less clear than in the case of dialogue, leading to potentially more drastic changes within theology.[24] Barbour argues that, in the case of religion and science, we must find a balance between unity and diversity, while avoiding both of the following extremes: a complete disconnection of science and religion, and an artificial fusion of the two fields. Although we cannot hope to develop a complete proposal on how to achieve such a balance,

---

21. I. G. Barbour, *Religion and Science. Historical and Contemporary Issues. A Revised and Expanded Edition of Religion in an Age of Science* (London: SCM Press Ltd, 1998). 'Science' is used here as shorthand for 'the natural sciences'.

22. Barbour, *Religion and Science*, 82.

23. Ibid., 89.

24. Ibid., 98

there are some interesting suggestions to be found in Schillebeeckx's work, as we shall see below.

In a lecture delivered by Schillebeeckx at the Concilium conference in 1970 in Brussels,[25] he points to the reduction of our concept of 'science' to 'the natural sciences' following the rise of positivism.[26] He first argues that the question of whether or not theology is a science is foremost a linguistic one, and thus only of secondary importance.[27] But his argument goes further than that: he describes theology as part of the sciences (i.e. a 'deel-wetenschap'), on equal footing with all other branches of science.[28] Schillebeeckx sees a need for interaction between all of these branches, not only to maintain the scientific nature of theology, but, moreover, to enable theology to perform its task.[29] As a 'science of faith', theology must offer 'research and reflection in service of the actualizing continuity of the history of Christian interpretation, which is actively pursued within and through the "communities of God"'.[30] When it comes to theology's role in this interaction, Schillebeeckx argues that theology needs to integrate the insights offered by the other sciences without, however, these other sciences ever becoming normative for theology's conclusions, or limitative for what theology can study.[31]

According to Barbour's fourfold typology, Schillebeeckx could be identified as a proponent of dialogue between theology and science, with the caveat that – at least in his presentation at the Concilium conference – he does not see theology and science as opposites. What Schillebeeckx suggests in this article is not a dialogue between theology, as something other than science, and science, as something other than theology. He suggests, rather, a dialogue between sciences, theology

25. E. Schillebeeckx, *Het kritisch statuut van de theologie*, 56–64.

26. The same argument can be found in E. Schillebeeckx, *God and Man* (London; Sidney: Sheed and Ward, 1969), 120.

27. Schillebeeckx, *Het kritisch statuut van de theologie*, 57.

28. However, when he discusses the sources of theology, Schillebeeckx distinguishes between theology and other humanities, on the one hand, and between theology and the natural sciences, on the other. Schillebeeckx, *Tussentijds verhaal*, 13. Later, Schillebeeckx criticizes the presumed objectivity of the sciences and questions their dominance in Western culture. See Schillebeeckx, *Mensen als Verhaal van God*, 22–3.

29. Schillebeeckx, *Het kritisch statuut van de theologie*, 58; 61. Schillebeeckx stresses that theology must prevent the opening of any gap between people's faith and their daily experience in the secular world.

30. Schillebeeckx, *Het kritisch statuut van de theologie*, 62.

31. Ibid. Schillebeeckx's explanation of the integration of biblical exegesis in systematic theology illustrates his understanding of the relation between theology and other sciences. Schillebeeckx, *Tussentijds verhaal*, 10. Sciences can never question the theological presupposition that God's saving activity is discernible in history. However, they can examine the cultural influences in human language about this saving activity. Schillebeeckx, *Tussentijds verhaal*, 103.

being one of them.[32] Although Schillebeeckx did not develop this suggestion systematically,[33] it could well be fruitful in two important respects. First, scientists could gain new perspectives on religion, or be pointed towards possible flaws in their research, if they acknowledge that theology has a unique contribution to the study of religion (a contribution that has become clear in the discussion of 'experience' above).[34] Second, and with respect to the scientific nature of theology – particular as it is and certainly differing from the natural sciences – Schillebeeckx's suggestion could convince Christians that the encounter between theology and science, or, moreover, between Christian religion and science, need not lead to a 'watering down' or 'hollowing out' of Christian religious beliefs. Schillebeeckx was very much aware of this fear, which he intended to prove unjustified by his use of historical sciences.[35] He did not mean to imply that theology has to confirm its methodological assumptions, for instance, regarding naturalism, to those of the natural sciences, or that theology should limit itself, as religious studies does, to talk *about* religion rather than *from within* religion.[36]

As stated above, a formal discussion of the distinctions between theology and scientific studies of religion – that is, delineating the delicate balance between, on the one hand, the unity of theology and science and, on the other hand, their diversity – is beyond the scope of this chapter. Nevertheless, we have learned from Schillebeeckx that establishing such a balance can be seen as inherent to theology, and even indispensable for a theology that puts itself in service of the continuous actualization of God's revelation. In order to develop this idea further, we now turn to Lutheran theologian Philip Hefner's work on the relation between theology and science.

4. Building a World View

When endeavouring to build bridges between theology and science, the first element that needs consideration is the purpose of such bridge-building. What do we want to accomplish by bringing theology and science together? In this regard, it is important to note that Schillebeeckx links experience and science.[37] In other

32. This does not imply that theology should, in turn, become normative or limitative to science. For a related discussion about religion influencing science, see M. Stenmark, *How to Relate Science and Religion: A Multidimensional Model* (Grand Rapids, MI: B. Eerdmans Publishing Co., 2004), 171–249. Stenmark argues that religion should be allowed to influence science with regard to formulating research questions, the methodology in the search for an answer, and the application of the results in society. However, religion should never be used to verify or falsify scientific results.

33. Schillebeeckx, *Het kritisch statuut van de theologie*, 62, n. 28.

34. Ibid., 63.

35. Schillebeeckx, *Tussentijds verhaal*, 38.

36. See Schillebeeckx, *Het kritisch statuut van de theologie*, 64.

37. Ibid., 60.

words, he sees science as part of the whole range of human experience, to which religious experiences also belong.[38] For Schillebeeckx, the interaction between theology and science is about grounding theology in reality, taking as much of human experience as possible into account because it is one of the two sources of theology; these are, namely, the Christian tradition and the variety of present human experience.[39] It is important to note that Schillebeeckx regards the latter as a constitutive element of the former. Lutheran theologian Philip Hefner, who has produced extensive theological reflections on the relation between religion and science,[40] in particular between religion and evolutionary theory,[41] assumes a similar position.[42] His analysis shows quite a few parallels with Schillebeeckx's, and, moreover, offers us an answer to our question about the intention of bridge-building.

Hefner argues that the significance of the interaction between science and theology lies in the meaning that emerges from it. This meaning is both expressed and recreated through language.[43] Hefner sees theology's role as interpretive. Science delivers the raw material upon which theology reflects in order to discover meaning.[44] Meaning and explanation are related concepts, according to Hefner. Explanation has to do with ordering experiences, and it functions as a filter when we search for meaning.[45] Hefner stresses the importance of science for explaining our world: 'Science explains the world more fully and more adequately than any other approach yet devised.'[46] He posits three criteria for meaning, in the form of questions. Is it coherent? Does it reveal what is valuable to me? Does it sustain me as a person? But meaning is not just the result of 'applying the tests'.[47] Hefner argues, based on Whitehead and James, that meaning cannot be drawn out of nature directly, but rather is mediated to us through thought and language.

---

38. Schillebeeckx, *Mensen als verhaal van God*, 44. This position is intellectually more honest than that of Dawkins and Dennett, who both argue for an evolutionary origin of human culture as a whole, but then single out religion as the one element of culture that is inherently irrational.

39. E. Schillebeeckx, *Tussentijds verhaal*, 13.

40. See, for example, his many editorials for *Zygon: Journal of Religion & Science*, for which he was the editor between 1989 and 2009.

41. P. Hefner, *The Human Factor: Evolution, Culture, and Religion. Theology and the Sciences* (Minneapolis, MN: Fortress Press, 1993).

42. P. Hefner, 'Theology and Science: Engaging the Richness of Experience', *Theology and Science* 1, no. 1 (2003): 95–111.

43. Hefner, 'Engaging the Richness of Experience', 95.

44. Hefner, 'Engaging the Richness of Experience', 95. Schillebeeckx employs a parallel view in his reflection on the role of interpretation in salvation history and on the structure of revelation. Schillebeeckx, *Mensen als verhaal van God*, 26, 28.

45. Hefner, 'Engaging the Richness of Experience', 96.

46. Ibid.

47. Ibid., 97.

The mediated character of meaning leads Hefner to three axioms, the first of which is described in the following manner:

> We may call this the Whiteheadian axiom, and it is critical for our understanding of how we approach nature: nature is not a given entity outside of ourselves that causes our experience, and our experience of nature is not an experience of the effects of those causes. On the basis of this axiom, Whitehead himself asserts, rather, 'nature is known to us in our experience as a complex of passing events'.[48]

This axiom implies the inability of human thought and language (or thought-and-language, as Hefner would write, stressing the intertwinement of both elements of this dyad) to express adequately the richness of experience.[49] Although there is no room to expound this point further in our investigation, it is interesting to note the parallels between Hefner's position in this regard and Schillebeeckx's view of the human being as a cultural being, which we have discussed above. A second axiom that Hefner posits is based on Ricoeur's work on metaphor, which he combines with the (explicit) proposition that language can never give adequate expression to the richness of experience. There is always a surplus of experience, and hence a surplus of meaning:

> From Ricoeur we may draw a second axiom, alongside that of Whitehead: Our ongoing transaction with nature is marked by an effort to stretch, relocate, the significations of our ideas and the language that articulates them. We are under a constant pressure to discover new significations and new ideas else we can neither understand our own experience of nature nor communicate it and reflect on its meaning.[50]

At this point, Hefner brings in the importance of our cultural inheritance. We inherit ideas, concepts, and expressions of experiences that our ancestors have had.[51] This inheritance itself bequeaths new meaning.[52] Another way of saying this is that this inheritance is part of the way we experience nature. Again, it is tempting to note a resemblance with Schillebeeckx's work, in this case with his views of the development of tradition. Metaphor is the nature of the process by which meaning is created, Hefner argues, because it allows for (inherited) meanings to shift and change, or even forces them to do so. This is Hefner's third axiom: 'New meanings merge in our understanding of nature when we forcibly equate concepts that exist in two different fields of meaning, thereby distorting our existing meanings so as to engender new worlds of meaning.'[53]

48. Ibid., 98.
49. Ibid.
50. Ibid., 99.
51. Ibid., 102.
52. Ibid., 103.
53. Ibid., 104.

The main significance of Hefner's article for our attempt to find a balanced relation between theology and science lies in one of the conclusions he draws from his three axioms. Hefner takes the position that theology should not take an apologetic approach to the encounter with science, but rather seek to use science in creating new meaning in the world as described by science:

> The point, however, is not to reformulate doctrines so that they can pass muster with scientists and philosophers of science. Rather, the aim of reformulating is to enable traditional faith to be a catalyst for the creation of new meaning – creating meaning that will enable us to understand our lives in the world meaningfully, in the world whose causes and coherence science describes. ... The aim is to serve the human community in its struggle to understand how the natural world can be a meaningful ambience for human living.[54]

This is where we can connect Schillebeeckx's theology with Hefner's. We discussed earlier how Schillebeeckx sees experience and interpretation as intrinsically connected. This becomes even more obvious in his discussion of negative contrast experiences.[55] This kind of experience cannot be interpreted from the safety of the proverbial armchair, but calls for praxis of a 'theologal life', praxis of the Kingdom of God.[56] From this idea of praxis, we suggest that a dialogue between science and theology should be regarded as part of a 'theologal life', and therefore as an inherent part of theology. The question that remains, however, is whether we can conceive a dialogue between theology and evolutionary studies of religion that overcomes the problem of retro-reductionism. We will discuss this in the final section of this chapter.

5. History as Vantage Point

Schillebeeckx describes how Christian tradition reaches back into the past in order to enable Christians to act in the present, in service of the future coming of the Kingdom of God. Religion is the anamnesis of God's salvific presence in the history of the world.[57] This view implies that knowledge of humanity's evolutionary

---

54. Ibid., 109.

55. Schillebeeckx, *Mensen als verhaal van God*, 24. Schillebeeckx defines negative contrast experiences as the humanly experienced 'veto' against the world in its present state, and calls them human, pre-religious, basic experiences.

56. Cf. Schillebeeckx, *Mensen als verhaal van God*, 49–50. See also Schillebeeckx, *Tussentijds verhaal*, 64, 72.

57. Schillebeeckx, *Tussentijds verhaal*, 64; Schillebeeckx, *Mensen als verhaal van God*, 33. It is beyond the scope of this chapter to examine the parallels between Schillebeeckx's position and Philip Hefner's proposal of tradition enabling humanity to 'co-create' the future according to God's will, as presented in Hefner, *The Human Factor*.

history, including knowledge of the emergence of culture from its biological roots, is an important source for a theology that strives to be a 'science of faith'. We have learned from our discussion of both Schillebeeckx and Hefner how experience and interpretation are intertwined, and how culture enables humans to discover meaning and to construct new meaning in the process of interpretation. But we have also seen how the discipline of evolutionary studies of religion argues that there is no critical element at the roots of religious experiences, that, whenever critical reflection is at play, it does not concern the real meaning of religious beliefs; such reflection is, rather, the superficial icing on an evolutionary cake. We have identified the assumption that religion does not entail critical reflection as the first step of retro-reductionism, which precludes a dialogue between theology and evolutionary studies of religion.

Robert Bellah's monumental study of religion[58] offers a way to avoid the assumption of retro-reductionism, while still acknowledging the insights offered by evolutionary studies of religion. The main idea that is advocated in this book is that religion developed through cultural evolution, eventually becoming a cultural tool that enables people to criticize and change the society they live in.[59] One of Bellah's central principles, 'nothing is ever lost',[60] is particularly interesting for our current discussion. This principle belongs to the very core of evolutionary theory. Natural selection does not throw away anything lightly. For instance, the gradual process of building on earlier developments is ultimately behind the human vulnerability to back pain, since our spinal cords were originally adapted for walking on four legs rather than two. The implication here is that the contingent course through evolutionary history can open or close gateways to certain possibilities, an idea which caused Stephen Gould to state that 'any replay of the tape [of evolutionary history] would lead evolution down a pathway radically different from the road actually taken'.[61] Bellah first introduces his principle of 'nothing is ever lost' in his discussion of the relation between religion, reality, and representation. He makes a distinction between different types of religious representations, following individual cognitive development.[62] For our discussion,

---

58. R. N. Bellah, *Religion in Human Evolution: From the Paleolithic to the Axial Age* (Cambridge, MA: The Belknap Press of Harvard University Press, 2011).

59. Bellah, *Religion in Human Evolution*, 268.

60. Ibid., 267.

61. S. J. Gould, *Wonderful Life: The Burgess Shale and the Nature of History* (New York: W. W. Norton, 1990), 51.

62. Bellah refers to Jean Piaget and Jerome Bruner as inspiration for his typology of religious representations. J. Piaget and B. Inhelder, *The Psychology of the Child* (New York: Basic Books, 1969), and J. Bruner, *Studies in Cognitive Growth* (New York: Wiley, 1966), cited by R. N. Bellah, *Religion in Human Evolution*, 13. The reason why Bellah grounds his typology of religious representations in individual human psychological development is twofold. First, Bellah argues that religious representations are fundamentally connected with representations of reality, and thus with reality itself (Bellah, *Religion in Human*

it is important to note Bellah's remark on the succession of these types, which he sees not as a replacement of the old by a novelty, but rather as an integration, or enfolding, of the old in the new.[63] When Bellah goes on to discuss the evolution of human culture, he points to the role of 'conserved core processes' (i.e. processes or structures that remain almost unchanged during long periods) as building blocks for natural selection, and conditions for the possible directions which evolutionary history can take. Translating this biological theory of 'facilitated variation' (i.e. variation conditioned by the presence of existing core processes or structures) to culture, Bellah makes what he considers to be his central claim: 'Perhaps each of these [different phases in cultural evolution] is a "conserved core process," never lost even though reorganized in the light of new core processes, each promoting variation, adaptive and innovative, but *each essential* to cultural integrity.'[64] There might be a parallel here with Schillebeeckx's proposals on tradition and its 'fluid permanence':

> The past is within the present on the way towards the future, which then, in its turn, via the present, fades into the past – a course which leads from interpretation to doing and then reinterpretation. In this *fluidity* in the development of tradition there is, in other words, an aspect of permanence, a dynamic self-identity which cannot in itself be expressed.[65]

Note that this non-essential view of the identity of tradition parallels the non-essential view of the identity of species in evolution, whether biological or cultural evolution.

This principle is relevant for our current discussion insofar as it implies that traits of earlier stages can still be noticed in current religious behaviour. Evolutionary theories of religion, most notably classic cognitive science of religion,[66] suggest that the past, the present, and the future are essentially the same, as mere variations on a theme. The principle, 'nothing is ever lost', pictures the

Evolution, 11). Second, Bellah traces the development of the capacity for symbolic transcendence (9). In short, Bellah assumes, in the first chapter of his voluminous study of religion, a psychological perspective, resembling in some respects evolutionary psychology and cognitive science (prioritizing mental features of the human species and presupposing these features to be universal). He does so in order to lay the groundwork for a broader, cultural perspective (43). It is interesting to see how Bellah thus makes a connection between ontogeny and phylogeny, without resorting to the flawed adagium of 'ontogeny recapitulates phylogeny'.

63. Bellah, *Religion in Human Evolution*, 13.

64. Ibid., 65. The different stages are explained at length in M. Donald, *A Mind So Rare: The Evolution of Human Consciousness* (New York; London: W.W. Norton & Company, 2001).

65. E. Schillebeeckx, 'Catholic Use of Hermeneutics', *GFM*, *CW* vol. 3, 26 [39]; my emphasis.

66. See Barrett, *Why Would Anyone Believe in God?*

present as entailing the past, building on the past, and passing on its legacy to the future. This implies that it is possible to combine the following elements: (i) an interest in the evolutionary past of religion; (ii) an appreciation for the importance of this past for our understanding of current religious phenomena; and (iii) an acknowledgement of more recent developments in the evolutionary history of religion, including the growing role of critical reflection. In other words, Bellah points us to a seemingly forgotten aspect of Darwinism: its historical character.[67] A growing number of scholars from different fields argue for an integration of cultural history with evolutionary history and even cosmological history; such an integrated history they label 'deep history' or 'big history'.[68] It therefore seems appropriate to regard evolution foremost as the historiography of humanity's deep history, rather than as a reductionist explanation of human culture.

This brings us to the suggestion that, in line with Schillebeeckx's remarks on the value and limits of social studies of religion, an evolutionary explanation of religion could be instrumental for embedding religion into the deep history of humanity, thus improving our understanding of religious experiences as part of human experiences, without reducing religion to a function of either the biological or cultural levels of reality.[69] As indicated above, such reduction would fail to engage the richness of religious experience. Avoiding retro-reductionism

67. See J. L. Gaddis, *The Landscape of History: How Historians Map the Past* (Oxford: Oxford University Press, 2002). See also the following: J. Beatty and E. C. Desjardins, 'Natural Selection and History', *Biology and Philosophy* 24 (2009): 231–46; W. Flinn, 'Culture and the Evolution of Social Learning', *Evolution and Human Behavior* 18 (1997): 23-67; T. Ingold, 'On the Distinction between Evolution and History', *Social Evolution & History* 1, no. 1 (2002): 5–24.

68. For an introduction to this topic, see the following: A. Shryock, D. Lord Smail, and T. Earle, *Deep History: The Architecture of Past and Present* (Berkeley: University of California Press, 2011); D. Smail, *On Deep History and the Brain* (Berkeley: University of California Press, 2008); G. D. Snooks, 'Big History or Big Theory? Uncovering the Laws of Life', *Social Evolution & History* 4, no. 1 (2005): 160–88. For a theological reflection on deep history, see N. H. Gregersen, 'Cur deus caro: Jesus and the Cosmos Story', *Theology and Science*, 11 no. 4 (2013): 370–93; J.-O. Henriksen, 'Challenges to the Traditional Christian Concept of History', *Zygon* 49, no. 4 (2014): 855–74.

69. Cf. Schillebeeckx, *Mensen als verhaal van God*, 77. See also Bellah's remark on evolutionary explanations of love: 'That parental care would lead to social bonding, the possibility of individual friendship, and even, eventually, to marriage and the family, are all unforeseen, and, though in turn adaptive, have given rise to meanings that go beyond adaptation. To find the origin of love in the adaptations of the earliest mammals and birds is not to reduce it to those origins but to marvel at the ways of nature in leading to something so central to our lives. Nonetheless, what humans have done with the practice and ideal of love should in no way make us overlook the whole evolutionary history or put down other species for not quite reaching some of the advances of our own' (Bellah, *Religion in Human Evolution*, 72).

might help evolutionary studies to appreciate the complex interplay of causes on different levels of reality when constructing a model to match the rich reality of religion. Moreover, since theology is accustomed to take history into account, it should be possible to consider evolutionary theory as the historiography of deep history. This will offer, we believe, new possibilities for theology to include the insights from evolutionary studies of culture and religion in its reflections. But, most important, it could well help Christians to appreciate the long, continuous relation between God and humanity, and will enable them to live this relationship today, to live 'a theologal life'.[70]

Bibliography

Barbour, I. G., *Religion and Science. Historical and Contemporary Issues: A Revised and Expanded Edition of Religion in an Age of Science* (London: SCM Press Ltd, 1998).

Barrett, J. L., *Why Would Anyone Believe in God?* (Walnut Creek: Altamira Press, 2004).

Beatty, J., and E. C. Desjardins, 'Natural Selection and History', *Biology and Philosophy* 24 (2009): 231–46.

Bellah, R. N., *Religion in Human Evolution: From the Paleolithic to the Axial Age* (Cambridge, MA: The Belknap Press of Harvard University Press, 2011).

Boyer, P., *Religion Explained: The Human Instincts That Fashion Gods, Spirits and Ancestors* [London: Vintage (Random House), 2001].

Bruner, J., *Studies in Cognitive Growth* (New York: Wiley, 1966).

Burkert, W., *Creation of the Sacred: Tracks of Biology in Early Religions* (Harvard University Press: Cambridge, MA, 1996).

Dawkins, R., *The God Delusion* (London: Black Swan, 2007); first published as ibidem (London: Bantam Press, 2006).

Dennett, D. C., *Breaking the Spell: Religion as a Natural Phenomenon* (New York: Viking, 2006).

Donald, M., *A Mind so Rare: The Evolution of Human Consciousness* (New York; London: W.W. Norton & Company, 2001).

Feierman, J. R. (ed.), *The Biology of Religious Behavior: The Evolutionary Origins of Faith and Religion* (Santa Barbara, CA, et al.: Praeger, 2009).

Flinn, W., 'Culture and the Evolution of Social Learning', *Evolution and Human Behavior* 18 (1997): 23–67.

Gaddis, J. L., *The Landscape of History: How Historians Map the Past* (Oxford: Oxford University Press, 2002).

Gould, S. J., *Wonderful Life: The Burgess Shale and the Nature of History* (New York: W. W. Norton, 1990).

Gregersen, N. H., 'Cur deus caro: Jesus and the Cosmos Story', *Theology and Science*, 11 no 4 (2013): 370–93.

Haught, J. F., *Resting on the Future: Catholic Theology for an Unfinished Universe* (New York: Bloomsbury, 2015).

Hefner, P., 'Editorials', *Zygon: Journal of Religion & Science* (1989–2009).

---

70. Cf. Schillebeeckx, *Tussentijds verhaal*, 70–1.

Hefner, P., *The Human Factor: Evolution, Culture, and Religion. Theology and the Sciences* (Minneapolis, MN: Fortress Press, 1993).

Hefner, P., 'Theology and Science: Engaging the Richness of Experience', *Theology and Science* 1, no. 1 (2003): 95–111.

Henriksen, J.-O., 'Challenges to the Traditional Christian Concept of History', *Zygon*, 49, no. 4 (2014): 855–74.

Hinde, R., *Why Gods Persist: A Scientific Approach to Religion* (New York: Routledge, 1999).

Ingold, T., 'On the Distinction between Evolution and History', *Social Evolution & History* 1, no. 1 (2002): 5–24.

Kirkpatrick, L. A., *Attachment, Evolution, and the Psychology of Religion* (New York: The Guilford Press, 2005).

Laland, K. N., and G. R. Brown, *Sense & Nonsense: Evolutionary Perspectives on Human Behaviour*, 2nd edn (Oxford: Oxford University Press, 2011).

Norenzayan, A., *Big Gods: How Religion Transformed Cooperation and Conflict* (Princeton: Princeton University Press, 2013).

Piaget, J., and B. Inhelder, *The Psychology of the Child* (New York: Basic Books, 1969).

Schillebeeckx, E., 'Het kritische statuut van de theologie', *De toekomst van de kerk: Verslag van het wereldcongres 'Concilium' te Brussel 12–17 September 1970* (Amersfoort, Bussum: De Horstink/Paul Brand, 1960), 56–62.

Schillebeeckx, E., *God and Man* (London; Sidney: Sheed and Ward, 1969).

Schillebeeckx, E., *Tussentijds verhaal over twee Jezusboeken, Bloemendaal* (Baarn: Nelissen, 1978) [Schillebeeckx, E., *Interim Report on the Books Jesus and Christ*, trans. John Bowden, *CW*, vol. 8 (London: Bloomsbury T&T Clark, 2014)].

Schillebeeckx, E., *Mensen als verhaal van God* (Baarn: Nelissen, 1989) [Schillebeeckx, E., *Church: The Human Story of God*, trans. John Bowden, *CW*, vol. 10 (London: Bloomsbury T&T Clark, 2014)].

Schillebeeckx, E., *God the Future of Man*, *CW*, vol. 3 (London: Bloomsbury T&T Clark, 2014).

Schloss, J., and M. Murray (eds), *The Believing Primate: Scientific, Philosophical, and Theological Reflections on the Origin of Religion* (Oxford: Oxford University Press, 2009).

Shryock, A., D. L. Smail and T. Earle, *Deep History: The Architecture of Past and Present* (Berkeley: University of California Press, 2011).

Smail, D. L., *On Deep History and the Brain* (Berkeley: University of California Press, 2008).

Snooks, G. D., 'Big History or Big Theory? Uncovering the Laws of Life', *Social Evolution & History* 4, no. 1 (2005): 160–88.

Stenmark, M., *How to Relate Science and Religion: A Multidimensional Model* (Grand Rapids, MI: B. Eerdmans Publishing Co., 2004).

Trigg, R., and J. Barrett (eds), *The Roots of Religion: Exploring the Cognitive Science of Religion* (Farnham: Ashgate, 2014).

Part IV

CROSSINGS OF THEOLOGY AND THE PUBLIC SPHERE

Chapter 13

EDWARD SCHILLEBEECKX AND SEXUAL TRAUMA: SALVATION AS HEALING

Julia A. Feder

Acts of sexual violence are horrific. Those who have experienced them first-hand suffer from their effects on a daily basis. Many who have experienced sexual violence second-hand – either through the intimacy of relationships with a victim or through merely the knowledge of disturbing events via a news report – live with the anxiety of protecting themselves and their loved ones. Sexual violence disorients the seer and rings in the ear of the hearer. It seems to those who experience the horror of sexual violence (either directly or indirectly) that these kinds of acts push against the natural order. The sexual violation of the bodies of children and teens threatens (what can feel like) a basic instinct of humanity to protect and nurture its youth, and the coercion of adults against their will into sexual acts distorts (what can feel like) the natural beauty and easy joy of sexual coupling. The feeling of 'unnaturalness' that accompanies these acts is what, in part, Edward Schillebeeckx is aiming to communicate when he discusses extreme suffering as senseless.[1] In other words, extreme suffering – in this case, the suffering of sexual violence – serves no higher purpose or greater human value. This kind of suffering pushes against all ways of making sense of the world as good and orderly.

And yet, it would *not* be accurate to describe acts of sexual violence as against the natural order if such a claim means that these acts are exceptional or rare. The United States Centers for Disease Control and Prevention has reported that almost one in five women (18.3 per cent) and one in seventy-one men (1.4 per cent) describe themselves as having experienced attempted or completed rape at some time in their lives.[2] In the

---

1. E. Schillebeeckx, *Christ: The Christian Experience in the Modern World*, trans. John Bowden, *CW*, vol. 7 (London: Bloomsbury T&T Clark, 2014), 717–23 [724–30].

2. Centers for Disease Control and Prevention, *Sexual Violence: Facts at a Glance*, https://www.cdc.gov/ViolencePrevention/pdf/SV-DataSheet-a.pdf.

more specific case of undergraduate students, as many as 19 per cent of women in the United States experience attempted or completed sexual assault while in college. Further, in a survey of American high school students in 2011, 11.8 per cent of girls and 4.5 per cent of boys reported having been raped at some point in their young lives.[3] As Judith Lewis Herman explains,

> It was once believed that such events were uncommon. In 1980, when post-traumatic stress disorder was first included in the diagnostic manual, the American Psychiatric Association described traumatic events as 'outside the range of usual human experience'. Sadly, this definition has proved to be inaccurate. Rape, battery, and other forms of sexual and domestic violence are so common a part of women's [and children's] lives that they can hardly be described as outside of the range of ordinary experience.[4]

Here, too, Schillebeeckx has some wisdom to offer in his description of all forms of senseless human suffering as 'the alpha and omega of the whole history of [hu] mankind'.[5] Sexual violence, though horrific and disorienting, is a salient feature of our common life together. It is widespread in our schools, our churches, and our homes.

Any contemporary articulation of Christian salvation must take into account the reality of widespread, senseless human suffering in our world, including the horrific realities of sexual violence. Christian salvation is the '"total sense" or "haleness", being whole' of human existence, not yet experienced but anticipated.[6] Because sexual violence threatens human wholeness in a diversity of arenas (viz. personal-material well-being, interpersonal well-being, and social-political well-being), the reality of sexual violence is a topic that theologians need to address.

In this chapter, I frame healing from sexual trauma as a component of Christian salvation through an appeal to Edward Schillebeeckx's analysis of experience. Schillebeeckx's analytical category of negative contrast experience allows for a dialectical understanding of experience: that is, God is present to the patient in her suffering and recovery, though does not sanctify it. God is 'for' humanity, desiring a complex version of human good, including – although not limited to – bodily-material, interpersonal, and political-institutional forms of well-being. According to Schillebeeckx's view, God's salvific work in the world is always mediated through human beings; this means that Christian faith in salvation is intrinsically

---

3. Centers for Disease Control and Prevention, *Sexual Violence, Facts at a Glance*, 2012, http://www.cdc.gov/ViolencePrevention/pdf/SV-DataSheet-a.pdf.

4. J. L. Herman, *Trauma and Recovery* (New York: Basic Books, 1992), 33.

5. Schillebeeckx, *Christ*, 718 [725].

6. E. Schillebeeckx, *Jesus: An Experiment in Christology*, trans. John Bowden, *CW*, vol. 6 (London: Bloomsbury T&T Clark, 2014), 7 [24].

connected to the responsibility to work towards this salvation, which embraces human liberation. Therefore, Christian salvation includes a comprehensive project of human healing. Schillebeeckx's thought gives us a contemporary framework for articulating the ways in which victims of sexual trauma work towards their own healing precisely as a salvific task, without eclipsing the salvific role of God in the recovery process.

1. Sexual Trauma and its Effects

Trauma is defined, broadly speaking, as the state of being overwhelmed, physically as well as psychologically, by an external threat of annihilation or total destruction.[7] Thus, the effects of traumatic violence are widespread: the traumatized person experiences threats that are personal-material, interpersonal, social, and spiritual. On the personal-material level, trauma can block the victim's attention to present and new experiences; consequently, trauma victims struggle to secure a sense of their own bodily integrity, a foundation for positive self-esteem, and a basic degree of autonomy and individual competence.[8] On the interpersonal level, sexual trauma can present barriers to healthy adult relationships, especially healthy sexual relationships.[9] On a social-political level, the prevalence of sexual trauma creates a culture of rape. Judith Herman muses, 'Rape and combat might thus be considered complementary social rites of initiation into the coercive violence at the foundation of adult society.'[10] The habitual violation of the bodies of those who are vulnerable in society creates a sense of normalcy surrounding grave acts of injustice, such that they become part of the fabric of the ordinary social order.[11] Yet, unlike war veterans, rape victims are largely unrecognized in the social realm (especially before the law).[12] On a spiritual-religious level, sexual trauma inevitably transforms the way that its victims view the world on the whole, as well as their understanding of God's relationship to created reality. Where individuals perhaps have perceived the world as a safe place, they now question their safety and the

---

7. See S. Jones, *Trauma and Grace: Theology in a Ruptured World* (Louisville, KY: Westminster John Knox Press, 2009), 13–15. In distinction from 'suffering', a form of pain which can be integrated into one's understanding of the world with time, 'trauma' is an extreme form of suffering that endures and cannot be integrated in time. S. Rambo, *Spirit and Trauma: A Theology of Remaining* (Louisville, KY: Westminster John Knox Press, 2010), 7.

8. Herman, *Trauma and Recovery*, 52–66.

9. B. Watson and W. K. Halford, 'Classes of Childhood Sexual Abuse and Women's Adult Couple Relationships', *Violence and Victims* 25, no. 4 (2010): 518; Herman, *Trauma and Recovery*, 53.

10. Herman, *Trauma and Recovery*, 61.

11. Ibid., 33.

12. Ibid., 72–3.

safety of those whom they love. Where individuals perhaps have perceived God as a protective figure, they now may perceive God as indifferent to human suffering, or perhaps even as one who is in the business of punishing unatoned sins with violence.

2. Edward Schillebeeckx on Salvation and Negative Contrast Experiences

How can we talk about Christian salvation in a world that is afflicted with so much destructive sin? Is it possible to carve out space for hope in the midst of experiences of violence of this sort? Edward Schillebeeckx approaches the good news of Christian salvation with a particular sensitivity to the reality that our experience in the world is characterized more by brokenness than wholeness. He acknowledges the destructive reality of human suffering in history[13] and, in particular, the 'barbarous excess ... [of] *unmerited* and *senseless* suffering'.[14] At the same time, however, Schillebeeckx argues forcefully that God is not the source of this suffering: 'God does not want [hu]mankind to suffer'[15] and is the 'author of good and the opponent of evil'.[16] Therefore, Schillebeeckx is able to identify salvation with the complete and total end of this kind of suffering. In the present moment, salvation is 'hidden' from us; it is 'merely announced and promised'.[17] He writes, 'Nowhere do I see signs of an "objectively completed" redemption'.[18] We now live an 'eschatological *borderline*' existence where experiences of positive meaning stand alongside of experiences of absolute negativity.[19] Though Schillebeeckx does not specifically address the reality of sexual trauma, one can easily talk about experiences of sexual violence as a prime example of the kind of senseless human suffering that God opposes. More specifically, experiences of sexual trauma are 'negative contrast experiences'. In discussing negative experiences specifically as 'contrast' experiences, Schillebeeckx is able to highlight that, although experiences of suffering are devastatingly evil, they reveal an underlying hope and sense of the good that remain in the experiencer despite the harm that was committed against her.

For Schillebeeckx, 'negative contrast experiences' are those that impress upon the human person an awareness of that which *ought not to be*. In these experiences, the individual's encounter with the negative is sharpened by previous 'positive experiences of meaning and joy'; thus, her perception of excessive suffering and resistance to it are strengthened.[20] The power of these experiences of suffering as

---

13. Schillebeeckx, *Christ*, 690–1 [699].

14. Ibid., 718 [725].

15. Ibid., 717–23 [724–30].

16. Ibid., 720 [727].

17. Ibid., 740 [745].

18. Ibid., 9 [25].

19. Ibid., 740 [745]; original emphasis.

20. Schillebeeckx, *Christ*, 815, n. 77 [819, n. 158].

negative contrast lies specifically in the subject's feeling of the contrast between what is and the incipient sense of what could be and should be. As Schillebeeckx explains, 'The *critical* practical force does not lie either in the positive or in the negative, but only in their dialectical tension, that is, *in* the contrast experience of suffering of people who receive and give meaning.'[21]

In lived experience, meaning and non-meaning abut and, on the whole, history is ambiguous and cannot be thematized neatly.[22] As a result, Christianity resists any attempt to offer a wholly systematic meaning of history.[23] Christians will experience universal meaning eventually, but, for now, history is 'still in the making'; history remains ambiguous and total meaning is not yet perceptible.[24] In experiences of negative contrast, however, one senses pre-reflexively, in a 'vague, yet real' way, what indeed ought to be.[25] In these experiences, one catches a glimmer of what total salvation will look like. Thus, the pain that one feels as one recognizes that what *should* be is not what *is*, together with the resistance which one exerts against that which *is*, reveals something more foundational: a hope that what *should* be *could* be. Schillebeeckx explains, 'Protest is possible only where there is hope. A negative experience would not be a contrast-experience, nor could it excite protest, if it did not somehow contain an element of positive hope in the real possibility of a better future.'[26] Though the vision of the expectant future of total liberation lacks definitive content, and complete salvation exceeds that which we are able to conceptualize, we are nevertheless able to experience in the midst of our contemporary experiences of suffering an authentic 'anticipation of "total sense" or "hale-ness", being whole'; we are privileged to genuine glimmers of what salvation will look like.[27] Experiences of negative contrast equip one with a dimly perceived sense of directionality, a kind of parabolic hope which aims towards the good without knowing, or being able to explain, exactly what this good is and will be.[28] It is only through a realization of what ought-not-to-be that one is able to experience some kind of positive (though indirect) vision of human meaning.[29] It is through these experiences that one possesses a 'knowledge that demands a future and opens it up'.[30]

21. Ibid.

22. Schillebeeckx, *Jesus*, 577–8 [615].

23. Ibid., 578–9 [616]. Schillebeeckx notes that to posit a total system of meaning is different than to claim total meaning in Jesus Christ because total meaning in Christ still resists 'any demonstrable, specific form in which that meaning is realized'. Schillebeeckx, *Jesus*, 580 [617].

24. Schillebeeckx, *Jesus*, 580–1 [618–19].

25. Schillebeeckx, 'Church, Magisterium and Politics', *God the Future of Man*, trans. N. D. Smith, *CW*, vol. 3 (London: Bloomsbury T&T Clark, 2014), 92–3 [154].

26. E. Schillebeeckx, 'The Church as the Sacrament of Dialogue', *GFM*, 83 [136].

27. Schillebeeckx, *Jesus*, 7–8 [24].

28. Ibid., 581–3 [620–1].

29. Ibid., 583–4 [622].

30. Ibid., 584 [622].

Schillebeeckx's language of negative contrast experience can help us to speak more clearly about the effect of traumatic violence upon the human person. Trauma is absolutely negative and yet can also function as a site of dialectical revelation. It is critical to note that the revelation of trauma is negative in nature. It is precisely in our *resistance* to traumatic violence, in our experience of trauma *as pain* or as that which *should not be*, that the truth of God and of our potential as human beings is revealed. The language of negative contrast experience allows us to identify traumatic violence as revelatory without in anyway sanctifying the violent act itself.

For Schillebeeckx, suffering, though not salvific in itself, has a critical, productive effect in the patient to reveal the shape of human good in its absence. The personal-material, interpersonal, social, and spiritual wounds of sexual trauma reveal the importance of human goods such as bodily integrity, individual competence, healthy adult sexual relationships, and a culture that supports non-dominating human relationships and emphasizes enthusiastic consent as prerequisite to sexual activity. In other words, the profundity of the wounds of trauma (especially insofar as traumatic violence affects all levels of human-being – personal-material, interpersonal, sociopolitical, and spiritual) reveals the profundity of salvation as it has been promised to us. The experience of suffering, in this context as in all others, reveals God as pure positivity, as one who is *against* evil and *for* the good of humanity. The good news of Christianity is precisely this: that 'these three, God, Jesus Christ and humanity, are one in the sense that they can never be set over against one another or in competition with one another'.[31]

Schillebeeckx employs the dual theological images, Kingdom of God and resurrection of the body, in order to argue that God's salvific activity in us transforms all levels of human reality. The Kingdom of God, a political-theological concept anticipating the salvific healing of human beings on a social-institutional level, represents a vision of the future in which healed human persons will live with each other in the freedom of egalitarian relationships.[32] Schillebeeckx explains that 'this symbolic central idea, the very message of Jesus, indicates that human being-whole is only possible when every human domination over other human beings is dissolved into the "reign of God," which brings peace and solidarity among all men and women, and puts an end to all master-slave relationships, all class struggle and every distinction between oppressor and oppressed'.[33]

This is a world other than that which already exists, but the seeds necessary for its growth have already been planted. Christian political praxis – in other words, the praxis of the Kingdom of God – is the embodiment of divine action, that is,

---

31. E. Schillebeeckx, *On Christian Faith: The Spiritual, Ethical and Political Dimensions* (New York: Crossroad, 1987), 31.

32. Schillebeeckx, *On Christian Faith*, 18, 20.

33. E. Schillebeeckx, 'Erfahrung und Glaube', in *Christlicher Glaube in moderner Gesellschaft*, Enzyklopädische Bibliothek in 30 Teilbänden, vol. 25, F. Böckle et al. (eds) (Freiburg et al.: Herder 1980), 99.

action springing from the concern for humanity.[34] The resurrection of the body is a companion image that anticipates healing on a personal level.[35] These two images are tightly interrelated, to the extent that they form a unified image of the comprehensive promise of salvation. Schillebeeckx writes,

> In the Kingdom of God and the resurrection of the body the socially oriented and the existential dimension of human life come fully and pregnantly to expression. The personal resurrection thus belongs also to the Gospel message of the coming of the political kingdom of God. The New Testament sees the individual and political destiny of human beings as an indissoluble unity.[36]

Taken together, these two images of salvific healing indicate that the multiple levels of human-being – the personal, the interpersonal, and the social (as levels of one complex reality) – are all marred by sin and require restorative healing. Consequently, the task of the Christian is to participate in the work of healing wherever brokenness can be found. In the case of sexual violence, the victim who experiences enduring trauma is compelled to commit herself to her own healing out of fidelity to the Christian mission. In addition, those who live in community with her are commissioned to support her and contribute to this task. This work of healing participates in the work of God's salvation of creation.

Christian salvation involves the healing of the whole human person in her relational and political context. As Schillebeeckx puts it,

> Christian salvation cannot be simply the 'salvation of souls'; it must be healing, the making whole of the whole man and woman, the person in all his or her aspects and the society in which the person lives. Thus Christian salvation includes ecological, social, and political aspects, though it is not exhausted by them. Although Christian salvation is more than that, it is at least that.[37]

As he explains in another text, the comprehensive meaning of salvation can be garnered etymologically: 'The root of the word *salus* or salvation is connected with *sanitas*, health; with being whole or with integrity.'[38] Therefore, Christian salvation concerns the broad health of the individual person in the wholeness of her historical reality. The trauma victim is in need of salvific healing not only spiritually, but also physically, relationally, and politically. Because Schillebeeckx places conditions of oppression and alienation in contrast to the Christian vision of redemption, the work of Christian salvation must involve concrete measures of

34. Schillebeeckx, *On Christian Faith*, 20.

35. Schillebeeckx, 'Erfahrung und Glaube', 99.

36. Ibid.

37. E. Schillebeeckx, 'Can Christology be an Experiment?', *Proceedings of the Catholic Theological Society of America* 35 (1980): 13.

38. Schillebeeckx, *Christ*, 741 [746].

human liberation. Eschatological salvation must be embodied and actualized in our human structures of existence in the form of liberation.[39] Salvation, therefore, includes, but is not limited to, human liberation. Schillebeeckx writes, 'A praxis of liberation supported by political love is, in its emancipation, at the same time (through every metanoia) a bit of Christian redemption. Of course, Christian redemption is more than emancipatory self-liberation. But real human liberation, borne up by political love, refers concretely to the worldly fruitfulness of Christian redemption. It is an interior ingredient of it.'[40]

Salvation cannot be reduced to human efforts aimed towards liberation, but political liberation is a key component of eschatological salvation. Salvation implies liberation, but also goes beyond it. It is identified with full human flourishing. Thus, Schillebeeckx's complex portrait of salvation can affirm (a) that healing from sexual trauma is related positively to salvation. In other words, healing from trauma has a *mystical* quality – that is, it brings about unity with God. It also affirms (b) that healing from sexual trauma is not merely a cognitive and individual enterprise; rather, healing involves material restoration, as well as relation and social elements. In other words, the *mystical* is never pure inwardness, but rather has a *political* nature to it. Healing, if it involves renewed intimacy with God, has not only an effect on personal-psychological well-being, but must also involve political and social elements. A theological response to trauma must imply a full range of healing – of the mind, body, social relationships, sexual relationships, familial relationships, social structures, political institutions, and so forth. A mystical approach that excludes the political would fail to restore the individual in the context of her external world. Conversely, a merely political approach would miss a key component of interior healing that is necessary following trauma.

If human liberation is a key component of Christian salvation, what does human liberation look like in the context of our overwhelmingly broken world? In short, we do not know. Schillebeeckx does not attempt to offer a positivistic definition of human good. This would betray his conviction that good can only be perceived indirectly this side of the eschaton. Instead of a concrete set of specific norms, Schillebeeckx offers seven anthropological constants that provide an orientation towards the articulation of human good.[41] All seven of his anthropological constants point to the meaning of 'personal identity within social culture',[42]

---

39. Schillebeeckx writes, 'By means of continually provisional and replaceable configurations, eschatological salvation must visibly, if fragmentarily, be realized within the basic framework of our human history, both in heart *and* structures, so that (especially in our present society) the heart of love may also be mediated by the structures.' E. Schillebeeckx, 'God, Society and Human Salvation', in *Faith and Society: Acta Congressus Internationalis Theologici Lovaniensis 1976*, M. Caudron (ed.) (Paris: Duculot, 1978), 91.

40. E. Schillebeeckx, 'The Church in the World Community', in *The Schillebeeckx Reader*, R. J. Schreiter (ed.) (New York: Crossroad, 1984), 273.

41. Schillebeeckx, *Christ*, 727–8 [733].

42. Ibid., 728 [734].

functioning as a 'system of co-ordinates' of humanity and human salvation.[43] First, human-being is inextricably bound up with materiality (both the materiality of the human body, as well as the material realities of the non-human natural world). Second, human-being involves interpersonal relationships. Third, human-being is tied to the realities of surrounding social structures and institutions. Fourth, human-being is conditioned by both time and space. Fifth, theory and practice are mutually conditioning. Sixth, human-being involves 'religious and "para-religious" consciousness'.[44] Seventh, these six anthropological constants form an 'irreducible synthesis'.[45] This last constant reinforces the notion that no one of these human realities can be prioritized over the others. An example which Schillebeeckx himself points to as particularly problematic is the tendency to elevate humanity's spiritual needs (the sixth anthropological constant) over its material needs (the first anthropological constant). Christian salvation refers to the wholeness of humanity according to all these levels; it cannot mean one to the exclusion of others.

We learn precisely what it means to be human negatively by means of contrast. Over the course of history, we gain 'painful insights into the conditions of true humanity'.[46] The results of these are Schillebeeckx's anthropological constants. He understands these anthropological constants of 'true humanity' as pointing towards the shape of eschatological salvation, however indirectly known in our state of negative contrast. Because these constants are not known positively in their fullness, but only in their lack or partiality, they can point us towards dimensions of human-being in need of present healing, especially in the case of those who are suffering from traumatization. For example, the first anthropological constant is motivated by the realization that it is an illusion to believe that true human freedom consists in rule over nature. Instead, freedom cannot exist outside of the limits of the bodily-material.[47] We can never be free of our bodies, especially insofar as our bodies place limits upon our ability to work without rest or live without pain. Yet, there are ways in which we can imagine our bodies as sources of joy and connection with others (in all their limitations), rather than as weapons to be used against each other and as holders of the shame and secrecy of sexual violation. The second anthropological constant is motivated by the realization that personal identity is not possible outside of the acknowledgement of one's relationships with others. Rather, we flourish relationally, and we harm each other relationally. The third anthropological constant is motivated by the realization that human freedom cannot be secured without the aid of institutional structures to support that freedom. In other words, healing from sexual trauma must be supported by institutional and social structures (e.g. ecclesial, familial, governmental, educational, economic, etc.) if it is to be accomplished at all. All

---

43. Ibid.
44. Ibid., 734 [740].
45. Ibid., 736 [741].
46. Schillebeeckx, 'Erfahrung und Glaube', 95.
47. Ibid., 95–6.

three of these confirm that 'to the very kernel of his [or her] innerness the individual is co-determined by the concrete society and its own nurtured needs'.[48] Human freedom is a 'situated and thematic freedom, not a free initiative in a vacuum or an airless room'.[49] 'True humanity' is an eschatological reality that we experience now only in hints and half-visions.[50] We live a borderline existence, experiencing salvation only in fragments and looking forward to a future in which we will be able to experience it more fully.[51] Thus, the fullness of healing from sexual trauma, while striven for now, is never fully experienced this side of the eschaton.

3. A Schillebeeckxian Trauma Theology: Salvation as Comprehensive Healing

Edward Schillebeeckx provides us with an understanding of Christian salvation that includes human healing in all the ways in which human beings experience woundedness. A theological response to sexual trauma informed by Schillebeeckx must, then, take into consideration a comprehensive vision of human healing precisely *as* a salvific transformation of the human person. This is a transformation accomplished by God with the cooperation of human beings in and through our resistance to that which *ought not to be*.

Schillebeeckx's category of 'negative contrast experience' lends itself to a dialectical theology of suffering in which God is present to the patient in the midst of suffering, yet not in such a way that legitimates any 'goodness' of the experience of suffering itself. This is significant for a responsible discussion of sexual trauma because it clearly casts the negativity of trauma as that which is not salvific.[52] Healing from trauma only becomes a value to be taken seriously by theological thinkers when traumatic violence itself is seen as an excessive evil.[53] Labelling sexual trauma as an evil places a responsibility upon Christians to protect each other's sexual integrity and work for each other's healing. If it is true that human liberation and Christian salvation are intimately related, we can then arrive at the

---

48. Schillebeeckx, 'God, Society and Human Salvation', 90.

49. Schillebeeckx, *Christ*, 726 [732].

50. Ibid., 725 [731].

51. Ibid., 740 [745].

52. Although this assertion may be obvious to the reader, this is certainly not a consistent message preached to the faithful.

53. See Schillebeeckx's comments on excessive suffering and evil in the following passage: 'There is an *excess* of suffering and evil in our history. There is a barbarous excess, for all the explanations and interpretations. There is too much *unmerited* and *senseless* suffering for us to be able to give an ethical, hermeneutical and ontological analysis of our adversity. There is suffering which is not even suffering "for a good cause," but suffering in which men, without finding meaning for themselves, are simply made the crude victims of an evil cause which serves others.' Schillebeeckx, *Christ,* 718 [725].

radical claim that those who work towards their own and others' healing from the detrimental effects of sexual trauma are working towards their own and others' salvation.

While Schillebeeckx maintains a clear condemnation of suffering as absolutely negative, he simultaneously opens up a discussion regarding the productivity of suffering. This is a fragile balancing act that Schillebeeckx is able to execute because of his concept of negative contrast. Negative contrast describes the way in which suffering is able to produce knowledge in the victim – suffering generates a spontaneous resistance to evil that underlies an inchoate sense of human good. We perceive this human good only in contrast, in faint glimmers of light shining through the cracks of the suffering and evil in our world. Schillebeeckx's dialectical approach to experience allows for the possibility that the survivor of sexual violence may, in some sense, have an epistemological privilege over those who have not experienced such abuse. In other words, she may know the depths of the darkness of the human situation with particular acuity. She may be particularly aware of the reality of human sin in the world and therefore may have a kind of privileged understanding of the shape of Christian salvation more than others since she can perceive its grave lack.[54]

Edward Schillebeeckx's anthropological constants map out the dimensions of Christian salvation, which we now perceive faintly and in contrast, in a way that makes clear the comprehensive nature of post-traumatic healing: Christian salvation must involve bodily healing (the first constant), egalitarian interpersonal relationships (the second constant), broad social change (the third constant), as well as a richly unitive relationship with God cultivated through spiritual disciplines (the sixth constant). All of these aspects of Christian salvation are deeply interrelated and cannot be considered without the others (the seventh constant). Thus, Edward Schillebeeckx's mysticism is a profoundly *incarnational* mysticism, attentive to the bodily, the concrete, and the worldly aspects of spirituality. Liberation on multiple levels of human-being is integral to salvation.

Because Schillebeeckx's discussion of liberation extends to the political or structural, he maintains an explicit unity of all three levels of human-being in his treatment of the anthropological constants. Schillebeeckx can be a helpful resource in stressing that we live within larger contexts in which specific behaviours are rewarded or condemned in a complex fashion according to broad social values.

---

54. Serene Jones makes a similar claim as she describes the imagined encounter between Mary of Nazareth and 'Rachel', a fictional mother of a young boy killed in the slaughter of the innocents ordered by Herod. She states that Mary must learn from Rachel, the more deeply traumatized individual, about 'the brokenness of the created order that can ... only be named and mourned ... for our grief bears witness to what *should not be* and therefore to what *actually is* and *should be*, according to God's creative and redemptive intentions'. Jones, *Trauma and Grace*, 121–2; original emphasis. Yet, she does not explore the relationship between experiences of suffering and insight into the shape of salvation with the precision that Schillebeeckx does.

For example, in a culture that emphasizes authority and orderliness more than transparency and open communication (such as the church or the patriarchal family), sexual abuse, if it happens, often remains unchallenged and undiscussed. Trauma researchers have found that the refusal to address and treat sexual abuse when it happens significantly affects an individual's chances of recovery. Victims who report what has happened to them, are taken seriously by their communities, and are given treatment often avoid developing post-traumatic stress disorder.[55] Ecclesial communities can, therefore, act in ways that either facilitate or stand in the way of traumatic healing. Is an ecclesial community's practice of communal prayer multivocal? Are there limits to inclusion, and, if so, are these delineated? In other words, are there clear boundaries about what kind(s) of behaviours are inappropriate, yet also open conversations about what constitutes breaking these boundaries? Does the community engage in practices that encourage authentic listening? These are all evaluative questions that Schillebeeckx's framing of human life, as indivisibly personal, interpersonal, and structural, can propose.

Christian salvation is the consummation of human good, now perceived 'through a glass, darkly' (1 Cor. 13:12), and therefore must include (but is not limited to) the healing of traumatized persons in multiple arenas of human-being – personal-material, interpersonal, social-political, and spiritual. Salvation is meaningless if it does not bring about this kind of comprehensive healing for those who bear the wounds of sexual violence. As long as women experience rape and the threat of rape as a deterrent to walking outside alone, as long as parents have legitimate fears of the sexual violation of their children in schools and religious communities, and as long as sexual violence functions as a common expression of relational dominance in areas of political conflict, as well as in the family homes of those living in 'politically stable' areas alike, salvation is not 'objectively completed'.[56] Total salvation is yet to come. Although we do not have access to a direct vision of eschatological human salvation, we can see that salvation must include (though certainly also extends beyond) healing from the wounds of sexual trauma.[57]

Bibliography

Beste, J., *God and the Victim: Traumatic Intrusions on Grace and Freedom* (New York: Oxford University Press, 2007).

Herman, J. L., *Trauma and Recovery* (New York: Basic Books, 1992).

Jones, S., *Trauma and Grace: Theology in a Ruptured World* (Louisville, KY: Westminster John Knox Press, 2009).

Rambo, S., *Spirit and Trauma: A Theology of Remaining* (Louisville, KY: Westminster John Knox Press, 2010).

55. J. Beste, *God and the Victim: Traumatic Intrusions on Grace and Freedom* (New York: Oxford University Press, 2007), 112–13.

56. Schillebeeckx, *Christ*, 9 [25].

57. Schillebeeckx, 'Can Christology be an Experiment', 13.

Schillebeeckx, E., 'God, Society and Human Salvation', in *Faith and Society: Acta Congressus Internationalis Theologici Lovaniensis 1976*, M. Caudron (ed.) (Paris: Duculot, 1978), 78–99.

Schillebeeckx, E., 'Can Christology be an Experiment?', *Proceedings of the Catholic Theological Society of America* 35 (1980): 1–14.

Schillebeeckx, E., 'Erfahrung und Glaube', in *Christlicher Glaube in moderner Gesellschaft*, Enzyklopädische Bibliothek in 30 Teilbänden, vol. 25., F. Böckle, F. X. Kaufmann, K. Rahner, B. Welte and R. Scherer (eds) (Freiburg et al.: Herder 1980), 73–116.

Schillebeeckx, E., 'The Church in the World Community', in *The Schillebeeckx Reader*, R. J. Schreiter (ed.) (New York: Crossroad, 1984), 243–74.

Schillebeeckx, E., *On Christian Faith: The Spiritual, Ethical and Political Dimensions* (New York: Crossroad, 1987).

Schillebeeckx, E., *Christ: The Christian Experience in the Modern World*, trans. J. Bowden, *CW*, vol. 7 (London: Bloomsbury T&T Clark, 2014).

Schillebeeckx, E., *God the Future of Man*, trans. N. D. Smith, *CW*, vol. 3 (London: Bloomsbury T&T Clark, 2014).

Schillebeeckx, E., *Jesus: An Experiment in Christology*, trans. J. Bowden, *CW*, vol. 6 (London: Bloomsbury T&T Clark, 2014).

Watson, B., and W. K. Halford, 'Classes of Childhood Sexual Abuse and Women's Adult Couple Relationships', *Violence and Victims* 25, no. 4 (2010): 518–35.

Chapter 14

AN EVER-STITCHED WHOLENESS: MULTIDIMENSIONAL RELATIONALITY IN TRAUMA THEORY AND SCHILLEBEECKX'S THEOLOGY OF SALVATION

Heather M. DuBois

Spiders have

> a knack for seeing and understanding the nature of their environment, the contours and potentialities of a given place. Spiders must think strategically about space, how to cover it, and how to create cross-linkages that stitch locations together into a net. And they must do this time and again, always at considerable risk and vulnerability to themselves.[1]

Using fragments of varying lengths, spiders can create webs that span almost any shape, connecting multiple dimensions of space. Their weaving entails continual reweaving, stitching together old and new fragments, to create a web that persists across time. The spider's web is a visual representation of the interconnectedness – the myriad, embedded layers of mutual influence – explored in analytical frameworks from systems theory and ecology to social psychology and global politics. The spider's capacity to creatively participate in environments that it cannot control makes it a suitable image for thinking broadly about what it means to be human in finite conditions.

Like their fellow creatures, the spiders, humans always already live in a web, indeed are always reweaving it. Yet only occasionally do some of us consider the vast whole on which we rest and our agency in relation to it. By virtue of his appreciation for Critical Theory's embrace of 'the fragment', his ethical framework of 'anthropological constants', and his theology of salvation, Edward Schillebeeckx can help us to ask, in what kind of web do we wish to live, and how do we actualize that vision? This chapter attends to these questions particularly in terms of seeking conditions that

---

1. J. P. Lederach, *The Moral Imagination: The Art and Soul of Building Peace* (New York: Oxford University Press, 2005), 81.

enable the possibility of psychosocial and spiritual healing from traumatic violence. First, it builds on the affinities between Schillebeeckx's anthropology and trauma theorists Judith Herman, Carolyn Yoder, and Ann Cvetkovich in order to emphasize the importance of holistic analytical inquiry and material response attuned to multidimensional, multidirectional impact. This chapter implicitly argues that describing the dimensions of life that are affected by violence – or articulating the webbed matrices in which we live – can enable greater participation in healing forms of relationality. Second, Schillebeeckx's seven anthropological constants are each related to discussions about healing in contemporary trauma theory. Third, the chapter considers how Schillebeeckx presents the what, who, where, and how of Christian salvation in order to test the capacity of his soteriology to communicate God's love to persons and communities affected by traumatic violence. Overall, Schillebeeckx offers an interpretive framework in which people need not attain wholeness to experience it. In other words, it becomes discursively possible to experience psychic health without being completely healed.[2]

1. The 'Fragment' in Schillebeeckx's Theology and Trauma Theory

In Schillebeeckx's theology, salvation is wholeness experienced in fragmentary or momentary fashion; eschatological fullness is mediated in and through history. He integrates the Christian understanding of mystical or contemplative glimpses of the whole of reality with Critical Theory's understanding of the integrity of the fragment in the light of the failures of grand narratives. In the resulting framework of interpretation, individual experiences of meaning remain possible, and religion is 'deliberately anticipated totality', but the 'total meaning' of history cannot be fully discerned because history is still in progress.[3] For religious anticipation of meaning to be an honest encounter with reality, rather than a self-surrender to ideology, it must take place in full view of the meaninglessness that is also present in history. According to Schillebeeckx, experiences of wholeness – which are ultimately encounters with God – are only possible through practical reason and liberating praxis that seek to reduce meaningless suffering. 'We do not find salvation primarily by means of a correct interpretation of reality, but by acting in accordance with the demands of reality.'[4] In short, ethical engagement with the

---

2. The insight that healing may be ongoing work has been difficult to establish firmly in mainstream medical settings. Yet, it is an important insight that is beginning to reframe therapeutic responses helpfully. The word 'recovery', for instance, is now used less frequently among trauma specialists, because it denotes an end-state that is problematic to posit, as well as a 'return' to that which may never have existed.

3. E. Schillebeeckx, *The Schillebeeckx Reader*, R. J. Schreiter (ed.) (New York: Crossroad, 1984), 47, 66–7.

4. E. Schillebeeckx, *Christ: The Christian Experience in the Modern World*, trans. John Bowden, *CW*, vol. 7 (London: Bloomsbury T&T Clark, 2014), 47 [61].

particular is necessary to mystical perception of the whole, which is always more than the sum of its fragments.

In mainstream trauma theory, the word 'fragment' does not have the constructive valence that it does in Critical Theory. As described in Judith Herman's classic text *Trauma and Recovery*, fragmentation of memory and sense of self are negative symptoms of trauma.[5] This is why cognitive therapy often focuses on narration, which is a way to put the pieces together. Coherence is prized in this view of trauma healing, and it is often understood in terms of language and memory, or 'telling one's story'. While Schillebeeckx's theology shares trauma theory's concern with multidimensional relationality, as will be shown below, it does not rely on coherence of this kind. Again, access to the whole – whether in terms of meaning or sense of self – is attained through praxis, and one does not need to have a coherent narrative in order to act. In this view of agency, Schillebeeckx aligns with a more recent trauma theorist, Ann Cvetkovich, who draws upon a performative understanding of the self. In this case, complete coherence is an impossibility, rather than an implied therapeutic goal.

The relationality that situates and animates fragments prevents Schillebeeckx's perspective from disintegrating the whole, obstructing healing, or tending towards nihilism. In terms of his anthropological constants, the relational lines that connect all of the constants are as important as the dimensions of ethical, salvific import that he names. Rather than a checklist, the constants form a 'system of coordinates'.[6] Like the spider's web-span, which is disproportionate to its size, Schillebeeckx ambitiously demands that theology attend to 'the height and breadth and depth of human salvation'.[7] At the same time, he asserts that theology after historicity be chaste in its universal prescriptions. The result is a schema that points to '*permanent* human impulses and orientations, values and spheres of value, but at the same time [does] not provide us with *directly* specific norms or ethical imperatives'.[8] The anthropological constants are each manifest distinctly in different temporal, geographic locations. Specifically, they include relationships to a person's corporeality, the natural world, other humans, social and institutional structures, culture, history, and narratives of hope.[9] The last constant is the interrelationship among the others, thus emphasizing the ecological quality of human flourishing.

Because the anthropological constants are designed as a flexible framework for interpretation and dialogue, in contrast to a definition of the human person, they allow for the compounding contingencies of socio-political, religio-cultural, and interpersonal forms of violence.[10] This facet corresponds with emerging

5. J. Herman, *Trauma and Recovery* (New York: Basic Books, 1992, 1997).

6. Schillebeeckx, *Christ*, 728 [734].

7. Ibid., 725 [731].

8. Ibid., 727 [733].

9. Ibid., 725 [731].

10. For me, this broad understanding of violence stems from peace researcher Johan Galtung's terminology, which distinguishes among direct, structural, and cultural forms of

complications regarding trauma's definition. The inclusion of post-traumatic stress disorder in the American Psychiatric Association's diagnostic manual in 1980 (DSM III) was an important clinical milestone, largely associated with returning veterans of America's war with Vietnam.[11] Quickly, however, clinicians working with other patient groups began to point to the limitations of a definition tied to punctual events, particularly when these are designated as 'outside the range of usual human experience'. Herman's work with survivors of chronic child abuse and domestic violence – not uncommon human experiences – prompted her to suggest the additional diagnostic term, 'complex PTSD'. Cvetkovich finds that this improvement does not sufficiently recognize the contextual specificities of trauma. Instead of privileging a medical approach to understanding, she treats trauma as 'a social and cultural discourse', one that emerges in varied forms as people respond to 'the psychic consequences of historical events'.[12] The expanding, multifaceted definition of trauma points to the ways in which it is embedded within relationships and systems. Further, it cautions against presumptive knowledge and one-size-fits-all responses. Cvetkovich necessarily emphasizes that 'trauma is a far from straight forward experience, and [that] no simple prescription, whether therapeutic or political, or both, can heal it'.[13]

2. Schillebeeckx's Anthropological Constants and the Relationality of Healing

Whether the starting point for discussing trauma is a clinical diagnosis or a cultural discourse, the conversation should entail Schillebeeckx's first anthropological constant, embodiment – in our own bodies and in the material environments that sustain us. The most often cited physical responses to trauma are related

---

violence. J. Galtung, 'Violence, Peace, and Peace Research', *Journal of Peace Research* 6, no. 3 (1969): 167–91; J. Galtung, 'Cultural Violence', *Journal of Peace Research* 27, no. 3 (1990): 291–305. See also S. Hamby and J. Grych, *The Web of Violence: Exploring Connections among Different Forms of Interpersonal Violence and Abuse* (New York: Springer, 2013).

11. The current diagnostic manual of the American Psychiatric Association (DSM 5, 2013), http://www.dsm5.org/Documents/PTSD%20Fact%20Sheet.pdf (accessed April 2015) defines post-traumatic stress syndrome (PTSD) as 'exposure to actual or threatened death, serious injury or sexual violation. The exposure must result from one or more of the following scenarios, in which the individual: directly experiences the traumatic event; witnesses the traumatic event in person; learns that the traumatic event occurred to a close family member or close friend (with the actual or threatened death being either violent or accidental); or experiences first-hand repeated or extreme exposure to aversive details of the traumatic event (not through media, pictures, television or movies unless work-related)'.

12. A. Cvetkovich, *An Archive of Feelings: Trauma, Sexuality, and Lesbian Public Cultures* (Durham, NC; London: Duke University Press, 2003), 18.

13. Cvetkovich, *An Archive of Feelings*, 117.

to 'the fight-or-flight response', such as hyperarousal, and to intrusive memory, such as flashbacks. In addition, responses to trauma may include polar opposite experiences, such as numbing or dissociative absence of memory. Though experts debate the neurobiological details,[14] the body as object of trauma is now accompanied by an understanding of the body as agent of healing. Somatic therapies, from dance to material arts to Eye Movement Desensitization and Reprocessing, are increasingly recognized as beneficial – at times necessary – pairings with talk therapy. The importance of communication is a constant in the literature, but trauma specialists are thinking more broadly than before about the modes in which this communication occurs.

The second constant is intersubjectivity, a vehicle for self-transcending love, as well as deep and lasting harms. In Kathleen McManus's words, Schillebeeckx makes it explicit that 'human beings are not only grace, but also threat to their fellow men and women'.[15] Herman puts human relationships at the centre of healing in her work, which helped to define the field in the 1990s. The scope of response begins in reliable safety and extends to relationships of acknowledgement and reconnection. It implicates interpersonal, familial, and communal dynamics. Herman explains that all of these are crucial:

> A supportive response from other people may mitigate the impact of the event, while a hostile or negative response may compound the damage and aggravate the traumatic syndrome. In the aftermath of traumatic life events, survivors are highly vulnerable. Their sense of self has been shattered. That sense can be rebuilt only as it was built initially, in connection with others.[16]

Such responses may be complicated by a desire or compulsion on the part of the victim to withdraw from sociality. In cases of group or societal trauma, sometimes the 'others' who would respond are themselves in need of safety and support. Carolyn Yoder, from her perspective working in communities where violence is ongoing, adds that 'perhaps the traditional wisdom about safety needs to be reframed: What *degree* of safety? What *kind* of safety?'[17] To these questions I will return.

14. See, for instance, the debate between psychiatrist Bessel van der Kolk and historian of psychiatry and psychology Ruth Leys, as exemplified in the following: B. van der Kolk, 'The Body Keeps Score: Approaches to the Psychobiology of Posttraumatic Stress Disorder', in *Traumatic Stress: The Effects of Overwhelming Experience on Mind, Body, and Society*, B. van der Kolk, A. McFarlane and L. Weisaeth (eds) (New York: Guilford Press, 1996), 214–41; and R. Leys, *Trauma: A Genealogy* (Chicago: University of Chicago Press, 2000), 229–65.

15. K. A. McManus, *Unbroken Communion: The Place and Meaning of Suffering in the Theology of Edward Schillebeeckx* (New York: Rowan & Littlefield, 2003), 145.

16. Herman, *Trauma and Recovery*, 61. While not directly quoting, Herman cites in her own notes here the following work: R. B. Flannery, 'Social Support and Psychological Trauma: A Methodological Review', *Journal of Traumatic Stress* 3 (1990): 593–611.

17. C. Yoder, *The Little Book of Trauma Healing: When Violence Strikes and Community Security Is Threatened* (Intercourse, PA: Good Books, 2005), 51.

Third, Schillebeeckx addresses 'social and institutional structures', highlighting how we often treat these as 'unchangeable natural' arrangements instead of as contingent creations that human choices develop and maintain.[18] Creating effective norms in terms of this constant requires appreciating the tension between structure and agency. Only in this way can societies intervene in their own systems when they 'enslave and debase [human beings] rather than liberate them and give them protection'.[19] To appreciate fully the salience of this constant for trauma responses requires fluid perceptions of trauma – as both 'everyday' and discrete event, as both private and public. Cvetkovich references, for example, the links between histories of racial trauma in the United States and everyday racism in order to track 'diffuse effects', seeing 'the connections between catastrophic events and very ordinary ones'.[20] From this perspective, the work of healing individuals cannot be separated from changing social systems. 'Once the causes of trauma become more diffuse, so too do the cures'.[21]

The fourth constant is the 'conditioning of people and culture by time and space', or humanity as a *'hermeneutical* undertaking'. Schillebeeckx cautions against processes of interpretation that abstract themselves from their locations, even calling them 'a danger to humanity'.[22] Trauma theory equally warns against ahistorical hermeneutics, for instance, as it emphasizes testimony and other practices of 'remembrance and mourning'.[23] In collective processes, this might entail a dual form of acknowledgement: what Yoder terms 'grieving our own story' and 'recognizing that "the other" has a story'.[24] Groups, like individuals, may have to mourn the loss of a past sense of identity, plans for the future, physical integrity, and previous relationships. They too have to choose how to deal with fantasies of revenge.[25] Communities and nations also face the additional challenge of discerning if and how to erect public monuments. For even societies that seem to have chosen amnesia eventually ask questions about which losses, and whose, are remembered.

18. Schillebeeckx, *Christ*, 731 [737].

19. Ibid., 732 [738].

20. Cvetkovich, *An Archive of Feelings*, 6.

21. Ibid., 33. In the light of increased attention to post-traumatic stress syndrome, in combination with a queer theory critique of psychotherapy's temptation to pathologize social 'deviance', Cvetkovich issues the following warning: 'It is wise to remain vigilant about the hazards of converting a social problem into a medical one' (45).

22. Schillebeeckx, *Christ*, 732–3 [738–9]; original emphasis.

23. Herman, *Trauma and Recovery*, 175, 181.

24. Yoder, *The Little Book of Trauma Healing*, 54–5.

25. Yoder deals with these in sections of *The Little Book of Trauma Healing* on forgiveness and 'healing justice approaches' (61–8), and she expressly addresses community responses to mass atrocities in chapter 6, 'What If? 9-11 and Breaking the Cycles'. With other staff and faculty of the Center for Justice and Peacebuilding at Eastern Mennonite University (Harrisonburg, Virginia, USA), Yoder founded the STAR programme (Strategies for Trauma Awareness and Resilience) in response to requests for support following September 11, 2001.

Fifth, Schillebeeckx names the relationship between theory and practice. Trauma studies emerged as a dialogue between theory and clinical treatment. However, as with other work that brings attention to the *causes* of violence, social power intervenes in the theory-practice cycle. Herman explains: 'Throughout the history of the field, dispute has raged over whether patients with post-traumatic conditions are entitled to care and respect or deserving of contempt, whether they are genuinely suffering or malingering, whether their histories are true or false and, if false, whether imagined or maliciously fabricated.'[26] The 'systematic study of psychological trauma', Herman concludes, 'depends on the support of a political movement'.[27] Simply put, the relationship between theory and practice does not exist in a vacuum; it also requires a strong network of relationships. Whether trauma can be discussed at all is a question that stymies personal and social healing. Moreover, a multidimensional response requires attending to *which* trauma and *whose* trauma appears in theory and/or practice, because 'the institutionalisation of public responses to trauma are unevenly distributed'.[28]

The sixth constant is the 'religious and "para-religious" consciousness' of humanity. Schillebeeckx here includes models and interpretations of reality, attributing constant value to our varied historical narratives of hope. He connects the capacity to envision, however ephemerally, a 'meaningful whole' with the capacity to 'make sense of contingency or finitude, impermanence and the problems of suffering, fiasco, failure and death'.[29] In a section of *Trauma and Recovery* entitled 'Reconstructing the Story', Herman writes:

> The traumatic event challenges an ordinary person to become a theologian, a philosopher, and a jurist. ... She stands mute before the emptiness of evil, feeling the insufficiency of any known system of explanation. Survivors of atrocity of every age and every culture come to a point in their testimony where all questions are reduced to one, spoken more in bewilderment than in outrage: Why? The answer is beyond human understanding.[30]

---

26. Herman, *Trauma and Recovery*, 8. In a chapter entitled 'A Forgotten History', Herman begins with an early example: Freud recanted his early findings about female 'hysteria' when they revealed that cases of sexual assault, abuse, and incest were as prevalent among the bourgeois as they were among the proletariat. She then describes how 'shell shocked' veterans of the Second World War were sent back to the front despite both research and clinical practice warning against this (26). In a third example, Herman notes that the women's movement opened the first US rape crisis centre in 1971. It was not coincidental, she writes, that the hundreds that would emerge in the next decade were organized 'outside the framework of medicine or the mental health system' (31).

27. Ibid., 9.

28. Cvetkovich, *An Archive of Feelings*, 68.

29. Schillebeeckx, *Christ*, 734–6 [740–1].

30. Herman, *Trauma and Recovery*, 178.

Juxtaposing this quotation with Schillebeeckx's anthropological constant regarding 'the whole' is a moment in which the exception seems to prove the rule. Part of the tragedy of meaning experienced by Herman's survivor is that there *should* be a 'system of explanation'. The lesson from trauma healing – and theologies like Schillebeeckx's – is that the banishment of empirical certainty from a cognitive model of reality need not equal the banishment of meaning. Even as 'the why question' may remain, Herman observes, many do find meaning, often especially in working to support other survivors and to prevent further violence.

Having arrived at the end of the list, Schillebeeckx undoes his own taxonomy by reminding the reader that his anthropological constants refer to an '*irreducible autonomous reality* (which cannot be reduced either idealistically or materially)'.[31] Philosophies and analytical categories, while vital to understanding, inevitably fail to capture or convey all that there is to the human condition; and, even as this condition is ours, it is ever more than our limited, contingent manifestations of it. Arguably, Schillebeeckx's capacity to combine conceptual articulation with respect for that which remains, exceeding analysis, enables him to appreciate the ubiquitous reach and import of relationality. It is not enough to attend to each of the constants: that which 'heals [persons] and brings them salvation lies in [their] synthesis'.[32] When salvation is understood as 'the conquest of all human, personal and social alienations',[33] obstacles to relationality are obstacles to salvation.

Thinking of healing in terms of relationality – instead of solely intervention – brings us back to Carolyn Yoder's proposition that trauma theory reframe its notion of safety to account for the datum of ongoing violence. Healing towards wholeness is desperately needed, precisely in the places some logics say it cannot occur. Part of the web-watching imperative – to recall the spider – is to pay attention to the cognitive or cultural outliers. Yoder, who has learned from people who do exhibit resilience in traumatic conditions, offers a series of questions that suggest such possibilities:

> Does being grounded psychologically, socially (in a community), emotionally, and spiritually create safe spaces, even an inner space, that allows healing to begin even without complete physical safety? Does knowing our ideals and values, and what we are willing to die for, provide an inner strength that pushes us beyond fear? Is 'acting well in spite of threat' the key to breaking, preventing and transcending the traumatic cycles of victimhood and violence that undermine long-term security? Do such actions surprise and throw the 'enemy' off guard, creating a chink in their defensive armor – and ours? And if so, how do we promote and cultivate this ability, both individually and as societies?[34]

31. E. Schillebeeckx, *Christ*, 736 [741].
32. Ibid., 735–36 [741].
33. Ibid., 810 [814].
34. Yoder, *The Little Book of Trauma Healing*, 51.

Schillebeeckx might say that Yoder probes here the shape and density of salvation in finite conditions, to which we now turn.

3. Salvation Amidst Traumatic Violence

To understand further the 'what' of salvation in Schillebeeckx's theology, it is helpful to consider the questions of where, who, and how. Schillebeeckx succinctly answers the question of 'where' by pointing to 'the world and human history': 'It is there that salvation is achieved in the first instance … or salvation is rejected and disaster is brought about. In this sense it is true that *extra mundum nulla salus*, there is no salvation outside the human world.'[35] Theologian Robert Schreiter reflects upon this statement in a way reminiscent of following a spider's complicated and risky walk: 'We need to attend closely to what God is doing in the world on behalf of humankind. Without keeping both world and salvation in critical tension we will fail to follow how God is among us.'[36] Parsing the 'where' question another way, Schillebeeckx finds that salvation occurs not always as an end to suffering, but also in its midst. It can occur 'in the non-identity, the finitude of suffering human existence'.[37] Indeed, he continues, 'Any positive experience of meaning, any fragment of redemption and liberation, takes place in "unredeemed" conditions.'[38]

Schillebeeckx's recommendation to identify positive fragments in ambiguous or clearly negative settings is a way of pursuing change that suits trauma healing defined as ongoing and inevitably incomplete work. Addressing trauma, especially that stemming from violence and its effects, requires hopeful vision always attuned to limitation. Herman writes about such liminal tension using the term 'integrity',

35. E. Schillebeeckx, *Church: The Human Story of God*, trans. J. Bowden, *CW*, vol. 10 (London: Bloomsbury T&T Clark, 2014), 11–12 [12]. This statement has prompted some confusion, as Schillebeeckx notes in a 2008 letter to a symposium on his theology. Some have thought *extra mundum nulla salus* refers to humanism rather than Christian salvation, which is always from God. 'This is because they put the accent on *mundum* instead of *salus*.' E. Schillebeeckx, 'Letter from Edward Schillebeeckx to the Participants in the Symposium "Theology for the 21st Century: The Enduring Relevance of Edward Schillebeeckx for Contemporary Theology" (Leuven – 3–6 December 2008)', *Edward Schillebeeckx and Contemporary Theology*, L. Boeve, F. Depoortere and S. van Erp (eds) (London: T&T Clark International, 2010), xiv.

36. R. Schreiter, 'The Relevance of Professor Edward Schillebeeckx, O.P. For the Twenty-First Century', *The Kathleen and John F. Bricker Memorial Lecture* (Tulane University, New Orleans, LA, 8 October 2009), 12, http://schillebeeckx.nl/wp-content/uploads/2008/11/Lecture-on-relevance-Schillebeeckx.pdf (accessed May 2014).

37. Schillebeeckx, *Christ*, 815 [819].

38. Ibid. It is worth noting here that Schillebeeckx has a relatively positive view of finitude; he does not equate it with sinfulness.

as expounded by psychoanalyst Erik Erikson. In her words, 'Integrity is the capacity to affirm the value of life in the face of death, to be reconciled with the finite limits of one's own life and the tragic limitations of the human condition, and to accept these realities without despair.'[39] In Schillebeeckx's terms, 'While [the human person] indeed is *potentiality-for-good*, the specific historical starting point for any ethics is not a pre-existing *order*, but [humanity] *who has already been damaged*.'[40] The work of healing begins and continues in imperfect conditions, even in the best of circumstances. Moreover, suppressing this reality hinders the good that persons would do for themselves and one another.

The third question about salvation involves who saves. Of course Christians claim that salvation is a gift from God, but more should be said. 'The expression *extra mundum nulla salus*', writes Schillebeeckx, 'has to do with the reality that the creative, saving presence of God is mediated in and through human beings.'[41] This raises the stakes of ethical praxis and loving relationships in that they affect persons' access to God's unconditional love. It also offers a synergistic understanding of divine and human agency; the latter is not eclipsed as it comes into contact with the grace of God. Instead, Schillebeeckx presents the interplay of divine and human as more of a game of hide-and-seek, which is how he at one point describes prayer.[42] This apparent paradox is a life-giving simultaneity. 'God is the origin, the ever-present ground, and the power of all good – a good that human beings themselves must do freely in order to make a better world. Yet, every human action for justice, peace, and the integrity of creation is at the same time the gift of the silent God.'[43] Synthesis, then, is intrinsic not only to the anthropological constants of human cultures. It also describes human involvement in God's acts of salvation.

The discussion of 'who' has already merged into the last question, the 'how' of salvation. Here one could trace a compelling genealogy of trauma that includes biblical narrations of Jesus 'healing the sick and driving out devils'.[44]

---

39. Herman, *Trauma and Recovery*, 154.

40. Schillebeeckx, *Christ*, 649 [659].

41. Schillebeeckx, 'Letter from Edward Schillebeeckx', xiv.

42. Schillebeeckx, *Christ*, 811–12 [816].

43. Schillebeeckx, 'Letter from Edward Schillebeeckx', xiv–xv.

44. E. Schillebeeckx, *Jesus: An Experiment in Christology*, trans. John Bowden, *CW*, vol. 6 (London: Bloomsbury T&T Clark, 2014), 158 [180]. One has only to think of the documentary *Pray the Devil Back to Hell*, which is about the Liberian civil war. G. Reticker, *Pray the Devil Back to Hell* [Amherst, MA: Balcony Releasing (US) ro*co films (International), 2008]. One might also explore connections mentioned by Herman. She writes, 'The language of the supernatural, banished for three hundred years from scientific discourse, still intrudes into the most sober attempt to describe the psychological manifestations of chronic childhood trauma.' Herman, *Trauma and Recovery*, 96. She cites author and incest survivor Sylvia Fraser: 'I have more compulsions as my body acts out other scenarios, sometimes springing from nightmares, leaving my throat ulcerated and my stomach nauseated. So powerful are these contractions that times I feel as if I were

Yet, given the continuing need to understand the everydayness of trauma, it is maybe more important to consider 'Jesus' caring and abiding presence among people', a presence which they 'experienced as salvation coming from God'. In addition to testimony of miracles as extraordinary occurrences, Christian witness entails the memory of Jesus's praxis.[45] It speaks of the liberating effects of Jesus's companionship: it was in the 'broad range of dealings Jesus had with other people in the ordinary affairs of life' that they came to know salvation.[46] Jesus shares 'conviviality' – he shares his life in mutuality – 'with outcasts, with tax-gatherers and sinners'.[47] Indeed, he 'has been sent to carry to the outcasts, and to them in particular, the message of restored communication with God and with other human beings'.[48] As the anthropological constants attempt to demonstrate, such relational communication affects the whole person – socially, psychologically, physically, and spiritually. With Schillebeeckx, one might say that Jesus's healing changes life in all its coordinates.

How to survive and how to flourish can be material and existential quandaries, not least for those who have experienced traumatic violence. Some persons may be so estranged from previous ways of being that safety and healthy forms of love feel foreign and uncomfortable. Some may never have been embedded in environments of consistent love and care, and so they do not know basically how to live in them. Therefore, ongoing healing requires intimate attention to the details of sensory living and communication. Yoder explains the salience of daily conduct in relation to others in this way: 'When we choose to act in new ways, the brain literally forms new neural pathways. Healthy encounters contradict the helplessness and paralysis of traumatizing events. They contradict the habitual way of responding to stressful triggers that further weaken feelings of control and connection. The rewards are palpable.'[49]Schillebeeckx writes about the quotidian in different terms, but with similar respect: 'People are always in search of a meaningful existence in their own lives. The question of salvation has to do with people's ordinary lives – work, family, politics – this is where they meet the Living God.'[50]

---

struggling for breath against a slimy lichen clinging to my chest, invoking thoughts of the incubus who, in medieval folklore, raped sleeping women who then gave birth to demons. … In a more superstitious society, I might have been diagnosed as a child possessed by the devil. What, in fact, I had been possessed by was daddy's forked instrument – the devil in man.' S. Fraser, *My Father's House: A Memoir of Incest and of Healing* (New York: Harper & Row, 1987), 222–3, cited by Herman, *Trauma and Recovery*, 97.

45. Schillebeeckx, *Jesus*, 157 [179].

46. Ibid., 176–7 [201].

47. Ibid.

48. Ibid., 186–7 [212].

49. Yoder, *The Little Book of Trauma Healing*, 60.

50. Schillebeeckx, 'Letter from Edward Schillebeeckx', xiv.

As markers of salvation, 'synthesis', 'wholeness', and 'presence' refer to what Christians are almost always ultimately referring to – love. At its best, love does not manifest in part; it affirms a person in totality. We may *like* someone 'because', but we *love* someone 'although', as the adage goes. Schillebeeckx writes, 'One might say that only love is redemptive, because it essentially guarantees a person's existence, accepts them, confirms them and endorses them.'[51] He further states that women and men 'appropriate God's salvation', help to make it manifest, 'in and through acts of love'. Salvation 'comes about … where good is furthered and evil is challenged in the human interest'.[52] This kind of loving and being loved is inevitably frail, contingent, and incompletely actualized, but the point is that humans can and do experience fragments of salvific wholeness here and now. Schillebeeckx boldly claims that this is love even as the Saviour Jesus lived it:

> As God's interpreter and one who practiced a way of life commensurate with the kingdom of God, Jesus did not act from a well-defined concept of eschatological or final salvation. Rather, he saw a distant vision of final, perfect and universal salvation – the kingdom of God – *in and through* his own *fragmentary actions*, which were historical and thus limited or finite.[53]

The story of the Christ, who 'went around doing good', highlights the power of love understood as daily, relational work.[54]

Conclusion

Schillebeeckx enables us to understand that 'fragment' can be as salvific a term as 'wholeness', when it designates the reality that the whole can subsist in fragments – indeed always does in human history. Transposed to psychic healing and health, this interplay between fragment and whole, part and totality can encourage those suffering from trauma, offering them a place from which to begin to heal. The alternative, speaking only of wholeness as if it were an all-or-nothing reality, mocks the traumatized subject and community, those who may have less resources for maintaining illusions of self-identical wholeness and complete health. Thus, words frequently used in Christian theology, words such as *re*-conciliation and *re*-storation, should be used with discretion and attention to context and detail. They may support hopeful movement towards the direction at which those struggling currently aim, or they may express presumption of a previous state that has never been lived, perhaps barely experienced. They may ring hollow, trigger painful

---

51. Schillebeeckx, *Christ*, 829 [834]. On this page, he continues: 'At least fragmentary salvation is realized where we encounter others in love.'

52. Schillebeeckx, *Church*, 12 [12].

53. Schillebeeckx, *Christ*, 787–8 [791]; original emphasis.

54. Schillebeeckx here reflects on Acts 10.38. Schillebeeckx, *Christ*, 788 [791]).

memories, and incite despair in those who have not yet truly known a loving home, community, or God.[55]

This insight from Schillebeeckx's theology of salvation helpfully challenges theorists like Herman when they use terms like 'shatter', as quoted above. Some victims and survivors look back to their previous selves as whole in comparison to what follows a traumatic event. Yet, a full discussion of trauma healing includes those whose trauma is chronic. Moreover, some contemporary theorists of subjectivity question whether any self is ever of one piece at the outset.[56] The common trauma narrative – of a self that is born then lost or damaged, potentially beyond repair – needs revision in order to balance the acknowledgement of an experience of psychic brokenness and the often-existing reality of resilience in spite of it.[57] Once more thinking of our exemplar the spider, its web must be continually rewoven, which is to say that it frequently breaks. Nonetheless, the web holds together more often and for longer periods of time than its thin, translucent threads would suggest. Likewise, and remarkably, Schillebeeckx's mystical-political theology finds that it is possible to perceive that the whole remains, that meaning persists, despite tears and holes within the fabrics of our lives. To borrow a phrase from McManus, the dynamic of salvation invites humans to access, no matter the circumstance, 'unbroken communion with God'.[58]

Bibliography

Butler, J., *Gender Trouble: Feminism and the Subversion of Identity* (New York: Routledge, [1990] 2007).

Butler, J., 'Violence, Mourning, Politics', *Studies in Gender and Sexuality* 4, no. 1 (2003): 9–37.

Cvetkovich, A., *An Archive of Feelings: Trauma, Sexuality, and Lesbian Public Cultures* (Durham, NC; London: Duke University Press, 2003).

Flannery, R. B., 'Social Support and Psychological Trauma: A Methodological Review', *Journal of Traumatic Stress* 3 (1990): 593–611.

55. As Schillebeeckx poignantly states: 'Before it is even possible to understand what Christians mean by liberation, it is necessary to have experienced some form of liberation. For what can love of God mean to anyone who has never been the "object" of liberating love from a fellow [human], who has never experienced human love?' Schillebeeckx, *Christ*, 740 [745].

56. For instance, see Judith Butler, especially the following: *Gender Trouble: Feminism and the Subversion of Identity* (London; New York: Routledge, 1990, 2007); and 'Violence, Mourning, Politics', *Studies in Gender and Sexuality* 4, no. 1 (2003): 9–37.

57. For example, my colleague Janna Hunter-Bowman has verbally expressed that the communities with whom she worked in Colombia preferred the word 'resilience' to 'trauma', because to them the latter implied that the violence was over, or that it had to stop before healing could begin.

58. McManus, *Unbroken Communion*.

Fraser, S., *My Father's House: A Memoir of Incest and of Healing* (New York: Harper & Row, 1987).

Galtung, J., 'Violence, Peace, and Peace Research', *Journal of Peace Research* 6, no. 3 (1969): 167–91.

Galtung, J., 'Cultural Violence', *Journal of Peace Research* 27, no. 3 (1990): 291–305.

Hamby, S., and J. Grych, *The Web of Violence: Exploring Connections among Different Forms of Interpersonal Violence and Abuse* (New York: Springer, 2013).

Herman, J., *Trauma and Recovery* (New York: Basic Books, [1992] 1997).

Lederach, J. P., *The Moral Imagination: The Art and Soul of Building Peace* (New York: Oxford University Press, 2005).

Leys, R., *Trauma: A Genealogy* (Chicago: University of Chicago Press, 2000).

McManus, K. A., *Unbroken Communion: The Place and Meaning of Suffering in the Theology of Edward Schillebeeckx* (New York: Rowan & Littlefield, 2003).

Reticker, G., *Pray the Devil Back to Hell* (Amherst, MA: Balcony Releasing 2008).

Schillebeeckx, E., *The Schillebeeckx Reader*, R. J. Schreiter (ed.) (New York: Crossroad, 1984).

Schillebeeckx, E., 'Letter from Edward Schillebeeckx to the Participants in the Symposium "Theology for the 21st Century: The Enduring Relevance of Edward Schillebeeckx for Contemporary Theology" (Leuven - 3-6 December 2008)', in *Edward Schillebeeckx and Contemporary Theology*, L. Boeve, F. Depoortere and S. van Erp (eds) (London: T&T Clark International, 2010).

Schillebeeckx, E., *Christ: The Christian Experience in the Modern World*, trans. J. Bowden, *CW*, vol. 7 (London: Bloomsbury T&T Clark, 2014).

Schillebeeckx, E., *Church: The Human Story of God*, trans. J. Bowden, *CW*, vol. 10 (London: Bloomsbury T&T Clark, 2014).

Schillebeeckx, E., *Jesus: An Experiment in Christology*, trans. J. Bowden, *CW*, vol. 6 (London: Bloomsbury T&T Clark, 2014).

Schreiter, R., 'The Relevance of Professor Edward Schillebeeckx, O.P. For the Twenty-First Century', *The Kathleen and John F. Bricker Memorial Lecture* (Tulane University, New Orleans, Louisiana, October 8, 2009).

Yoder, C., *The Little Book of Trauma Healing: When Violence Strikes and Community Security Is Threatened* (Intercourse, PA: Good Books, 2005).

Van der Kolk, B., 'The Body Keeps Score: Approaches to the Psychobiology of Posttraumatic Stress Disorder', in *Traumatic Stress: The Effects of Overwhelming Experience on Mind, Body, and Society*, B. van der Kolk, A. McFarlane and L. Weisaeth (eds) (New York: Guilford Press, 1996), 214–41.

Chapter 15

TOWARDS A THEOLOGY OF VULNERABILITY: AN ANALYSIS AND CRITIQUE OF WHITE STRATEGIES OF IGNORANCE AND INVULNERABILITY

Eleonora Hof

Human beings are characterized, to some degree, by their porous borders to society and the world. As such, humans fundamentally are affected by a myriad of factors, both known and unknown. In the work of authors such as Kristine Culp,[1] the fundamental openness of humanity is indicated by the word 'vulnerability'. 'Vulnerability' is, in this case, the openness towards both the human other and the divine. This fundamental human openness provides for one's being affected in both positive and negative ways. In the words of Erinn Gilson, 'Simply put, it is only because one is vulnerable that one can be harmed (or benefited).'[2]

Across a range of disciplines, it is now recognized that the opposite of vulnerability, invulnerability, accounts for a spate of societal problems. For example, from the perspective of disability studies, invulnerability as a societal norm leads to the downplaying of the experiences of people with disabilities, thereby reducing them to abnormal creatures in need of tutelage or repair.[3] In addition, from the perspective of critical race theory, new theories are emerging that challenge the ideal of invulnerability, which is analysed as a constituent element of racism. Only by positing oneself as the invulnerable, impenetrable person does one allow oneself to become impervious to the gaze of the other and their critical reflection(s) on one's behaviour.[4] Finally, from a feminist

---

1. K. A. Culp, *Vulnerability and Glory: A Theological Account* (Louisville, KY: Westminster John Knox, 2010).

2. E. Gilson, 'Vulnerability, Ignorance, and Oppression', *Hypatia* 26, no. 2 (2011): 309.

3. A. E. Beckett, *Citizenship and Vulnerability: Disability and Issues of Social and Political Engagement* (New York: Palgrave Macmillan, 2006).

4. A. Bailey, 'On White Shame and Vulnerability', *South African Journal of Philosophy* 30, no. 4 (2011): 472–83; Gilson, 'Vulnerability, Ignorance, and Oppression'.

theological perspective, a number of forays have been made into a dialogical and multireligious understanding of vulnerability.[5]

1. Statement of the Problem

One pressing area in which a stance of invulnerability leads to societal problems is found within race relationships. In particular, white privilege is maintained by a strategy of invulnerability. White privilege can be understood as a pervasive feature of a raced society, in which white people continue to benefit from structural advantages by virtue of their whiteness. White privilege is hampering the flourishing of particular societies as a whole, because it fosters and maintains unjust and asymmetrical connections between diverse groups in such societies.

In this chapter, I will outline a theology of vulnerability as a constructive proposal – within the broader project of a public theology – that seeks to do the following: to contribute to efforts of countering and resisting white privilege and unjust race relationships. In order to develop such a theology, I first need to show that the opposite of vulnerability, namely invulnerability, is a contributing problem to white privilege and whiteness. Second, I will seek to answer the main question of this chapter: In what ways may a theology of vulnerability help to dismantle the invulnerability which is a constitutive element of whiteness? Because strategies of invulnerability occupy a central place in the maintenance of whiteness, I will seek resources that flow in the opposite direction, namely those that are discovered in a theology of vulnerability.

Recently, (Catholic) theology has made headway in assessing whiteness and working in collaboration towards just race relationships. For example, the edited volume of Laurie Cassidy and Alexander Mikulich is a laudable attempt to research actively and question white privilege from a theological perspective.[6] Other authors, such as George Yancy,[7] Bryan Massingale,[8] and Karen Teel,[9] have made significant strides in combatting racism from an explicitly theological angle. Yet, as far as I know, no explicit attempts have been made to work in this realm from the particular angle of a theology of vulnerability. While my work acknowledges the

---

5. Arbeitsstelle Feministische Theologie Und Genderforschung, http://www.uni-muenster.de/FB2/aktuelles/tff/ESWTR_Konferenz2014.html (accessed 23 February 2015).

6. L. M. Cassidy and A. Mikulich, *Interrupting White Privilege: Catholic Theologians Break the Silence* (Maryknoll, NY: Orbis Books, 2007).

7. G. Yancy, *Black Bodies, White Gazes: The Continuing Significance of Race* (Lanham. MD: Rowman & Littlefield Publishers, 2008); G. Yancy, *Christology and Whiteness: What Would Jesus Do?* (New York: Routledge, 2012).

8. B. N. Massingale, *Racial Justice and the Catholic Church* (Maryknoll, NY: Orbis Books, 2010).

9. K. Teel, *Racism and the Image of God* (New York: Palgrave Macmillan, 2010).

endeavours of these authors, I have opted for an approach rooted in 'vulnerability' due to the perilous nature of constructing oneself as invulnerable.

In the most common reading of the term, vulnerability is understood as a privative category, a *privatio boni*, or the lack of something that should be present and is considered desirable.[10] Being vulnerable, then, is a shortcoming, a lack of possession of the ideal, which is invulnerability. Invulnerability is connected with being strong, self-sufficient, and controlled. There are two factors that foster and uphold the ideal of invulnerability. The first factor is the desire to consider oneself as invulnerable, a factor which is related to the unacknowledged norm of invulnerability in contemporary society. Showing control and possessing self-mastery are prerequisites for being taken seriously as an actor in society. The negative perception of vulnerability is the second factor in the production of invulnerability. The negative perception of vulnerability, as weakness and dependence, results in the desire for the opposite characteristics: strength and independence. Yet, as Judith Butler has shown, there are high costs involved in the denial of human vulnerability and attempts to strive towards invulnerability. The denial of vulnerability could result in violence (in myriad forms), which ultimately begets even more violence. Butler therefore advocates engaging in the 'mindfulness of this vulnerability'.[11]

Consequently, this present discussion on whiteness and vulnerability falls squarely within the realm of public theology, which insists that theology should join the public debate in order to reflect upon topics of common interest and provide complementary approaches with regard to human flourishing in the public sphere.[12] The debate on whiteness and white privilege is a pressing issue that needs to be engaged in, particularly given the systemic nature of racism in a raced society and its deadly consequences. For example, Cobus van Wyngaard is one of the few voices that have wrestled with the interplay of public theology and whiteness, writing from a South African perspective. He argues that public theology should wrestle with matters of white privilege and whiteness. Public theology is ultimately concerned with the common good of society; as such, a necessary prerequisite is that all voices are heard within the debate, not silenced by structures of racial exclusion.[13]

This investigation will proceed by outlining the phenomenon of whiteness and white privilege, as well as by searching for ways of redemption through concrete

10 M. Moyaert, 'On Vulnerability: Probing the Ethical Dimensions of Comparative Theology', *Religions* 3, no. 4 (2012): 1144–61.

11. J. Butler, 'Violence, Mourning, and Politics', in *Precarious Life: The Power of Mourning and Violence* (New York: Verso, 2004), 28–9, cited by E. Gilson, 'Vulnerability, Ignorance, and Oppression', 308.

12. S. C. H. Kim, *Theology in the Public Sphere* (London: SCM Press, 2011), 3.

13. C. van Wyngaard, 'Race-Cognisant Public Theology in Contemporary South Africa: Tentative Thoughts from a Privileged Location', 2012, http://uir.unisa.ac.za/handle/10500/5585.

protest in the midst of dehumanizing circumstances. In so doing, various themes which are present in the work of Edward Schillebeeckx emerge as apropos. For example, I am interested in the theme of salvation within the world and connecting this with human wholeness and human flourishing. The human experience, in this case the experience of racial injustice, forms a powerful *locus theologicus*.[14] In addition, Schillebeeckx turned out to be critical of modernity, analysing the acute horrors and nameless suffering it has produced. His criticism of modernity was inspired by the Frankfurt School, especially its leading figures, Max Horkheimer and Theodor Adorno.[15] His critique of modernity and its totalizing tendencies is shared by theorists who work to dismantle oppressive societal patterns manifested in systemic racism.[16] Schillebeeckx aptly criticizes 'abstract Enlightenment universalism' because it fails to give attention to concrete human circumstances, on which he primarily focuses.[17] My theology of vulnerability is guided by concrete attention to the 'sinned against', especially as this idea is featured in the work of Schillebeeckx. Since the production and maintenance of whiteness are aided by ignoring the perspective of those who are sinned against, the impetus of Schillebeeckx (i.e. to concrete experiences of those who suffer) acquires additional importance.[18] In order to dismantle whiteness, then, we need the recovery of the force of the contrast experience, since whiteness flourishes through diminishing the impact of the contrast experience.[19]

2. Introducing Whiteness

Before delving deeper into the possibility of a theology of vulnerability, I will first outline the nature of whiteness and white privilege. White privilege is a

---

14. K. P. Considine, *Salvation for the Sinned-Against: Han and Schillebeeckx in Intercultural Dialogue* (Eugene, OR: Pickwick Publications, 2015), 33; E. Schillebeeckx, *Christ: The Christian Experience in the Modern World*, trans. J. Bowden, *CW*, vol. 7 (London: Bloomsbury T&T Clark, 2014), [529].

15. Considine, *Salvation for the Sinned-Against*, 39; E. Schillebeeckx, 'The New Critical Theory', *The Understanding of Faith: Interpretation and Criticism*, trans. N. D. Smith, *CW*, vol. 5 (London: Bloomsbury T&T Clark, 2014), 89–107 [102–23]; E. Schillebeeckx, 'The New Critical Theory and Theological Hermeneutics', *UF*, 109–35 [124–55]; Schillebeeckx, *Christ*, [817–21]; E. Schillebeeckx, *Church: The Human Story of God*, trans. J. Bowden, *CW*, vol. 10 (London: Bloomsbury T&T Clark, 2014), 171–3.

16. For an elaborate account on modernity and the production of whiteness, see P. Gilroy, *The Black Atlantic: Modernity and Double Consciousness* (Cambridge, MA: Harvard University Press, 1993).

17. Schillebeeckx, *Church*, 177.

18. Bailey, 'On White Shame and Vulnerability'.

19. E. Schillebeeckx, *Geloofsverstaan: Interpretatie En Kritiek*, Theologische Peilingen 5 (Bloemendaal: H. Nelissen, 1972), 152–9.

pervasive feature of a raced society in which white people continue to benefit from structural advantages by virtue of their whiteness. White privilege is hampering the flourishing of a society as a whole because it creates and fosters unjust and asymmetrical connections between diverse groups in society. I will reflect upon theological resources which might be beneficial for challenging white privilege and the whiteness from which it follows. Whiteness is a 'socially and historically constructed category of racial identity'.[20] It is bolstered by a strategy of invulnerability, which aids white persons, or selves, in their perception of the world and hinders them from critically engaging their own positions as subjects. Whiteness is characterized as the particular outlook of whites on the world, an outlook which is perceived as the default and normative way of viewing the world. The perspective of whites on the world is therefore normalized as 'the way things are'.[21] Whiteness is therefore a multidimensional phenomenon that is both actively produced and unconsciously maintained. Bodily behaviour and patterns of thought both constitute whiteness. Three interlocking perspectives have been distinguished by Ruth Frankenberg, one of the early theorists of whiteness: Whiteness is first perceived as a structural advantage enjoyed by white selves. Second, it denotes a standpoint, a location from where white selves perceive the world. Third, it is understood as a conglomerate of cultural practices.[22] In addition, Marilyn Frye has pointed to the concomitant beliefs that whites hold about themselves and their underlying nature: they generally entertain the deep-seated conviction that they are good people who behave in morally appropriate ways.[23] Whiteness and white privilege are therefore related ideas, but are not to be equated with each other. Whiteness refers to being white in the world and thus signifies an identity. In raced societies, whiteness results in the accompanying white privilege, whereby whiteness is valued over other racial ways of being in the world.

3. Invulnerability and Whiteness

Whiteness is produced and maintained by at least two strategies, which mutually enable each other. In the first place, the strategy of invulnerability limits the knowledge of, and access to, other perspectives. Consequently, the resources to challenge the normalization of the white perspective are out of reach. In this vein, Erinn Gilson has argued that invulnerability is a dis-identification

---

20. R. Frankenberg, *Displacing Whiteness: Essays in Social and Cultural Criticism* (Durham, NC: Duke University Press, 1997), 36–7.

21. S. Vice, "'How Do I Live in This Strange Place?'", *Journal of Social Philosophy* 41, no. 3 (2010): 324.

22. R. Frankenberg, *White Women, Race Matters: The Social Construction of Whiteness* (Minneapolis: University of Minnesota Press, 1988), 1.

23. M. Frye, 'White Woman Feminist', *Willful Virgin: Essays in Feminism, 1976–1992* (Freedom: The Crossing Press, 1992), http://www.feminist-reprise.org/docs/fw2.htm.

with vulnerability.[24] As was demonstrated above, invulnerability is maintained by two factors: (i) the desire to see one's self as invulnerable, in the light of the unacknowledged norm of invulnerability in contemporary society; and (ii) the negative portrayal of vulnerability as weakness and dependence. As I will outline in the following section, the negative depiction of vulnerability is fundamentally flawed and should be replaced with a more nuanced and ambiguous account. In the final analysis, the negation of vulnerability functions as a foundation on which other forms of ignorance are built. The strategy of invulnerability feeds, therefore, into the second strategy, that of ignorance.

The strategy of ignorance is an epistemic practice that is sustained by the benefits of not knowing. Recently, the field of agnotology – that is, the study of ignorance and its production – has been developing.[25] A key assumption in agnotology is that ignorance is not merely the absence of knowledge, but must also be understood and analysed along the lines of power and interest. The production of knowledge is not necessarily progressive because there may be structural benefits which result from not knowing. Wilful ignorance is maintained by selectively ignoring perspectives that challenge prevailing views. In the context of whiteness, wilful ignorance is the cultivation of a stance in which the white self is allowed to consider itself as morally pure and untainted.

Whiteness is accompanied by the phenomenon of 'white talk'. 'White talk' is the evasive and scripted responses of white people who are confronted with the issue of racism and the possibility that they might be responsible for the continuation of racist structures. 'White talk' is often highly predictable and takes recourse to clichés, anecdotes, and stereotypes in order to avoid difficult questions and an introspective stance. Alison Bailey, for example, has coined an entire conversation made up of 'white talk', using the following utterances: 'I'm a good person. ... I have black friends. ... I'm from a poor white family. We suffered too and you don't hear us complaining.' These are all examples of the evasiveness that characterizes 'white talk'.[26] The problem of whiteness is not solved by the expression of innocence or solidarity with sufferers of racism. What could be a solution to white talk? Even posing this question is indicative of the presence of white talk because white people like to adhere to scripts, or rules, as an indication that white selves are moral and responsible. The white perspective on the world considers adherence to the right script a contribution to solving the problem of racism.

Yet, following a script is no solution to the problem of white talk precisely because the (underlying) problem, the construction of invulnerability, remains untouched. Alison Bailey suggests, therefore, replacing the treatment of 'white talk'

---

24. Gilson, 'Vulnerability, Ignorance, and Oppression', 312.

25. R. Proctor and L. Schiebinger (eds), *Agnotology: The Making and Unmaking of Ignorance* (Stanford: Stanford University Press, 2008).

26. Bailey, A., '"White Talk" as a Barrier to Understanding the Problem with Whiteness', in *White Self-Criticality beyond Anti-racism: How Does It Feel to Be a White Problem?*, G. Yancy (ed.) (London: Lexington Books, 2015), 37–56.

with a 'discourse of vulnerability'.[27] This latter discourse has the ability to dismantle the boundaries of the white self. White talk is, at its roots, an attempt to direct the attention away from the culpability of the white self towards its moral purity. In the account of Bailey, fear is a fundamental characteristic of white talk: fear of exposure, fear of not being as morally pure and untainted as one should be, and fear of not living up to one's standards. Fear tries to cover itself up by maintaining invulnerability, thereby neglecting the fundamental vulnerability beneath it. Bailey suggests, therefore, exposing the hidden vulnerability and treating it as a source of knowledge instead of as a source of shame and disgust. In other words, she suggests a discourse of vulnerability instead of white talk.

4. Vulnerability from the Perspective of Disability

I will here respond to Bailey's suggestion to develop a 'discourse of vulnerability' further, doing so along theological lines. What are the theological sources of a discourse of vulnerability? The foundation for a theology of vulnerability is given with the life and death of Christ and the character of God revealed in Christ. In recent years, an increasing number of theologians have advanced the idea of a suffering, vulnerable God. The Council of Chalcedon renounced the view that God was capable of suffering as implausible.[28] Yet, William Placher, in his monograph *Narratives of a Vulnerable God: Christ, Theology and Scripture*, remarks upon the diversity of contemporary theologians who affirm the possibility of God's suffering.[29]

One of these theologians is Thomas Reynolds, who develops a theology of vulnerability from the perspective of disability. He takes disability as his epistemological focal point, from where he argues that the church should be imagined as a hospitable and vulnerable community.[30] Reynolds construes his theological proposal from the margins of society by placing experiences of disability in the foreground; such experiences have not yet acquired a significant place in theological thought. Reynolds parts ways with accounts of disability that are grounded primarily in physical impairments, instead striving to provide a holistic and integrative definition of disability. A key concept in his work is the 'cult of normalcy', defined as the tendency in society to focus attention on the able-bodied, and to label those who do not adhere to the norm of ability as deviant. His denouncement of the 'cult of normalcy' opens up the conceptual

27. Bailey, '"White Talk" as a Barrier to Understanding the Problem with Whiteness', 12.

28. W. C. Placher, *Narratives of a Vulnerable God: Christ, Theology, and Scripture* (Louisville, KY: Westminster John Knox, 1994).

29. Placher, *Narratives of a Vulnerable God*, 6.

30. T. E. Reynolds, *Vulnerable Communion: A Theology of Disability and Hospitality* (Grand Rapids, MI: Brazos Press, 2008).

space in which disability may be defined according to the interplay between the physical and the social. Disability is, in Reynold's account, intrinsically connected with the vulnerability shared by all human persons. In this sense, no human being is perfectly 'abled'. Consequently, disability and ability are conceived as a continuum rather than as two radically opposed conditions. Because Reynolds has identified disability along a continuous scale, everyone shares at one point or another in the experience of disabilities. Without taking up the medical ideal of healing, Reynolds searches for other dimensions of wholeness. In his opinion, wholeness is not defined as the restoration of disability into a state of ability, but rather is imagined along the lines of community and interdependence. Wholeness is the result of a radical, inclusive community in which everyone opens her/himself up to the vulnerability of the other, which provides a window into one's own vulnerability. Sharing one's humanity with others is exemplified in the vulnerability of God, who fully enters the human condition, thus sharing in the vulnerability of humanity. The vulnerability of God is revealed in the full humanity of Jesus Christ. If vulnerability is a basic element of human life, it follows that being vulnerable is the default state. Invulnerability, then, is not the proposed ideal for human flourishing. Instead, receiving one's existence from the other is desirable. Consequently, the prevalent ideal, of rational, autonomous, and individual personhood, to which people with disabilities cannot ascribe, is neither attainable nor profitable.

How does the position of Reynolds bear upon my plea for a theology of vulnerability to counteract white privilege? Reynolds makes it clear that, by taking disability as an epistemological priority, the full humanity of people with disabilities should be safeguarded. All people are, to a certain extent, disabled, and it is not possible to relegate people with disabilities to a completely different group or class of humanity altogether. Disability is a continuum. By conceiving the category of disability in this manner, one can maintain that the core of human personhood cannot be defined merely in terms of autonomy and ability: because all people exist on the continuum, disability cannot be excluded from full humanity. For our investigation, this view safeguards the vulnerability of humans and indicates that maintaining whiteness in the form of detachment undermines human flourishing. Dependence needs to be fostered instead of denounced. If white privilege is constructed, in part, by a strategy of invulnerability, it follows that the theology of Reynolds might offer an alternative account of human interaction. Disability is a powerful window into vulnerability and could therefore function as an investigatory locus to overcome constructions of invulnerability. A theology of disability is especially helpful for this project because it strives to formulate ideas of wholeness from which no person is, a priori, excluded, and to which people with disabilities are no exception. Theorizing from the perspective of disability thus turns the ideal of invulnerability on its head, because it searches for a description of humanity in which persons with disability are fully included. The ideal of wholeness and community is therefore placed primarily within the realm of interdependence, where the vulnerability of persons is clearly in view. As such, the radical, inclusive nature of theorizing from the perspective of disabilities allows us to expand our definitions of wholeness, community, and human flourishing. The ideals hidden behind the fortification of white privilege thus crumble away. The ideal of invulnerability, self-reliance, and independence give way to inclusive definitions of human flourishing.

5. *Exploring Resistance*

Our interpretation of Reynolds's account leaves open the question of how a theology of vulnerability can contribute to a stance of resistance with regard to the unjust situations continually generated by white privilege. To elaborate this potential contribution, I now turn to the approach of Kristine Culp, who provides an account of the ambiguity of vulnerability.[31] For Culp, vulnerability has an affinity with the idea of openness. In this case, vulnerability denotes the openness either to be blessed or to be harmed. The main question her work seeks to answer is whether it is possible to align together the principal vulnerability of existence, the fundamental ambiguity of life, and the affirmation of life as a gift of God.[32] Because vulnerability is ambiguous in character, she offers two trajectories of response: the first is a trajectory of resistance, and the second is an itinerary of delight and gratitude.

The trajectory of resistance is aimed at the creation of a place of shelter. Through the action undertaken by movements of resistance, a place of shelter is created for vulnerable persons.[33] Acts of resistance are characterized by both an individual and a communal dimension. The communal dimension of resistance emerges when the creation of a shelter extends beyond the shelter for oneself. The communal factor consists of a movement of inclusive welcome and active resistance. Wisdom is a necessary component in the discernment process of what should be resisted and who should be welcomed. Resistance is able to direct attention to the concrete materiality of struggle and engagement with the world. In addition, resistance has the ability to connect a multitude of movements with each other and to see the connections between widely diverging movements.[34]

According to Culp, in polar tension – not polar opposition – to the trajectory of resistance is the trajectory of delight and gratitude.[35] The movement towards God's glory and the enjoyments of God's blessings do not take place by an erasure of vulnerability. It is precisely '*in their vulnerability*'[36] that humans turn towards

---

31. Culp, *Vulnerability and Glory*, 5.

32. Ibid., 4, 6.

33. Ibid., 157.

34. Connections between grass-roots movements of resistance and the academic world are also possible insofar as both are, on different levels, contributing to a just society.

35. Culp, *Vulnerability and Glory*, 161.

36. Ibid., 160; original emphasis.

the glory of God. The recognition of vulnerability directly correlates with the experience of joy.[37] Delight emerges in the same recognition of vulnerability and functions to orient life towards God in a grateful acknowledgement of blessing.[38]

The contribution of Culp is primarily found in the two responses she created in the engagement of shared vulnerability. Vulnerability necessitates the creation of a shelter by resisting elements that are detrimental to the flourishing of life. Applied to the pervasive problem of white privilege, holding onto the necessity of vulnerability with an active stance of resistance is much needed. Her approach could be applied to the resistance of racism in all its permutations. What does the creation of a shelter mean in practice, particularly regarding the problem of a raced society? It means, first of all, that resistance against the harming of vulnerable life is closely connected with resisting the ills of discrimination and racism. In a raced society, resistance is needed not only in outwardly directed movements, but also inwardly. As such, resistance signals the introspective stance in/from which one opens oneself up for the following possibility: that one needs to resist self-inflation, self-flattery, and self-entitlement. Whiteness often manifests itself surreptitiously, in learned and internalized behaviour. Whiteness thus operates at an unconscious level and oftentimes goes unchecked.[39] An important part of a trajectory of resistance in this case is the resistance of these learned and internalized patterns of white entitlement. The work of Culp helps to point us towards an important trajectory of resistance, which is characterized both by an active, outward turn and by an inward, introspective turn. By revealing one's hidden and ingrained stances of whiteness, one undertakes important groundwork for resistance and the creation of shelters for vulnerable life.

In order to arrive at resistance, contrast experiences as they are defined by Schillebeeckx, that is, as the intense experience of how the world should *not* be, will prove to be illuminating. Contrast experiences arise out of the context of oppression. Some people are able to see the contrast experience more clearly because they live this oppression and injustice on a daily basis. However, when one benefits from whiteness, it is oftentimes much harder to discern these contrast experiences, because one profits from the unjust status quo, or one is even actively involved in its maintenance. Resistance, protest, and a prophetic voice can only be expressed when this contrast experience is indeed personally felt.[40]

What if this experience is not present? Schillebeeckx says that, in the contrast experience, people *become aware* ('*bewust worden*') that a better existence is

---

37. Culp, *Vulnerability and Glory*, 178.

38. Ibid., 179.

39. S. Sullivan, *Revealing Whiteness: The Unconscious Habits of Racial Privilege* (Bloomington: Indiana University Press, 2006).

40. Schillebeeckx, *Geloofsverstaan: Interpretatie en Kritiek*, 156.

indeed possible.[41] The problem, however, is that the awareness of a better life is hard to imagine for people who benefit from white privilege, since they, wrongly, feel that they benefit from segregation in the areas of housing, the school system, and within churches. In this context, it is hard to understand racial discrimination and injustice as a *collective ailment* (*collectieve kwaal*) although Schillebeeckx explicitly names racial discrimination as one example of collective ailments.[42] It is exactly the awareness of a collective ailment through a contrast experience that leads to the formulation of an ethical imperative actually to change the situation. In this chapter, I thus offer the praxis of vulnerability as a way to help white people experience the contrast in this regard. If one is vulnerable, one allows the perspective of the other to influence one's own experience and perspective. Mutual interdependence and vulnerability are therefore attitudes that one can develop in order to perceive racial injustice as the *collective* ailment that it is. A contrast experience can be realized through mutual vulnerability and interdependence in which the other functions as a mirror through which one may perceive the contrast experience. The oppressed other can therefore function as a 'disagreeable mirror' in which one can detect the moral taintedness of one's self by being confronted with the concrete ramifications of racism.[43]

Although I have been arguing for vulnerability as a response to whiteness and white privilege, my endorsement should not be read as an uncritical condoning of all types of vulnerability. Vulnerability is a multi-layered concept that has potential both for good and for evil. Evil arises with the distortion and violation of vulnerability. Evil could thus be seen as the violation of the boundaries of the vulnerable self, as has been argued convincingly by Mary Potter Engel.[44] Let me thus state unequivocally that not all forms of vulnerability are contributing to human flourishing. I am searching, therefore, and similar to Sarah Coakley, for the 'right' forms of vulnerability;[45] I am neither looking for nor defending 'an undiscriminating adulation of vulnerability'.[46] One should be careful, then, to make distinctions between the 'right' form(s) of vulnerability and the types of vulnerability that are open to abuse.[47] The goal of this engagement has been to show how vulnerability is a given of human life, and that wilful postures of

41. Schillebeeckx, *Geloofsverstaan*, 157; original emphasis.

42. Ibid., 153.

43. Bailey, 'On White Shame and Vulnerability', 478.

44. M. Potter Engel, 'Evil, Sin and Violation of the Vulnerable', in *Lift Every Voice: Constructing Christian Theologies from the Underside*, S. Brooks Thistlethwaite and M. Potter Engel (eds) (Maryknoll, NY: Orbis Books, 1998), 159–72.

45. S. Coakley, 'Kenosis and Subversion: On the Repression of "Vulnerability" in Christian Feminist Writing', in *Swallowing a Fishbone? Feminist Theologians Debate Christianity*, D. Hampson (ed.) (London: Society for Promoting Christian Knowledge, 1996).

46. Coakley, 'Kenosis and Subversion', 106.

47. Ibid., 109.

invulnerability lead to the ideas of superiority and self-congratulation that are ingrained within white privilege.

What does the type of vulnerability for which I am looking entail? Coakley's work is helpful in this regard. Vulnerability should not be equated with powerlessness, according to her. She draws upon the work of Michel Foucault to argue that all persons possess power, however limited this power may be. Accounts of vulnerability that determine this idea (i.e. vulnerability) as the absence of power are therefore ruled out. Instead, Coakley opts for the possibility of a power-in-vulnerability. This possibility, moreover, signals the opening up towards the divine as a practice of self-emptying. Coakley writes that this is 'not a negation of the self, but the place of the self's transformation and expansion into God'.[48] The power that was manifested in Christ, the power-in-vulnerability, is a totally distinct form of power compared to occurrences of destructive (patriarchal) power. As Coakley has touched upon in her book *God, Sexuality and the Self*,[49] desiring this type of 'power-in-vulnerability' is challenging. It might even be accompanied by a loss of social standing because of the prophetic stance it requires.[50] The power-in-vulnerability that I have here embraced from the work of Coakley is to be read as a thoroughly spiritual practice in which one seeks to be connected with the mind of Christ. This thoroughly Cristo-centric mysticism leads not to an opposition to empowerment. On the contrary, empowerment (by divine power) and vulnerability are in close relationship with each other – they do not cancel each other out. The result of striving for power-in-vulnerability is not necessarily quietist either, but leads to the empowerment to speak out with a prophetic voice. As a result, power-in-vulnerability has the possibility to subvert the status quo of a racist society from the inside out.

As we have seen in the work of Bailey and Gilson, the maintenance of a position of whiteness stems from deep-seated habits about what it means to possess power as a white person. The spiritual road suggested by Coakley orients us towards the practice of self-searching in which wrongful forms of power and privilege will be brought to light and relinquished. By seeking the same mind that Christ had – Christ who challenged harmful and abusive forms of power – a space opens up for prophetic utterances and societal transformation.

Conclusion

My insistence on racial justice through the dismantling of white privilege, thereby striving to find reconciliation and human flourishing, connects me clearly with the theology of Edward Schillebeeckx. I take from Schillebeeckx a concrete attention

---

48. Ibid., 108.

49. S. Coakley, *God, Sexuality, and the Self: An Essay 'On the Trinity'* (Cambridge: Cambridge University Press, 2013).

50. Coakley, *God, Sexuality, and the Self*, 85.

to those who are sinned against; in this case, the sinned against are those who suffer from racial injustice today. As Kevin Considine argues in his description of Schillebeeckx's theology, attention to the signs of the times[51] is a paramount task for those who practice theology.[52]

At the present moment, the problem of racial injustice as a sign of the times is impossible to ignore. One need only look at the months that have passed between the original presentation of this chapter (in August 2014) and its final drafting (in June 2015), months which were characterized by large-scale police violence against black and brown persons. For example, the scandalous deaths of Michael Brown and Eric Garner brought massive outrage and protest all over the United States of America. Catholic theologians in the United States responded to these egregious killings by issuing a statement on racial justice, which has been signed by over 450 theologians at this present moment.[53] The massive outcry against racial injustice might very well be one of the most poignant signs of the times that we are experiencing presently. Therefore, it is my hope that a robust theology of vulnerability will be read in accordance with the 'signs of the times' and might contribute to addressing the issue of white privilege, creating innovative, helpful pathways for resistance.

Bibliography

Bailey, A., 'On White Shame and Vulnerability', *South African Journal of Philosophy* 30, no. 4 (2011): 472–83.

Bailey, A., '"White Talk" as a Barrier to Understanding the Problem with Whiteness', in *White Self-Criticality beyond Anti-racism: How Does It Feel to Be a White Problem?*, G. Yancy (ed.) (London: Lexington Books, 2015), 37–56.

Beckett, A. E., *Citizenship and Vulnerability: Disability and Issues of Social and Political Engagement* (New York: Palgrave Macmillan, 2006).

Butler, J., 'Violence, Mourning, and Politics', *Precarious Life: The Power of Mourning and Violence* (New York: Verso, 2004).

Cassidy, L. M., and A. Mikulich, *Interrupting White Privilege: Catholic Theologians Break the Silence* (Maryknoll, NY: Orbis Books, 2007).

Coakley, S., 'Kenosis and Subversion: On the Repression of "Vulnerability" in Christian Feminist Writing', in *Swallowing a Fishbone? Feminist Theologians Debate Christianity*, D. Hampson (ed.) (London: Society for Promoting Christian Knowledge, 1996).

51. The phrase 'signs of the times' originates from *Gaudium et Spes*: 'To carry out such a task, the Church has always had the duty of scrutinizing the signs of the times and of interpreting them in the light of the Gospel' ('Pastoral Constitution on the Church in the Modern World – *Gaudium et Spes*', 1965, paragraph 4, http://www.vatican.va/archive/hist_councils/ii_vatican_council/documents/vat-ii_cons_19651207_gaudium-et-spes_en.html.

52. Considine, *Salvation for the Sinned-Against*, 37.

53. Statement of Catholic Theologians on Racial Justice, http://catholicmoraltheology.com/statement-of-catholic-theologians-on-racial-justice/ (accessed 30 May 2015).

Coakley, S., *God, Sexuality, and the Self: An Essay 'On the Trinity'* (Cambridge: Cambridge University Press, 2013).

Considine, K. P., *Salvation for the Sinned-Against: Han and Schillebeeckx in Intercultural Dialogue* (Eugene, OR: Pickwick Publications, 2015).

Culp, K. A., *Vulnerability and Glory: A Theological Account* (Louisville, KY: Westminster John Knox, 2010).

Frankenberg, R., *White Women, Race Matters: The Social Construction of Whiteness* (Minneapolis: University of Minnesota Press, 1988).

Frankenberg, R., *Displacing Whiteness: Essays in Social and Cultural Criticism* (Durham, NC: Duke University Press, 1997).

Frye, M., 'White Woman Feminist', *Willful Virgin: Essays in Feminism, 1976–1992* (Freedom: The Crossing Press, 1992).

Gilroy, P., *The Black Atlantic: Modernity and Double Consciousness* (Cambridge, MA: Harvard University Press, 1993).

Gilson, E., 'Vulnerability, Ignorance, and Oppression', *Hypatia* 26, no. 2 (2011): 308–32.

Kim, S. C. H., *Theology in the Public Sphere* (London: SCM Press, 2011).

Massingale, B. N., *Racial Justice and the Catholic Church* (Maryknoll, NY: Orbis Books, 2010).

Moyaert, M., 'On Vulnerability: Probing the Ethical Dimensions of Comparative Theology', *Religions* 3, no. 4 (2012): 1144–61.

Placher, W. C., *Narratives of a Vulnerable God: Christ, Theology, and Scripture* (Louisville, KY: Westminster John Knox, 1994).

Potter Engel, M., 'Evil, Sin and Violation of the Vulnerable', in *Lift Every Voice: Constructing Christian Theologies from the Underside*, S. Brooks Thistlethwaite and M. Potter Engel (eds) (Maryknoll, NY: Orbis Books, 1998), 159–72.

Proctor, R., and L. Schiebinger (eds), *Agnotology: The Making and Unmaking of Ignorance* (Stanford: Stanford University Press, 2008).

Reynolds, T. E., *Vulnerable Communion: A Theology of Disability and Hospitality* (Grand Rapids, MI: Brazos Press, 2008).

Schillebeeckx, E., *Geloofsverstaan: Interpretatie En Kritiek*, Theologische Peilingen 5 (Bloemendaal: H. Nelissen, 1972).

Schillebeeckx, E., *Christ: The Christian Experience in the Modern World*, trans. J. Bowden, *CW*, vol. 7 (London: Bloomsbury T&T Clark, 2014).

Schillebeeckx, E., *Church: The Human Story of God*, trans. J. Bowden, *CW*, vol. 10 (London: Bloomsbury T&T Clark, 2014).

Schillebeeckx, E., *The Understanding of Faith: Interpretation and Criticism*, trans. N. D. Smith, *CW*, vol. 5 (London: Bloomsbury T&T Clark, 2014).

Sullivan, S., *Revealing Whiteness: The Unconscious Habits of Racial Privilege* (Bloomington: Indiana University Press, 2006).

Teel, K., *Racism and the Image of God* (New York: Palgrave Macmillan, 2010).

Van Wyngaard, C., 'Race-Cognisant Public Theology in Contemporary South Africa: Tentative Thoughts from a Privileged Location', 2012.

Vice, S., '"How Do I Live in This Strange Place?"', *Journal of Social Philosophy* 41, no. 3 (2010): 323–42.

Yancy, G., *Black Bodies, White Gazes: The Continuing Significance of Race* (Lanham, MD: Rowman & Littlefield Publishers, 2008).

Yancy, G., *Christology and Whiteness: What Would Jesus Do?* (New York: Routledge, 2012).

INDEX